THE HOUSING ACT 1996
A PRACTICAL GUIDE

General Editor:
David Cowan

Contributors:
Professor D N Clarke
David Cowan
Devonshires, Solicitors
Margaret Richards
Matthew Waddington

JORDANS

1996

Published by
Jordan Publishing Limited
21 St Thomas Street
Bristol BS1 6JS

© Jordan Publishing Limited 1996
Reprinted November 1996
Reprinted March 1997

British Library Cataloguing-in-Publication Data
A catalogue record for this book is available from the British Library.

ISBN 0 85308 394 0

Typeset by Mendip Communications Ltd, Frome, Somerset
Printed by Biddles Ltd, Guildford and King's Lynn

DEDICATION

For our Mother, Father,
Sylvia, Jo and Helen
and
for Ruth Arwen,
born the same year as the Act,
and for her mother

'One of the delegates, a Bakers' Union shop steward, who had lost his job in one of the big mergers of the local bakeries, got up and said, in an Irish accent, "It's the morality of housing that we're after. Society is a chain, and the strength of a chain is its weakest link, and the wealth of a society is the wealth of its poorest members". Tremendously moving.'

Tony Benn *Conflicts of Interest: Diaries 1977–80* (Arrow, 1990) p 15

David Cowan

David Cowan is lecturer in law at the University of Bristol, specialising in housing law and policy, and community care. He is the author of numerous articles in academic journals on housing and homelessness. He is the author of the forthcoming *Specific Issues of Homelessness* (Dartmouth, 1997).

David Clarke

David Clarke, Solicitor, is Professor of Law at the University of Bristol and a consultant with Osborne Clarke, Bristol. He is the author of various articles and books on leasehold law, including *Leasehold Enfranchisement – The New Law* (Jordans, 1994) and *Rent Review Manual* (FT Law and Tax). He is also a part-time chairman of Rent Assessment Panels.

Devonshires

Devonshires is one of the largest specialist housing law practices and acts for more than a hundred housing associations and a number of funders to the sector. The firm is at the forefront of advice on the new local housing company market. Its legal services span the whole range of social landlords' activities. For further information about Devonshires, telephone 0645 940091.

Margaret Richards

Margaret Richards, Solicitor, is a part-time chairman of a Rent Assessment Panel. She is also a board member of a special needs housing association. She lectures extensively on social welfare law and is the author of *Community Care for Older People: Rights, Remedies and Finances* (Jordans, 1996).

Matthew Waddington

Matthew Waddington is a housing solicitor at Salford Law Centre and a freelance trainer. He was formerly a housing specialist at the Law Centres Federation during the consultations leading up to the introduction of the Housing Bill. He has also jointly set up a World Wide Web Site monitoring the legislation (http://www.ferret.co.uk/housing/).

PREFACE

As co-ordinator of the various contributors and contributions, it falls to me to write the Preface to this book on the new Housing Act 1996. However, from the outset, the production of this book would have been impossible without the expert assistance, encouragement, and know-how of the contributors. Devonshires, who are responsible for the drafting of Part I and Chapter 3 in Part III, are a renowned, respected firm of solicitors specialising in housing associations. Matthew Waddington, who is responsible for Part II and Chapter 8 in Part V, is a housing solicitor at the Salford Law Centre and a freelance trainer in housing law. In addition, Matthew worked as a housing specialist at the Law Centres Federation during the consultations leading up to the Bill. Professor DN Clarke, who is responsible for Chapter 5 in Part III, combines the difficult roles of legal academic, colleague and solicitor. He is an acknowledged expert in the field of leasehold enfranchisement, commonhold and property law. I am also grateful to him for beginning the process by introducing me to Jordans. Margaret Richards, who is responsible for Chapter 6 in Part IV, is a solicitor specialising in all aspects of community care and is a board member of a special needs housing association. Against this intellectual and knowledgeable panel, my own expertise somewhat dims.

As will be apparent from the range and diversity of the contributors, the new Housing Act 1996 is an amalgam of different provisions affecting different sectors of the housing world. There are several innovations which will command universal or near universal support, such as the introduction of non-profit-making local housing companies as a force in the provision of housing; improvements upon the current leasehold enfranchisement scheme, reflecting the fact that leasehold is a largely outmoded form of land tenure (no doubt, commonhold will be with us shortly); a more current definition of housing need; and, possibly better methods of challenging local authority decision-making.

Nevertheless, the Act is also highly political. Whilst we have all endeavoured to write in a value-free style, there are many aspects of the Act which have caused and will cause deep concern. For example, further deregulation of the system of protection and security for tenants (or short leaseholders) has been made against a backdrop of uncertainty as to the success of the initial scheme. And whilst there are more properties available for rent, this may be only until the housing market picks up again.

Personally, I cannot think of a worse system of Parliamentary justice than the removal of long-term protection for homeless persons. The Judicial Committee of the House of Lords had already decided (wrongly in my view) that long-term protection was not the purpose of the original homelessness legislation. A simple amendment would have cured that. The Government's argument is that so many people have complained to them about homeless persons 'jumping the housing queue' that the legislation is necessary. It is yet another example of minority groups being prejudiced as a result of seemingly majority opinion. The scheme created in the Housing Act 1996 may not have achieved that result but, whether or not that is correct, the reason for defining 'housing need' was precisely to enable other groups to 'jump the housing queue'. It may well be that the homelessness legislation had failed – a view which I now hold – but this was entirely because of the failure of the supply side of the equation to match the demand.

The Labour Party is committed to re-introducing the protection of the homelessness legislation as it was originally intended. How they will match up the supply/demand equation remains a difficult and, as yet, in my opinion, unanswered question.

A further dimension to the Act is that, in similar vein to other legislation passed over the past 20 years or so, it is largely an enabling Act. That is, the various Secretaries of State (the Housing Corporation and Housing for Wales in Part I) retain huge powers to regulate, make Guidance, Orders, or Directions. This is now an accepted facet of our system of Parliamentary democracy and derives from the increasing regulation, down to the minutiae, of local democracy. The task of the authors, therefore, is somewhat different. Rather than describing substantive rules and their effect, we are often left describing the breadth of such powers. Furthermore, the size of the Act increased by 52 sections and seven Schedules through its Parliamentary passage. Substantial Government changes were even made on the Third Reading in the House of Lords. These increases suggest that when the Bill was initially introduced, much of it was ill-thought through.

I fear that I also made the authors' task rather more difficult by asking for a style that would not exclude non-lawyers. As Lord Woolf has recently observed, housing law needs to become more consumer-oriented. Such an approach also appeals to publishers who can foresee a wider market for their product. The 1996 Act makes this much more difficult because of its complexity and the constant need to refer back to other statutes, which it amends and updates.

It would be impossible to finish this Preface without thanking three people. First, Martin West of Jordans has been a tower of strength, full of encouragement, efficient, and consistently helpful; indeed, Jordans has been a model publisher. Secondly, Clare Haley, who acted as my research assistant through the latter stages of the Bill. Her depth of knowledge, enthusiasm, and appreciation of housing law throughout the year has been a joy. I hope that she continues with housing. Finally, to my partner, who has endured some of my blackest moods and temperamental outbursts and met them with consoling advice and equanimity.

The law is stated as at 1 August 1996.

David Cowan
September 1996

CONTENTS

TABLE OF CASES

References in the right-hand column are to paragraph numbers.

TABLE OF STATUTES

References in the right-hand column are to paragraph numbers.

TABLE OF STATUTORY INSTRUMENTS

References in the right-hand column are to paragraph numbers.

TABLE OF EUROPEAN MATERIAL

References in the right-hand column are to paragraph numbers.

TABLE OF NON-STATUTORY MATERIAL

References in the right-hand column are to paragraph numbers.

TABLE OF CONSULTATIONS AND PARLIAMENTARY DEBATES

(i) Consultation Documents

DoE *Access to Local Authority and Housing Association Tenancies* (HMSO, 1994)

DoE *Our Future Homes* (HMSO, 1995)

(ii) Documents Linked to *Our Future Homes*

The Future of Private Housing Renewal Programmes – Explanatory Paper Linked to the Housing White Paper Our Future Homes (DoE, 1995)

Rough Sleepers Initiative: Future Plans – Consultation Paper Linked to the Housing White Paper Our Future Homes (DoE/Department of Health/Department of Social Security/ Home Office/Department for Education and Employment, 1995)

Rough Sleepers Initiative: The Next Challenge – Strategy Paper Linked to the Consultation Paper Rough Sleepers Initiative: Future Plans (DoE/Department of Health/Department of Social Security/Home Office/Department for Education and Employment, 1996)

More Choice in the Social Rented Sector – Consultation Paper Linked to the Housing White Paper Our Future Homes (DoE, 1995)

Proposals for a Purchase Grant Scheme for Housing Association Tenants – Consultation Paper Linked to the Housing White Paper Our Future Homes (DoE, 1995)

Improving Standards in Houses in Multiple Occupation – Consultation Paper Linked to the Housing White Paper Our Future Homes (DoE, 1995)

The Legislative Framework for Private Renting – Consultation Paper Linked to the Housing White Paper Our Future Homes (DoE, 1995)

(iii) Press Releases

These can be found at the DoE site on the internet: http://www.coi.gov.uk/coi/depts/GNV

"Government to Crack Down on Neighbour Nuisance on Council Estate" 5 April 1995

(iv) Parliamentary Debates

Note: The First Reading of Bills in both Houses are formal. Since the Second Reading debates are concerned with the principal of the proposed legislation, ministerial statements tend to be concerned with the general policy and purpose. Clauses receive detailed consideration in the Committee and Report Stages.

With the exception of Standing Committee G, references are to the volumes of the House of Commons, Official Report, Parliamentary Debates (Hansard) and to the parallel House of Lords, Official Report, Parliamentary Debates (Hansard), London, HMSO.

	DATE	REFERENCE
HOUSE OF COMMONS		
Second Reading	29 January 1996	Vol 270, cols 647–750
Committee Stage	Considered in Standing Committee G in 26 sittings, between 6 February and 2 April 1996	
Report	29 April 1996	Vol 276, cols 770–876
	30 April 1996	Vol 276, cols 913–1047
Third Reading	30 April 1996	Vol 276, cols 1047–1052
HOUSE OF LORDS		
Second Reading	16 May 1996	Vol 572, cols 560–625
Committee Stage	6 June 1996	Vol 572, cols 1367–1419, 1434–1480
	11 June 1996	Vol 572, cols 1577–1645, 1654–1706
	13 June 1996	Vol 573, 1839–1892, 1908–1958
	18 June 1996	Vol 573, cols 165–243, 256–308
	19 June 1996	Vol 573, cols 319–386, 390–446
	25 June 1996	Vol 573, cols 767–834, 849–914
Report	8 July 1996	Vol 574, cols 12–76, 83–166
	10 July 1996	Vol 574, cols 298–364, 368–434
	11 July 1996	Vol 574, cols 445–532
Third Reading	17 July 1996	Vol 574, cols 837–978
HOUSE OF COMMONS		
Consideration of Lords Amendments	22 July 1996	Vol 282, cols 33–120
HOUSE OF LORDS		
Consideration of Commons Reason and Amendments	23 July 1996	Vol 574, cols 1290–1315

TABLE OF ABBREVIATIONS

CA 1985: Companies Act 1985

DoE: Department of the Environment

DSS: Department of Social Security

HAA 1985: Housing Associations Act 1985

HAG: Housing association grant

HAT: Housing Action Trust

HATOS: Housing Association Tenants' Ombudsman Scheme

HMO: House in multiple occupation

HRA: Housing Revenue Account

LTA 1985: Landlord and Tenant Act 1985

LTA 1987: Landlord and Tenant Act 1987

LVT: Leasehold Valuation Tribunal

RDG: Revenue deficit grant

RSL: Registered social landlord

SHG: Social housing grant

SNMA: Special needs management allowance

SSAA: Social Security Administration Act 1992

the 1967 Act: Leasehold Reform Act 1967

the 1985 Act: Housing Act 1985

the 1988 Act: Housing Act 1988

the 1989 Act: Local Government and Housing Act 1989

the 1993 Act: Leasehold Reform, Housing and Urban Development Act 1993

INTRODUCTION

Scheme of the Act

The Housing Act 1996 is in eight Parts.

(i)   Part I incorporates, amends, and updates provisions in the Housing Associations Act 1985. It makes provision for the social rented sector of the housing market. More specifically, it covers housing associations, local housing companies and the Housing Corporation, Housing for Wales and their powers.

(ii)   Part II reinforces the law on houses in multiple occupation, by amending the Housing Act 1985.

(iii)   Part III concerns itself with three particular aspects of landlord and tenant: first, it provides for certain protection, rights and remedies of tenants faced with large service charges; second, it amends the private sector security of tenure legislation in the Housing Act 1988, making it easier to grant assured shorthold tenancies and regain possession of rented property; third, it extends the rights of leaseholders to enfranchise found in the Leasehold Reform, Housing and Urban Development Act 1993.

(iv)   Part IV makes certain changes as regards housing benefit administration.

(v)   Part V creates a scheme of probationary tenancies to enable local housing authorities and housing action trusts to cope with nuisance tenants. It further enables some landlords to gain possession where tenants have caused a nuisance or annoyance, domestic violence, or have committed an arrestable offence. Finally, it gives the courts power to attach a power of arrest in certain circumstances.

(vi)   Part VI radically revises the scheme of allocation of local authority housing (formerly, in the Housing Act 1985, ss 21 and 22).

(vii)   Part VII significantly amends the homelessness legislation, formerly contained in the Housing Act 1985, Part III.

(viii) Part VIII makes miscellaneous and supplementary changes.

Whilst, as a rule, this book follows the structure of the Act, certain self-contained sections of the Act (particularly in Part III) are given separate chapters of their own. In addition, some sections are taken out of order in chapters where their role is better explained in conjunction with earlier or later sections.

Application to the UK

The Act generally applies only to England and Wales.[1] It applies also to the Isles of Scilly, although the Secretary of State may make an order excepting, adapting and modifying it. Such order is to be made by Statutory Instrument and is subject to negative resolution.[2] The only provision which may apply in Northern Ireland relates to the payment of housing benefit to third parties. However, this can be done by Order in Council and is subject to negative resolution in either House of Parliament.[3] Finally, any power given by the Act to make consequential amendments or repeals of enactments extends to any part of the UK.[4]

The Act applies to Scotland only in the following parts: Part IV (housing benefit and related matters);[5] repeal of tenant's choice.[6] Certain other amendments and repeals specifically do not apply to Scotland.[7]

Commencement

The following sections come into force immediately on Royal Assent:[8]

s 110 (new leases: valuation principles);
s 120 (payment of housing benefit to third parties);
ss 223–226, 228–233 (general provisions).

The following sections and Schedules come into force two months after the Act receives Royal Assent:[9]

ss 81 and 82 (restriction on termination of tenancy for failure to pay service charge);
s 85 (appointment of manager by the court);
s 94 (provision of general legal advice about residential tenancies);
s 95 (jurisdiction of county courts);
s 221 (exercise of compulsory purchase powers in relation to crown land);
Schedule 18, paras 24 and 26–29 and, so far as they relate to these paragraphs, ss 222, 227 and Sch 19.

---

1 Section 231.
2 Section 225.
3 Section 225(2).
4 Section 231(5).
5 Section 231(2).
6 Schedule 18, para 1.
7 Section 231(4).
8 Section 232(1).
9 Section 232(2).

All other sections and Schedules come into force on such day as the Secretary of State determines by statutory instrument, although this may be staggered according to areas and or purposes.[10]

10 Section 232(3), (4).

PART I

CHAPTER 1

THE SOCIAL RENTED SECTOR

I: Registered social landlords

The register of social landlords

1.1   Section 1 of the Housing Act 1996 imposes an obligation upon the corporation to maintain a register of social landlords.[1] The Corporation is defined as being either Housing for Wales or The Housing Corporation depending on whether the social landlord has its registered office in Wales or England.[2] The register is not a new creation. It existed under the Housing Associations Act 1985 ('HAA 1985').[3] It has always been a linchpin and remains so as only registered social landlords ('RSLs') will qualify for social housing grants and the other benefits granted to social landlords by the Act.

The register is to contain brief details of the social landlord, including: (a) its registration number; (b) its date of registration; (c) its name; (d) its registered office address; (e) its correspondence office address; (f) the number and date of the Corporation's minute confirming registration; and (g) the name and number of the approved independent ombudsman scheme. In addition, a new public information file will be maintained and certain information will be kept at regional offices of the Corporation.[4] The register will be open for inspection by the public at the appropriate head office of the Corporation.[5]

Eligibility for registration

1.2   One of the underlying purposes behind the new provisions is to widen the types of body that are eligible for registration as social landlords. The Housing White Paper had proposed that, in addition to the charities and industrial and provident societies which already qualify for registration, both profit-making and non profit-making Companies Act companies should be eligible for registration as social landlords.[6] However, all references to profit-making bodies being

---

1 Section 1(1).
2 Section 56.
3 HAA 1985, s 5.
4 See further HL Debs, Vol 572, col 1368.
5 Section 1(1).
6 DoE *Our Future Homes* (HMSO, 1995).

eligible for registration had been dropped from the Act.[7] The substantive change that the Act makes to eligibility for registration is to provide that 'not for profit' companies registered under the Companies Act 1985 ('CA 1985') are now eligible for registration.[8] This opens the door to 'local housing companies', in which local authorities have a minority interest, becoming registered as RSLs.

Types of body eligible

1.3   Eligible bodies are divided into three classes:[9]

(i)   registered charities which are also housing associations – being charities registered with the Charity Commission;

(ii)   industrial and provident societies registered under the Industrial and Provident Societies Act 1965; and

(iii) companies registered under the CA 1985.

All existing housing associations which immediately before the commencement of the Act were registered under Part I of the HAA 1985 are automatically registered under the Act as social landlords.[10]

Conditions of eligibility

1.4   In the case of a registered charity which is a housing association,[11] no further conditions are laid down[12] and it is eligible for registration. In all other cases, three further conditions are laid down.[13]

(i)   The body is non profit-making.[14] A body is non profit-making if either: (a) it does not trade for profit; or (b) its constitution or rules prohibit the issue of capital with interest or dividend exceeding the rate prescribed by the Treasury.[15] The body can, however, make surpluses. Many existing housing associations make large surpluses which are ploughed back. On the other hand, the body cannot pay any profit that it makes to its proprietors by way of distribution or dividend.[16]

---

7 Apparently, this is because the Government felt that 'the needs of leaseholders are more important in the immediate term'. Nevertheless, the Government said that it would introduce a separate Bill 'that covers that issue, which I hope will soon be introduced': HC Debs, Vol 270, col 647.

8 For discussion about the gestation and future of such companies, see R Bayley, 'Companies Advance to Go' (1996) July/August *Roof* 34. See also, HL Debs, Vol 574, cols 480–2, for the way in which the Government anticipates they will operate and the difficulties in advising people whether to become directors of such companies. It should be noted that these companies remain regulated by the Companies Acts; the 1996 Act merely overlays additional regulations: HC Debs, Vol 572, cols 2373–4.

9 Section 2.

10 Section 1(2).

11 The term 'housing association' is defined by reference to HAA 1985, s 230.

12 Section 2(1)(a).

13 Section 2(1)(b) and (c).

14 Section 2(2).

15 Section 2(3), following HAA 1985, ss 1(1) and 5.

16 *Goodman v Dolphin Square Trust Ltd* (1979) 38 P & CR 257.

(ii) The body must be established for, or have as its objects or powers, the provision, construction, improvement or management of any one or more of the following:[17]

    (a) houses[18] for letting (which includes licences to occupy);

    (b) houses for occupation by members of a co-operative body where the rules of the body restrict membership to those entitled to occupy a house provided or managed by the body; or

    (c) hostels.[19]

(iii) Any additional objects or purposes must be among the following list of conditions:[20]

    (a) the provision of land or amenities or other services, or the provision, construction, repair or improvement of buildings for the body's residents either exclusively or together with other persons;[21]

    (b) the acquisition, repair, improvement or creation by the conversion of houses or other property of houses for sale or shared ownership leasing;

    (c) the construction of houses to be disposed of on shared ownership leases;

    (d) the management of houses or blocks of flats not falling within (ii)(a) or (b) above;

    (e) the provision of services for owners or occupiers of houses in carrying out or facilitating works of maintenance or improvement to their houses;

    (f) the provision of advice or services for housing associations or other voluntary organisations concerned with housing.

Powers of the Secretary of State

1.5 The Secretary of State retains the power to extend these objects or powers. So, whilst the provision of an alarm system would come within para (a) if provided to a housing association property, the extension of such a scheme to other properties would require an execution of the power. The Government did not wish to see the movement 'fossilise'.[22] In Committee, the Government undertook to bring forward an Order at commencement to cover the additional

---

17 Section 2(2), re-enacting HAA 1985, s 4(2).

18 This includes flats, yards or gardens forming part of a house, throughout this Part of the Act: s 63(1).

19 This takes a similar meaning to s 106(1) of the Housing Act 1985: s 63(1).

20 Section 2(4). These provisions appear to be lifted straight out of the 1985 Act to such an extent that even the reference in s 24(f) is to 'housing associations' rather than to 'social landlords'.

21 The phrase 'together with other persons' is in the Act 'specifically to envisage the possibility that where what is required is more than plain and simple housing ... the development should be done in conjunction with people who take the risk of those commercial activities and who are expert in providing and managing them': HL Debs, Vol 572, col 1380.

22 Section 2(7); see HL Debs, Vol 572, cols 1382, 1388.

items included in the secondary legislation under the HAA 1985[23] and indicated that it would, when bringing forward such order, consider including in it possible new activities which might include community alarm systems and the question of the provision of care, both of which were activities raised as possible additional purposes. It is likely that others will come forward as well if social landlords continue to diversify their activities.

Exceptions

1.6　The second and third conditions are qualified by providing that a body is not ineligible for registration as a social landlord by reason only that its powers include power to:[24]

(i)　acquire commercial premises or businesses as an incidental part of an activity which falls within either of the second or third conditions;

(ii)　repair or improve or convert such commercial premises or to carry on for a limited period any such businesses;

(iii)　repair or improve houses or blocks of flats after a disposal by the landlord to the tenant.

The powers relating to commercial premises or trading are restricted to powers which are an incidental part of activities or projects which fall within the list of permitted objects. Such powers relating to commercial premises or businesses cannot stand on their own and exist as independent objects; they can only be carried on for a limited period.

This list of purposes or objects is exhaustive. A company which has a memorandum of association containing the wide objects clause invariably found in a commercial company's memorandum of association will not be eligible for registration under the Act. Therefore, careful drafting of the memorandum of a Companies Act company seeking registration as a social landlord will be necessary. Under the previous regime for the registration of housing associations, the National Federation of Housing Associations (which changed its name to the National Housing Federation in September 1996) published model sets of rules for industrial and provident society housing associations and it is likely that a similar model memorandum of association will be produced for Companies Act companies wishing to seek registration as social landlords.

23 Housing Associations (Permissible Additional Purposes) (England and Wales) Order 1994, SI 1994/2895.
24 Section 2(5), repealing HAA 1985, s 4(4).

Registration and removal

Registration powers of the Corporation

1.7   The Corporation has a discretion to register any eligible body.[25] The Act imposes a duty on the Corporation to establish criteria which may be varied but which should be satisfied. Further, in deciding whether to register a body as a social landlord, the Corporation must have regard to whether those criteria are met.[26] It must consult representative bodies of RSLs and bodies representative of local authorities as it thinks fit before establishing or varying them.[27] They are to be published by the Corporation in such manner as it considers appropriate to bring them to the attention of such bodies.[28] There are no rigid criteria for RSLs; the responsibility for registration is left to the Corporation. During the Committee stage of the Bill, Mr David Curry (the Minister for Local Government Housing and Urban Regeneration) stated, in relation to local housing companies, that it was agreed that a housing company must be in the private sector and that no one should have a dominant share in that company, but as to the other criteria the Corporation must consider each case as it comes – in his words, 'suck it and see'.

The Corporation has issued a Consultation Paper on its proposals for the registration of stock transfer applicants which, it is anticipated, will largely be local housing companies. This will lead to criteria which will probably extend to: (a) the role of the RSL; (b) its management; (c) the checks and controls within the body; (d) its general conduct; and (e) its ability to comply with the Corporation's existing standards.

A body seeking registration as a social landlord must apply in such manner as the Corporation may determine. There is power for the Corporation to levy a fee.[29] As soon as it has registered the social landlord, the Corporation is to give notice of that fact, in the case of a registered charity, to the Charity Commissioners; in the case of an industrial and provident society, to the appropriate registrar; and in the case of a Companies Act company (including a company which is a registered charity), to the Registrar of Companies.[30] The Act also provides that a body which at any time is, or was, registered shall, for all purposes, other than rectification of the register, be conclusively presumed to be, or to have been, at that time a body eligible for registration.[31] This is to protect those dealing with social landlords.

---

25 Section 3(1).
26 Section 5(1), (2).
27 Section 5(3).
28 Section 5(4).
29 Section 3(2).
30 Section 3(3).
31 Section 3(4).

Power to remove from the register

1.8   Having been registered, a body can only be removed from the register in accordance with the following procedure:[32]

(a)   if it appears to the Corporation that the body is no longer eligible for registration;

(b)   if it appears to the Corporation that the body has ceased to exist or does not operate; and

(c)   on the request of the registered social landlord.

Under (a) and (b),[33] the Corporation must give at least 14 days' notice to the social landlord. Furthermore, under these provisions, the duty to remove is mandatory. If it appears to the Corporation that either applies, the Corporation must take steps to remove the body from the register.

In the case of (c), notice can be served at the address last known to the Corporation to be the principal place of business of the body.[34] This discretionary power can only be exercised after the Corporation has consulted the local authority in whose area the body operates; and the Corporation must also inform those authorities of its decision.[35] However, the Act also provides that the Corporation must establish (and may from time to time vary) criteria. In deciding whether to remove a social landlord from the register, the Corporation is to have regard to whether those criteria are met.[36] The procedure to be followed under (c) above is a change from the previous law.

Notice on removal

1.9   As soon as the Corporation has removed a body from the register of the social landlords, the Corporation must give notice of the removal, in the case of a registered charity, to the Charity Commissioners; in the case of an industrial and provident society, to the appropriate registrar; and in the case of a Companies Act company (including a company which is a charity), to the Registrar of Companies.

Challenging the Corporation's decision

1.10   Any body aggrieved by a decision of the Corporation:

(a)   not to register it as a social landlord; or

(b)   to remove or not to remove it from the register of social landlords,

may appeal against the decision to the High Court.[37] If an appeal is brought against a decision relating to the removal of a body from the register, the

---

32 Section 4(2) and (4).
33 These are a re-enactment of HAA 1985, s 4.
34 Section 4(3).
35 Section 4(5).
36 Section 5(3) and (4).
37 Section 6(1).

Corporation is not to remove the body until the appeal has been finally determined or is withdrawn.[38] The Corporation must give notice of the appeal as soon as possible to the Charity Commissioners (in the case of a registered charity) and to the appropriate registrar or Registrar of Companies (in the case of industrial and provident societies and Companies Act companies).

II: Disposal of land and related matters

Introduction

1.11 There have always been powers for housing associations to sell land, which are controlled by the Corporation. These provisions are re-enacted. What is new in the 1996 Act, however, is the right of tenants to acquire, subject to control by the Corporation, the property of a registered social landlord (hereafter 'RSL'). This was promised in the White Paper and further Consultation was produced on the funding mechanism.[39] No doubt, it makes sense for these tenants to be able to purchase their properties, as local authority tenants have had this right for some time and so the effect has been disproportionate between sectors. Within Parliament, the most controversial provisions related to which properties should be excluded from this new right.

Power to dispose of land

General power of disposal

1.12 An RSL is given a general power[40] to dispose of its land in such manner as it thinks fit, subject to control by the Corporation.[41] The power to dispose of property does not arise except under this provision.[42] Section 39 of the Settled Land Act 1925 (duty to obtain 'best consideration in money') is excluded.[43] This creates some difficulties in relation to the tenant's right to acquire, even though requirement for the Corporation's consent is expressly excluded.[44] As all

---

38 Section 6(2).

39 DoE *Our Future Homes* (HMSO, 1995) p 15; DoE *Proposals for a Purchase Grant Scheme for Housing Association Tenants: Consultation Paper Linked to 'Our Future Homes'* (DoE, 1995).

40 Section 8(1).

41 Section 8(3).

42 Section 8(1).

43 See s 8(2). The duty under s 39 of the Settled Land Act to obtain best consideration is applied to the trustees of a charity by s 29 of that Act, and, but for s 8(2) of this Act, any RSL which is a registered charity would be subject to the duty to obtain the best consideration which would prevent the RSL from selling at a discount. It is, however, made clear that this exemption from that duty is not to be treated as authorising any breach of the trusts of the charity.

44 Section 10(3).

disposals must be through this section, there is a potential conflict between the *right* to acquire and the *power* to dispose. No doubt, the former overrides the latter but the obligations of the RSL do not require it to dispose of the property. Furthermore, whilst, throughout Parliamentary debates, it was assumed that an RSL would receive market value for the property, the exclusion of s 39 of the Settled Land Act does not require this. No doubt, the Corporation would be concerned if market values were not being received, particularly in the light of the problems uncovered in Westminster by the district auditor.

Corporation's consent to disposals

1.13   The consent of the Housing Corporation under seal is required for any voluntary disposal[45] under this power.[46] This replaces the familiar s 9 of the HAA 1985. The Corporation may give:[47]

(a)   a general consent to all RSLs;
(b)   a consent to a particular landlord or description of landlords;
(c)   a consent in relation to particular land;
(d)   a consent in relation to a particular description of land.

In each case, the consent may be given subject to conditions or unconditionally. The Corporation has in the past used a general consent to deal with most ordinary course disposals.[48] A new duty requires the Corporation to consult representative bodies of RSLs before giving any general consent.[49]

A disposal of a house[50] without consent is void, unless the disposal is: (a) made to one or more individuals; and (b) the landlord reasonably believes that he or they intend to use the house as his or their principal dwelling.[51] In all other cases, failure to obtain consent does not affect the disposal's validity in favour of the purchaser, who does not need to inquire whether the consent has been given.[52]

---

45 Defined as a sale, lease, mortgage, charge or other disposition. Difficult questions generally arise as to the meaning of 'disposition' in property and revenue law: see *Grey v IRC* [1960] AC 1; *Oughtred v IRC* [1960] AC 206; *Vandervell v IRC* [1967] 2 AC 291; *Re Vandervell's Trusts* [1974] Ch 269.

46 Section 9(1), replacing HAA 1985, s 9. If an RSL is removed from the register maintained under s 1 of the Act, any subsequent disposal of land which it owned at the time of such removal will nevertheless continue to be governed by s 9: s 9(6).

47 Section 9(2).

48 See R2–20/95.

49 Section 9(3).

50 The expression 'house' is used in Part I of the Act to include any part of a building which is occupied or is intended to be occupied as a separate dwelling – see s 63(1).

51 Section 9(4).

52 Section 9(5).

Exemptions from consent

1.14   The following are exempt from the consent requirement:[53]

(i)   lettings under assured tenancies, secure tenancies, or assured agricultural occupancies or those which would be so but for certain exclusions;

(ii)   disposals to which ss 81 and 133 of the Housing Act 1988 apply, where, in any event, the Secretary of State's consent is required;

(iii) disposals under Part V of the Housing Act 1985 (right to buy), and under s 16 of this Act (RSL tenant's right to acquire).

Covenant to be made in disposals to which Corporation's consent required

Recovery of discount under 'voluntary purchase grant' scheme

1.15   As promised in the White Paper,[54] a new scheme known as 'voluntary purchase grant' was introduced, with effect from 1 April 1996, to enable RSLs to grant discounts when selling voluntarily to certain tenants.[55] This scheme complements the new right to acquire. Eligible tenants are those of two years' standing in total (not necessarily continuously), except those in arrears, undischarged bankrupts and those against whom the landlord is seeking possession.

(i) The covenant

Where a purchaser from an RSL receives a discount, that person has to undertake to repay all or part of the discount if there is a further disposal within three years, unless the Corporation's consent provides to the contrary.[56] The undertaking takes the form of a covenant in the instrument effecting the sale, binding the purchaser and successors. If there is a further disposal of the house within three years, the person making the disposal must pay to the landlord a sum equal to all or part of the discount, as follows:[57]

Disposal in first year	Repay 100 per cent
Disposal in second year	Repay two-thirds
Disposal in third year	Repay one-third
Disposal after third year	No repayment[58]

---

53 Section 10.

54 DoE *Our Future Homes* (HMSO, 1995) p 15.

55 Housing Corporation Circular F2–06/96 (March 1996).

56 Section 11(1).

57 Section 11(2).

58 These replace the corresponding provisions in HAA 1985, Sch 2, paras 1 and 2. The provisions for repayment on an early disposal are similar to those applicable under Part V of the Housing Act 1985, where the 'right to buy' has been exercised.

The obligation to repay all or part of the discount arises only where the further disposal is a 'relevant disposal' but not an 'exempted disposal'.[59]

(ii) Security

There is a statutory charge in favour of the RSL on the house, which is subject to protection in accordance with s 59 of the Land Registration Act 1925.[60] Where a charge arises to secure a potential obligation to repay a discount, it ranks immediately after any charge securing the amount left outstanding by the purchaser or lent to him by an 'approved lending institution'[61] for the purposes of acquiring the interest.[62] The RSL may agree to postpone its charge to an advance or further advance made by the institution,[63] but must do so where the purpose of the advance or further advance is to enable the purchaser to pay for: (a) the cost of any works to the house; (b) any service charge payable for works in respect of the house (whether or not the works are to the house); (c) insurance; (d) the discharge of any loan secured by a charge ranking in priority to the charge, including arrears of interest and costs of enforcement of repayment or payment of any such loan or interest.[64]

Right to impose covenant limiting further disposals in National Parks

1.16 There is a provision intended to safeguard the integrity of rural communities by giving RSLs powers to prevent the onward sale of former social housing.[65] Apart from the substitutions of references to RSLs for references to housing associations, the new provisions produce no change in the law. The effect is to impose on the purchaser a covenant limiting the freedom to sell on the property, although there is no requirement to impose the covenant. There can be no 'relevant disposal' other than an 'exempted disposal' without the consent of

---

59 Section 11(2) – and see s 15 (and paras **1.17** and **1.18** below).

60 Under s 11(3). The charge takes priority over any other charge other than charges securing any part of the price left outstanding when the RSL is sold, or charges to secure advances by approved lending institutions to enable the tenant to acquire an interest in the property. It can be protected only by registration of a notice, caution or other prescribed entry. The notice is the most efficient remedy although see *Mortgage Corporation v Nationwide Credit Ltd* [1993] 3 WLR 769 (effect and priority of notice); *Clark v Chief Land Registrar* [1994] 3 WLR 593 (effect of caution).

61 Section 12(5). An approved lending institution is defined as a bank, building society, insurance company, friendly society, the Corporation and a body specified in an order made under s 156 of the Housing Act 1985.

62 Section 12(1).

63 Section 12(2).

64 Section 12(3) and (6).

65 Sections 13–15, re-enacting HAA 1985, Sch 2, paras 3–5.

the RSL.[66] No doubt, a more prohibitive covenant could be inserted. The areas affected are National Parks, areas of outstanding natural beauty[67] and designated rural areas.[68]

(i) Consent must be given where there is a disposal to a person who has, for the previous three years, worked or lived in a designated[69] region or regions within the National Park or area concerned.[70]

(ii) Security: where the limitation applies, it is protected as a local land charge and, where the land is registered under the Land Registration Act 1925, it is to be further protected by means of a restriction under s 58 of that Act.[71] This says that the landlord will receive notification prior to any transfer – an unusual way of protecting a local land charge.

Meaning of 'relevant disposal'

1.17 This means (a) a freehold conveyance, (b) an assignment of a lease, or (c) the grant of a lease (not at a rack rent) for a term of more than 21 years.[72] The avoidance device of granting a short lease with an option to renew will not be effective.[73]

Meaning of 'exempted disposal'

1.18 This category covers a number of situations where the house remains in the ownership of a member of the same family or where the disposal is, in effect, involuntary (or both). It means any of the following:[74]

(a) a freehold conveyance, or assignment of a lease, of an entire house:

(i) by co-owners to one (or more) of their number; or

(ii) to the spouse or former spouse of the person (or one of the people) making the disposal; or

(iii) to a member of the family of the person (or one of the persons) making the disposal, who has lived throughout the previous 12 months with that person (or one of those persons);[75]

---

66 Section 13(2).
67 Designated under s 87 of the National Parks and Access to the Countryside Act 1949.
68 Designated by orders made under s 157 of the Housing Act 1985 (SI 1981/397, SI 1982/21, SI 1982/187, SI 1986/1695, SI 1988/2057 and SI 1990/1282 (all England)).
69 Under s 157 of the Housing Act 1985.
70 Section 13(3).
71 Section 13(5).
72 Section 15(2).
73 Section 15(3).
74 Section 15(4).
75 Section 15(5).

(b)   a vesting of the entire house in a beneficiary under a will or on an intestacy;

(c)   a disposal pursuant to a property adjustment order or order for the sale of property in connection with matrimonial proceedings, or pursuant to an order as to financial provision to be made from the estate of a deceased person, or pursuant to a property adjustment order or an order for the sale of property after overseas divorce or pursuant to an order for financial relief against parents;

(d)   a disposal pursuant to a compulsory purchase order, or to someone who has made (or would have been made) a compulsory purchase order or for whom such an order had been or would have been made had the disposal not taken place voluntarily;

(e)   a disposal of a yard, garden or outhouse or appurtenance belonging to or usually enjoyed with a house.

Tenant's right to acquire

Introduction

1.19   The new scheme differs from that contained in the HAA 1985 in one important respect. Under the old scheme, sale proceeds went to the Housing Corporation. Under the new scheme, which applies only to properties built or acquired with public money after the Act comes into force, sale proceeds are due to the RSL itself and must be used to replace the sold stock.[76]

Qualifying tenants

1.20   An RSL tenant qualifies for the right to acquire provided that he or she (i) has an assured or secure tenancy[77] and (ii) satisfies the qualifying conditions under Part V of the Housing Act 1985.[78] The conditions in Part V require the tenant to have occupied the property for at least two years with certain exceptions.[79]

Qualifying dwellings

1.21   In addition to the tenant conditions, there are also certain conditions as to the dwelling:[80]

(a)   It was 'provided with public money'. It must have been:

---

76 See DoE *Our Future Homes* (HMSO, 1995) p 15 and Standing Committee G, Third Sitting, col 76. See also ss 24 and 25.
77 Section 16(1)(a), excluding assured shortholds and long tenancies.
78 Section 16(1)(c).
79 See ss 118–121.
80 Section 16(1)(b).

(i)   provided or acquired wholly or in part by means of the new social housing grant under s 18;[81] or

(ii) provided or acquired wholly or in part by applying all monies standing in the disposal proceeds fund of an RSL under s 25;[82] or

(iii) acquired by an RSL (after the relevant provision of the Act comes into force) from a public sector landlord at a time when it was capable of being let as a separate dwelling.[83]

(b)   It has 'remained in the social rented sector'. This occurs if, at all times since it was built or acquired with public money, the freeholder has been either an RSL or a public sector landlord.[84] It is also necessary that anyone with any leasehold interest (other than as a mortgagee) has been either an RSL or a public sector landlord, or an individual not holding under a long tenancy.[85]

Powers of the Secretary of State

1.22   The Secretary of State has enormous powers in relation to the tenant's right to acquire.[86]

(a)   There is power to specify the amount or rate of discount which is to be given when a tenant exercises the right.[87] The Government proposes to follow the amounts already available under the tenant's incentive scheme (which enables tenants to buy in the private sector).[88]

(b)   There is power to designate rural areas in which the right will not apply. Before making an order which would result in an area ceasing to be designated, the Secretary of State must consult the local housing authority or authorities concerned (or local housing authorities in general if the order is general in its effect), and such bodies as appear to him to be representative of RSLs as he considers appropriate.[89] This consultation is ongoing at the time of writing. The bones of the exemption are as follows:[90]

---

81 This occurs if the Corporation, when making the grant, told the recipient that the dwelling would be so regarded. Before doing so the Corporation must warn the applicant for the grant that it intends that the dwelling will be so regarded, and allow an opportunity to withdraw the application.
82 HC Debs, Vol 276, col 789.
83 Section 16(2).
84 Section 16(3)(a).
85 Section 16(3)(b).
86 Section 17.
87 Section 17(1)(a).
88 Standing Committee G, Fourth Sitting, col 113.
89 Section 17(6).
90 See HL Debs, Vol 572, cols 1582–1584.

    (i)   In England, settlements[91] where less than 3,000 people live are to be designated. In Wales, there is a test of population density of fewer than 150 persons per square kilometre.[92]

    (ii) Exclusions will be based on parish areas wherever possible, although maps may have to be used to delineate the area.

    (iii) Assessments are based on the most recent census and will be updated on each subsequent census.

    (iv) The Government was willing to consider areas where there might be a special case. In addition, the figure of 3,000 was only a rough-and-ready guide.

    (v) There is no intention of removing exemptions, once made, save in special circumstances.

(c)   There is extensive power to amend Part V of the Housing Act 1985 as it applies to the tenant's right to acquire. RSLs will have discretion to sell where the costs of reprovision are greater than the outstanding private debt.[93] The rent-to-mortgage scheme under the 1985 Act will also be excluded (take-up has, in any event, been very low).[94] The Government has confirmed that the following will be excluded from the right to acquire:

> 'first, the types of supported group developments for the physically or mentally disabled, or the elderly which are excluded from the existing right to buy; secondly, supported housing schemes for special needs accommodation – we have still to define the details of this – and, thirdly, properties where the attributable debt is more than the market value.'[95]

Special needs dwellings excluded will include groups of houses for women who have suffered domestic violence.[96]

However, properties where restrictive covenants apply, limiting, for example, user, type of occupant, or tenure of the property, will be subject to the right to acquire. RSLs who have entered into such restrictive covenants will be subject to liability for breach of these covenants (if enforced), although the sale proceeds will be recycled into new properties subject to the same conditions. Rather than applying for the removal of the restrictions through the Lands Tribunal under s 84 of the Law of Property Act 1925, RSLs should negotiate with the holders of the restrictive covenants for their removal at once (unless the properties are exempt). Equally, areas where planning restrictions by virtue of s 106 agreements are in force will be

---

91 This is the Rural Development Commission's concept: Standing Committee G, Third Sitting, col 87.
92 Using the Organisation for Economic Co-operation and Development's definition of rurality: Standing Committee G, Third Sitting, col 89.
93 Standing Committee G, Third Sitting, col 110.
94 Standing Committee G, Fourth Sitting, cols 118–120.
95 HL Debs, Vol 572, col 1458.
96 HL Debs, Vol 572, col 1472.

subject to the right to acquire, even though new properties will not be able to be built in those areas.[97]

III: Grants and other financial matters

Introduction

1.23 Chapter III empowers the Corporation to make grants and the Public Works Loan Commissioners to make loans to RSLs. In very broad terms, these provisions mirror those of ss 50–59 of the Housing Act 1988 governing the housing association grant ('HAG') and revenue deficit grant ('RDG'), which they supersede.

This Chapter extends the grant (to be known as 'social housing grant' or 'SHG') to all registered social landlords – not just housing associations. Further, it provides for a grant to be made available to landlords to cover the discount they suffer when tenants exercise their right to acquire. As under current legislation, the Act simply sets out a basic framework for the making of SHG. The detailed provisions are left to be set by the Corporation. The Corporation is currently updating its Circulars which will set out its requirements for SHG. However, SHG is unlikely to be implemented before the start of the 1997/8 fiscal year at the earliest.

Social housing grants

Transitional arrangements

1.24 Once SHG becomes available, it will entirely replace HAG and no further claims for HAG may be made. RDG will only be available for deficits from the years beginning 1 April 1994, 1995 and 1996.[98] It is not yet clear to what extent the Corporation will make other revenue grants available once RDG is superseded. The Corporation currently makes a revenue grant, known as special needs management allowance ('SNMA'), under the general HAG provisions to associations which provide special needs accommodation (eg for disabled or frail elderly tenants) and this is likely to continue. In practice, other revenue grants are rare.

Other reforms

1.25 In the White Paper *Our Future Homes*, the Government announced its intention to allow profit-making bodies to compete for SHGs. In order to create a

---

97 For discussion, see HL Debs, Vol 572, col 1469.
98 Section 28(1) and (2).

level playing-field for profit-making companies, the Chancellor announced in the November 1995 Budget that he proposed to withdraw tax relief grant for non-charitable social landlords. This grant currently covers non-charitable associations' liability to corporation tax and stamp duty (but not, for example, value added tax). Charitable associations are, in any event, able to claim exemption from these taxes under general law.

In the event, the Government did not introduce either of these reforms into the Act at any stage of its passage through Parliament, although it still intends to introduce them later in the year. Tax relief grant is only available to non-charitable registered housing associations under the existing legislation and is not extended by the Act to other categories of social landlords (such as local housing companies). A recent DoE Consultation Paper has invited comments on some suggested ways for its withdrawal.

The role of the Corporation

1.26   SHG is to be made only to cover expenditure 'incurred or to be incurred' in connection with the RSL's housing activities.[99] The Corporation will distribute the grant in accordance with such principles as it may from time to time determine. There is no general written requirement that these principles should be set out although, in practice, they will be promulgated in Corporation Circulars. However, the Corporation is required to specify the following:[100]

(a)   the method of grant application;
(b)   the circumstances in which the grant is payable (or not payable);
(c)   the way the grant will be calculated and any limitations; and
(d)   how and when the grant is to be paid.

General determinations relating to SHG require the approval of the Secretary of State (but not, as previously required, the Treasury) and consultation with representatives of RSLs which the Corporation considers appropriate.[101] This is generally interpreted to mean the National Housing Federation. The Corporation may also impose specific conditions on individual RSLs to whom the grant is paid.[102]

Despite some initial concern that the administration of SHG might pass to the Audit Commission, responsibility has remained with the Corporation. Indeed, the Corporation's role remains extremely wide and the number of bodies it must deal with (and thus the scope of its function) has grown.

---

99 Section 18(1).
100 Section 18(2).
101 Sections 53(4) and 54.
102 Section 18(3).

The role of local authorities

1.27 As under existing legislation, the Corporation may appoint a local housing authority to act as its agent for the assessment and payment of SHG.[103] This method of administering the grant can be useful even though it may not be entirely attractive for local authorities. The authority acts as the Corporation's agent and so does not have a free hand in deciding how the grant is to be used. At the same time, the grant is generally treated as counting against the authority's own housing investment programme. Any delegation to a local authority will need the approval of the Secretary of State and the consent of the Treasury.[104]

Transfers of properties with outstanding claims

1.28 If a grant is payable to an RSL in relation to certain property, and that property comes under the ownership of another RSL, then an appropriate proportion of the grant becomes payable to that other RSL.[105] The Corporation may either publish determinations as to how it will allocate a grant between RSLs or make specific determinations for particular cases.[106] Where the relevant property is transferred from a social landlord registered with the Housing Corporation to one registered with Housing for Wales, they must agree a suitable split.[107]

General financial assistance powers

1.29 The Corporation currently has a general power to give financial assistance for specified matters relating to the promotion, formation and management of associations, including tenant participation in management. This power is broadened so as to apply to all RSLs and co-operative housing associations. It allows financial assistance generally to facilitate the proper performance of their functions.[108]

Exclusions

1.30 A new provision excludes from the scope of SHG any land which is managed by an RSL under a management agreement entered into under s 27 of the Housing Act 1985. That enables local housing authorities with the consent of the Secretary of State to appoint another person, such as a housing association, as agent to manage housing or land held for a related purpose.[109]

---

103 Section 18(4), replacing Housing Act 1988, s 50(4).
104 Section 18(5).
105 Section 18(6).
106 Section 18(7).
107 Section 18(8).
108 HAA 1985, s 87(1), replaced by Sch 3, para 7.
109 Section 19.

Purchase grants

1.31 The Corporation is required to make grants to RSLs, in order to cover discounts given to people exercising their right to acquire. The grant given in any year will equal the total of discounts given by the RSL that year to people who exercise the right to acquire.[110]

Powers of the Corporation on distribution

1.32 Whilst grants are mandatory, the Corporation is given power: (a) to impose conditions for the making of this grant;[111] (b) to set out the procedure for grant applications; and (c) to determine how and when the grant is to be paid. This will be done in Circulars.[112]

Other grants

1.33 The Corporation has a parallel power to make grants to cover sales by RSLs of homes to tenants at a discount, in cases not covered by the new right to acquire. The grant is not intended to cover discounts for tenants who exercise the existing right to buy,[113] even though the Act would arguably be wide enought to include this. In these cases, the grant will normally be discretionary.[114] However, where a tenant would be entitled to a right to acquire but buys a different home, the grant is mandatory but limited to the discount the tenant would have had under the right to acquire.[115] Again, the Corporation can impose similar conditions.[116]

Local authorities

1.34 The Act gives local authorities power to promote and assist RSLs. This builds on existing legislation, under which local authorities have corresponding powers in relation to housing associations although certain of these only apply to registered associations.[117] A local authority may promote the formation of bodies to act as RSLs, and the extension of the objects or activities of such landlords.[118] The types of assistance a local authority may give to an RSL are:

(i)   to subscribe its share or loan capital;
(ii)   to make grants or loans to the RSL; or

---

110 Section 20(1) and (2).
111 For example, audits, record-keeping, etc: HL Debs, Vol 572, col 1594.
112 Section 20(3) and (4).
113 Housing Act 1985, Part V.
114 Section 21(1).
115 Section 21(2).
116 Section 21(3) and (4).
117 HAA 1985, ss 58–61.
118 Section 22(1).

(iii) to guarantee or join in guaranteeing payment of interest and capital on borrowings, and interest on share capital issued.[119]

Care is needed since in many cases the assistance given will amount to 'financial assistance' for which the consent of the Secretary of State is required under existing legislation.[120] If this consent is not obtained, the assistance will be void. Following recent court decisions,[121] many funders and others are now wary of relying on guarantees or similar support from local authorities. However, those cases concerned guarantees given by authorities in cases for which there was no statutory power to give them. Where, as here, there is a clear statutory power and the conditions set out in the Act are strictly followed, then it is unlikely that the validity of the guarantee or other assistance could be successfully challenged, although some of the cases suggest the assistance could be void if the authority had acted improperly – in particular if it had taken into account 'impermissible reasons'.

At present, where a local authority has made certain loans or grants to a registered housing association, then either party (with or without the consent of the other) may apply to the Secretary of State to vary or terminate the relevant agreement. This right is repealed by the Act.[122] The Act empowers local housing authorities to sell, or supply on hire-purchase (or by way of conditional sale), furniture to occupants of houses provided by an RSL, and to buy furniture for that purpose.[123] Once again this extends an existing power which currently only applies to housing associations.[124]

Public Works Loan Commissioners

1.35 The Public Works Loan Commissioners are currently empowered to make loans to registered housing associations for specified purposes.[125] Their powers are extended by the Act so as to enable these loans to be made to any RSL.[126] As previously, the Act is fairly specific as to the purposes for which loans may be made.[127]

---

119 Section 22(2) and (3).
120 Local Government Act 1985, s 25.
121 For example *Crédit Suisse v Waltham Forest Borough Council* and *Crédit Suisse v Allerdale Borough Council* (unreported), 8 May 1996, CA.
122 Schedule 3, para 4, repealing HAA 1985, s 69(1)(e) and (g).
123 Section 22(4).
124 HAA 1985, s 61.
125 HAA 1985, s 67.
126 Section 23.
127 Section 23(1).

Security cover requirements

1.36   A loan by the Commissioners (together with interest on the loan) must be secured by a mortgage on the land on which the loan is to be spent, and other property may also be charged as security. The Act contains a 'loan to value' ratio: the amount lent must not in general exceed three-quarters of the value of the charged properties. However, where a local authority guarantees payment of principal and interest on the relevant loan, the maximum loan rises to 90 per cent of the value of the charged properties.[128] The Act does not specify how the property is to be valued except to say that this must be 'to the satisfaction of' the Commissioners. This in itself could lead to extensive arguments in due course given the number of methods of valuation currently used for social housing.

The Act contains an apparent contradiction, in that if the amount lent exceeds two-thirds (not three-quarters) of the value of the security and is not guaranteed, the Commissioners may require further security for their loan. In view of this, it would appear prudent for landlords to comply with the stricter of the two limits, ie the loan not to exceed two-thirds of the value of the charged property.[129] Loans may be made in instalments as the building work on the charged property progresses.[130]

Loan term

1.37   In general, a loan from the Commissioners must be repayable within no more than 40 years and any property to be charged must be either freehold or leasehold with at least 50 years to run at the date of the loan.[131] However, where the purpose of the loan is to carry out a housing scheme approved by the Secretary of State, the maximum length of the loan is 50 years instead of 40 and the term of any charged leasehold property must continue for at least ten years beyond the loan period.[132]

Use of net disposal proceeds

Introduction

1.38   In return for purchase grants, the Act controls the way in which an RSL deals with the proceeds received from a tenant who exercises a right to acquire. This is the only requirement on social landlords to apply receipts in a specific way. Under the existing legislation, a registered housing association which had received a grant could be required to show separately in its accounts surplus rental income arising from housing activities to which the grant related.[133] The

---

128 Section 23(2).
129 Section 23(4).
130 Section 23(3).
131 Section 23(5).
132 Section 23(6).
133 Housing Act 1988, s 55(1).

Secretary of State could require any of this surplus income fund to be paid to him.[134] In practice, associations are not generally required to pay over surplus income in this way although recently there has been growing speculation about the safety and prudent level of housing association reserves and surpluses. This provision has not been carried forward into the Act for SHG and will no longer apply to HAG under the Housing Act 1988, although it remains in place for allocations of old-style grants under previous legislation.[135]

Calculation of net disposal proceeds

1.39 Under the Act, RSLs are required to show separately in their accounts the 'net disposal proceeds'.[136] The net disposal proceeds are:

(a) net proceeds of sale (after deducting an amount to be determined by the Corporation)[137] received on sale of land to a tenant under the right to acquire[138] or for which a purchase grant was available; plus

(b) payments of purchase grant received by the association; plus

(c) any repayments by a tenant of discount for which any purchase grant was given; plus

(d) any other sale proceeds or grant payments which the Corporation determines should be included.[139]

The Corporation will determine (in a Circular) what interest is to be added to the net disposal proceeds fund[140] and how it is to be accounted for.[141] Where the Corporation has directed how disposal proceeds are to be used, it cannot then require the SHG on the relevant property to be repaid to it.[142]

The Corporation is to issue determinations (in the form of Circulars) stating how amounts shown in an RSL's disposal proceeds fund may be disposed of.[143] The Corporation has already issued Guidance on voluntary purchase grant schemes, which states that the account is to be used to provide new social housing units for rent, or to bring existing long-term voids into use or prevent the need for demolition.[144] It seems likely that a similar approach will be taken in relation to statutory purchase grants. If an RSL fails to comply with any directions given, then the Corporation may require part or all of the disposal proceeds to be paid to it.[145]

---

134 Housing Act 1988, s 55(6).
135 Housing Act 1985, s 41, and any prior provision for grant to associations: s 28(5). The Government will return to the issue of long-term surpluses when introducing legislation on profit-making RSLs: Standing Committee G, Fifth Sitting, col 158.
136 Section 24(1).
137 Section 24(3).
138 Section 16.
139 Section 24(2).
140 Section 24(6).
141 Section 24(5) and Sch 1, para 16.
142 Section 24(7).
143 Section 25(1).
144 Circular F2–06/96, paras 7 and 8.
145 Section 25(2).

The Corporation may require all RSLs, or all of a particular description, or individual RSLs to supply any information which it reasonably requires in relation to the disposal proceeds fund.[146]

Supplementary powers of the Corporation

1.40

(i)   The Act contains provisions similar to existing legislation[147] under which the Corporation can reduce, suspend or cancel SHG and recover SHG which has actually been paid.[148] (In fact, the Act does not limit the amount recoverable to SHG actually received.) It is left to the Corporation to publish Circulars identifying when this is to happen.[149] Under the current Circulars (relating to repayment of HAG), in general terms, the principal matters which would result in the Corporation reclaiming HAG are either a sale of the property for which the grant was paid, or a breach of the terms on which the grant was made. In practice, the Corporation may well give an association an opportunity to put right a breach of a grant condition before reclaiming.

(ii) One slight extension is made to the powers of the Corporation where a grant has already been paid. Under the existing legislation, the Corporation could only direct an association to repay the grant to it.[150] Under the Act, the Corporation can direct an RSL either to pay the money to the Corporation, or to apply it for any other purpose which the Corporation may specify.[151] This change is also made to the existing legislation in relation to HAG.[152] The Corporation is still considering in what circumstances it would cancel or claw back SHG and what type of direction it may make as an alternative to requiring repayment to itself.

(iii) Where the Corporation requires any amount to be repaid to it (or paid elsewhere), it can require interest to be payable, at a fixed or variable rate, from a time it specifies. It may also provide that if a payment is made by a specified time, then either no interest or a reduced rate of interest will be payable on it.[153]

(iv) Where an RSL has received grant on a property, and that property then falls within the ownership of another RSL (or is leased to another RSL) that RSL will take over responsibility for any repayment of SHG, as if the grant had originally been made to it. In appropriate cases, the Corporation can direct the proportions.[154] Any directions regarding payment of interest, or the

---

146 Section 26.
147 Housing Act 1988, s 52.
148 Section 27.
149 Section 27(1).
150 Housing Act 1988, s 52(2)(c).
151 Section 27(2).
152 Section 28(3).
153 Section 27(3)–(5).
154 Section 27(6).

proportion of grant to be attributed to a new RSL, may be set out either generally or specifically.[155]

(v) Some housing associations are still entitled to receive payments direct from the Secretary of State of 'special residual subsidy'. This is a form of grant which was originally provided for in the Housing Finance Acts 1967 and 1972. Under the Act, the Secretary of State is now entitled to 'commute' payments which would be due for years 1998/9 and subsequent years into a single lump-sum payment. It if turns out that that payment was too high or too low, then the Secretary of State can make, or require to be made, compensation payments.[156] The Secretary of State may delegate this process to the Corporation.[157]

IV: General powers of the Corporation

Information

Power and procedure

1.41 The Corporation is given extended powers to obtain information from certain specified people and this is backed up by the creation of offences.[158] Furthermore, specified persons and bodies may disclose information to the Corporation, in certain circumstances, and it may disclose information to them.[159] The Corporation may,[160] for any purpose connected with the discharge of any of its functions in relation to RSLs, serve notice under its seal on:[161]

(a) an RSL;

(b) any person who is, or has been, an officer, member, employee or agent of an RSL;

(c) a subsidiary or associate of an RSL;[162]

(d) any person who is or has been an officer, member, employee or agent (including banker, solicitor and auditor) of a subsidiary or associate of an RSL;

(e) any other person whom the Corporation has reason to believe is, or may be, in possession of relevant information.

---

155 Section 27(7).
156 Section 29(1)–(3).
157 Section 29(4).
158 Sections 30–31.
159 Sections 32–33.
160 Section 30.
161 Section 30(2).
162 Defined in s 60(1) and (2).

The notice may require the person to give to the Corporation at a time and place, and in the form and manner specified therein, such information relating to the affairs of the RSL as may be specified or described in the notice. Alternatively, the person may be required to produce to the Corporation, or a person authorised by the Corporation, at a time and place specified in the notice, any documents relating to the affairs of the RSL which are described or specified in it and are in his custody or under his control. The expression 'document'[163] includes anything in which information of any description is recorded. This must be produced in legible form.

Nothing requires disclosure to the Corporation of anything which a person may refuse to disclose on grounds of legal professional privilege in High Court proceedings, or by a banker of anything in breach of any duty of confidentiality owed by him to a person other than an RSL or a subsidiary or associate of an RSL.[164] Any person to whom documents are produced is entitled to take extracts and copies of the documents produced.[165]

Default

1.42   Upon any default in complying with the notice, the Corporation may apply to the High Court for such order as the court thinks fit for requiring the default to be made good.[166] This order can provide that all the costs or expenses of or incidental to the application are to be borne by the person in default, or by any officers of a body who are responsible for its default. There are also two offences:

(a)   a person who, without reasonable excuse, fails to do anything required of him by a notice under s 30 will be liable on summary conviction to a fine not exceeding level 5 on the standard scale;[167]

(b)   a person who intentionally alters, suppresses, or destroys a document which he has been required by notice under s 30 to produce will be liable on summary conviction to a fine not exceeding the statutory maximum and on conviction on indictment to a fine.[168]

Proceedings for these offences can only be brought by or with the consent of the Corporation or the Director of Public Prosecutions.[169]

Disclosure to the Corporation

1.43   The following bodies and persons may,[170] subject to any express restriction on disclosure imposed by or under any other enactment, including an

---

163 Section 30(1).
164 Section 30(4).
165 Section 30(7).
166 Section 31(4).
167 Section 31(1).
168 Section 31(2).
169 Section 32(1).
170 Section 32(1).

enactment comprised in subordinate legislation,[171] disclose any information received by that body or person under or for the purposes of any enactment, to the Corporation:[172]

(a) any government department, including a Northern Ireland department;
(b) any local authority;
(c) any constable;
(d) any other body or person discharging functions of a public nature (including a body or person discharging regulatory functions in relation to any description of activities).

Any such disclosure must be for the purpose of enabling the Corporation to discharge any of its functions relating to RSLs.

Disclosure by the Corporation

1.44 Once the Corporation has the information relating to an RSL, it may disclose it to the same list of persons as may disclose information to the Corporation,[173] except that a person discharging functions of a public nature can also include extra-nationals. However, the disclosure should be for the purpose of the discharge of the functions of the Corporation in relation to such landlords or for the purpose of enabling or assisting the person disclosed to to discharge any of its functions.[174] For example, the Government envisages the Corporation exchanging information with a local authority in support of its functions.[175]

If information disclosed is subject to any express restriction on further disclosure, then the Corporation may only exercise its power to disclose subject to that restriction. Any person who discloses information in contravention commits an offence and is liable on summary conviction to a fine not exceeding level 3 on the standard scale.[176] In its turn, the Corporation may also make a restriction on the further disclosure of information and the same fine would be leviable on a person disclosing that information.[177]

The consent of the Corporation or the Director of Public Prosecutions is required for these proceedings.[178]

Performance standards

1.45 The Corporation is given the power to determine standards of performance in the provision of housing and to arrange for their publication. It must also

---

171 Section 211.
172 Section 32(2).
173 Section 33(2).
174 Section 33(1).
175 HL Debs, Vol 572, col 1401.
176 Section 33(3).
177 Section 33(4) and (5).
178 Section 33(5).

collect information as to levels of performance achieved and publish information to tenants and potential tenants.[179]

Standards of performance

1.46 The Corporation may, after consultation with people or bodies it considers to be representative of RSLs (eg the National Housing Federation), from time to time determine standards of performance in connection with the provision of housing which, in the Corporation's opinion, ought to be achieved by the landlords. It may arrange for the publication, in such form and manner as it considers appropriate, of these standards.[180] It has already put performance standards in place[181] and will, no doubt, update, revise and extend these.

Levels of performance

1.47 The Corporation is given a duty to collect information from time to time as to levels of performance achieved by RSLs in connection with the provision of housing.[182] The Corporation is to make a direction specifying a date in each year by which information is to be given by the RSL as to its level of performance.[183] The information is to be given in regard to each standard determined as the standard of performance. Similar systems are already in place.

Failure without reasonable excuse by an RSL to comply with the direction is an offence subject to a fine not exceeding level 5, and proceedings need the consent of the Corporation or the Director of Public Prosecutions.

Publication

1.48 The Corporation is under a duty at least once in every year to arrange for publication, in such form and manner as it considers appropriate, of the information collected or provided as it thinks expedient to give to tenants or potential tenants of RSLs.[184] It is to have regard to the need for excluding (so far as that is practicable) any matter which relates to the affairs of an individual where publication would or might, in the opinion of the Corporation, seriously and prejudicially affect the interests of that individual, and similarly for any body whether corporate or unincorporate.[185] Presumably, that information that would give an unfair advantage to competitors or unjustifiably prejudice the operations of or reputation of the RSL may be so excluded.

---

179 Sections 34–35.
180 Section 34.
181 Performance Standards for Housing Associations 1994.
182 Section 35(1).
183 Section 35(2).
184 Section 35(4).
185 Section 35(5).

Housing management

1.49   The Corporation is given power to issue Guidance, on housing management. Certain matters are mentioned specifically but the power is general. It can be a gauge for the measurement of the affairs of an RSL.[186] If the Corporation considers that any RSL is failing to maintain or repair any premises in accordance with Guidance it has issued, it is given a new power to enter the property, make a survey and recover the costs from the RSL. It is an offence to hinder the entry.[187]

Before issuing Guidance, the Corporation is to consult such bodies as appear to it to be representative of RSLs. It also has to submit a draft to the Secretary of State for approval.[188] It must then issue it in a manner appropriate to bring it to the notice of RSLs, presumably by Circular.[189] It may then be revised or withdrawn following the same procedure.[190] The Guidance can differentiate in its provisions between different cases, areas, and descriptions of accommodation and of RSLs.[191]

The Corporation may have regard among other matters to the extent to which this Guidance is being, or has been, followed in considering whether action needs to be taken to secure the proper management of the affairs of an RSL, or whether there has been mismanagement.[192]

Powers of entry

1.50   It is logical for the Corporation to have powers of entry when so much of an RSL's work depends on the state of repair of its property. Where it appears to the Corporation that an RSL may be failing to maintain or repair any premises in accordance with the Guidance,[193] a person authorised in writing by the Corporation may enter the premises at any reasonable time to survey and examine on giving not less than 28 days' notice of such intention to the RSL concerned.[194] The authority must state the particular purpose or purposes for which the entry is authorised and must, if required, be produced for inspection by the occupier or person acting for him or her.[195] It is the duty of the RSL, where

---

186 Section 36.
187 Section 37.
188 Section 36(3).
189 Section 36(4).
190 Section 36(5).
191 Section 36(6).
192 Section 36(7).
193 Section 37(1).
194 Section 37(2).
195 Section 37(5).

such a notice is given, to give the occupier or occupiers of the premises not less than seven days' notice of the proposed survey and examination. Failure by the landlord to give this notice or obstruction of the surveyor by the RSL or any of its officers or employees is an offence.[196] Proceedings can be brought only by or with consent of the Corporation or the Director of Public Prosecutions.[197] The landlord is liable on summary conviction to a fine not exceeding level 3 on the standard scale. The landlord is entitled to a copy of the survey and may have to pay the costs of the surveyor.[198]

Insolvency

1.51 Sections 39–50 of the Act contain an entirely new procedure that must be followed in the event that an RSL is in broad terms insolvent, where action is to be taken to enforce any security over its land or where it is to be put into an insolvency procedure. The circumstances in which these provisions apply are wider than in a pure insolvency situation and, where they apply, the provisions of the Act take precedence over the Insolvency Act 1986.[199] For example, where a creditor seeks to enforce security over land held by the RSL it does not necessarily follow that in such circumstances the RSL will be insolvent.

Considerable private funds are being lent to the social housing sector by banks and other institutional lenders and are usually secured against land owned by the social landlord. The rationale behind these provisions was to protect tenants by putting in place a system that would enable such land to be transferred from one RSL to another should the original owner become insolvent.

In common with all UK insolvency legislation, these provisions recognise the importance of secured creditors over unsecured creditors. There is little comfort in the Act for unsecured creditors.

Notice procedure

1.52 Sections 40 and 41 incorporate a twofold notice procedure designed to ensure that the Corporation is kept informed where an RSL is in immediate peril

---

196 Sections 37(3) and 38(1).
197 Sections 37(4) and 38(3).
198 Section 37(6) and (7).
199 Together with the Insolvency Rules 1986/1925, the Insolvency Act 1986 contains most of the relevant statutory provisions regarding the various insolvency procedures, individual and corporate. For information as to the procedures to be followed in an insolvency, for example the procedure to liquidate a company, reference must be made to the relevant provisions of this legislation.

of insolvency or losing control over all or part of its land to a secured creditor. The consequences of failing to follow the notice procedure are in the case of the first notice (s 40) fatal, and in the case of the second notice (s 41) damaging but not necessarily fatal.

The first notice

1.53 The Corporation must be given written notice *before* certain defined steps are taken against the RSL.[200] There is no set form for the notice, only that it must be written but it obviously must give proper notice of the step or action that is intended to be taken. The only timing requirement is that it is given *before* the step is taken. It must follow that the only obligation on the person charged with giving the notice is to show that it was received by the Corporation before the person took the step/action in respect of which notice is required to be given: 'before' means one minute, one hour, one day or one week before. This notice can be given by facsimile which will create a timed record of when it was sent.

The Act provides for a number of specified acts in respect of which the written notice must be given to the Corporation by a specified person. The Act provides for various notices to be given where the social landlord is an industrial and provident society, a company or a charitable trust:

Step	*Person to give notice*
1 Any step to enforce any security over land held by the landlord[201]	The person proposing to take the step
2 Presenting a petition for the winding-up of the landlord[202]	The petitioner
3 Passing a resolution for the winding-up of the landlord[202]	The landlord
4 Applying for an administration order[203]	The applicant

The notice must be given by the specified person. For example, if a creditor intends to enforce security over land held by an RSL then the fact that the Corporation may be aware of the creditor's intention from a third party is irrelevant. It is the duty of the creditor to give the prescribed notice.

Failure to give the first notice[204] renders any action taken ineffective.[205] So where one of the defined steps is taken without the prescribed notice, the proceedings

---

200 Section 40(1).

201 This applies to all three categories of social landlord.

202 This applies to an industrial and provident society or company.

203 This only applies to a company. For administrative provisions, see the Insolvency Act 1986, Part II, ss 8–27.

204 See the very limited exception in s 40(5) where the Corporation will in any event be aware of the insolvency as its consent is required.

205 Section 40(6).

are of no effect. This is a trap for the unwary. For example, if a petition is served without first a s 40 notice and a liquidator appointed, that person would be a trespasser acting without authority and liable to make good any loss the RSL suffers. Furthermore, as petitions are usually issued by solicitors, the creditor instructing the solicitor would have a cause of action in negligence to recover the wasted costs and any loss suffered as a result of the delay.

The second notice

1.54   This 'must be given to the Corporation as soon as may be after any of the steps [mentioned in s 41] are taken in relation to an RSL'.[206] These steps are the logical consequence of the above. They are:

Step	Person to give notice
1 The taking of a step to enforce any security over land held by the landlord	The person taking the step
2 The making of an order for the winding-up of the landlord	The petitioner
3 The passing of a resolution for the winding-up of the landlord	The landlord
4 The making of an administration order	The applicant

The consequence of failing to give the second notice is that it delays and prevents any disposal of land (without the Corporation's consent) because the 28-day moratorium does not start to run until the second notice has been given. Any disposal without cause is void.

Examples

1.55   It is quite possible that both notices may be given within a very short time frame:

(i)   A creditor decides to appoint receivers over land owned by a defaulting RSL. Prior to the appointment a s 40 notice must be given. The receivers may then be appointed and as soon as possible thereafter a s 41 notice given. These events could all happen during the course of one working day.

(ii)   A creditor decides to issue a petition for the winding-up of an RSL. A s 40 notice must be given and the petition can then be issued: this could happen in the same day. There is then likely to be a delay of several weeks before the making of the order for the winding-up and it is notable that if a creditor wanted to appoint a provisional liquidator[207] then the Corporation need not be given specific notice of that application.

---

206 Section 41(1).
207 A provisional liquidator has the power to collect and preserve assets.

(iii) Where a landlord is entering voluntary liquidation and is passing a resolution for that purpose, the s 40 and s 41 notices may be given again on the same day before and after the meeting.

(iv) In the case of an application for an administration order, that is a relatively quick process and it will be possible for the s 40 notice to be given one day, with the application to take place in court the following day. Such applications usually last a couple of hours and the s 41 notice can be given thereafter if an administration order is made.

Meaning of 'the taking of a step to enforce the security'

1.56 This raises difficult issues. Security means any mortgage, charge or other security and in most cases it is likely to be a charge.[208] The Secretary of State may make provision by order defining what is meant by a step to enforce security over land but no such provisions have been made yet.[209] The taking of a step is the doing of a positive act and that act must be done to enforce security over land. The creditor's appointment of a receiver would be such an act, but consulting a solicitor for advice probably would not. A grey area is the sending of a letter of demand which will almost certainly be required as the trigger under the loan agreement to establish an act of default to appoint a receiver. Until the position is clarified by order the safest course for a creditor is, before sending such a letter, to give the Corporation a s 40 notice.

Moratorium

1.57 Insolvency legislation is increasingly using the concept of the moratorium.[210] This moratorium applies only to the disposal of land held by the RSL. Therefore, if a creditor petitions for an RSL's liquidation and gives the s 40 notice, but fails to give the s 41 notice following the appointment of a liquidator, the only constraint on the liquidator is that no disposal of land can be made.[211] The liquidator would, for example, be able to take control of all assets and dispose of all assets other than land. Once the moratorium is in place, the consent of the Corporation is required for any disposal of land held by the RSL, whether directly or indirectly, ie in a subsidiary company. The Corporation can give consent both in advance and subject to conditions.[212]

The moratorium is for a minimum period of 28 days from the day on which the s 41 notice is given and can then be extended with the consent of all the RSL's

---

208 Section 39(2).

209 Section 39(3).

210 See, for example, individual voluntary arrangements, administration orders and proposals to change company voluntary arrangements – this concept was imported from the US Chapter 11 procedure.

211 Disposal for these purposes has a wide definition under s 39(2) and it means sale, lease, mortgage, charge or any other disposition, and includes the grant of an option.

212 No consent is required for the disposal of land let under an assured tenancy or an assured agricultural occupancy or other land within the meaning of s 10(1) of the Act – see s 42(3).

secured creditors.[213] In such circumstances the Corporation must give notice to the RSL and any liquidator, administrative receiver, receiver or administrator appointed in respect of the RSL or any land held by it. During the period of the moratorium, land can only be disposed with the Corporation's consent.

The purpose of the moratorium is to enable the Corporation to put forward proposals for the proper management of the land, so where it considers that the proper management can be secured without making proposals, then it retains the power to direct that the moratorium shall cease to have effect, ie within the 28-day period.[214] There is no obligation on the Corporation to make proposals.[215] If the Corporation chooses to do so then it is required to consult the RSL, but only 'so far as is practicable, its tenants' in formulating proposals.[216] In addition, the Corporation 'shall have regard to the interests of all the landlord's creditors, both secured and unsecured', but there is no obligation to consult and it is difficult to see what practical benefit such a provision will have.[217] If the secured creditors have security over land (which is likely) then in any event their agreement is a prerequisite to binding proposals.

No proposals shall be made affecting the preferential creditor's rights, unless with the consent of the creditor concerned,[218] but unsecured creditors have no such protection. The only requirement on the Corporation and secured creditors is 'so far as practicable no proposals shall be made which have the effect that unsecured creditors of the landlord are in a worse position than they would otherwise be' (ie in a liquidation).[219] The term, 'so far as practical', leaves much room for argument and may, in practice, provide no protection to unsecured creditors in most cases.

The Corporation is obliged to serve its proposals on the landlord and its officers, the secured creditors and any liquidator/administrator, administrative receiver or receiver appointed in respect of the landlord or its land. This excludes members, tenants and unsecured creditors, where the only requirement on the Corporation is that it will 'make such arrangements as it considers appropriate to see that [they] are informed of the proposals'. This gives a wide discretion and will cover, for example, informing tenants at a public meeting or notifying them by letter.

Agreed proposals
1.58   Where the Corporation and all the secured creditors agree proposals, they bind all concerned including preferential creditors, unsecured creditors, tenants

---

213 Section 43(3).
214 Section 43(4).
215 Section 44(1).
216 Section 44(2)(a).
217 In addition, the Corporation shall also consult the appropriate Registrar in the case of an industrial and provident society or in the case of a registered charity the Charity Commissioners – see s 44(3).
218 Section 44(4).
219 Section 44(5).

and members. Such categories of person can challenge the proposals if they infringe the provisions of s 44(4)–(6) (see above). It is conceivable that committee members, directors and trustees will not have been party to the discussions formulating proposals, which will most probably take place between the secured creditor and the Corporation. To prevent such persons refusing to co-operate, the Act provides that it is their duty to do so to the extent that it does not conflict with any fiduciary or other duty owed by them.[220] To the extent that such officers refuse to co-operate, they could be compelled to do so by court order and may be liable for any loss sustained by a breach of these provisions.[221]

The Corporation is under a duty to serve a copy of the agreed proposals on:

(i)   the RSL and its officers;
(ii) the secured creditors of the landlord;
(iii) any liquidator, administrator, administrative receiver or receiver appointed in respect of the landlord or its land;
(iv) where the landlord is an industrial and provident society or registered charity, the appropriate Registrar of the Charity Commissioners as the case may be.

The only obligation on the Corporation regarding members, tenants and unsecured creditors is to make such arrangements as it considers appropriate to inform them of the proposals.[222]

Where no proposals are agreed
1.59   If the Corporation is unable to agree proposals with all secured creditors then at the conclusion of the 28-day period the moratorium will come to an end unless all the secured creditors agree to an extension. In the absence of any such agreement the moratorium will end after 28 days, and for the next three years if any further steps are taken which would require a s 41 notice, the moratorium will not be reinstated unless the RSL's secured creditors consent; the notices must still be given otherwise any action is ineffective. Once the moratorium is at an end the secured creditor is free to dispose of the land, and in such circumstances does not have to sell to another social landlord although in practical terms it is highly likely that the only purchasers in the market will be other RSLs.

The appointment of a manager

1.60   The Corporation and the secured creditors can agree to appoint a manager to oversee and implement the agreed proposals.[223] The manager, who is likely to be (but does not necessarily have to be) a licensed insolvency

---

220 Section 45(3)(c).
221 See s 50.
222 Section 45.
223 If the landlord is a registered charity, the Corporation must give notice to the Charity Commissioners of the appointment – see s 46(2).

practitioner, will then implement the proposals subject to the direction of the Corporation. If the manager wishes to clarify any particular matter, application may be made to the High Court for directions.[224] Given the wide powers the Corporation has, the Parliamentary draftsman has found it necessary to include a provision that a court direction supersedes the direction of a Corporation.[225]

The manager has very wide powers to administer the land pending sale and then to sell.[226] The manager is the landlord's agent and does not attract personal liability on contracts entered into. Furthermore a person dealing with the manager in good faith is not concerned to inquire whether the manager is acting within the powers. So far as is practicable, the manager is to consult/inform the RSL's tenants regarding the exercise of any powers which are likely to affect them and inform them about any such exercise of the powers. What is practicable will depend upon the circumstances and it may be that in some circumstances it is not practical to consult the tenants at all.

Where the RSL is an industrial and provident society, the manager is empowered to make and execute any instrument transferring the engagement of a society on its behalf. The manager is required to send a copy of the instrument to the appropriate registrar within 14 days from the date on which the instrument is executed. In the event that the document is not sent in time, this does not invalidate registration after 14 days.

High Court

1.61 Section 50 contains two distinct mechanisms by which applications can be made to the High Court to secure compliance with the agreed proposals.

(i)   The RSL or any creditor of the RSL can apply to the High Court on the ground that an action of the manager is not in accordance with the agreed proposals.[227] The court has power to 'confirm, reverse or modify any act or decision of the manager, give him directions or make such other order as it thinks fit'. It is unlikely in such circumstances that the court would make any order or award of damages unless the manager had breached the duty of good faith. In any event, if there is a dispute regarding the manager's actions, it is likely that the manager would apply to the High Court for directions.

(ii) The Corporation or any other person bound by the agreed proposals may apply to the High Court on the ground that any action, or proposed action, by another person bound by the proposals is not in accordance with those proposals. For example, this would apply where committee members were refusing to ratify a sale or transfer of land that had been agreed. The court

---

224 Thus, in this respect, the position of the manager is very similar to that of an insolvency
     office-holder or supervisor of a voluntary arrangement under the Insolvency Act 1986.
225 Section 46(5).
226 Section 47(2).
227 Section 50(1).

has wide power under s 50(2) on the hearing of an application and may declare any action to be ineffective, and more importantly can grant an injunction, an award of damages or other relief as appears appropriate. The Parliamentary draftsman has used much harsher language than in s 50(1). Where people bound by agreed proposals are for any reason dissatisfied with those proposals they should take advice and consider making an application to court for directions (if applicable) rather than seek to frustrate the proposals by direct action which could result in individuals being liable for costs and damages.

Assistance by the Corporation

1.62 Section 49 provides for the Corporation to give assistance as it thinks fit to the landlord to preserve the position pending the making and agreement of proposals, and if agreed to the RSL or manager for the purpose of carrying out the proposals.[228] Such assistance includes (non-exclusively) lending to staff, paying or securing the payment of the manager's reasonable remuneration and expenses or giving such other financial assistance as appears appropriate. However, the powers of the Corporation are limited in that it requires the consent of the Secretary of State to:

(i)   make grants or loans;
(ii)   indemnify the manager in respect of liabilities incurred in connection with his functions;[229]
(iii) pay or guarantee payment of the principal debt secured on the land.[230]

---

228 Section 49(1).

229 A licensed insolvency practitioner carries a bond that should cover him in such circumstances. If not then the manager will have to obtain insurance cover.

230 Preventing the Corporation from stepping into the secured creditors' shoes.

1.63

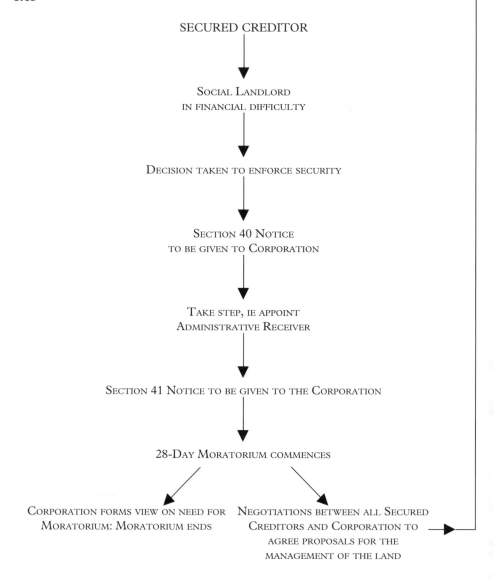

SECURED CREDITOR

SOCIAL LANDLORD
IN FINANCIAL DIFFICULTY

DECISION TAKEN TO ENFORCE SECURITY

SECTION 40 NOTICE
TO BE GIVEN TO CORPORATION

TAKE STEP, IE APPOINT
ADMINISTRATIVE RECEIVER

SECTION 41 NOTICE TO BE GIVEN TO THE CORPORATION

28-DAY MORATORIUM COMMENCES

CORPORATION FORMS VIEW ON NEED FOR
MORATORIUM: MORATORIUM ENDS

NEGOTIATIONS BETWEEN ALL SECURED
CREDITORS AND CORPORATION TO
AGREE PROPOSALS FOR THE
MANAGEMENT OF THE LAND

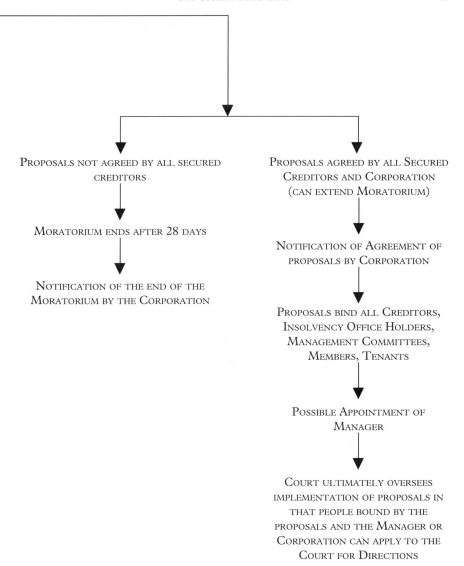

V: Miscellaneous and general provisions[231]

Housing complaints

1.64   Section 51 and Sch 2 deal with the establishment of housing ombudsman schemes, under which tenants can make complaints against social landlords. The Act puts the requirement of a housing ombudsman scheme on a statutory footing, imposes detailed obligations on social landlords and gives wide-ranging powers to housing ombudsmen. However, an ombudsman's sanctions have little teeth as they are limited to publishing (or requiring the association to publish) details of non-compliance with the statutory scheme.

Housing Association Tenants' Ombudsman Scheme

1.65   At present, registered housing associations subscribe to the Housing Association Tenants' Ombudsman Scheme ('HATOS'). There is no direct statutory requirement to join HATOS, but the Corporation has issued a Circular[232] under its general powers[233] requiring registered associations to join HATOS and to abide by its terms of reference. HATOS may notify the Corporation of any breach of its requirements. The Corporation's ultimate sanction for those who fail to join or abide by HATOS would be to cut off their grant. HATOS is independent of the Corporation. Its terms of reference cover, in general terms, complaints from tenants or disappointed applicants for tenancies arising from an association's duties as landlord.

New schemes

1.66   The new schemes are based on the schemes which apply to building societies.[234] Whereas at present the only scheme is HATOS, the Act envisages that several schemes may run concurrently. Each must be approved by the Secretary of State.[235] The existing HATOS scheme is applying for recognition under the Act. Membership of a scheme will be compulsory for 'social landlords', defined as:

(i)   registered social landlords;
(ii) a transferee of housing under a qualifying disposal;[236]
(iii) a new landlord which has acquired housing under the 'tenants' choice' mechanism in Part IV of the Housing Act 1988 (abolished in this Act);

---

231 Concentration in this text is upon the new provisions.
232 'The Responsibilities of Registered Housing Associations with Respect to the Housing Association Tenants' Ombudsman', HC39/93.
233 HAA 1985, s 36A.
234 Building Societies Act 1986, s 83 and Sch 12.
235 Section 51(1).
236 Leasehold Reform, Housing and Urban Development Act 1993, s 135.

(iv) any other body which has at any time been registered with the Corporation and owns or manages 'publicly funded dwellings'.[237]

'Publicly funded dwellings' are those provided by means of SHG or HAG since 1974, or which have been acquired from a public sector landlord.[238]

The Secretary of State may, after appropriate consultation, vary the definition of 'social landlords' to which the housing ombudsman provisions are to apply by statutory instrument.[239]

Types of new schemes

1.67 Every social landlord must join at least one appropriate scheme, which must cover all its housing activities.[240] If a social landlord fails to join a scheme or schemes covering its activities, it can be ordered to do so by the High Court (on an application by the Secretary of State).[241]

The actual contents of a scheme are left to be set by its promoters. Schedule 2, para 2 lists matters which must be addressed but, in general, leaves open what the scheme should say on each point. The overriding restriction is that the Secretary of State must find the scheme 'satisfactory' before approval.[242]

Role of the Corporation

1.68 The Corporation must maintain a register of housing ombudsman schemes identifying membership of each scheme, which must be made available to the public.[243] Each social landlord which joins an approved scheme (or a scheme which becomes approved) has 21 days to give notice to the Corporation of this. Failure to do so is an offence.[244] If a social landlord wishes to withdraw, notice must be served on the Corporation demonstrating adequate regulation by other schemes after withdrawal. If the Corporation is not satisfied, it can refuse to accept the withdrawal and the social landlord will remain bound by the first scheme.[245]

Determinations by ombudsman

1.69 A housing ombudsman must determine each complaint by reference to what is fair in the circumstances[246] and may order a scheme member to pay compensation. The complainant or the social landlord may be directed not to

---

237 Section 51(2).
238 Section 51(3).
239 Section 51(4) and (5).
240 Schedule 2, para 1(1).
241 Schedule 2, para 1(2).
242 Schedule 2, para 3(2)(b).
243 Schedule 2, para 6.
244 Schedule 2, para 4.
245 Schedule 2, para 5.
246 Schedule 2, para 7(1).

exercise or insist on rights or obligations under the contract between them. Thus, for example, the ombudsman could prevent an RSL from exercising a power to evict a tenant.[247] If a member of an ombudsman scheme does not comply with an ombudsman's ruling, the ombudsman's default powers are somewhat limited as follows:

(i)   the ombudsman can order a landlord to publish that fact;
(ii) in the case of a landlord who is not a 'social landlord', the ombudsman can expel that landlord, publish a notice of expulsion and the reason;
(iii) if the member fails to publish a notice as required, the ombudsman can do this and recover the cost.[248]

If the ombudsman makes any order against the complaining tenant, there are no enforcement powers.

Members of a scheme cannot claim that they have no power to do what an ombudsman requires, except that a charitable member cannot be required to act against its charitable trusts.[249]

Orders and determinations

1.70   An order made by the Secretary of State under Part I of the Act may make different provisions for different cases or descriptions of case: for different bodies or descriptions of body; for different housing activities; and for different areas.[250] An order may contain any supplementary, incidental, consequential or transitional provisions and savings which the Secretary of State considers appropriate.[251]

Determinations are made by the Secretary of State or by the Corporation.

The word 'determination' is not defined and is wide enough to cover the issue of general criteria,[252] the granting of consent[253] or the issue of a notice.[254] In each case it is a means of making more detailed regulations for a matter which is simply mentioned in the Act. The most familiar manifestation is in the form of Corporation or DoE Circulars. Determinations are, however, separate from the power of the Corporation to issue Guidance to registered social landlords.[255]

Where the Secretary of State or the Corporation is to make a general determination (defined as a determination which does not relate solely to a

---

247 Schedule 2, para 7(2).
248 Schedule 2, para 7(3), (4) and (5).
249 Schedule 2, para 7(6).
250 Section 52(2).
251 Section 52(3).
252 See, for example, s 5.
253 See, for example, s 9.
254 See, for example, s 30.
255 Section 36 (replacing HAA 1985, s 36A).

particular case),[256] the entity making the determination must consult any bodies representative of registered social landlords which it considers appropriate. But consultation must be genuine and sufficient time given to formulate a proper response.[257] The final determination must be publicised 'in such manner as they consider appropriate'.[258] Any general determination by the Corporation dealing with accounting and audit requirements of registered social landlords,[259] or recovery, etc of social housing grants,[260] requires the approval of the Secretary of State.[261]

Minor amendments to certain acts

1.71 The Act makes a number of amendments to existing statutes:[262]

Finance Act 1981

This Act exempts conveyances relating to houses sold at a discount by such bodies as local authorities and registered housing associations from stamp duty on the discounted element which is contingently repayable, for example, if the property is sold within a certain period.[263] The amendments take account of the creation of the definition of an RSL and also provide that a purchase grant under the Act is to be treated in the same manner as a discount for the purposes of exemption.

Local Government Finance Act 1982

New sections[264] give the Audit Commission powers to agree programmes of comparative studies with the Corporation with a view to making recommendations for improving the economy, efficiency and effectiveness of RSLs. The cost of these programmes is to be borne by the Corporation. When the Corporation and the Audit Commission fail to agree the implementation of a programme, the matter can then be referred to the Secretary of State who may direct that the programme be carried out with or without modification. The Corporation may authorise the Audit Commission to obtain information or documents from RSLs for the purposes of carrying out such a study. Information obtained can be disclosed to the Corporation by the Audit Commission. The amendments also give the Audit Commission the power to provide the Corporation with

---

256 Section 53(3).
257 Section 53(4) and see *R v Secretary of State for Social Services ex parte AMA* [1986] 1 WLR 1.
258 Section 53(5).
259 Schedule 1, para 16.
260 Section 27.
261 Section 54.
262 Schedule 3.
263 Finance Act 1981, s 107.
264 Sections 28B–28E.

consultancy services relating to the audit of accounts of RSLs and to charge for these.

Housing Associations Act 1985

The provision in this Act which allows the Secretary of State to recognise a central association advising housing associations and to make grants to cover its expense is abolished.[265] A number of the general functions of the Corporation are also amended.[266]

The most important amendment concerns the sale of the Corporation's loan book originally announced in the November 1995 Budget. The Corporation has made loans to housing associations since about 1974. Typically, the loans were made to fund the acquisition or development of a particular property or set of properties and were secured by a charge on those properties. The loans were entered into for a term of 30 or 60 years and most were at a fixed rate of interest, although in a minority of cases a variable or stepped interest rate was charged. Associations which have entered into a number of loans may 'consolidate' the financial terms of the loan so that all become subject to an 'average' rate of interest and final repayment date, and there is a single pool of security. In doing so, under the latest Corporation Circular, certain covenants (both legal and financial) must be entered into in favour of the Corporation.

Over the years, the Corporation has made a substantial number of changes to the standard terms which apply to these loans. One point of particular concern in the context of the sale was whether mortgages entered into on a number of the earlier sets of terms were assignable at all. The Act resolves this difficulty by giving the Corporation an express power to sell all or part of its loans portfolio and permitting the release of security for those associations which have not already consolidated their security. Any arrangement for sale must be approved by the Secretary of State, and the Secretary of State may direct the Corporation to enter into such an arrangement. Any sale may involve the transfer of any interest in land of the Corporation, or alternatively the creation of separate economic interests without involving such a transfer (eg the creation of trusts). This could enable the division of the Corporation's loan book when it is sold.[267]

Income and Corporation Taxes Act 1988

This Act exempts co-operative housing associations from corporation tax on chargeable gains as well as specifying that rent received from members is to be disregarded for tax purposes, the yearly interest being treated for tax purposes as payable by the members of the association in proportion to the rents which they pay. For this exemption to apply, the co-operative housing association in

---

265 HAA 1985, s 33.
266 HAA 1985, s 75(1)(a), (b) and (c).
267 Schedule 3, para 6 (inserting HAA 1985, s 76A).

question must be approved by the Secretary of State.[268] The amendments provide for the Secretary of State to delegate his functions of approval to the Housing Corporation. Similar provisions exist in relation to self-build societies[269] and the amendments provide for similar delegation.

VI: Regulating the RSL[270]

Control of payments to members, etc

1.72   Schedule 1, Part I replaces, with minor and consequential amendments, HAA 1985, ss 13–15. These controls are imposed with the intention of ensuring that an RSL cannot distribute profits or, with certain exceptions, pass benefits to shareholders, officers or other specified persons connected to the RSL. To date, they have done much to ensure the continuance of the good name of the housing association movement. However, the provisions have caused, and will continue to cause, great difficulties in practice, particularly in small communities. Where, for example, a local trader joins the committee or board of an RSL, he can no longer supply to the RSL, even at a discount, despite being, say, the only supplier for 15 miles. The embargo continues for a year after the trader resigns from the committee.

The Corporation has expected registered housing associations to comply not just with the letter but also with the spirit of the law, which they have seen as the legal embodiment of the good reputation of the housing association movement.[271] This attitude will continue in respect of RSLs. As public money and the confidence of lenders are both involved, RSLs must be, and be seen to be, above not only wrongdoing but also any such suspicion.

RSLs other than industrial and provident societies and companies that are registered charities

1.73   The Corporation has in the past expected all such registered housing associations which are charities to comply with the spirit of HAA 1985, s 15 (now para 2) and to adopt their standards. It will expect RSLs to do the same.

Gifts, loans, dividends or bonuses to members and others

1.74   All RSLs are forbidden to make a gift or pay a sum by way of dividend or bonus to:[272]

---

268 Income and Corporation Taxes Act 1988, s 488.
269 Income and Corporation Taxes Act 1988, s 489.
270 These provisions are contained in Sch 1. Concentration is upon the new provisions.
271 Housing Corporation Circular HC 11.93, para 8.
272 Schedule 1, para 1(1).

(i)   A person who is or has been a member of the body.
(ii)   A person who is a member of the family of the person within para (i). A member of another's family for the purposes of Part I of the Act[273] is:

    (a)   a spouse of that person, or someone who lives together with that person as husband and wife; or

    (b)   a parent, grandparent, child, grandchild, brother, sister, uncle, aunt, nephew or niece of that person. Relationships by marriage are treated as relationships by blood. Half-blood relationships are treated as whole blood relationships and the stepchildren of a person are treated as children.[274]

(iii) A company of which a person within para (i) or (ii) is a director.

However, payment of interest on capital lent or subscribed by way of shares is permitted if it is in accordance with the constitution or rules of the body.[275] These must, for registration purposes, prohibit the issue of capital at greater than certain interest or dividend rates,[276] and may not be amended without sealed consent from the Housing Corporation.[277] Therefore, this is not an important relaxation.

Also permitted are payments by a fully mutual housing association to a person, who has ceased to be a member, of the sum due under the relevant tenancy agreement with the association, or under the terms of the agreement under which that person became a member of the association.[278] This relaxation is required by co-operative and co-ownership associations whose members may be entitled to repayment of a share at par or a sum paid to meet an equity share on leaving the association.

Payments and benefits to officers, employees, etc

1.75 This applies to RSLs that are industrial and provident societies or companies other than companies which are registered charities. They are forbidden,[279] with exceptions,[280] to make a payment or grant a benefit to:

(i)   Their officers[281] or employees.
(ii)   People who at any time within the preceding 12 months have been officers or employees. For example, subject to any relaxation by determination, it is essential to renegotiate, without ending, the contracts of employees who

---

273 Section 62 (previously HAA 1985, s 105).
274 Children born outside marriage are already treated the same as other children: Family Law Reform Act 1987, s 1.
275 Schedule 1, para 1(2)(a).
276 Section 2(3)(b).
277 Schedule 1, paras 9, 10 and 11.
278 Schedule 1, para 1(2)(b).
279 Schedule 1, para 2(1).
280 Schedule 1, para 2(2).
281 For definition, see s 59.

wish to continue to work part time after, perhaps, giving up full-time employment.

(iii) Close relatives of those in para (i) or (ii). It has been assumed that close relatives are a smaller class than a member of the family. The definition has intentionally been left vague. It would seem safest to consider that the meaning is as wide as a member of the family. However, the Housing Corporation has expressed the view that a close relative is a relative by blood or marriage who is so close to the person involved that there is a real risk that the decision of the association to grant him/her a benefit could be influenced by that relationship.[282] The examples they give exclude nephews, nieces, aunts, and uncles, but clearly these could be within the class.

(iv) Businesses trading for profit of which a person falling within para (i), (ii) or (iii) above is either a principal proprietor or directly concerned in the management.

However, the following are permitted:[283]

(i) Payments to officers or employees under contracts of employment with the body. This can lead to difficulties in regard to settlement of claims upon dismissal[284] or retirement. Matters like pensions and other benefits must be considered before commencement of (or during) any employment, and contract terms and conditions should be kept up to date. Concern was expressed that this would lead to a change in ethos within the movement, as allowing paid officers. The Housing Corporation is likely to want to limit the numbers of employee directors or committeemen on a Board.

(ii) Payment of remuneration or expenses to an officer who has no contract with the body. Remuneration has been added to the HAA 1985 wording but maximum payments will be specified.

(iii) Payments permitted as set out at para **1.74**.

(iv) For co-operative housing associations, the grant or renewal of a tenancy.

(v) Grants of tenancies of the same or another dwelling to an existing tenant where that person or that person's close relative later became an officer or employee.

(vi) Payments made or benefits granted in accordance with any determination by the Housing Corporation. This determination may specify the class or classes of case when a payment may be made, or benefit granted, and may specify the maximum amount.[285] The latter is new. It has been included to ensure 'that the voluntary ethos of housing associations is not lost' so that 'they do not become commercial organisations hiring their directors or council members on a voluntary basis'.

---

282 Housing Corporation Circular HC 11.93, paras 21 and 22.
283 Schedule 1, para 2(2).
284 Housing Corporation Circular HC 11.93.
285 Schedule 1, para 2(3).

Maximum fees and expenses

1.76   The Corporation may specify from time to time the maximum amounts (and different amounts for different purposes) payable by an RSL which is an industrial and provident society or company (but not a company registered as a charity):

(i)   by way of fees or other remuneration or expenses to a member of that body who is not its officer or employee; or

(ii)   by way of remuneration or expenses to an officer of the body who has no contract of employment with the body. This picks up and regulates the new departure in Sch 1, para 2(2)(b).

No determination was made by the Corporation under its previous similar powers but the Corporation will use its powers under para (ii) at least. The Government has said that any payments allowed will be modest and based on loss of earnings using established systems such as jury service or magistrates' allowances as a basis for the new system.[286] There seems to be a possibility that payments will be below jury service levels. However, the Housing Corporation will consult before using its powers.[287]

Enforcement

1.77   In each case where an industrial and provident society or a company, despite the relevant prohibitions,[288] pays a sum, makes a gift, grants a benefit or makes a payment in excess of a permitted maximum specified, it may recover the sum or the value of the gift or benefit or the excess, and shall take proceedings for recovery if the Corporation so directs.[289] If a payment is made in excess of a maximum specified by a determination made by the Corporation, it is possible that the whole payment is recoverable. However, the Corporation has required partial recovery in the past and would possibly do so again.

Constitution, change of rules, amalgamation and dissolution

1.78   Schedule 1, Part II, re-enacts ss 16–23 inclusive of HAA 1985 with the consequential amendments that are necessary to apply the various powers of the Corporation to the extended list of bodies now entitled to be registered as RSLs. In particular, the Corporation is given powers over companies registered under the Companies Act 1985 which are registered.

During the passage of the Housing Bill through the House of Lords, the Government was at pains to make clear that the powers in the Act over

286 HL Debs, Vol 572, col 1409.
287 HL Debs, Vol 574, col 483.
288 Schedule 1, paras 1(1), 2(1) and 3(1).
289 Schedule 1, paras 1(3), 2(4) and 3(3).

Companies Act companies were intended to supplement and overlay the Companies Act with additional requirements designed to allow the Corporation to fulfil its purpose of protecting public funds and tenants. Thus, for example, the Corporation's power to remove a director and appoint a new director is a power independent of the company's shareholders' power to do the same thing. The power must be given to the Corporation so that it is able to act in the public interest whether or not the shareholders agree or are concerned.

The shareholders of a company are entitled to dismiss directors and could, in theory, dismiss directors appointed by the Corporation and seek to reappoint directors whom the Corporation has dismissed. In those circumstances the Corporation might consider that the proper management of the company as an RSL has been put at risk and may bring its further powers in Sch 1, Part IV into play.

Accounts and audit

1.79 Schedule I, Part III re-enacts with some amendments HAA 1985, ss 24–27. The general requirements to be set and policed by the Corporation relating to the accounts of RSLs apply to all types of social landlord, registered charities, industrial and provident societies and Companies Act companies. It is to be noted that these requirements are to be determined by the Corporation whereas under the earlier legislation they were set by the DoE. Paragraphs 17 and 18 are aimed specifically at industrial and provident societies and registered charities respectively. Paragraph 19 makes those that are responsible in a management capacity for the preparation and audit of accounts, also responsible for ensuring that provisions applicable to the particular RSL are complied with.

Apart from making Companies Act companies liable to comply with the general requirements as determined by the Corporation, there are no specific accounting and audit requirements on Companies Act companies, it presumably being felt that existing legislation governing companies contains sufficiently stringent provisions. Therefore companies will have to comply with all the provisions in the Companies Act relating to audit and accountancy as well as the general requirements that the Housing Corporation will determine for RSLs' accounts and the form of them. Companies will, like other RSLs, be responsible for complying with those requirements which relate to them under para 19.

The principal effect of paras 17 and 18 which relate to industrial and provident societies and charities is to apply the accounting and audit requirements in the Friendly and Industrial Provident Societies Act 1968 to industrial and provident societies, whatever the volume of receipts and payments, the number of members or the value of its assets, and to apply those requirements to RSLs which are registered charities.

Inquiry into the affairs of RSLs

1.80   Schedule I, Part IV re-enacts, with amendments and modifications, HAA 1985, ss 28–32, which enabled the Housing Corporation to institute an inquiry into the affairs of housing associations where it suspects misconduct or mismanagement. The powers are to some extent strengthened, and may be exercised on an interim basis where, for example, immediate action is necessary to protect tenants and assets. The powers include suspension or removal of anyone responsible for or involved in the misconduct or mismanagement, the freezing of the RSL's assets and the disqualification of a person from acting as an officer of the RSL. A register of persons so disqualified is to be kept by the Corporation.

The Corporation can also direct the transfer of land to another RSL or to itself, but this power is not available in relation to RSLs which are registered charities, and where the transferor RSL has charitable objectives, the transfer must be to an RSL with like objectives.

PART II

CHAPTER 2

HOUSES IN MULTIPLE OCCUPATION

Introduction

2.1 Part II of the Act amends the law on 'houses in multiple occupation' (hereafter 'HMOs'). Traditionally, these properties are viewed as the worst end of the rented sector for safety, facilities, repairs and harassment. Indeed, the record of deaths attributed to them makes this one of the most emotive parts of the Act. The Government estimates that there are over 300,000 HMOs in England, excluding self-contained flats. Changes to housing benefit and the general thrust of the Act to make more use of the private sector may lead to their increased frequency, while the weakening of private tenants' security will leave them less able to insist on protection.

The latest improvements were in the Local Government and Housing Act 1989 (hereafter 'the 1989 Act'). The Government's deregulation initiative led, in 1993, to considering abolishing registration schemes and common lodging house controls. The Campaign for Bedsit Rights and others have long lobbied for a national mandatory licensing scheme. The first consultation for the 1996 Act was open to all ideas including this.[1] The final one was limited to improvements on the existing scheme, in a similar manner to the 1989 Act.[2]

Limits of the 1996 Act

2.2 The 1996 Act leaves the pre-existing structure intact, but aims to strengthen and streamline it. Local authorities have a range of powers specifically for HMOs, including powers both to intervene directly and to set up registration schemes. These are in Part XI of the Housing Act 1985 (hereafter 'the 1985 Act') and various statutory instruments and DoE Circulars. The law will continue to be the amended 1985 Act, with the 1989 Act changes, rather than the 1996 Act in its own right.

The main items not affected (except for fines increases) are the definition of HMOs, HMO overcrowding, and the Management Code. The powers on unfit and overcrowded general housing, which apply also to HMOs, are unaffected. There is also a major, separate, impact from environmental protection, fire, planning, and building regulations. This book does not cover the pre-existing

---

1 DoE *HMOs: Consultation Paper on the Case for Licensing* (DoE, 1994).

2 DoE *Improving Standards in HMOs: Consultation Paper Linked to the Housing White Paper 'Our Future Homes'* (DoE, 1995), referred to hereafter as 'the final consultation'.

law. Readers are referred to the Campaign for Bedsit Rights and to the usual housing law texts.[3]

Changes in the 1996 Act

2.3   The main changes are on fitness provisions and works notices, and on registration schemes, introducing ongoing regulation and 'special control' provisions. Fines are increased throughout.[4] Some planned changes are not in the 1996 Act itself, but instead will come in through Regulations and Guidance under the 1985 Act. These include: (a) increasing registration fees; (b) changing exclusions from registration schemes; (c) extending the mandatory fire safety duty; and (d) drawing up Codes of Practice for the new fitness duty.

Registration schemes

2.4   Registration schemes are of two basic types: with and without control provisions. The latter are known as 'notification' schemes and are used for information gathering to target other enforcement powers. They cannot be used to control the HMO itself by a refusal to register. Many local authorities complain that such schemes divert effort to good landlords who come forward to register. Some have preferred voluntary accreditation schemes with incentives like homeless referrals, bond boards or advice. The Government said that local authorities which proactively locate properties and enforce standards under their other powers may have had no need for the old registration schemes.[5] The changes make them easier to introduce and more effective as enforcement tools. However, many local authorities may wait, expecting a Labour Government to introduce a national mandatory licensing scheme.

2.5   The offences related to registration schemes are now grouped together and fines for breach of a registration scheme's provisions are increased from level 2 to level 4.[6]

Adoption of schemes

2.6   The changes allow adoption of schemes without Government approval and improve the ability to fund the scheme through fees. Under the old law, all schemes needed DoE confirmation. The DoE developed non-statutory model schemes and would give confirmation readily to schemes fitting the models, while others would need to be justified by local conditions. The new law effectively makes model schemes statutory, dispenses with the need for confirmation when a model is used, and retains the old system for cases where a model is not used.[7]

---

3 For example, D Hughes and S Lowe *Social Housing Law and Policy* (Butterworths, 1995), ch 8.
4 Standard levels for fines are currently set at level 1–£200, level 2–£500, level 3–£1,000, level 4–£2,500, level 5–£5,000.
5 DoE Circular 12/93, para 4.12.9.
6 Section 68(1) (inserting new s 348G of the 1985 Act).
7 Section 65(1) (amending s 346B and s 346(1) and (3) of the 1985 Act).

2.7   The register and the scheme are both to be made public in the same way.[8] For schemes based on the models, the publicity is to be timed around the date of adoption,[9] and evidence in court of the scheme's validity is based on proving it did not need confirmation.[10]

HMOs covered by model schemes

2.8   A fundamental difficulty with the HMO powers is that the definition of an HMO is wide-ranging but unclear.[11] The Government's Consultation Papers set out the variety of types of possible HMOs, including bedsits, student shared houses, families with lodgers, and hostels. The case-law on women's refuges and student shared houses has established that whether the occupants form one household or several is an arcane question of fact and degree on various tests, none of which is definitive (such as whether they eat together, select later tenants, or pool money).[12] There is also an unclear dividing line between hostels and hotels, which fall outside the definition as would hospitals, prisons or barracks. The Campaign for Bedsit Rights suggests avoiding these difficulties by licensing all private renting, not just HMOs. On the status of occupiers of bedsits, hostels and shared houses, there are similar difficulties over whether individual households have exclusive possession of separate dwellings or whether there is one joint tenancy of the whole house.[13]

The Government plans to limit the sizes and types of property included in the model schemes, and to target enforcement to match risk analysis. It plans to consult over the models before bringing these sections into force.[14] It suggests excluding smaller properties, self-contained leasehold flats, universities and housing associations, and those covered by other regulations like registered care homes. This would allow a local authority to spread its net wider, but it would have to show particular local reasons in seeking approval. Special control provisions are not likely to be included in the model schemes.[15] Another example of targeting particular categories of HMO is fire-escape enforcement.[16]

Registration under schemes

2.9   One of the objections to the old registration schemes system was the difficulty of using them for enforcement, given registration was once and for all.

---

8 Section 69(1) (amending s 349(4) of the 1985 Act).
9 Section 69(1) (amending s 349 of the 1985 Act).
10 Section 65(2) (amending s 351(1)(c) of the 1985 Act).
11 Section 345 of the 1985 Act.
12 For example, *Simmons v Pizzey* [1979] AC 37 and *Barnes v Sheffield City Council* (1995) 27 HLR 719.
13 For example, *Central YMCA Housing Association Ltd v Saunders* (1990) 23 HLR 212 and *AG Securities v Vaughan* (1988) 21 HLR 79.
14 HL Debs, Vol 572, col 1675 (Lord Lucas).
15 See below.
16 See below.

Landlords will now have to apply for re-registration every five years,[17] giving an opportunity to recheck eligibility. While not directly linked, this has a parallel in the five-year limit on repeat fitness works notices.[18]

Schemes must now include a positive duty on landlords to register and re-register.[19] Previously there was simply a power to include provisions imposing duties to notify and a power to require information, on which there are increased fines.[20] This therefore really only clarifies the position. It will not necessarily be clear to landlords, or anyone else, whether their properties fit the definition of an HMO. This may encourage limiting schemes to the more readily identifiable types of HMO.

Charging for registration

2.10   Another objection was that the costs of the old schemes outweighed the benefits. A power to charge for registration was introduced in 1991.[21] The new law incorporates it into the statute,[22] and allows for half-fees on the new five yearly re-registrations. The Government says it intends to use its order-making power 'substantially to increase' the levels.[23] The final consultation suggested doubling fees to £60 per room and said this should help pay for improved enforcement.[24] However, Guidance on the old charges was emphatic that the fees were a maximum and should be limited to covering the costs of registration, not of enforcement.[25]

Control provisions

2.11   Control provisions are optional in a registration scheme and move it from just 'notification' to a 'regulatory' scheme, governing conditions in HMOs through its own mechanism.[26] They should not be confused with control orders,[27] which are independent of registration schemes. The old control provisions only applied effectively on first registration or expansion of the HMO and did not add enough to the other HMO powers to be worth the bureaucracy of a registration scheme in many local authorities' eyes.

---

17 Section 65(1) (inserting s 346A(2) of the 1985 Act).
18 See below.
19 Section 65(1) (inserting s 346A(1) of the 1985 Act).
20 Section 78(1) (amending s 350(2) of the 1985 Act).
21 SI 1991/982, issued under ss 150–152 of the 1989 Act.
22 Section 65(1) (inserting s 346A(4)–(6) of the 1985 Act).
23 HL Debs, Vol 572, col 1665 (Lord Lucas).
24 Paragraph 3.9.
25 DoE Circular 6/91 *HMOs: Charges for Registration Schemes.*
26 Section 65 (amending ss 347–348A of the 1985 Act).
27 See below.

The old law contained limits on the types of HMO which control provisions could affect. The new law leaves these out,[28] but new limits will feature in the new model schemes instead. The Act also clarifies that pre-existing HMOs can be registered for occupation levels to be reached by not replacing tenants who leave.[29] Fines for over-occupation in breach of control provisions are increased to level 5 from level 4.[30]

Management conditions and alteration of registered numbers are major changes enabling use of schemes to regulate management of HMOs during the currency of their registration. The local authority can impose conditions on management at registration, renewal or variation applications. Registration can be revoked at any time for breach or because the person controlling or managing the HMO is not a fit and proper person.[31] The power is broad but local authorities must act under Guidance and the usual principles of administrative law.[32] There are rights of appeal against conditions and revocation, modelled on ordinary control provision appeals and allowing the court to vary conditions.

Where there is a change in circumstances in the HMO, rather than in local authority standards, then the local authority can at any time require works, revoke registration, or change the numbers of people registered to occupy it, to ensure the property and the registered number are suitable for each other.[33] Again there are similar appeal rights.

These changes are so broadly drafted that there is now potentially far wider scope for regulating HMOs through control schemes than through other powers. Although this may be limited by Government Guidance, the limits on the other powers are statutory.

Special control provisions

2.12   Special control provisions are completely new.[34] They were inspired by tales of behaviour of benefit claimants in hotels converted to hostels damaging the tourist industry in seaside resorts, but are drafted more widely. Model schemes will not include special control provisions.[35] Local authorities will have to make out a strong case for specific approval, and Guidance will at first be limited.[36] They may, however, also attract inland local authorities keen to use all available powers on ordinary neighbour nuisance. Fears were expressed in

---

28 Section 66 (removing s 347(3)(a) and (b) of the 1985 Act).
29 Section 66 (amending s 347(3) of the 1985 Act).
30 Section 67(1) (inserting s 348G(2) of the 1985 Act, previously s 347(4)).
31 Section 66 (inserting ss 348(1)(d), (2)(c), (3)(c), (7) and 348A(3) of the 1985 Act).
32 Discussed HL Debs, Vol 574, col 522.
33 Section 66 (inserting s 348A(1)–(2) and (4)–(6) of the 1985 Act).
34 Section 67 (creating ss 348B–F of the 1985 Act).
35 HL Debs, Vol 572, col 523 (Lord Lucas).
36 HL Debs, Vol 572, col 1684–5 (Lord Lucas).

debate about 'not in my backyard' attitudes, 'ethnic cleansing' and the appropriateness of local authorities stopping poor neighbours from moving in and 'lowering the tone' of a neighbourhood. There were also fears that these could be used to stop special needs hostel developments. However, the Government stated in debate that it expects equivalents of the model scheme exclusions to be applied to special control schemes, so that most social landlords and care homes should not be covered.[37]

Special control provisions are different from other aspects of the HMO legislation in that they are concerned with protecting the neighbourhood from the tenants, rather than protecting the tenants from the conditions of the property. This recalls the origins of HMO law in the protection of neighbours against hovels spreading fire, disease, crime and immorality.

Other regulations

2.13   Planning legislation also regulates the establishment of HMOs.[38] These changes introduce reference to the amenity of the neighbourhood which is a consideration traditionally dealt with during the planning process, so case-law may have to be taken from that field. It will also increase the importance of inter-departmental HMO strategies, to ensure that planning and environmental health departments do not undermine each other's decisions, avoiding differences where appropriate and being clear as to the reasons for any differences where the two systems cannot be reconciled.

Relevant management failure

2.14   The purpose of special control provisions is to stop the amenity or character of an area from being adversely affected by the existence of the HMO or the behaviour of its tenants. A 'relevant management failure' is a failure by the person with control, or the person managing, to take reasonably practicable steps to prevent or reduce these effects.[39] This failure is a key to the other provisions including refusal of registration, the reduction of numbers of occupiers, enforcement of conditions on registration, and revocation of registration. There are rights of appeal modelled on those for control provisions.

Relevant management failure is the only ground for refusing an application for registration by a pre-existing HMO. A new HMO can also be refused where the local authority believes there are too many HMOs in the area already. Relevant management failure is necessary before an existing registration can be revoked, and the HMO must also be either over-occupied, or there must be a breach of a

---

37 See n 35, above.

38 The Use Classes Order was changed in April 1994, tightening rules on changing hotels to hostels.

39 Section 67(1) (creating s 348F of the 1985 Act).

condition. Conditions can be imposed on management of the HMO or on behaviour of the tenants. However, as no consequences flow without relevant management failure, the distinction is not as significant.

Occupancy directions

2.15 A relevant management failure with a serious adverse effect allows the local authority to make use of occupancy directions.[40] This is an additional enforcement power, directing the HMO effectively to cease operating as such, with at least 28 days' notice. Enough tenants must be required to leave to reach a level of occupation not covered by the scheme.[41] Contrast a closing order, where no person would be allowed to remain. It is an offence to fail to take all reasonable steps to comply with the occupancy direction, carrying a level 5 fine.[42] Again, there is an appeal system modelled on the other provisions.

To enable landlords to reduce occupation, the consequent evictions operate outside the 1988 Act assured system, though 'protected' and 'secure' tenants are unaffected. Tenants will not qualify for rehousing under s 39 of the Land Compensation Act 1973 as the occupancy direction is not a 'housing order'. This would be very harsh on those who were suffering nuisance from others, only to find themselves evicted too. The rights of appeal apply to 'a person aggrieved', which presumably cover tenants. However, they do not receive notice of reasons, although the new s 348D(3) of the 1985 Act requires consideration of tenants' interests.

Fitness for number of occupants

2.16 This and the following provisions operate independently of registration schemes and apply to all types of HMO. The HMO-specific standards on fitness for number of occupants differ from the overcrowding provisions in dealing with numbers of people in relation to the facilities available (eg for washing, cooking and fire prevention) – instead of space for sleeping – and in giving additional powers to force works to improve the facilities.

Directions limiting the number of occupants are tightened to stop replacement of tenants who leave, and the fines are increased.[43] Directions issued are also made local land charges,[44] so any buyer of the HMO will be bound by them. Works notices on these provisions had already previously been made local land charges.[45]

---

40 Section 67(1) (creating ss 348D–E of the 1985 Act).
41 See above.
42 Section 68(1) (creating s 348G(3) of the 1985 Act).
43 Sections 79(1) and 78(2)–(3) (amending ss 355(1), (2) and 356(2) of the 1985 Act respectively).
44 Section 74 (inserting s 354(8) of the 1985 Act).
45 By the 1989 Act.

New fitness duty

2.17　There is a new duty on landlords to keep properties up to the standard of fitness for the number of occupants.[46] Breach of this duty is both a crime and a tort. This new duty fills another gap, because under the old regime landlords were not breaking the law if the HMO was not fit for the number of occupants, provided that, for whatever reason, the local authority had not served any notice.

2.18　Landlords will be in breach of this new duty irrespective of whether notice is served, as long as they fail to take 'such steps as are reasonably practicable' to stop the HMO's condition 'calling for'[47] service of a notice by being 'not reasonably suitable' for the number of occupants. This means landlords will have broad defences, including those cases (referred to in debate) where tenants themselves damage equipment or refuse entry to builders.[48]

Two particular problems are associated with the enforcement of this new duty:

(i)　There will be a new Code of Practice on the new duty,[49] and this was relied on heavily in debate as giving adequate certainty for all parties.[50] The problem is that the new duty rests entirely on the standards of fitness which are still not fixed. Government Guidance has for some time insisted that the standards are a matter for local authority discretion, and that the Guidance is therefore only advisory.[51] The duty and the Code do not change the discretionary nature of the law on what facilities are adequate, so there will still not be an objective basis for prosecutions or civil claims. With the offence of ignoring a notice, there is at least an objective question of whether a notice has been served. The Code of Practice for the new duty will be only evidential, and so not as strong as the 'Management Code'[52] for s 369 of the 1985 Act, breach of which is an offence. Broadly, the new duty is about provision of enough facilities while the Management Code concerns their maintenance.

(ii)　There may be complications from the overlap with other provisions. The option to prosecute for breach of this new duty should not have any direct effect on a local authority's discretion on whether also, or instead, to serve a fitness works notice.[53] In debate, it was also suggested that neither compliance with a fitness works notice nor registration under a control

---

46 Section 73(1) (creating s 353A of the 1985 Act).

47 Cf ss 354(1) and 379(1)(d) of the 1985 Act, but also s 47(1) of the National Health Service and Community Care Act 1990.

48 HL Debs, Vol 574, cols 524–6.

49 See below.

50 For example, HL Debs, Vol 572, col 1693 (Lord Lucas).

51 See, most recently, DoE Circulars 12/92 and 12/93.

52 See below.

53 It is unlikely to give tenants any new rights to expect local authority action, after *Ephraim v Newham LBC* (1992) 25 HLR 207.

scheme would be conclusive evidence that the landlord had complied with this new duty.[54]

2.19 The new duty is also enforceable as a tort, giving tenants and others affected a right to sue landlords for compensation for the effects on them of a breach. This is unique among the HMO provisions, though prosecutors should also bear in mind criminal compensation. A civil action will attract legal aid, which could (for example) fund an independent expert on fitness. The effectiveness of the new tort is limited by the Act's other changes imposing assured shorthold tenancies,[55] given that there is nothing, it seems,[56] to prevent a landlord from using the mandatory shorthold eviction ground against a tenant for taking action over conditions, and there is no 'retaliatory eviction' defence.[57] Tenants could record conditions to claim when they leave, as these claims do not expressly rely on reporting faults at the time.[58]

The new tort also highlights tenants' difficulties when wishing to sue on the ground of unfitness for human habitation. The Law Commission recently called for a broader implied term in residential tenancies on fitness for human habitation.[59] Until that is implemented, there will be anomalies from the differences between tenants' rights under the two fitness standards.

Fitness works notices

2.20 Local authorities also continue to be able to enforce the fitness standard by serving notices requiring works to make the property fit. The following changes, on periods and costs, apply only to fitness works notices. There are separate changes applying to both these notices and Management Code works notices.[60]

(i) Following the deregulation initiative, once landlords have been ordered to carry out works, then for the next five years they can only be ordered to improve on those works because of a change in the circumstances of the property, not just because the local authority raise standards.[61] This will mean advisers have to check back five years for previous notices where a property fails current standards.

(ii) Local authorities are now able to claim from landlords the costs of preparation and service of fitness notices, not just the costs of carrying out works in default.[62] The Government will set a maximum, and has suggested

---

54 HL Debs, Vol 572, col 527 (Lord Lucas).
55 See s 96 of the 1996 Act.
56 Although perhaps management conditions could forbid it – see above.
57 Contrast ss 44 and 100 of the Employment Rights Act 1996 protecting employees.
58 Contrast s 11 of the Landlord and Tenant Act 1985.
59 Law Commission No 238 *Landlord and Tenant: Responsibility for the State and Condition of Property* (HMSO, 1996).
60 See below.
61 Section 71 (inserting s 352(7)–(8) of the 1985 Act).
62 Section 72 (creating s 352A of the 1985 Act) – compare s 87 of the Housing Grants, Reconstruction and Regeneration Act 1996.

£300.[63] This is like the increased registration fees in helping local authorities fund use of their HMO powers, but has the advantage of raising the money only from defaulting landlords.

Other changes

HMO overcrowding

2.21   Overcrowding in HMOs is governed by the standard for general housing in Part X of the 1985 Act and by HMO-specific powers. The latter are additional and rely on the local authority's judgement, instead of a set calculation, on appropriate numbers of people for the sleeping space. The fines for ignoring overcrowding information notices are increased.[64]

Means of escape from fire

2.22   The Campaign for Bedsit Rights' bulletin *Bedsit Briefing* chronicles the gruesome tally of fire deaths. Although estimates vary widely, the risk of dying by fire in an HMO is significantly greater than in general housing. Research is pending which may lead to further action. The Government plans separately to broaden the mandatory enforcement duty to apply to all HMOs covered by registration scheme models which are over a certain number of storeys, irrespective of floor-space.[65]

The regime in s 365 of the 1985 Act is amended by s 75 of the 1996 Act. Fire precautions, not just means of fire escape, are now covered by the power to accept undertakings and make s 368 closing orders, and consequently by the related enforcement duties. The requirement for consultation with the fire authority before enforcement action will also be wider than previously, although it is now restricted to types of HMO attracting mandatory enforcement or specified by the Secretary of State under a new order-making power.

Management Code

2.23   The Management Code is the statutory instrument giving details on standards of management for HMOs.[66] This has been a major means of regulation since the 1989 Act made its application to all HMOs automatic. It is to be distinguished from the new 'management conditions'[67] in control provisions of registration schemes, and the proposed Code of Practice[68] on the new duty on

---

63 The final consultation, para 3.12.
64 Section 78(4) (amending s 364(2) of the 1985 Act).
65 Standing Committee G, Sixth Sitting, col 213 (Mr Gwilym Jones), by altering SI 1981/1576, under s 365(2) of the 1985 Act.
66 SI 1990/830.
67 See above.
68 See below.

fitness for number of occupants. The fine for the offence of breaching the Management Code is increased to level 5 from level 3.[69]

Works notices

2.24 Works notices allow local authorities to specify works to be done by the landlord to make the building fit for the number of occupants or to meet the Management Code requirements.[70] In default, local authorities can do the works themselves and recoup the costs from the landlord. The fines for ignoring works notices are increased to level 5.[71]

Works notices can now be tied to the standard procedure for enforcement notices in s 5 of the Deregulation and Contracting Out Act 1994.[72] An order from the Secretary of State will create a new stage before deciding to serve a works notice, in which the local authority will first serve a warning and possibly also give reasons as well as a right to have representations considered. Local authorities will be able to dispense with this where it appears necessary, and will not have to disclose information against the public interest. The change sits uneasily with the new fitness offence, the purpose of which is to allow prosecution of landlords as soon as a situation could lead to a notice, matching the position under the Management Code.

Works notices used to be linked to means-tested grants. The Housing Grants, Reconstruction and Regeneration Act 1996 broadly makes such grants discretionary, and its Guidance is expected to urge treating works as normal business overheads, negotiating nomination rights for grants, and targeting grants to an HMO strategy based on risk assessment. That, with this Act's rehousing changes,[73] may ease some local authorities' reluctance to use works notices.

Control orders

2.25 These are the most complicated enforcement methods for local authorities, in which they essentially take over the management of the HMO from the landlord. The associated fine for failing to permit carrying out of works is increased from level 3 to level 5.[74] The time is increased from four to eight weeks after service of a control order, for the local authority to decide whether to make a compulsory purchase order which delays the 'management scheme'.[75] This then matches the eight weeks to serve the management scheme.

---

69 Section 78(6) (amending s 369(5) of the 1985 Act).
70 See above for changes to fitness notices alone.
71 Section 78(7)–(8) (amending ss 376(1)–(2) and 377(3) of the 1985 Act).
72 Section 76 (creating s 377A of the 1985 Act).
73 See Parts VI and VII.
74 Section 78(9) (amending s 387(5) of the 1985 Act).
75 Section 79(3) (amending Part IV, Sch 13, para 22 to the 1985 Act).

Codes of Practice

2.26 There is a new power to approve Codes of Practice,[76] which should not be confused with the Management Code or Government Guidance in Circulars. The key to them is that they will be admissible as evidence in court proceedings where relevant, rather than being directly enforceable.[77] They can relate to particular subjects or areas, and the Government can approve Codes drawn up by other agencies. The most significant is likely to be the one planned on the new fitness duty,[78] but others can be added.

Obstruction

2.27 There is an offence of obstructing local authority officers, and others authorised to enter premises, from exercising their HMO powers. The fine is increased from level 3 to level 4.[79]

'Person managing' definition

2.28 This is a key definition for responsibility for conditions under the HMO regime. The new law extends it by adding people who would receive rents but for having made arrangements with others to do so instead, not just as trustees or agents.[80] This consequently extends the wider definition in the Management Code.[81]

Common lodging houses

2.29 The old law giving additional powers to govern common lodging houses is simply abolished,[82] leaving them to be covered just by the ordinary HMO regime instead. The decision follows the Government's deregulation initiative. The powers were little used, not effectively updated since the first Victorian housing legislation, and have always been mainly about local authorities having powers to make local bye-laws to implement them. The DoE advised local authorities to use the HMO regime instead of its model bye-laws as they were so out of date.[83] The irony is that new voluntary night shelters are being opened for asylum seekers and others made destitute by changes connected to this Act, and the old law could have covered those.

---

76 Section 77 (creating s 395A of the 1985 Act).
77 In this they are similar to those in discrimination law such as the Commission for Racial Equality's *Code of Practice on Rented Housing*.
78 See above.
79 Section 78(10) (amending s 396(2) of the 1985 Act).
80 Section 79(2) (amending s 398(6) of the 1985 Act).
81 SI 1990/830, para 2(1).
82 Formerly Part XII of the 1985 Act, repealed by s 80.
83 For example, DoE Circular 12/86, para 4.7.

Implementation

2.30   The registration scheme changes are planned to come in with most of the rest of the Act in January 1997, after consultation on the model schemes and their exclusions. However, s 70 will leave pre-existing registration schemes in force under the old regime for up to two more years, unless revoked by the local authority or replaced with schemes under the new regime.

The other changes are planned to be brought in later in 1997. The new fitness duty will need consultation on its accompanying Code of Practice. Other Codes could be approved at different times later. The provisions on costs and periods for works notices do not apply to notices served before those sections come into force.[84] The various other items which need regulations will depend on when those are introduced. Finally, the various Guidances will have to be reissued.

2.31   The real effects remain to be seen on the take-up of registration schemes, the use of the new fitness duty, and any reductions in the record of deaths. The most unpredictable factor will be the new special control provisions. It may be that local authorities hold back on registration schemes to see if a national mandatory licensing scheme comes in with a change of Government.

The registration changes will create further complexity over the next two years for anyone wanting to know the legal position locally. For this they need first to know the national legislation, the Management Code, DoE Guidance, and now any Codes of Practice. They then need to find the local authority's annually reviewed policy and work out which of eight broad situations apply on registration. These are: no scheme at all; an old scheme with or without control provisions; a new model scheme with or without control provisions; or a new local version with or without control provisions, or with special control provisions as well.

The debates on local powers versus a national mandatory system and the concern over tenants' behaviour in hostels reflect the Victorian arguments over what to do about lodging-houses as the haunt of mendicants, prostitutes and thieves in the days of milestone legislation such as the Public Health Act 1848 and the 1851 Shaftesbury Acts. There will be more changes to come as these debates continue and further Government research bears fruit.

---

84 Sections 71(2) and 72(3).

PART III

CHAPTER 3

TENANTS' RIGHTS

Introduction

3.1 Chapter 1 of Part III of the Act contains provisions which seek to improve tenants' and lessees' rights to challenge unreasonable service charges and bad management by landlords. The Chapter was introduced into the Bill at a late stage following concerns raised in Parliament about landlords exploiting the leasehold system to levy excessive service charges and to evade their management obligations. The problem had been highlighted, in particular, by the London *Evening Standard* which ran a series of articles in autumn 1995 drawing attention to a supposedly new breed of landlords who were systematically exploiting the scope for levying service charges.[1]

Whilst the clear intention behind the proposals is to improve the lot of long leaseholders, some of the provisions will also apply to periodic tenants of both private and social landlords. Indeed, the Chapter is headed 'Tenants' Rights'.[2]

Forfeiture

3.2 The Act restricts the right of a landlord to seek forfeiture of a tenancy on the grounds of non-payment of service charges[3] whether by exercising a right of re-entry or by forfeiture proceedings. This only applies to residential premises: business and agricultural tenancies are specifically excluded.[4] Nor does it affect the landlord's right to forfeit on any other grounds, for example non-payment of rent (provided no part relates to the cost of services) or breaches of other covenants.[5]

Procedure

3.3 The landlord will only be able to forfeit by issue of proceedings or re-entry if (a) the tenant has agreed or admitted the amount of service charge claimed by

---

1 See Standing Committee G, Twenty-Third Sitting, cols 881 and 893–4 giving concerns about an outfit known as 'The Ground Rent Brokers'.

2 'Tenant' and 'tenancy' have the same meaning as lessee and lease. Both expressions include sub-leases or sub-tenancies as well as contracts for the same: s 229.

3 The same broad meaning of 'service charge' as is in s 18(1) of the Landlord and Tenant Act 1985 applies: s 81(5).

4 Section 81(4).

5 Section 81(6).

the landlord or (b) the amount of the charge has been determined by a court or a tribunal set up under an arbitration agreement (referred to in the Act as 'arbitral tribunal').[6] Since forfeiture is deemed to take place at the time of service of proceedings, it is clear that a landlord will not be able to seek a determination within the forfeiture proceedings. A separate application to the court will need to be issued for a determination to be made before forfeiture proceedings can be instituted.

Where a court (or arbitral tribunal) has made a determination, a landlord must wait a further 14 days before seeking forfeiture.[7] However, a tenant's appeal against the determination will not prevent the landlord forfeiting after the 14-day period.[8]

The landlord is not prevented from serving a s 146 notice,[9] although the threat posed by such a notice will presumably be minimal if the landlord is restricted from issuing proceedings on expiry. However, any s 146 notice served on the grounds of service charge arrears will be ineffective unless it sets out the effect of the above.[10] The Secretary of State is given specific power to prescribe by statutory instrument the form of words to be used and, in any case, requires the wording to be in characters no less conspicuous than those used in the notice.[11]

Practical effect

3.4   This will undoubtedly assist leaseholders in disputes over service charges by removing the threat of forfeiture proceedings or peaceable re-entry (although the latter course was unlikely in any event in view of the protection afforded by s 3 of the Protection from Eviction Act 1977). It remains to be seen whether attempts will be made in the drafting of leases to obtain blanket agreements/ admissions from leaseholders in advance as to recoverable service charge. There are no anti-avoidance provisions in this section although s 19(3) of the Landlord and Tenant Act 1985 ('LTA 1985') may be effective to strike down any such agreements/admissions.

Service charges

3.5   Since the above only applies to forfeiture proceedings and not ordinary possession proceedings, it will not affect a landlord's right to seek possession

---

6 This was considered particularly important because 'it has unfortunately been the practice of building societies to pay up any disputed service charges over the leaseholder's head at the first sign that a forfeiture application is under way': Standing Committee G, Twenty-Third Sitting, col 908.

7 Section 81(2).

8 Section 81(3).

9 Section 82(1).

10 Section 82(2).

11 Section 82(2)–(4).

against periodic tenants (eg the assured, assured shorthold and secure tenants of social landlords) on the ground of non-payment of service charges. However, s 83 will apply to periodic tenants and long leaseholders alike (but not to tenants of regulated tenancies under the Rent Act 1977 where the rent is registered but not registered as variable, and certain other tenants, eg of local authorities).[12]

Role of the Leasehold Valuation Tribunal

3.6 The Act gives tenants the right to seek a determination as to the reasonableness of any service charge claimed by a landlord by applying to a Leasehold Valuation Tribunal ('LVT').[13] The right is in addition to the existing right to seek a declaration in the county court as to the reasonableness of a service charge.[14] However, the LVT should be a more attractive option for tenants since no costs will be recoverable in proceedings before it.[15]

A fee will be payable on issuing an application and the LVT will be entitled to require one party to pay the whole or part of the other party's fee.[16] The fees to be charged were originally expected to be sufficient to meet the costs of providing the LVT service. When it became apparent that the fee might have to be as high as £2,000 to cover the cost of the service, there was considerable Parliamentary debate.[17] Following a Government defeat in the Lords, an amendment was agreed to in the Commons in the present form which provides that the fee will not exceed £500.[18] The figure may be changed by the Secretary of State by statutory instrument. Special provision for reduction or waiver of the fee payable will be made in accordance with a means-testing regime also to be introduced by statutory instrument.[19]

Regulations under the Rent Act 1977 relating to the procedure of Rent Assessment Committees will also be used to prescribe the procedure in applications to the LVT.[20] The procedure established by the Secretary of State is expressly expected to include provisions enabling similar cases to be dealt with together (eg separate applications by several tenants in the same block) and to empower the LVT to throw out vexatious claims or claims which constitute an abuse of process.[21] The latter is aimed at dealing with the difficult tenant who is out of kilter with all his neighbours and to prevent unscrupulous landlords attempting to wear down tenants by taking each and every dispute to the LVT.

---

12 Sections 26 and 27, LTA 1985.
13 Section 83(1) (inserting LTA 1985, s 2A).
14 LTA 1985, s 19(4).
15 Section 83(3) (inserting LTA 1985, s 31A(4)).
16 Section 83(3) (inserting LTA 1985, s 31B).
17 See, for example, HL Debs, Vol 574, cols 337–50.
18 LTA 1985, s 31B(3). The debates can be found at HC Debs, Vol 282, cols 33 et seq and HL Debs, Vol 574, cols 1290 et seq.
19 Ibid, s 31B(5) and (6).
20 Ibid, s 31A(2).
21 Ibid, s 31A(3).

Furthermore, Rent Assessment Committees will have jurisdiction to exercise the powers of LVTs (they will also be known as LVTs)[22] and there will be a limited right of appeal to the Lands Tribunal but only with leave of the tribunal or the LVT itself.[23] Rights of appeal to the High Court by way of appeal or case stated are specifically denied by adopting the supplementary provisions of Sch 22 to the Housing Act 1980. The same provisions also empower the LVT to obtain information from tenants, landlords and superior landlords on pain of summary conviction.[24]

The powers of the LVT are similar to those given to the county court in the LTA 1985 (to decide whether service charges have been reasonably incurred, whether works/services are of a reasonable standard and whether any amount payable before costs are incurred is reasonable).[25] The LVT also has power to make a determination regarding anticipated costs and services.[26] No application will be permitted where the tenant has already agreed or admitted the service charge claimed or where the matter is to be arbitrated or where the court or an arbitral tribunal has already made a determination.[27]

Practical effect

3.7 No doubt, most leases will be drafted so as to enable landlords to add any costs incurred in proceedings to the lessee's service charge. This would defeat the provision that no costs be awarded in proceedings before the LVT, so the Act enables the tenant to apply to the LVT for an order that the landlord may not add his/her costs of the proceedings to the tenant's service charge.[28] This applies to proceedings before an LVT, the court, the Lands Tribunal, or in connection with arbitration proceedings. The application may be made during the proceedings or afterwards to any county court, to any LVT, or to the Lands Tribunal, depending on the original forum.[29]

A landlord will also be able to apply to the LVT, but is unlikely to take that route since the restriction on forfeiture requires a determination by a court (or an admission by/agreement of the tenant) and the Act makes it clear that 'court' means county court (and, in certain circumstances the High Court) and not an LVT.[30] In other words, landlords can be expected to use the court procedure and tenants that of the LVT.

---

22 Ibid, s 31A(1).
23 Ibid, s 31A(6).
24 Ibid, s 31A(5).
25 Ibid, s 19(4).
26 Section 83(1) (inserting LTA 1985, s 19(2B)).
27 Section 83(1) (inserting LTA 1985, s 19(2C)).
28 Section 83(4) (inserting LTA 1985, s 20C).
29 Ibid.
30 Section 95.

Transfer to LVT

3.8   The Act gives power to the court to transfer to the LVT for determination any question falling within the LVT's jurisdiction and, further, that any determination subsequently made by the LVT will be treated as a determination for the purposes of s 81.[31] This means in practice that a landlord will be obliged to apply to the court for a determination under s 81 but that the application may well be shunted off to the LVT anyway. This will also enable the court to transfer issues relating to service charges raised in other actions (eg debt recovery), to which landlords are almost certain to have recourse because of the restrictions on issuing forfeiture proceedings. Once the LVT has made its determination, the proceedings will return to the court to give effect to the decision of the LVT.[32] If the service charge issue was only part of the landlord's claim, the court could either adjourn the whole action pending the decision of the LVT on the service charge element or dispose of the remainder of the claim, thereby enabling the landlord to enforce that part of the claim not in dispute or in respect of which the tenant has no defence.[33]

Choice of insurer

3.9   Tenants already have the right to challenge a landlord's choice of insurer in the county court.[34] Section 83(2) of the Act enables LVTs to deal with such challenges. There are also some supplementary changes: to prevent any such challenge where the matter has already been agreed or admitted by the tenant, or where the matter is to be referred to arbitration or has already been the subject of a determination by a court or arbitral tribunal;[35] to enable any determination made by the LVT to be enforced as if it were a court order (with leave of the court);[36] and to include an anti-avoidance provision to prevent landlords circumventing the section in well-drafted leases.[37] The inclusion of this provision serves to highlight the absence of an equivalent in s 81.

---

31 Section 83(3) (inserting LTA 1985, s 31C(3)).
32 LTA 1985, s 31C(2).
33 LTA 1985, s 31C(1).
34 Schedule to the LTA 1985, para 8.
35 Ibid, para 8(3).
36 Ibid, para 8(5).
37 Ibid, para 8(6).

Right to appoint surveyor

3.10   The Act empowers a recognised tenants' association[38] to appoint its own surveyor[39] to advise the association on matters arising from service charges payable by one or more of the association's members. This new right supplements the existing rights of tenants under the LTA 1985 to obtain copy documents and other information relating to service charges.[40]

There is nothing to prevent a tenant or a tenants' association from appointing its own surveyor at present. However, the Act gives the surveyor rights of access to documents held by the landlord and the right to inspect common parts, on written notice to the landlord.[41] If the landlord fails to oblige within a certain period (one month for inspection of documents, reasonable time for access to premises), the county court can order the landlord to comply.[42] The tenants' association must apply for such an order within four months of the original notice to the landlord.[43] Similar provisions apply to obtain inspection of documents held by a superior landlord.[44] If a landlord disposes of his/her reversionary interest after a notice has been served and which remains to be complied with, the obligation to deal with the notice rests with the person acquiring the reversion unless the original landlord is in a position to discharge the outstanding obligations notwithstanding the transfer.[45]

Appointment of manager

3.11   A court currently has the power to order the appointment of a manager to carry out a landlord's management functions where the landlord is in breach of his/her obligations and that breach is likely to continue.[46] This is amended by ss 85–87.[47]

---

38 Defined in LTA 1985, s 29.

39 The appointed surveyor must be a qualified surveyor and the appointment will not be effective for the purposes of the section until written notice has been given to the landlord, or to the person who receives rent on behalf of the landlord (ie the landlord's agent), by the association giving details of the surveyor, the ambit of his/her instructions and the duration of his/her appointment: s 84(2)–(3).

40 LTA 1985, ss 21 and 22.

41 Schedule 4.

42 Schedule 4, para 5.

43 Ibid.

44 Schedule 4, para 6.

45 Schedule 4, para 7.

46 Landlord and Tenant Act 1987 (hereafter 'LTA 1987'), s 24.

47 For the avoidance of doubt, Sch 5 sets out in full the text of Part II of the LTA 1987, as amended by s 85.

(i)   The jurisdiction of the court to deal with applications to appoint is transferred to the LVT and the jurisdiction of the court, both statutory and inherent is specifically ousted.[48] Similar provisions to those contained in s 82 are made with regard to the make-up of LVTs, dealing with multiple claims and vexatious applicants, the non-recovery of costs, the limited rights of appeal and the payment and recovery of fees on the application.[49]

(ii)   The previous requirement that the court (now LVT) should be satisfied that the landlord's breach of obligation is likely to continue before appointing a manager,[50] is removed. A landlord will not be able to avoid appointment of a manager by giving assurances to the LVT about their future conduct as has been possible in the past, although the LVT will still be able to take that into account in deciding whether it is 'just and convenient' to make an order.[51]

(iii)   There are two further new circumstances in which the LVT may make an order:

(a)   where the LVT is satisfied that unreasonable service charges have been made or are proposed or are likely to be made by a landlord. Express guidance is given on the matters which the LVT shall take into account in deciding whether a service charge is unreasonable, including whether the amount payable is unreasonable having regard to the items paid for, whether the items paid for are of an unnecessarily high standard, or whether those items are of an insufficient standard such that further charges may be incurred.[52] The new provision is interesting in that it attempts to define unreasonableness whereas in LTA 1985, s 19 the term was left undefined;

(b)   where the landlord has failed to comply with any provision under any Code of Practice introduced in orders made by the Secretary of State pursuant to s 87 of the Leasehold Reform, Housing and Urban Development Act 1993.[53] The only Code of Practice which the Secretary of State has so far approved is in respect of sheltered housing, so the effect of this is limited for the time being.

(iv)   The existing procedure for the discharge of a management order[54] is tightened so as to prevent a landlord obtaining discharge of the order on presenting spurious proposals for changes to the management arrangements. The new amendment requires the LVT to be satisfied that new management arrangements will not result in a recurrence of the circumstances which led to the order being made in the first place.[55]

---

48 Section 86(1)–(4).
49 Section 86(5).
50 LTA 1987, s 24(2)(a)(ii).
51 LTA 1987, s 24(2)(a)(iii).
52 Section 85(4) (inserting LTA 1987, s 24(2A)).
53 Section 85(3) (inserting LTA 1987, s 24(2)(ab) and (ac)).
54 LTA 1987, s 24(9).
55 Section 85(6).

Acquisition orders

3.12　Section 88 of the Act amends s 29(3) of the LTA 1987 so as to reduce from three years to two years the period during which an appointment under s 24 of a person to act as manager must have been in force as one of the pre-conditions to an acquisition order being made (ie a court order providing for a person nominated by the qualifying tenants of certain premises to acquire their landlord's interest in the premises without his consent). Acquisition orders are rarely encountered in view of the other stringent pre-conditions contained in s 29 and this amendment is unlikely to change the position.

Right of first refusal

3.13　Under Part I of the LTA 1987 certain 'qualifying' tenants of residential flats have the right of first refusal when their landlord proposes to dispose of their interest in the property. In brief, Part I applies to long leaseholders and some tenants (although not assured or secure, protected shorthold, business, or assured agricultural tenants, or tenants on employment-terminable tenancies) where the landlord is not a resident or 'exempt' landlord (eg local authority, registered housing association and others) and the premises are relevant premises (two or more flats held by qualifying tenants with the number of flats so held exceeding half the total number of flats in the premises).

The provisions of Part I are notoriously difficult and came in for judicial criticism in *Denetower Ltd v Toop*.[56] Equally, when the provisions were originally introduced it was not anticipated that landlords would have any reason to object to selling to their lessees and so sanctions to deal with defaulting landlords were considered irrelevant and not provided for. In practice, however, landlords have often deliberately avoided their obligations, either to escape protracted negotiations with lessees or to ensure a sale to a particular purchaser. This Act, therefore, introduces various amendments to clarify and tighten-up the provisions of Part I and to close the various exploited loopholes:

(i)　New provision is made to curtail the practice of corporate landlords avoiding their obligations by taking a share in a purchasing company (so making it an associated company and any disposal thereby an excluded disposal) by requiring the purchasing company to have been an associated company for at least two years.[57]

---

56 [1991] 1 WLR 952G–H.

57 Section 90. 'The exemption for sales to associated companies is necessary to allow groups to carry out corporate restructuring in an orderly way. It is not easy to think of a way around the problem which will be watertight ...': Standing Committee G, Twenty-Fourth Sitting, col 923.

(ii) It becomes a criminal offence for a landlord to sell his or her interest without
       first having served notices on qualifying tenants under LTA 1987, s 5
       offering them their interest in the premises.[58] Any contravention of other
       requirements relating to the procedure under Part I (as amended) will also
       render a landlord liable to prosecution.[59] Thus a landlord who serves notice
       but goes ahead with a sale without waiting for the tenants' response will also
       be caught. A convicted landlord will face a fine.[60] Directors and/or other
       officers of corporate landlords, who consent to an irregular disposal or are
       negligent in permitting such a disposal to proceed, will also be liable to
       prosecution.[61] Local housing authorities have power to bring prosecutions
       under these provisions.[62] However, a conviction will not affect the validity of
       the disposal.[63]

(iii) An amendment is introduced into Part I to specify precisely when a relevant
       disposal takes place. Curiously, the 1987 Act failed to clarify whether a
       relevant disposal takes place at exchange of contracts or completion.
       Surprise that the point had not been considered was expressed in
       Mainwaring v Trustees of Henry Smith's Charity.[64] That case was the subject
       of some debate during consideration of the proposed amendments by
       Parliament[65] and was acknowledged by the Government to be the impetus
       behind the inclusion of this amendment[66] which confirms that where there is
       an exchange of contracts, that exchange will be the relevant disposal.[67] The
       section also deals with assignments of rights under a contract and contracts
       to assign such rights.[68]

Changes to the LTA 1987, Part I

3.14 Further changes are made to the statutory procedure by amending
ss 5–10 of the LTA 1987. Again, the changes are aimed at tightening-up the
procedure and curbing abuses by landlords. In view of the number of
amendments (mainly due to the complications arising from recognising
contracts to purchase as relevant disposals) the Act recasts Part I of the 1987 Act

---

58 Section 91(1) (inserting LTA 1987, s 10A).

59 Section 10A(1)(b).

60 Section 10A(2), at level 5 on the standard scale. The fines were felt to be sufficient because
    they will affect people with 'reputations to preserve': Standing Committee G, Twenty-Fourth
    Sitting, col 923.

61 Section 10A(3).

62 Section 10A(4).

63 Section 10A(5).

64 [1996] 2 All ER 223C–D.

65 See, for example, Standing Committee G, Twenty-Fourth Sitting, cols 925–30.

66 HL Debs, Vol 574, col 895.

67 The Court of Appeal in *Mainwaring* in fact concluded the opposite, following the authority of
    Wilkins v Horowitz (1990) EGLR 217.

68 Section 89(1).

in its totality and the new Part I appears as a Schedule to the Act.[69] The most important changes in the new Part I are considered below.

(i) Section 5 is amended to deal with the different circumstances in which a relevant disposal may arise (ie contract to be completed by conveyance, sale at auction, grant of option/right of pre-emption, conveyance not preceded by contract, or disposal for non-monetary consideration) and to prescribe the required wording of offer notices according to the type of disposal.[70]

(ii) Under the new s 6, landlords are forbidden from disposing of their interest after service on the qualifying tenants of an offer notice but before the period of the notice has expired to anyone other than the person(s) nominated by the tenants. Breach of this obligation will, as with breaches of any prohibition or restriction imposed by the amended ss 6–10, constitute a criminal offence.

(iii) As in the old Act, qualifying tenants may serve an acceptance notice in response to the offer notice and, thereafter, serve notice of their nominated purchaser. The period for doing so remains the same (two months in each case) although it is now known as the 'protected period'.[71] Under the old Part I, the qualifying tenants could also reject the landlord's initial offer and make a counter-offer. It was then open to the landlord to make a new offer and start fresh negotiations, or, treat the rejection of the original offer as final, disregard the counter-offer and go on to dispose of his/her interest to another purchaser. The counter-offer provisions could therefore work to the tenants' disadvantage and they are scrapped under the new legislation.

(iv) The new ss 7, 8 and 8A further simplify the procedure by requiring each party to comply with certain steps or withdraw. Once the qualifying tenants have served an acceptance notice and nominated their purchaser, the landlord must send the nominated person the requisite contract within one month of receiving the tenants' notice or send to the nominated person notice that the landlord no longer wishes to proceed with the disposal. If the landlord sends out the contract within the one-month period, the nominated person is obliged to offer to exchange contracts (by signing and sending the contract back to the landlord with the necessary deposit[72] within two months) or serve notice indicating their intention not to proceed. If that person offers to exchange, the landlord then has seven days to complete or withdraw. If he or she withdraws or fails to send out the contract or complete or, alternatively, the nominated person withdraws or fails to offer to exchange, then new ss 9A and 9B apply and the withdrawing party will be liable for any costs incurred by the other party after the first four weeks of the nomination period specified in the offer notice.

This new procedure removes a loophole which landlords have previously

---

69 Schedule 6.

70 Schedule 6, Part I (inserting LTA 1987, ss 5A–5E).

71 New s 6(4).

72 The amount in the contract or 10 per cent, whichever is less (s 8A(4)).

exploited. Under the old Act,[73] if the landlord failed to enter into a binding contract within two months of the end of the period for nominating a purchaser, the whole process effectively lapsed thereby allowing the landlord to proceed with a sale to another person. Under the new provisions landlords must either proceed with the next step in the transaction or withdraw the proposed disposal. Note, however, that the new Part I does allow for negotiations by specifically permitting extensions of the relevant periods by agreement between the parties.[74]

(v) The landlord's right to proceed with a sale to a third party, if a majority of qualifying tenants fail to serve an acceptance notice or nominate, are preserved by an amended s 7. As under the original section, the landlord has 12 months beginning with the end of the 'protected period' to dispose of his/her interest to another person. If the landlord is permitted and does in fact proceed with a sale to a third party then, as in the old Part I, the sale must be on the same terms and at the same price as set out in the offer notice.[75]

(vi) Specific provisions are made to apply the 'withdraw or proceed' scheme to sale by auction, disposals for non-monetary consideration and disposals pursuant to options or rights of pre-emption.[76]

(vii) Sections 11–17 of the 1987 Act conferred on qualifying tenants a right to buy exercisable against a new landlord when the original landlord sells their interest without first offering it to the tenants in accordance with the first refusal provisions. The new s 11A assists tenants by extending from two to four months the time by which they must serve notice requiring the new landlord to furnish them with particulars of the disposal. New provisions at ss 12A–12D rewrite the original sections dealing with the tenants' rights to compel the new landlord to sell to their nominated person or to compel the grant of a new tenancy where the original disposal consisted of a surrender and also include a new provision to deal with contracts entered into by landlords in breach of their obligations (contracts now being specifically recognised as relevant disposals under the Act). The new provision allows qualifying tenants to take the benefit of the contract in place of the person with whom the landlord has contracted.[77] The new sections also assist leaseholders in these situations by extending the time-limit for serving the necessary 'purchase notices' (compelling sale, electing to take the benefit of a contract, or requiring the grant of a new tenancy) by extending the time-limit for service on the landlord from three to six months.

(viii) Under the 1987 Act, the time period for service of the tenants' notices (whether requiring particulars or a purchase notice) was triggered by, inter alia, service by the new landlord of notice under s 3 of the LTA 1985 informing the tenants of the disposal. Under the new Act the new landlord

---

73 LTA 1987, s 10(4).
74 New s 6(1)(b).
75 New s 7(3).
76 New ss 8B–8D.
77 New s 12A.

must, in addition to the s 3 notice, serve on all qualifying tenants a notice under a new s 3A[78] where Part I of the LTA 1987 applies. The time-limits for service of a notice requiring particulars or a purchase notice will only begin to run from the date the new s 3A notice is served on the requisite majority of qualifying tenants. The notice must inform the tenant that Part I applies, that the tenant may have the right to serve a notice requiring particulars and a purchase notice, and must advise the tenant of the time-limits for serving notices.[79] If the landlord fails to serve a s 3A notice, then, as with non-service of the s 3 notice, the landlord will be liable to prosecution and a fine if convicted.

General legal advice

3.15   Section 94 gives power to the Secretary of State to give financial assistance to providers of 'general advice' about the law of landlord and tenant as it relates to residential tenancies or in connection with Part I, Chapter IV of the Leasehold Reform, Housing and Urban Development Act 1993 (estate management schemes in connection with enfranchisement). It is assumed that such funding will go to the Leasehold Enfranchisement Advisory Service which already deals with advice on leasehold enfranchisement and is co-funded by the Government.

---

78 Section 93(1) (inserting LTA 1985, s 3A).
79 LTA 1985, s 3A(2).

CHAPTER 4

ASSURED TENANCIES

I: Introduction

4.1 Part III, Chapter II makes alterations to the scheme of private sector tenancies first devised in the Housing Act 1988. The aim of the 1988 Act was to bring the grant of tenancies into line with notions of market forces and so, rather than have strict rent controls as had been the case under the Rent Act 1977, the notion of a 'market rent' was adopted. Given certain conditions, the rent assessment committee was enabled to determine the market rent on application. Furthermore, rights of succession to 1988 Act tenancies were narrowed from the 1977 Act position.

The success or failure of the market approach in the 1988 Act has been hotly debated. Research has suggested an increase in the number of tenancies available in the private sector after a gradual decrease throughout this century. However, the reasons for this are unclear.[1] The provisions of the 1996 Act are drafted on the basis that deregulation of the rental market has been the major cause of this increase.

The scheme of the 1988 Act

4.2 Under the 1988 Act, two types of tenancies can be created – an assured tenancy and an assured shorthold tenancy. The latter has to have a minimum term of six months. In order to create the latter, the landlord had to serve a notice informing the tenant that the letting was to be on an assured shorthold basis. In this sense, the default tenancy (that is, the tenancy granted where no notice had been served) was the assured tenancy. An assured shorthold tenancy, but not an assured tenancy, can be terminated by the landlord giving not less than two months' notice and a court order. Otherwise, an assured shorthold tenancy, together with the assured tenancy, can be terminated by one of eight mandatory and eight discretionary grounds for possession, contained in Sch 2 to the 1988 Act, which can only be granted by the courts.

---

1 See M Bevan, P Kemp and D Rhodes *Private Landlords and Housing Benefit* (University of York, 1996).

Outline of changes to the 1988 Act

4.3   The principal changes to this regime made by the 1996 Act is that the default tenancy will now be the assured shorthold tenancy; the conditions enabling a person to have their rent determined by the rent assessment committee have been circumscribed; a mandatory ground for possession (relating to arrears of rent) has been altered; and, finally, the 1988 Act is brought into line with the Agricultural Tenancies Act 1995, so that tenancies created under the latter Act are excluded from the 1988 Act and consistent with the 1996 Act.[2] There was also some debate about whether certain tenancies should allow succession rights between same sex partners.

II: The 1996 Act

Creation of assured shorthold tenancies

4.4   The first central change to the Housing Act 1988 is that the assured shorthold tenancy will now become the default tenancy. The reason for this amendment is that apparently a number of landlords were being caught out by the requirement to provide a notice of an assured shorthold tenancy and so created greater security of tenure than they had intended.[3]

This change is ensured by adding a new section and Schedule to the 1988 Act. This will mean that after this provision of the 1996 Act comes into force and subject to certain exclusions, any new tenancy granted will be an assured shorthold tenancy. In addition, a fixed-term assured tenancy, which comes to an end in accordance with s 5 of the 1988 Act[4] after the introduction of this section, becomes an assured shorthold tenancy at that time.[5] The wording of the new provisions make it clear that notice of an assured shorthold tenancy is no longer required. Also, such a tenancy is no longer required to be more than six months' duration[6] and, furthermore, can now be created orally.

Exclusions

4.5   Schedule 2A to the 1988 Act, as inserted by the 1996 Act, provides a list of exclusions to these provisions:

---

2 See 1996 Act, s 96(2) and Sch 7, para 9.

3 DoE *The Legislative Framework for Private Renting: Consultation Paper linked to 'Our Future Homes'* (DoE, 1995) para 2.7. The removal of all potential obstacles on persons renting out their property is considered to be a valuable aim.

4 Where the tenancy ends otherwise than under a court order, surrender or other action by the tenant, an assured shorthold will now arise.

5 Section 19A of the 1988 Act, as inserted by s 96(1) of the 1996 Act.

6 See para **4.10** below; however, note that there must still be a fixed maximum duration: *Prudential Assurance Ltd v London Residuary Body* [1992] 2 AC 386.

(i)   where the landlord serves a notice, before or after the tenancy has been created, on the tenant which states that the tenancy is to be an assured tenancy;[7]

(ii)   if the tenancy contains a provision expressly saying that it is an assured tenancy, it will be such;

(iii) certain tenancies, granted under the Rent Act 1977, Housing Act 1980 and Sch 10 to the Local Government and Housing Act 1989, entered the 1988 Act structure at certain points and became assured tenancies. These are also unaffected by the 1996 Act changes.[8]

(iv) certain assured agricultural occupancies are also excluded from the effect of the 1996 Act.

Safeguards with oral tenancies

4.6 It was noted above that assured shorthold tenancies can, under the 1996 Act, be granted orally. Concerns were expressed that this would lead to unscrupulous practices.[9] Consequently, the Government introduced, during Third Reading stage in the House of Commons, an amendment designed to remedy this predicted problem. The tenant[10] may request a written statement from the landlord during the currency of the lease providing details of any of the following, which have not been evidenced in writing: the date on which the tenancy commenced; the rent and date(s) on which it is payable; any rent review clause; details of any fixed term. If this statement is not provided by the landlord within 28 days of receipt of the request, the landlord is subject to criminal liability.[11]

It may well be that such a notice will be ineffective in any subsequent proceedings because it will not be regarded as conclusive of the agreed terms.[12] This was included because of any problems which might arise where terms are agreed

---

7 1996 Act, Sch 8, paras 1 and 2. If the notice has been served after the tenancy was entered into, the tenancy will have been an assured shorthold. If during that period the tenant has applied for a determination of the rent by a rent assessment committee, that determination will go ahead on the basis that it is an assured shorthold: Sch 8, para 6, 1996 Act.

8 1996 Act, Sch 7, paras 4–6.

9 See, for example, Standing Committee G, Twelfth Sitting, cols 471–477; HL Debs, Vol 573, cols 1849–1860.

10 References to the tenant and landlord include one or both of joint tenants and landlords: s 20A(7) of the 1988 Act, as inserted by s 97 of the 1996 Act.

11 The maximum penalty is a fine not exceeding level 4 on the standard scale (s 97(4)).

12 Section 20A(5).

orally between the landlord and the tenant but these terms seem to have been subsequently varied in the notice issued by the landlord. Proof that the written terms will correspond with the orally agreed terms will no doubt be on the usual standard of probability. In order to solve these problems, as well as take advantage of the accelerated possession procedure under the 1988 Act, the prudent landlord will, no doubt, continue to provide a written tenancy agreement and that will be good practice.

Determination of rent

4.7 Under an assured shorthold tenancy, the tenant may apply to a rent assessment committee for the determination of a rent 'which, in the committee's opinion, the landlord might reasonably be expected to obtain' under the tenancy.[13] The Government noted, in a Consultation Paper linked to the White Paper, that fewer than 1,500 such applications are made per annum and proposed to repeal this section.[14] Subsequently, they decided that it would be more appropriate to limit the right. Added to s 22(2) of the 1988 Act is a further exclusion where the original or replacement assured shorthold tenancy[15] has been in existence for longer than six months.[16]

Grounds for possession

Notice under section 21 of the 1988 Act

4.8 Assured shorthold tenancies can be brought to an end by a notice of not less than two months and a court is satisfied that such a notice has been given. Section 97 inserts a requirement that this notice must be given in writing, although there will be no prescribed form.

Restriction on section 21 of the 1988 Act

4.9 It was noted above that an assured shorthold tenancy does not now need to have any minimum fixed term, subject to common law requirements. However, s 99(2) of the 1996 Act, does not allow any order, as a result of a s 21 notice, to be given effect earlier than six months after the commencement of the tenancy and, where the tenancy is a replacement tenancy, no earlier than six months after the commencement of the original tenancy. This ensures that the minimum period of the tenancy remains at six months.

---

13 1988 Act, s 22(1).

14 *The Legislative Framework for Private Renting*, para 2.12.

15 To which s 19A of the 1988 Act applies.

16 If the landlord of an assured shorthold serves a notice increasing the rent, the tenant may similarly apply to the rent assessment committee: Sch 8, para 2(2) of the 1996 Act.

Essentially, an original tenancy refers to the original assured shorthold tenancy, even where this has been replaced by a succession of additional tenancies.[17] A replacement tenancy arises at the end of the assured shorthold tenancy but the landlord and the tenant must be the same people and the premises must be the same or substantially the same. An example should suffice: if X grants Y a tenancy for one month at a rent, that will be the original assured shorthold tenancy; at the end of that period, the replacement tenancy kicks in on a monthly basis. X, even though the term is just one month, will not be able to use the notice provisions to end the tenancy until six months after the grant of the original assured shorthold tenancy.

Rent arrears as ground for possession

4.10 In addition to the notice provision by which an assured shorthold tenancy can be terminated, landlords of both assured shorthold *and* assured tenancies are entitled to apply to the county court for an order for possession on one of eight mandatory and eight discretionary grounds, contained in Sch 2 to the 1988 Act. Mandatory Ground 8 is where the rent is in arrears for certain periods. Two of these periods are: where rent is payable weekly or fortnightly, 13 weeks' arrears; and where rent is payable monthly, three months' arrears.

Somewhat controversially, the Act shortens these periods to eight weeks and two months respectively.[18] This is controversial because housing benefit is soon to be paid four weeks in arrears and, although most housing benefit claims are settled within 14 days of the housing authority receiving all necessary documentation, about 30 per cent of such claims take a significantly longer time (particularly as recent announcements and changes have made authorities more conscious of the pressing need to seek out fraudulent claims).[19] Where a prospective tenant is in receipt of housing benefit, or might in the future be in receipt of housing benefit, particular problems may arise, giving the landlord the opportunity to seek this mandatory ground of possession.[20]

The Government's rejoinder to this argument was that the required court order will take about another three months for the landlord to obtain. In the meantime, housing benefit claims should have been settled and so the mandatory ground will cease to exist. Furthermore, local authorities are entitled to make a payment on account of housing benefit until a final determination of any claim.[21] However

---

17 The initial definition of an original tenancy was, in part, described as gobbledegook: Standing Committee G, Twelfth Sitting, col 480.

18 Section 101.

19 See Standing Committee G, Thirteenth Sitting, col 508.

20 The University of York study has found that many landlords do not wish to rent their properties to persons in receipt of housing benefit.

21 Housing Benefit (General) Regulations 1987, SI 1987/1971, reg 91.

optimistic this assessment may be, it is clear that in such circumstances the landlord will be able to apply for costs in the action.

Further discretionary ground for possession

4.11   A further discretionary ground for possession is also added by the 1996 Act to the eight such grounds already existing. This is where the tenant, or one tenant if there is more than one, induced the landlord to grant the tenancy by a false statement made knowingly or recklessly by that tenant or a person acting at the tenant's instigation.[22] This new ground was not mooted in the Consultation Paper and there has been no discussion upon it in Parliament, although it does exist in the Housing Act 1985.[23] Three matters must be proved by the landlord: first, the statement was false; secondly, that it was made knowingly or recklessly; and, finally, it induced the landlord to grant the tenancy. To a certain extent, this new ground enables a landlord to claim an order for possession based on the fraudulent misrepresentation of the tenant. If this is correct, then the falseness of the statement must be considered according to the meaning which the tenant attributed to it. Recklessness includes the situation where the tenant deliberately does not consider the honesty of the statement or purposely abstains from investigation.[24]

Succession of same sex partner

4.12   At present, succession to an assured periodic tenancy is limited to a person who was living with the original tenant as their wife or husband.[25] An attempt was made to expand the definition of wife or husband to include same sex partners. This attempt was successful in Standing Committee[26] but overturned on Third Reading in the House of Commons. The Housing Minister undertook to send unequivocal Guidance to local authorities requiring them to grant joint tenancies to same sex partners. In this way, the common law would operate the rule of survivorship on the death of one of the joint tenants. This would only apply to tenancies granted by the local authority.[27] Such Guidance has now been issued as Circular 7/96.

---

22 Section 102. The third party extension was added at Report Stage in the House of Lords (HL Debs, Vol 574, col 336) to extend to references provided by third parties, as well as other statements, written or oral, by third parties. Ground 5 contained in Sch 2 to the 1985 Act is similarly extended.

23 Ground 5 contained in Sch 2 to the 1985 Act.

24 See Cheshire, Fifoot and Furmston *Law of Contract* 12th edn (Butterworths, 1991), pp 277–279; *Derry v Peek* (1889) 14 App Cas 337, esp 374 per Lord Herschell.

25 1988 Act, s 17(4); *Harrogate BC v Simpson* (1985) 17 HLR 205.

26 Standing Committee G, Thirteenth Sitting, cols 513–522.

27 HC Debs, Vol 276, cols 977–979, 984–990.

CHAPTER 5

LEASEHOLD REFORM

Introduction

5.1 The leasehold reform provisions of the 1996 Act occupy 14 sections (ss 105 to 119) and three Schedules (Schs 9 to 11). The original Bill contained just five sections (and no Schedules), the preamble describing them as minor amendments to the leasehold reform provisions in the Leasehold Reform, Housing and Urban Development Act 1993.[1] In its Parliamentary passage, the Government had to concede one major change alleviating the low rent test and further modifications to both the 1993 Act and to the earlier Leasehold Reform Act 1967,[2] mostly designed to make leasehold enfranchisement more accessible. The basic structure of the leasehold reform provisions remains unchanged. Even with the liberalisation of the low rent test, there remains some justification in the Opposition charge that the new provisions will not achieve any further significant reform but merely tidy up unclear or unsatisfactory elements in previous legislation.[3] For an analysis of the earlier legislation onto which these amendments are grafted, the reader is referred to the standard texts.[4]

5.2 The changes can be conveniently considered in three categories. These are as follows.

(i) *New rights to enfranchisement.* There are four.
    (a) The sting of the existing low rent test has been drawn by granting the right to enfranchisement to certain long leaseholders who fail to qualify only because of the low rent test. In the case of both houses under the 1967 Act, and for flat enfranchisement under the 1993 Act, the principal beneficiaries are tenants with an initial term of 35 years.
    (b) There are technical amendments to the low rent test to deal with nil rateable values.
    (c) The Act closes the door on one of the more notorious avoidance devices by permitting collective enfranchisement of flats against more than one freeholder.

---

1 Hereafter the '1993 Act'.
2 Hereafter the '1967 Act'.
3 Standing Committee G, Twenty-Second Sitting, cols 860–861 (Mr Raynsford).
4 For the 1993 Act, see DN Clarke, *Leasehold Enfranchisement – The New Law* (Jordans, 1994) or P Matthews and D Millichip, *A Guide to the Leasehold Reform, Housing and Urban Development Act 1993* (Butterworths, 1993); for the 1967 Act see N Hague, *Leasehold Enfranchisement* 2nd edn (Sweet & Maxwell, 1987).

(d) One glaring omission in the 1993 Act is remedied by giving beneficiaries under trusts the same rights they would enjoy as legal owners of
the flats that they occupy.

(ii) *Procedural modifications to valuation.* There is a modest saving of cost in
removing a requirement of a professional valuation before a collective
enfranchisement can proceed. The valuation formulae are clarified to
prevent arguments to increase the price that might become payable.

(iii) *Minor miscellaneous changes.* Some of these are consequential.

New rights to enfranchisement

Long-term leases not at a low rent

5.3 Additional rights to enfranchisement are conferred on both long leaseholders of houses and of flats. Although the details differ in important respects,
the unifying principle is the wish to accord rights to secure the freehold on certain
leaseholders who previously failed to qualify solely because the rent payable
under their leases did not meet the low rent test. The existing low rent test has
been persistently criticised.[5] It permits lessors to grant long leases at rents just
above the limit. Many existing leases were so drafted to put the rents just above
the statutory limit. Indeed, the essential element of the low rent test – a rent less
than two-thirds of the letting or rateable value – not only appeared in the 1967
Act but in earlier legislation.[6] As amended by the 1993 Act,[7] the low rent test
provides that a lease is a lease at a low rent under any of the following
circumstances.[8]

(i)   Where no rent was payable under it in respect of the flat during the initial
year.[9]

(ii) Where the lease was entered into before 1 April 1963, the aggregate amount
of rent so payable during the initial year did not exceed two-thirds of the
letting value (on the same terms) on the date of commencement of the
lease.[10]

(iii) Where the lease was either entered into on or after 1 April 1963 but before 1
April 1990 (or on or after 1 April 1990 if in pursuance of a contract made
before that date) and had a rateable value[11] at the date of commencement of

---

5 It only survived the final attempt at amendment in 1993 on a tied vote in the House of Lords,
Vol 546, cols 187–204.

6 For example, the Landlord and Tenant Act 1954.

7 Which amended the 1967 Act to bring the two statutes into harmony.

8 Section 8 of the 1993 Act; added as an alternative low rent test for enfranchisement of houses
by s 65 of the 1993 Act introducing s 4A into the 1967 Act.

9 Section 8(1). This provision means that, in new leases, particular care must be taken when
rent-free periods, for whatever reason, are being considered.

10 Section 8(1)(a).

11 For the purpose of determining the amount of rateable value of a flat on a particular date, the
Rent Act 1977, s 25 applies (s 8(2)(c)).

the lease or at any time before 1 April 1990, the aggregate amount of rent so payable during the initial year did not exceed two-thirds of the rateable value on the appropriate date.[12]

(iv) In any other case, the aggregate amount of rent payable during the initial year did not exceed £1,000 in Greater London or £250 if elsewhere.[13]

The problems with this low rent test concern the arbitrary distinctions that result, the particular difficulty of proving letting values in the case of pre-1 April 1963 leases and the large number of long leaseholders excluded by the expedient over the years of setting rents just above the statutory limits. Avoidance continues with new lettings. For this reason, the Opposition tabled an amendment in the Commons Standing Committee which would have deleted the low rent test and permitted all long leases of houses and flats over 21 years to enfranchise. This amendment was carried with the assistance of backbench Conservative support.[14] The response of the Government, facing considerable pressure from its own side, was to introduce what is now s 106 of and Sch 9 to the 1996 Act. This preserves the low rent test unchanged but introduces an alternative right to enfranchisement so that some long leases do not need to meet the low rent test. The details differ depending on whether the property is a house within the 1967 Act or a flat within the 1993 Act.

Leasehold houses for terms exceeding 35 years

5.4 The additional right to enfranchise in the case of houses is given by para 1 of Sch 9 which introduces a new s 1AA into the 1967 Act.[15] It applies to those tenancies of houses excluded from the provisions of the 1967 Act solely on the grounds that the lease is not at a low rent – so all other statutory requirements must first be satisfied. If a tenancy is within s 1AA, the tenant has the same right to acquire the freehold as if it were a tenancy at a low rent. Tenancies within the new section are principally those granted for a term of years certain exceeding 35 years.[16] The section also ensures that tenancies which are equivalent to such a term are included so that tenancies with an obligation for perpetual renewal, those taking effect as leases for 90 years terminable by death or remarriage,[17] and those which by virtue of a right to renewal without payment of a premium have a combined term in excess of 35 years are also within the section.[18] There was

---

12 Section 8(1)(b).

13 Section 8(1)(c).

14 Standing Committee G, Twenty-Third Sitting, cols 875–912, with the support of Mr David Ashby from the Conservative benches.

15 The consequential drafting amendments to the rest of the 1967 Act are set out in Sch 9, para 2 to the 1996 Act.

16 Section 1AA(2)(a). If property is comprised in two or more separate tenancies but both tenancies are within subs (2), then the Act's provisions to treat them as a single tenancy are applicable (subs (4)).

17 Under the Law of Property Act 1925, s 149(6).

18 Section 1AA(2)(b)–(d).

cross-party consensus[19] that there was a case for exemption of properties in rural areas let as part of agricultural arrangements involving long leases but with no premium payable.[20] This exemption is the basis of s 1AA(3) which excludes tenancies in rural areas[21] of a house owned with adjoining land not occupied for residential purposes and granted before s 106 of the 1996 Act comes into force.[22] The result is to grant the right to enfranchise to nearly all tenancies of houses exceeding 35 years at whatever rent.[23] As introduced into the Commons, the benefit was given to houses with leases exceeding 50 years.[24] Disquiet was expressed on all sides of the House that 50 years was too long.[25] Pressure in the House of Lords led the Government to accept a proposed amendment to reduce the length to 35 years.[26] The result is that the only leases with initial terms of between 21 and 35 years will still need to meet the low rent test.[27]

Leasehold flats for terms exceeding 35 years

5.5   A similar reform is introduced for leaseholders of flats who cannot either collectively enfranchise nor have a right to a new lease under the 1993 Act because their leases are not at a low rent. The reform is achieved by amending s 5 of the 1993 Act[28] so that a 'qualifying tenant' is a tenant of a flat under a long lease which is either at a low rent or for a particularly long term. 'Particularly long term' is defined by a new s 8A of the 1993 Act primarily as one granted for a term of

---

19 See HC Debs, Vol 276, col 939 (30 April 1996).

20 It was estimated that less than 300 such leases were involved.

21 Designated by the Secretary of State.

22 This is to avoid the freeholder of a house in a rural area buying an adjoining plot of non-residential land to take advantage of the rural exemption (see HL Debs, Vol 574, col 377 (10 July 1996)).

23 It was said in the Commons Debates that there were no residential leases known for terms over 50 years at or near rack rents. If any such exist, now at terms in excess of 35 years, the tenants can enfranchise, although the higher the rent, the greater the premium payable on an enfranchisement. The Minister, Mr John Gummer, contended there were significant numbers at rack rents with terms between 21 and 50 years (HC Debs, Vol 276, col 925) but this assertion was later alleged to be on the basis of only six unsubstantiated examples proffered by the British Property Federation (HL Debs, Vol 574, col 373 (10 July 1996)).

24 Fifty years was originally chosen as it is the point at which a lease starts to depreciate so that terms for longer than this period are treated at the outset as freehold for accounting purposes (HL Debs, Vol 573, col 194).

25 Reference was made to particular cases in London with 45-year leases.

26 The amendment was made at Third Reading in the Lords (HL Debs, Vol 574, col 967) after the Government had conceded the principle of 35 years at Report Stage (HL Debs, Vol 574, col 384). It was accepted that any line drawn cannot be exact and a line drawn at 35 years is as arbitrary as any other but 35 years is the threshold for stamp duty and the point at which it is generally accepted that the freehold value rises to about one-third of the total interest in the property (see also HC Debs, Vol 282, col 79 (22 July 1996)).

27 The probability must be that future legislation will remove the low rent test altogether. Consequently, it is unwise to rely on the rule remaining unchanged. New leases for terms for over 21 years but less than 35 years at just above the low rent level should not be granted if it is desired to ensure enfranchisement will never occur.

28 By para 3(2) of Sch 9 to the 1996 Act.

years certain exceeding 35 years whether or not terminable before the end of that term by notice, re-entry, forfeiture or otherwise.[29] Once again, the section ensures that tenancies which are equivalent to such a term are included so that tenancies with an obligation for perpetual renewal, those taking effect as leases for 90 years terminable by death or remarriage,[30] and those which by virtue of a right to renewal without payment of a premium have a combined term in excess of 50 years are also within the section.[31] Leases granted in pursuance of the right to buy under the Housing Act 1985 or shared ownership leases may also qualify as leases for a particularly long term.[32] Consequential amendments ensure that the right to a new lease given to individual tenants is available in the case of particularly long leases.[33] Tenants under leases of Crown land may also benefit.[34] There is no exception for flats in rural areas to match that given in respect of houses.

Low rent test and nil rateable values

5.6 A small number of properties have been unable to meet the low rent test because they had a nil rateable value at the relevant date. An example would be a property which was uninhabitable at the relevant date. The lessee would undertake the substantial works of reconstruction under the terms of a long lease. The position is particularly anomalous when compared to newly constructed buildings which first became rated on completion. In response to concerns expressed,[35] s 105[36] amends both the 1967 Act and the 1993 Act to ensure that properties with a nil rateable value on the relevant date are able to enfranchise. The relevant date becomes the date on which it first had a rateable value after the commencement of the tenancy.[37] A consequential amendment is s 114 of the 1996 Act. This recasts s 1(1)(a) of the 1967 Act which sets out the dates on which the rateable value limits are effective.[38]

---

29 Section 8A(1)(a), inserted by para 3(3) of Sch 9 to the 1996 Act.

30 Under the Law of Property Act 1925, s 149(6).

31 Section 8A(1)(b)–(d).

32 Section 8A(2).

33 Made by Sch 9, para 4.

34 Schedule 9, para 5; and see DN Clarke, *Leasehold Enfranchisement – The New Law* (Jordans, 1994) paras 3.4.7 and 11.3.3.

35 In the Lords' Committee Stage, HL Debs, Vol 573, cols 183 and 187 by Lord Dubs and Lord Carnock.

36 Introduced as a Government amendment at Report Stage, HL Debs, Vol 574, col 368.

37 Section 105(2)(b) and (3)(b) amending s 4A of the 1967 Act and s 8 of the 1993 Act.

38 The Minister, Lord Lucas, also claimed that the new wording removes a potential lacuna in the former wording of the section (HL Debs, Vol 574, col 370).

Resident beneficiaries of flats[39]

5.7 Tenants wishing to participate in a collective enfranchisement of a flat do not have to be resident in their flat, but one-half of the participating tenants do need to satisfy a residence condition. A tenant desiring to exercise the individual right to a new lease must satisfy a residence requirement.[40] The 1993 Act made no provision for the case of beneficiaries under a trust where the title to the flat is vested in trustees and the beneficiary occupies. Such beneficiaries could not make a claim to a new lease since they were not tenants who were resident. Their inability to meet the residence condition for a collective enfranchisement might prevent an initial notice being possible if there were insufficient other tenants who were resident. This was an obvious lacuna in the 1993 Act.[41] Section 111 remedies the defect in respect of a collective enfranchisement by repealing subs 6(4) of the 1993 Act[42] and substituting three new subss (4)–(6). When the lease is vested in trustees,[43] a qualifying tenant is treated as satisfying the residence condition if an individual with an interest under the trust occupies the flat. The periods of occupation are naturally identical to those already required for a collective enfranchisement, namely, for the last 12 months or periods amounting to three years in the last ten years. It is immaterial whether the occupation by that individual arises by virtue of the trustee's lease or in some other way. Any initial notice under s 13 of the 1993 Act will set out the details of the residence by the beneficiary.[44] A beneficiary under a trust may exercise the right to acquire a new lease by virtue of s 112 which amends s 39 of the 1993 Act. The residence requirement is satisfied if the lease is vested in trustees and an individual having an interest under the trust (whether or not that individual is also a trustee) has occupied the flat as his only or principal home. The period of residence needed is identical to that provided for in the 1993 Act – which is different to that for a collective enfranchisement – namely, occupation for the last three years or for periods amounting to three years in the last ten.[45] There is the consequential amendment to s 42 of the 1993 Act to cover the particulars to be included in a tenant's notice.[46]

---

39 Sections 111–113; these were three of the original five sections in Chapter III of the Bill as published.

40 See DN Clarke *Leasehold Enfranchisement – The New Law* (Jordans, 1994) paras 3.6.1 and 11.2.3 for details of the residence which is needed in each case.

41 Provision is made in the case of enfranchisement of houses under s 6(1) of the 1967 Act. The omission from the 1993 Act may be the result of the residence provisions being introduced into the 1993 legislation at a late stage.

42 Which deals only with leases held by joint tenants.

43 Property vested in a sole tenant for life under the Settled Land Act 1925 is excluded. Leases held by joint tenants will be covered by the new provisions.

44 Section 111(2) amending s 13(3)(e)(iii) of the 1993 Act.

45 Section 39(2A).

46 Section 112(5).

Powers of trustees

5.8   Resident beneficiaries might be hindered in their wish to participate in a collective enfranchisement or exercise their right to a new lease by the terms of the trust. To ensure that this does not occur, it is now provided that where trustees are a qualifying tenant of a flat, their powers under the trust instrument shall include power to participate in a collective enfranchisement or to exercise the right to a new lease.[47] This power can only be excluded by an explicit direction to the contrary in a trust instrument taking effect on or after the day the 1996 Act is brought into force. The power is exercisable subject to any consents or direction required by the instrument for exercise of the trustee powers. Trustees are enabled to pay expenses incurred in connection with participation in a collective enfranchisement or new lease application.[48]

Collective enfranchisement against multiple freeholders

5.9   Under the 1993 Act, the right to collective enfranchisement is only available if the freehold of the building (or self-contained part) is owned by the same person. In order to deny the right to enfranchise, freeholders have been creating flying freeholds of one or more of the flats in any block. Normally, this is against their interest since the disposal triggers the right of first refusal given to the tenants[49] and the uncertainty of any flying freehold created would reduce the value of what is retained.[50] Circumvention of the 1987 Act rights and the use of controlled companies to hold the flying freehold permitting reconveyance when desired meant that landlords used this loophole to prevent enfranchisement. Section 107 not only closes the loophole but restores the right to collective enfranchisement where creation of flying freeholds has prevented it. This is achieved by the following provisions.

(i)   A collective enfranchisement is now possible where premises are owned by more than one person. The requirement in s 3 of the 1993 Act that the freehold of the whole of the relevant premises be owned by the same person is deleted.[51]

(ii)   If a building is made up of several self-contained parts, and there is more than one freehold interest in the building, the right of enfranchisement applies only to the self-contained part.[52] This is to prevent one group of leaseholders buying up more than the freehold interest in which their flats are located. By way of example, in a row of terraced houses, the flat tenants in a larger house could not enfranchise in a way to include a smaller one next

---

47 Section 113.

48 See s 113(2)–(4) for these issues.

49 By virtue of the Landlord and Tenant Act 1987.

50 The right of an individual tenant to a new lease also remains, see DN Clarke *Leasehold Enfranchisement – The New Law* (Jordans, 1994) para 10.4.2.

51 Section 107(1).

52 Section 107(2), adding s 4(3)(a) to the 1993 Act.

door.[53] By contrast, they can, by virtue of this section, enfranchise their own house, even if there is a flying freehold within it. In other words, where there are multiple freeholders, only a self-contained part of a building can be subject to a collective enfranchisement.

(iii) Any additional property which may be acquired under a collective enfranchisement no longer has to be owned by the same person as freeholder.[54] 'Additional property' has to be demised to the tenants by their leases or they must have the right to use it. It can then be acquired as part of the enfranchisement process. Examples would be gardens or a block of garages. Selling or transferring such additional property to another freeholder would not prevent a collective enfranchisement but might make it much less attractive. That loophole has also been closed.

Consequential amendments

5.10   The change to permit collective enfranchisement where there is more than one freeholder necessitated a substantial number of amendments to the rest of the 1993 Act. These are set out in Sch 10 to the 1996 Act.[55] The most important provisions to note are the following.

(i)   The collective enfranchisement process depends upon identifying the 'reversioner', the person who deals with the claim and upon whom notices are served. This is usually the freeholder.[56] With a claim against two or more freeholders, it became necessary to decide who the reversioner is to be. The simple solution was preferred: the reversioner is the freeholder specified in the leaseholders' initial notice.[57] They simply choose.[58] If the freeholders agree to change the reversioner, he or she can be appointed with agreement of the court.[59] Freeholders who consider that a claim for collective enfranchisement is likely, perhaps after receipt of a preliminary enquiry notice under s 11 of the 1993 Act,[60] may wish to anticipate the initial notice and inform the tenants or nominee purchaser which freeholder they would prefer to be the recipient of the notice and consequent reversioner.

---

53 An example given by the Under Secretary of State, Mr Clappison in Standing Committee G, Twenty-third Sitting, col 871, when introducing the clause.
54 Section 107(3), amending s 1(3) of the 1993 Act.
55 Which takes up no less than ten pages of the statute.
56 It could be the holder of an intermediate leasehold interest.
57 See para 4 of Sch 10 and para 15 which inserts a new Part 1A into Sch 1 to the 1993 Act.
58 A copy of the initial notice must be given to the other freeholders (Sch 3, Part II, para 12A to the 1993 Act, inserted by Sch 10(4) to the 1996 Act).
59 Paragraph 5A of Sch 1 to the 1993 Act. Paragraphs 5B and 5C give the court power to remove a reversioner or, in appropriate circumstances, appoint a replacement. The provisions mirror the existing Part I of the Schedule to the 1993 Act, on which see DN Clarke *Leasehold Enfranchisement – The New Law* (Jordans, 1994), paras 5.8.4 and 5.8.5.
60 On which see DN Clarke *Leasehold Enfranchisement – The New Law* (Jordans, 1994), para 4.7.2.

(ii) Paragraph 18 of Sch 10 sets out the basis for calculating the price to be paid for the freehold and intermediate leasehold interests in a multiple freeholder case. The nominee purchaser will pay a separate price for each of the freehold interests. Each amount is to be calculated separately as for any other enfranchisement purchase and so will comprise the three elements of open market value, the freeholder's share of any marriage value and any compensation due. It may well be that the open market value to be paid in total for the two or more divided freehold interests will be less than the open market value of the undivided freehold.[61] If this is the case, there may well be a reunification of freeholds into a single person before the 1996 Act is brought into force.[62]

(iii) There are new provisions to deal with the share of the marriage value between freeholder of part and any intermediate leaseholders.[63] It is determined by reference to the proportionate value of their respective interests in that part of the freehold.

Valuation

Collective enfranchisement – no need for a prior valuation

5.11 At present, one of the necessary steps before proceeding with a collective enfranchisement is that a valuation must be prepared by a qualified surveyor of the freehold and any intermediate leasehold interests. The initial notice must confirm that the tenants have done so and name the surveyor. The idea was to inform the tenants of the financial commitment they were entering into. This requirement has been removed by s 108.[64] The Government was convinced, after representations and complaints at Committee Stage, that the need for a formal valuation was overprescriptive. It led to unnecessary costs, particularly in straightforward cases and in cases where an agreement to sell the freehold in the light of the provisions of the 1993 Act can be made once an initial notice is served. A collective enfranchisement is now brought into line with enfranchisement of houses and lease extensions where there has never been such a requirement. After nearly three years' experience, some guidance on valuation is given by leasehold valuation tribunal decisions and the advisory service offered by the

---

61 This would reflect the inherent disadvantages of flying freeholds and difficulties of the mutual enforcement of covenants; the inability or grave difficulty of raising a mortgage on a flying freehold may also depress the price.

62 If there remain divided freeholders at the time of a collective enfranchisement, it is open to argument that the price for each part of the divided freehold should not be reduced since it can be argued that the other freeholders will be purchasers in the market seeking to buy (see para **5.13**).

63 Schedule 10, para 18(8), inserting new para 9A into Sch 6 to the 1993 Act.

64 It provides that s 13(6) of the 1993 Act shall cease to have effect. The section was introduced at Report Stage in the Commons: HC Debs, Vol 276, col 913.

Leasehold Advisory Service is continuing. In many cases, it may still be advisable to seek professional advice on valuation but this may be done more informally.

Clarification of valuation formulae

5.12   Sections 109 and 110 of the 1996 Act[65] amend Schs 6 and 13 respectively of the 1993 Act. They make essentially technical amendments to the valuation framework for assessing either the price to be paid on a collective enfranchisement or the premium on the grant of a new lease. The aim overall is to ensure that the price or premium cannot be artificially inflated.

Valuation and collective enfranchisement

5.13   On a collective enfranchisement, the first element in the price is the open market value of the freeholder's interest. To prevent the price being inflated, the 1993 Act provided that the value was to be assessed on the basis that neither the nominee purchaser nor any of the participating tenants were seeking to buy. This was done because it may otherwise be argued that they would be 'special purchasers' willing to pay higher than market price. Section 109 widens and redefines the category of special purchasers to prevent arguments that other categories of special purchaser might be wishing to purchase the freehold. The open market value is now assessed on the basis that neither the nominee purchaser, nor any tenant of property within the specified premises, nor any intermediate leaseholders of additional property are seeking to buy. In essence, no one with an interest in the property being acquired is seeking to buy. The open market price is that which an outsider would pay. When valuing the open market value of any intermediate leasehold or other interest in the property, the owner of any freehold interest is similarly treated as not seeking to buy.[66] There may be a drafting slip here. Since a collective enfranchisement can now be made against two or more freeholders, it may be argued that the freeholder should have been disregarded as a category of special purchaser in valuation of the freehold as well. Without such explicit direction, it remains open for a freeholder of part to argue that the other freeholder(s) of the other part(s) would pay a higher price to unite the freeholds into one title, thereby inflating the price to be paid by the nominee purchaser. The riposte to such an argument is that the ultimate price paid for both or all parts of the freehold, as the case may be, should not in any event exceed the value of the whole if held by one person. If that is right, the retention of any other freeholder as a special purchaser is not a drafting slip but merely ensures that the price paid by the nominee purchaser is not reduced by the fact of a split freehold.[67]

---

65 These were two of the five original sections in the Bill and provoked little debate. Unlike the rest of Chapter III, s 110 came into force immediately on Royal Assent.

66 Section 109(4) and (5).

67 See para **5.10**.

Valuation and the grant of a new lease

5.14 A number of changes are made to the valuation principles applicable to ascertainment of the premium on the grant of a new lease. The first mirrors the changes noted in the previous paragraph. The category of special purchaser is widened so that the owner of any intermediate interest, as well as the tenant, is not seeking to buy when the open market premium for the grant of a new lease is calculated.[68] The other changes are all points of clarification to the valuation of the landlord's share of the marriage value element in the premium payable by the tenant for the new lease. They close another lacuna in the 1993 Act which was permitting artificial transactions designed to increase the premium payable. The marriage value is found by calculating the difference between two aggregate sums.[69] The principal element of one sum is the value of the interest of the tenant under the present lease; the principal element in the other is the value to be held by the tenant under the new lease. The 1993 Act did not give any elucidation or valuation framework of assumptions and disregards for these two valuations. This is in marked contrast to the clear framework set out for valuing the landlord's interest.[70] The 1996 Act remedies that defect by inserting new ss 4A and 4B into Sch 13 to the 1993 Act.[71] They conform in detail very closely to the framework already provided for valuing the landlord's interest.[72] Section 110 is not, however, retrospective. It only applies to claims for a new lease made after 19 January 1996.[73] Consequently, the provision to prevent the value of the tenant's interest being increased or the value of the new lease being decreased by any artificial or other transaction[74] only applies to transactions after 19 January 1996. Any transactions prior to that date will be taken into account.

Miscellaneous amendments

Enfranchisement of houses – determination of costs

5.15 Section 115[75] extends the power of leasehold valuation tribunals when resolving disputes in the enfranchisement of houses under the 1967 Act. At present, any dispute on costs needs to be settled by separate court proceedings. Power is now given for the leasehold valuation tribunal to determine the amount of any landlord's costs. This brings proceedings under the 1967 Act in line with

---

68 Section 110(2).

69 See DN Clarke *Leasehold Enfranchisement – The New Law* (Jordans, 1994), para 20.4.1.

70 See Sch 13, para 3, when calculating the diminution in value of that interest.

71 Section 110(4) and (5) respectively.

72 Schedule 13, para 3.

73 Section 110(5). 19 January 1996 is the day after the First Reading of the Housing Bill 90 (HC Debs, Vol 269, col 902) when it was ordered to be printed.

74 Paragraphs 4A and 4B of Sch 13 to the 1993 Act inserted by s 110(4).

75 Inserted by way of Government amendment at Committee Stage, HL Debs, Vol 573, col 200.

the jurisdiction already available to tribunals under the 1993 Act when dealing with a collective enfranchisement or lease extension.[76]

Priority of interests on the grant of a new lease

5.16 Section 117[77] guarantees third party interests when a leaseholder is granted a new lease under the 1993 Act. There is already provision that if the tenant's existing lease is subject to a mortgage, then that mortgage takes effect against the new extended lease in the same way that it applied to the old lease.[78] To meet the uncertainty that had arisen where there is more than one third party interest to an existing lease, a new s 58A is inserted into the 1993 Act so that all the interests that applied to the old lease apply to the new lease in the same priority.[79] This is subject to agreement to the contrary.[80] Finally, there is protection for any rights of occupation under the Matrimonial Homes Act 1983 so that those existing on the grant of the new lease are treated as a continuation of rights to which he or she was entitled just before the surrender of the old lease.[81]

Estate management schemes

5.17 The relaxation of the low rent test[82] enfranchises a new class of leaseholders. This necessitated the granting of a further opportunity for any landlord to apply for an estate management scheme. Both the 1967 Act and the 1993 Act gave landlords a limited opportunity to apply for an estate management scheme and thereby retain some control over properties in the area. The two-year period permitted by the 1993 Act expired on 31 October 1995. By s 118,[83] landlords are given a fresh two-year opportunity to apply for an estate management scheme on the basis that the property will become enfranchisable after the 1996 Act comes into force. The same procedures and criteria will apply as in the 1993 Act.[84] A leasehold valuation tribunal may only approve a scheme if satisfied that it is necessary to maintain adequate standards of appearance and amenity or to regulate development. A case for a scheme under the 1996 Act may only be on the basis of property newly enfranchisable by virtue of the 1996 Act.[85] If granted, however, the scheme may apply to all property within its area.

---

76 See s 91(3)(d) of the 1993 Act.
77 Inserted by way of Government amendment at Committee Stage, HL Debs, Vol 573, col 201.
78 Section 58 of the 1993 Act.
79 Section 58A(1).
80 Section 58A(2).
81 Section 58A(3).
82 See para **5.3**.
83 Inserted by way of Government amendment at Committee Stage, HL Debs, Vol 573, col 201.
84 See DN Clarke *Leasehold Enfranchisement – The New Law* (Jordans, 1994), ch 23. The two-year period will run from the date s 118 comes into force.
85 These may either be houses, and therefore enfranchisable under the 1967 Act, or flats and therefore collectively enfranchisable under the 1993 Act.

Enfranchisement procedure – pre-trial reviews

5.18   Provision is made for pre-trial reviews to streamline leasehold valuation tribunal procedures (s 119).[86] Regulations may be made to permit preliminary hearings before a single qualified member. The aim is to permit the points in dispute to be clarified in advance of the full hearing and indicate the evidence that will be brought forward. It is hoped that parties will be better prepared, time and effort will be saved and costly adjournments to prepare responses to unanticipated evidence will be avoided. It will also be easier to identify the length and complexity of a case to assist in setting dates for the full hearing.

Compensation when an existing tenancy is prolonged

5.19   The leasehold reform provisions of the 1996 Act bring little cheer for landlords. The exception (although any benefit is delayed until after 15 January 1999) is contained in s 116 of and Sch 11 to the 1996 Act.[87] The complexities of Sch 11, which introduces parallel provisions into the 1967 and 1993 Acts,[88] attempt to resolve what was described as a fairly simple problem. If a claim for enfranchisement or a new lease is made just before the expiry of the existing lease, then the lease is continued until the claim is finally determined and for three months thereafter. The existing lease will be at a low rent. If the claim does not succeed, the landlord is denied the market rent from the end of the existing term until the end of the process. There is every incentive for tenants to spin out procedures or make spurious claims. The new provisions will apply only when the claim is made within two years of expiry of the long lease term and even then only to claims made on or after 15 January 1999.[89] Once such a claim has been determined as unsuccessful, the tenant becomes liable to pay to the landlord the difference between what the tenant would have paid in market rent and what has actually been paid in ground rent over the appropriate period. This is a period from the earliest date on which the lease could have terminated, usually the expiry of the term, and the date when the claim for enfranchisement or a new lease ends. One complexity of the new sections are the provisions to cope with changes in the leaseholders' immediate landlord. The new compensation was criticised by the Opposition.[90] At least tenants have adequate time to submit a claim before the new rules come into force. Whether the compensation provisions will survive to come into force on 15 January 1999 remains to be seen.

---

86 Introduced by way of Government amendment at Report Stage, HL Debs, Vol 574, col 398.

87 Introduced at a very late stage (Report Stage in the Lords, HL Debs, Vol 574, col 388, 10 July 1996). Schedule 11, which extends to over nine pages, was described by the Minister as 'of inordinate length'.

88 New s 27A in the 1967 Act for enfranchisement of houses, new s 37A in the 1993 Act for a collective enfranchisement and new s 61A in the 1993 Act where there is a claim for a new lease.

89 This is the changeover date for statutory regimes applicable to the holding over after a long lease expires. Schedule 10 to the Local Government and Housing Act 1989 will replace Part I of the Landlord and Tenant Act 1954 on that date.

90 See HL Debs, Vol 574, col 389 and HC Debs, Vol 282, col 82 (22 July 1996).

Conclusion

5.20   There were attempts to incorporate many other changes into the leasehold reform section of the Act. The two changes that got closest were the complete abolition of the low rent test and the further widening of enfranchisement in favour of blocks of flats with a commercial or non-residential element of up to 25 per cent.[91] Both succeeded in Commons Standing Committee, but were overturned at Report Stage,[92] the low rent test abolition by only two votes.

The changes that did not make it this time are not the only indication that the 1996 Act will not be the last word on leasehold reform. There is now every prospect of an early enactment of commonhold reform on which there is cross-party consensus.[93] In addition, the Opposition have indicated that in Government they will introduce a 'proper and comprehensive measure of leasehold reform' to give leaseholders of flats greater benefits.[94] It would be unwise to make arrangements let alone grant or accept leases on the basis that the present law will remain fixed for any long period of time.

---

91 The present limit is 10 per cent.

92 HC Debs, Vol 276, cols 949 and 991.

93 See *Commonhold, Draft Bill* and *Consultation Paper,* Lord Chancellor's Department, July 1996. The expectation is that the Commonhold Bill will be introduced into the final session of the current Parliament.

94 See the remarks of the frontbench spokesman, Mr Raynsford, at HC Debs, Vol 282, col 83 (22 July 1996).

PART IV

CHAPTER 6

HOUSING BENEFIT AND RELATED MATTERS

Introduction

6.1 The discussion in Standing Committee G and subsequently in the House of Lords on Part IV of the Housing Bill[1] was notable in two respects: (1) for the absence of any detailed discussion of the clauses as they stood; and (2) for the vain attempts made to introduce wholly unconnected general amendments to the housing benefit regime. Part IV itself may be adjudged to be largely uncontentious. It makes some discrete changes to the arcane system of housing finance, and otherwise effects a few detailed adjustments to the rules for payment of the housing benefit. None of the provisions is likely to carry major practical consequences for housing advisers or their clients.

Nevertheless, 1996 has seen major changes in entitlement to housing benefit which will have a considerable impact on claimants and their families. These changes are all regulatory and have been subject to a consultation process, rather than to parliamentary scrutiny. In January 1996, controversial extensions to the previous regulations 'capping' the amount of benefit payable to individuals were brought into force.[2] From October 1996, benefit for single people under the age of 25 will be further restricted, to cover only the cost of shared accommodation.[3] A further proposal to redefine the service charges which can be met by housing benefit, which would have sabotaged much provision for housing with care, has now been put back for a further review following very extensive lobbying by agencies involved in the provision of community care.

Given the extent of the 'other' legislative activity, this chapter aims to consider the Housing Act amendments to the housing benefit scheme within a general policy and financial context and, in so doing, to point out the policy reasons for the changes as a whole, which signify yet another phase in the complex legal history of the housing benefit scheme.

---

1 See, for example, Standing Committee G, Fifteenth Sitting, cols 530, 533 and 541.
2 Housing Benefit (General) Amendment Regulations 1995, SI 1995/1644.
3 Housing Benefit (General) Amendment Regulations 1996, SI 1996/965.

The housing benefit scheme

6.2   Housing benefit is a means-tested subsidy paid to individuals to meet rented housing costs. It is a financial lifeline for people on low incomes, and a majority of rent payers receive housing benefit.[4] It is therefore a major constituent of overall social housing expenditure and, since 1979, has accounted for an increasing proportion of that expenditure as rent increases have far outstripped inflation.

Historically, housing benefit dates back to the inter-war period when the municipal housing programme geared to provide decent and affordable 'homes fit for heroes' was at its peak.[5] The Housing Act 1930 encouraged local authorities to introduce means-tested rent rebate schemes. The original schemes were confined to slum clearance projects, to help the poorest tenants to afford new properties, but from then on provision for rebates on rents or cash allowances has been a constant feature of housing policy. There has been an uneasy co-existence between what is essentially a targeted subsidy for certain individuals, which allows rent levels generally to rise, and the 'bricks and mortar' approach to housing investment subsidy which was a main platform of central Government policy from the 1920s right through to 1980. Latterly, however, the pendulum has swung sharply towards supporting individual households within an overall rent system which has become much more market orientated, even within the social housing sector.[6] The White Paper acknowledges this transition:

> 'Since 1979 we have switched spending from "bricks and mortar" expenditure which helps all social tenants, to housing benefit which is targeted better on households with low incomes. We have done this by increasing rents in the social sector; by increasing use of private finance in providing new social housing; and by making greater use of the private rented sector. Better targeting has helped keep down public expenditure'.[7]

The role of local authorities in administering housing benefit

6.3   Administrative responsibility for paying housing benefit has always lain with local authorities. In the early days, authorities were empowered to set up and administer their own schemes. Later on, a national scheme was brought into operation to iron out variations and inequities between the different local

---

4 Currently, there are well over 4.5 m recipients of housing benefit, of whom 1.2 m are tenants in the private rental sector. Benefit accounts for 12 per cent of all social security expenditure (*Journal of the Institute of Rent Officers* (JIRO) July 1996, p 10).

5 D Hughes and S Lowe: *Social Housing Law and Policy* (Butterworths, 1995) ch 1.

6 Expenditure on housing benefit has increased by almost 300 per cent since implementation of the Social Security Act 1986 and the Housing Act 1988 (JIRO, July 1996, p 10).

7 DoE *Our Future Homes* 1995, p 8.

schemes,[8] but local authorities continued to be responsible for administration. This responsibility now rests in district councils, borough councils or other unitary authorities.

Given that the current emphasis in housing finance is on targeting subsidies through individual means-tested allowances, it could be argued that, in the interests of efficiency, housing benefit should be integrated with the rest of the social security system, and administered by central government. Indeed, the Social Security Act 1986 cleared the way for such a change by harmonising the means test for all income-related benefits[9] and standardising the rules in respect of claiming and paying benefit.

History, however, has not and probably will not, allow this to happen. In the early 1980s, there was a considerable amount of debate about the fragmented approach of the social security system to the payment of benefit to help with housing costs. Housing benefit, paid by local authorities, was available to help tenants on low incomes, whilst the Department of Health and Social Security, a central government agency, paid out supplementary benefit to help owner–occupiers with their mortgage interest. To make matters worse, tenants who relied on supplementary benefit as an income-replacement benefit would receive their housing costs from the DHSS and not from local authorities. At the time, the proposed rationalisation of this untidy system relied on the argument that it would be advantageous if the responsibility for running what was to be a 'unified' housing benefit scheme were to be given to local authorities.[10]

It was against this background that, in 1993, the Audit Commission affirmed the 'strong reasons for local government to undertake the task of administration'[11] in terms of the fact that council tenants account for more than 70 per cent of housing benefit recipients, and that local authorities can reduce costs and increase security for their tenants by operating a rebate system rather than having tenants receive cash benefits from another source.[12] Behind this is also the fact that there is now, and always has been, a close link between housing benefit and permitted reliefs on local taxes (domestic rates, community charge and, since 1993, council tax)[13] as regards the prescribed means test, general administration, and central government subsidy.

Nevertheless, central government finance meets approximately 95 per cent of the cost of housing benefit payments and about 60 per cent of the cost of

---

8 Housing Finance Act 1972.

9 Then income support, family credit, housing benefit; disability working allowance and council tax benefit have since been added to the list.

10 Social Security and Housing Benefits Act 1982.

11 *Remote Control: The National Administration of Housing Benefit*, Audit Commission 1993, p 1.

12 Notwithstanding that housing costs for owner occupiers on low incomes are now almost universally met by direct payments from the DSS to mortgage lenders; Income Support (General) Regulations 1987/1967, Sch 3.

13 Local Government Finance Act, 1992.

administering the scheme. In addition, the new Department of Social Security is responsible for policy regarding benefit entitlement and for the primary and secondary legislation which implements it. Legally, local authorities now operate the housing benefit scheme under the Social Security (Contributions and Benefits) Act 1992 and the Social Security Administration Act 1992 ('SSAA'), plus various sets of regulations, the most important of which are the much-amended Housing Benefit (General) Regulations 1987.[14] Central government has, therefore, a considerable interest in the quality of administration of housing benefit achieved by local authorities.

In this respect, the track record of local authorities has been far from exemplary. When the present 'unified' housing benefit system was introduced in 1983,[15] *The Times'* leader report referred to 'the worst administrative fiasco in the history of the welfare state'.[16] Since then, there has been constant criticism of the quality of the service from academics and voluntary agencies as well as from landlords and tenants, and the Local Government Ombudsman has referred to 'administrative chaos'.

There is also an inevitable tension as the administering agency, at the sharp end of practice, criticises the paymaster for underfunding.[17] Whatever the merits of that particular debate, objectively it is clear that the obsessive detail of the Housing Benefit Regulations, coupled with the necessity for local authorities to liaise with the Benefits Agency over payment of multiple benefits – a major characteristic of the system – raise very considerable problems for the administering agencies. In addition, the legislative changes since 1982 have made enormous demands on local authorities.[18]

Housing benefit finance

6.4 Public money spent on housing benefit includes the benefit payments themselves, and the local authority's administrative costs, such as salaries, computer costs and giro charges. The subsidy to meet these costs comes either from central government or from funds which local authorities raise themselves through local taxes. In order to understand the highly complex subsidy arrangements, it is important first to be aware that the generic label 'housing benefit' in fact comprises two distinct elements:

---

14 SI 1987/1971.
15 Social Security and Housing Benefits Act 1982.
16 Standing Committee G, Fourteenth Sitting, col 529.
17 Audit Commission, op cit, para 9.
18 These include the Social Security Act 1986; Housing Act 1988; Local Government Finance Act 1988; Local Government Finance Act 1992.

(a) *Rent allowances*

Rent allowances are usually paid directly to tenants of private landlords. Recipients of rent allowance include fair rent tenants[19] and tenants holding under assured tenancies or assured shorthold tenancies,[20] including housing association tenants who are on low incomes.

(b) *Rent rebates*

Rent rebates are credited to council tenants via an entry on their rent account, so that claimants do not actually receive cash payments.

Generally speaking, the rules of entitlement for rent allowances and rent rebates are identical but, in prescribed circumstances, a rent allowance may be paid direct to a landlord rather than to the tenant (see **6.11**). Housing association tenants usually agree that payment should be made direct to the landlord association.[21]

The SSAA gives power to the Secretary of State to pay subsidies to local authorities, calculated as specified in a subsidy order.[22] There is now a sharp demarcation between 'rent allowance subsidy' and 'rent rebate subsidy'.

Housing benefit subsidy

6.5 The subsidy which underpins rent allowances comes from central government as part of its general housing subsidy to local authorities. The rent allowance element of the general subsidy is not earmarked, so enabling central government to influence rent levels.

Housing revenue account subsidy

6.6 All local authorities are obliged to maintain a housing revenue account (HRA),[23] to which authorities' own rental income plus government housing subsidy are credited, and from which housing expenditure is met, including rent rebates for mainstream council tenants. The HRA is 'ring fenced' from other local authority accounts, so that, in effect, rent rebates have to be balanced against rental income, with the consequence that council tenants who pay their full rents subsidise the housing benefit paid to their less well-off neighbours.

It must be emphasised that rent allowance subsidy is not credited to the HRA, and rent allowances paid to private or housing association tenants are not included in HRA expenditure. In addition, housing benefit paid to homeless people[24] placed in bed and breakfast accommodation by the local authority is also

---

19 Rent Act 1977.
20 Housing Act 1988.
21 Audit Commission, op cit, para 31.
22 Section 135(1) and (2); the 1996 Act replaces this provision with new ss 140A and 140B.
23 Local Government and Housing Act 1989, s 79.
24 Part III of the Housing Act 1985, replaced by Part VII of the Housing Act 1996; see Ch 10.

excluded from HRA, as are rent rebates on accommodation leased by the local authority from a private landlord.

Administrative cost subsidies

6.7 All administrative costs, including those relating to council tenants and other recipients of rent rebates, lie outside the HRA. A separate subsidy is provided, as to 50 per cent by a cash limited grant, which is allocated amongst local authorities by reference to a formula geared to type of case, case-load, turnover data and tenure and as to 50 per cent by an increase to the revenue support grant. The central government subsidy for benefit administration covers a lower percentage of the overall costs (approximately 60 per cent) than do the subsidies in respect of benefit payments. This carries the 'perverse incentive' that local authorities may place a higher weighting on administrative savings than on savings in other areas, for example, fraud prevention.[25] The administration formula is also weighted towards rent allowances and against rent rebates, so that the more private tenants there are within a local authority's area, the higher the administration grant. This means, for example, that the Large Scale Voluntary Transfer of council stock to a housing association produces increased subsidy for a local authority.[26]

The distinction between rent allowances and rent rebates

6.8 Two points need to be emphasised:

(i) Ninety five per cent of rent allowances in respect of private sector tenancies (together with allowances in respect of bed and breakfast accommodation and accommodation leased by local authorities from private landlords) are met from the housing benefit subsidy referred to above. This subsidy is paid by the Department of Social Security (DSS).

(ii) The subsidy for rent rebates in respect of tenants of HRA dwellings is paid by the DoE, although the DSS remains responsible for regulating entitlement to rebates. On average the DoE contributes about 96 per cent of the cost of rent rebates, the remaining 4 per cent being met by local authorities themselves.

Relationship between central and local government

6.9 Central government uses the benefit subsidy mechanism in order to encourage good administration of housing benefit.[27] Both the HRA subsidy

---

25 *Remote Control: The National Administration of Housing Benefit*, Audit Commission 1993, para 30.

26 *Our Future Homes*, op cit, p 28.

27 *Remote Control: The National Administration of Housing Benefit*, Audit Commission 1993, para 27.

mechanism and the DSS housing benefit subsidy contain 'incentives' for local authorities. In particular:

(a) the HRA subsidy is reduced if the rents of council tenants receiving rent rebates have been raised relatively to those of other tenants;

(b) since tenancies under the Housing Act 1988 present the possibility of rent inflation, the DSS subsidy is reduced where rent allowance is paid in respect of rents which are considered to be excessive.

Restricting eligible rents

Under the Housing Benefit Regulations 1987, rent allowances may be paid up to the value of the 'eligible' rent, depending on the tenant's means.[28] It has always been the policy that housing benefit should meet *reasonable* rents but, nevertheless, local authorities have power to limit the eligible rent where individual accommodation is excessively large or luxurious in relation to the tenant's needs.[29] In addition, from 1990 onwards, most new private sector lettings had to be referred to the rent officer for a determination of a reasonable market rent. In addition, the rent officer was asked to make a judgment as to the appropriateness of the accommodation for the particular tenant and, in some cases, to determine an eligible rent based on a more suitable hypothetical letting. The rent officer's determination had no direct bearing on the local authority's decision on housing benefit,[30] but it meant that no DSS subsidy was payable on benefit attributable to the proportion of any rent which exceeded the rent officer's valuation.

Notwithstanding these indirect controls on local authority decision-making, the Government came to the conclusion that too many tenants were receiving benefit in respect of rents above the general level of market rents in a given area, with inflationary consequences. As a result, the regulations were further amended from January 1996 so as to give rent officers a more direct and systematic role in determining housing benefit entitlement. In particular, they are now required to set maximum eligible rents for new tenancies by reference to a prescribed formula[31] and the previous safe-guards for certain vulnerable claimants have been removed, leaving only local authorities' general powers to make provision in cases of hardship.[32] Rent officers are also empowered to make pre-tenancy determinations of the maximum eligible rent at the request of prospective tenants, the idea

---

28 SI 1987/1971, reg 8.
29 Ibid, reg 11; in theory, this power extends to council tenants as well as private sector tenants.
30 J Zebedee and M Ward, *SHAC Guide to Housing Benefit and Council Tax Benefit, 1993/94*, para 10.44.
31 SI 1987/1971, reg 11.
32 Ibid, reg 61.

being that, given such information, tenants can then seek to re-negotiate the asking rent.[33]

(c)   Private sector tenancies created before the deregulation of the private rented sector are considered to be unlikely to involve exploitation of housing benefit if rents have been registered by the rent officer,[34] or if fair rents have been determined by a rent assessment committee.[35] Where, however, the rent has not been registered, each local authority has a 'threshold' set by the DSS for the purposes of calculating subsidy. If the rent for housing benefit purposes is above the threshold, subsidy is reduced. Housing benefit paid to homeless people placed in bed and breakfast and other types of temporary accommodation by local authorities is affected by a similar mechanism.

(d)   Where benefit is overpaid penalties are again incurred, but the loss to the local authority is tapered depending on the reason for the overpayment. In order to encourage local authorities to engage in dealing with benefit fraud, overpayments made as a result of claimant fraud still qualify for 95 per cent subsidy, once they are identified. On the other hand overpayments made as a result of a local authority's own error attract no subsidy at all.

The new measures

6.10   Sections 120 to 123 of the 1996 Act make the following detailed changes to the system outlined above:

(1)   Section 120 amends s 5 of the SSAA to extend the Secretary of State's powers to make regulations in respect of methods of paying benefit, in this instance to enable the Secretary of State to *require* rather than simply to *permit* housing benefit to be paid to a third party on the claimant's behalf.

(2)   Section 121 gives effect to Sch 12, which contains substantial amendments to Part VIII of SSAA, concerned with arrangements for housing benefit and subsidies to local authorities.

(3)   Section 122 creates a new statutory basis for rent officers' functions in respect of housing benefit and rent allowance subsidy.

(4)   Section 123 gives effect to Sch 13, which contains consequential amendments necessitated by ss 120 to 122.

Payment of housing benefit to third parties

6.11   As noted in para **6.4**, rent rebates are not paid directly to tenants but are netted off against the rent due to the local authority. This mechanism prevents tenants from diverting resources which are intended to meet housing costs. Rent allowances, however, like other cash benefits, are paid direct to tenants,

---

33 Ibid, reg 12A(1).
34 Section 67 of the Rent Act 1977.
35 *Remote Control: The National Administration of Housing Benefit*, Audit Commission 1993, p 13.

consistently with the general principle that those who have statutory entitlement to benefit must generally be allowed freedom to plan their own financial affairs, rather than being forced by, for example, voucher systems, to allocate their expenditure in certain ways. Departures from this principle must be expressly prescribed. For income support, payments of benefit direct to the claimant's creditors are authorised in some circumstances;[36] the most notable recent addition to the rules here is the new provision that virtually all income support payments in respect of mortgage interest must be paid direct to mortgagees.[37]

As far as housing benefit is concerned, circumstances are prescribed in which a local authority must withhold benefit from a tenant and make payment directly to the landlord instead.[38] Instances are: where the tenant has fallen into arrears with rent; where the local authority decides that it is in the tenant's interest to make direct payments; and where the tenant either requests or consents to direct payments. Section 5 of SSAA is a generic provision which lays down a broad and somewhat open-ended power to prescribe circumstances in which any of the income-related benefits may be paid to a third party in order to discharge an obligation of the beneficiary.[39] Section 120 of the 1996 Act adds a new subs 6 which is specific to housing benefit and which authorises provision 'requiring the making of payments of benefit to another person, on behalf of the beneficiary, in such circumstances as may be prescribed'. Section 20(2) deems this amendment always to have had effect, suggesting that there may have been some doubts as to the legality of the regulations in respect of housing benefit made under s 5(1)(p). Practically speaking, however, this amendment makes no difference to the existing rules on payment of benefit to landlords. There is in fact much evidence of housing benefit fraud attributable to direct payments to landlords in respect of tenants who either do not exist or have moved on. The DSS clearly has power to seek to control this situation through regulations, should it wish to do so.

Schedule 12 to the Housing Act 1996

6.12   Part VIII of SSAA defines rent allowances and rent rebates and sets out the subsidy arrangements referred to earlier in this chapter. The new Sch 12 introduces new ss 140A to 140G, and heavily amends s 134 (arrangements for housing benefit) and s 138 (community charge benefit). Sections 135, 136 and 137 are repealed.

To a large extent, these amendments are cosmetic; the drafting is tightened up, and the terminology is brought up to date to reflect more accurately and clearly the previously explained distinction between the subsidy arrangements for rent rebates and rent allowances.[40]

---

36 Schedule 9, Social Security (Claims and Payments) Regulations 1987, SI 1982/1968.
37 Ibid, Sch 9A.
38 SI 1987/1971, reg 93.
39 Section 5(1)(p).
40 This in fact dates from the implementation in 1990 of the Local Government and Housing Act 1989.

The substantive amendments designed to 'clarify and simplify' the subsidy arrangements are as follows:

(i)   Benefit subsidy and administration subsidy payable to local authorities may be specified as fixed amounts rather than as percentages (s 140B) and there is power to specify that certain expenditure should receive nil subsidy.

(ii)   There are new powers to impose conditions for the payment of subsidy and to recover subsidy paid in breach of any conditions, or subsidy which has been overpaid (s 140C). Recovery may be made by withholding or reducing further subsidy.

(iii)   The Secretary of State is empowered to specify permitted totals for local authorities' discretionary expenditure, and s 134(11) is amended in this respect. The discretion is to pay extra benefit in exceptional circumstances, and in the past has accounted for approximately 0.1 per cent of benefit expenditure.[41] 'Exceptional circumstances' would include losses incurred through crime, high outgoings in respect of fuel, non-payment of wages etc.

Determinations by the rent officer

6.13 Section 122 restates the general power to require rent officers to carry out functions in relation to housing benefit and rent allowance subsidy[42] and s 122(3) makes it clear that benefit may be limited simply by reference to a rent officer's determination. In the past, subsidy limits themselves have not directly limited the amount of housing benefit payable in respect of a particular tenant in that the regulations have not permitted local authorities lawfully to restrict eligible rents by reference only to the subsidy rule, without taking other circumstances into account. Technically, this is still the position, although the imposition since January 1996[43] of a mathematical formula for the calculation of eligible rent together with the restriction on local authorities' powers to make exceptional provision have considerably increased central government control over the amount of housing benefit which is paid. Although, therefore, benefit decisions are still for the local authority and not for the rent officer, in future entitlement or disentitlement will be related directly to the rent officer's determinations.

Section 122(4) further empowers the Secretary of State for Social Security to calculate and, where he considers appropriate, make deductions from rent allowance subsidy by reference to determinations made by rent officers. It further undermines the local authority's own powers of determination in respect of housing benefit.

---

41 SI 1987/1971, reg 61(2).
42 Section 121 of the Housing Act 1988.
43 SI 1987/1971, reg 11.

Section 122(2) contains a new power to require a rent officer to make a pre-tenancy determination at the instigation of a prospective landlord, and on payment of a fee. Regulations may also require a landlord to provide copies of such determinations to the local authority, and may permit the local authority to seek a redetermination when a tenant has been identified, and makes a claim for housing benefit.

Conclusion

6.14 The Parliamentary debates referred to at the beginning of this chapter reflected Members' frustration that a major piece of primary housing legislation did not address public concerns about the operation of the housing benefit system, although recent or pending regulatory changes mean that many tenants living at poverty level will receive significantly less housing benefit than their contractual rent.[44] The demarcation of responsibility between the DoE, the DSS and local authorities has been noted. It does not wholly explain why the Government has not seen fit to tackle in primary legislation the well-documented administrative problems which have blighted the system for so long.

---

44 Standing Committee G, Fourteenth Sitting, col 529.

PART V

CHAPTER 7

INTRODUCTORY TENANCIES

The general scheme

7.1 Local housing authorities and Housing Action Trusts (HATs) will be entitled to set up an introductory tenancy scheme for all their new tenants. The scheme will apply to all new tenancies granted after the authority or HAT commences the scheme. The tenancies will last for a trial period of one year and tenants can only be evicted by court order. This is a mere formality and so there is provision for an internal review of the decision to evict. There are limited succession rights to an introductory tenancy. Such tenants have the same right to be consulted about housing management, as well as to be provided with information about their tenancies, as secure tenants. As the Housing Minister has said, '. . . local authorities will put their own lubrication into the system'; thus, the general legislative scheme offers broad discretion to the authority. Guidance is expected from the DoE on the operation of schemes, which may be less than exhaustive.[1]

Entering the scheme

Electing to commence a scheme

7.2 The introductory tenancy scheme is entirely discretionary. Local authorities and HATs can choose whether to operate it or not.[2] Before operating it, the local authority or HAT must elect to do so, although this election may be revoked at any time.[3] In addition, they will also need to consult their current tenants as this will represent a change in housing management.[4] If the authority or HAT elect to commence a scheme, then every periodic tenancy of a dwelling-house[5] can only be granted as an introductory tenancy.[6] It cannot be a secure tenancy.[7] Periodic

---

1 Standing Committee G, Ninth Sitting, col 337.
2 Section 124(1).
3 Section 124(1) and (5)
4 Housing Act 1985, s 105 (applies both to local authorities and HATs. 1988 Act, s 83(4)).
5 A dwelling-house may be the whole or part of a house and includes any land let together with it (s 139).
6 Section 124(2).
7 Schedule 14, para 5.

tenancies include licences, although not licences granted to a person who originally entered the property as a trespasser.[8]

Exclusions

7.3   There are three exceptions to the rule that every subsequent tenancy is an introductory tenancy:[9]

(i)   where the tenant or one of the tenants was a former secure tenant (in any area) immediately before the tenancy was entered into or adopted;

(ii)   where the tenant or one of the tenants was an assured tenant[10] of any RSL immediately before the tenancy was entered into or adopted;

(iii) where the tenancy was entered into or adopted as a result of a contract entered into before the election was made.

A tenancy is adopted if the local authority or HAT become the landlord either through purchasing the property or surrender to them.[11] These exemptions only cover former local authority and housing association tenants, not private sector tenants.[12]

Length of tenancies

7.4   The general rule is that an introductory tenancy lasts for one year from the date on which the tenancy was entered into or, if later, the date on which the tenant (or one of joint tenants) was first entitled to possession. In the case of tenancies adopted by the authority or HAT, the date of adoption provides the commencement.[13] If the tenant held an introductory tenancy or an assured shorthold from an RSL (ie a housing association or local housing company) immediately preceding the grant or adoption of the new introductory tenancy,[14] then the period during which the person was a tenant is counted. If there was more than one preceding introductory or assured shorthold tenancy from an RSL, provided they were consecutive, they all count towards the trial period.[15]

---

8 Section 126. Presumably, squatters who are subsequently granted licences of, say, a short life property will not be included.

9 Section 124(3) and (4).

10 This does not apply to those formerly holding under an assured shorthold tenancy (s 124(3) (b)).

11 Section 124(4).

12 This is apparently because 'Private sector tenants are not subject to the same housing management regime as social landlords', HL Debs, Vol 574, col 413.

13 Section 125(1)–(2).

14 Where the introductory tenancy is granted to two or more joint tenants, the earliest qualifying tenancy is the commencement point (s 125(4)).

15 Section 125(3). The tenant must have occupied those properties as their only or principal home.

Exiting the scheme

Determining events

7.5 There are several determining events of the introductory tenancy, other than the one-year period ending and the landlord revoking its election:

(i) the tenancy will end if it would not otherwise have been a secure tenancy. This is a reference to the fact that, if the tenant or none of the joint tenants does not occupy the property as their only or principal home, the tenancy will end;[16]

(ii) where the landlord ceases to be a local authority or HAT;

(iii) where the election setting up the introductory tenancy regime is revoked;

(iv) where the succession rights to an introductory tenancy have been exhausted.[17]

Where the introductory nature of the tenancy ends, a tenancy still exists and takes the form of a secure tenancy. An introductory tenancy which has ceased to be such a tenancy cannot, at a later time, again become introductory.[18]

Possession

7.6 The most Draconian determining event, however, is where proceedings are brought for possession of the property and the court makes an order for possession.[19] If the landlord applies to the court for a possession order and the one-year period ends or the tenancy determines as in para **7.5**, the tenancy will retain its introductory nature.[20] If the determining events specified in para **7.5** occur and proceedings have already been commenced, the old or new landlord can continue with the proceedings and the tenancy will again determine on the date specified in the court order.[21] If this is the case, the tenant will not be entitled to exercise the right to buy under the Housing Act 1985, Part V, unless the proceedings are determined in the tenant's favour.[22]

---

16 See s 81 of the Housing Act 1988. For the meaning of 'only or principal home', see *Brown v Brash* [1948] 2 KB 247; *Crawley BC v Sawyer* (1988) 20 HLR 98.

17 Section 125(5). See para **7.11** for succession rights.

18 Section 125(6).

19 Section 127.

20 Section 130(1), (2) and (5). The determining event is then either: (i) the tenant is required to give up possession by virtue of a court order; (ii) the proceedings are discontinued; (iii) any appeal is abandoned; or (iv) no appeal is lodged within the requisite time-limit.

21 Section 130(3).

22 Section 130(4).

Procedure

7.7   The procedure to be followed before the landlord can bring an action for possession is simple. The landlord must serve a notice of procedure on the tenant specifying the following matters:

(i)   the court will be asked to make an order for possession;[23]

(ii)   the reasons why a possession order will be sought;[24]

(iii) the date after which possession proceedings will be brought;[25]

(iv) that the court shall not hear any possession proceedings until after that date;[26]

(v)   the right to request a review of the decision and the time within which such a request must be made;[27]

(vi) the tenant should seek advice from a Citizens Advice Bureau, housing aid or law centre, or a solicitor, if required.[28]

Internal review

7.8   The right to request a review of the decision to seek possession of the property is contained in s 129 of the 1996 Act. The request must be made by the tenant within 14 days of receipt of the notice of proceedings.[29] The landlord must then review its decision before the date specified in the notice as the date after which possession proceedings will be brought.[30] The Secretary of State retains a regulation-making power as to the procedure to be followed on the review.[31] Such regulations are subject to the negative resolution procedure of the House of Commons and will be made by way of Statutory Instrument so that they will have the force of statute.[32] This provision is general but some examples are given on the face of the Act as to the content of the regulations: the decision on review should be conducted by an appropriately senior person not involved in the original decision, and the circumstances in which an oral hearing should take place.[33] Whilst the Government will be issuing 'detailed and firm Guidance' on introductory tenancies (including review procedures), this section is an attempt to respond to criticism about the earlier provision which gave authorities a free

---

23 Section 128(2).

24 Section 128(3). The requirement to give reasons is similar to that in s 184 on the homelessness provisions.

25 Section 128(4) – this cannot be before the date on which the tenant is notified of the result of any internal review.

26 Section 128(5).

27 Section 128(6).

28 Section 128(7).

29 Section 129(1).

30 Section 129(2) and (6) respectively.

31 Section 129(3).

32 Section 142.

33 Section 129(4).

rein.[34] At the time of writing, the Government is consulting on the content of the regulations.

Once the review has been conducted, the landlord is required to inform the tenant of the result of the review. If the review confirms the original decision, the landlord must notify the tenant of the reasons for the decision.[35] It will be these reasons which are challenged in any further proceedings.

Those proceedings should be conducted by way of judicial review in the High Court. There is procedure for determining questions in county court proceedings[36] but, it is submitted, this will not apply to a challenge to the internal review procedures. In judicial review proceedings, the scope of enforceable regulations and the content of Guidance will be critical. There are also certain basic minimum requirements which the internal review must meet to accord with the common law notion of natural justice.[37] Broadly, this involves a duty to be fair to the tenant, particularly as those conducting the review will be in a quasi-judicial position.[38] The duty to be fair differs according to the circumstances of the review body. It can safely be assumed that this type of review body will be required to act impartially, and weigh all aspects of the evidence. However, there is no requirement for the review to be conducted externally or independently of the local authority or HAT.[39] Although the review should be conducted as quickly as possible, this should not prejudice the concept of fairness. Any breach of these rules, other procedural unfairness, illegality, or where the landlord has come to a decision 'so unreasonable that no reasonable person could have reached that decision', will result in a successful application for judicial review of the review body's decision.[40]

An evidential question

7.9 The most difficult question is whether the tenant should be entitled to comment upon any evidence given by witnesses. The usual answer to this is that the tenant is so entitled.[41] However, there are arguments both ways. On the one

---

34 See, for example, HL Debs, Vol 574, cols 417–419.

35 Section 129(5).

36 Section 138, as to which, see below.

37 See, generally, H Wade and C Forsyth, *Administrative Law* 7th edn (Oxford, 1994), chs 13–15.

38 See, for example, *Lloyd v McMahon* [1987] 1 All ER 1118.

39 The reason given for this exclusion was that such decisions need to be taken with the maximum of speed and efficiency, see HL Debs, Vol 573, cols 268–274.

40 The usual rules of judicial review will apply, as to which see *Council of Civil Service Unions v Minister for the Civil Service* [1985] AC 374; *Associated Provincial Picture Houses Ltd v Wednesbury Corporation* [1948] 1 KB 223. Whilst the doctrine of proportionality has not yet been accepted in English law, it is possibly a guide as to the reasonableness of a decision and should be considered, see *R v Barnsley MBC, ex parte Hook* [1976] 1 WLR 1052; *R v Secretary of State for the Home Department, ex parte Brind* [1991] 2 WLR 588.

41 See, in different context, although with similar width to the provision, *R v Director General of Gas Supply, ex parte Smith* (unreported, 31 July 1989).

hand, the tenant must know the arguments as well as the identity of those putting forward the arguments in order to be able to fully answer the case against them. This will be particularly true where there is even a mere possibility that the tenant is being persecuted as a result of race, creed, living habits, or some other difficulty (such as, for example, schizophrenia). On the other hand, in notifying the tenant as to the identity of those putting forward the arguments, this might put the latter in some fear of reprisals. On balance, it may well be that, given the severity of the penalty (ie possession), the former argument should prevail, although regard must be had to individual circumstances.

Role of the court

7.10   The Act does not set out any ground or grounds that the landlord must prove to gain possession. The role of the court in such matters is to check that the procedure specified in the Act – that the tenant has been given the requisite notice – has been correctly completed.[42] Once that has been done, the court's role is simply to provide the appropriate order, the grant of which is mandatory. Eviction could occur even where there was a challenge to the procedures operated on an internal review.

Considerable concern has been expressed that those who 'might not fit into the neighbourhood' will be unnecessarily penalised. For example, if complaints are made to the landlord because the tenant has mental difficulties or is of different racial origin to the community, such complaints could, without further investigation, lead to eviction of the tenant. Guidance will be issued dealing with this point. One member of the Standing Committee had this to say: 'If [Guidance is not strong and clear, the Government] ... will fall foul of the European Convention on Human Rights, because the Bill will deny people the chance to go to court on the substantive issue.'[43] The Government has accepted that a person with mental health problems, who is evicted from an introductory tenancy, 'would probably be intentionally homeless' under Part VII.[44]

Succession and assignment

Rights of succession

7.11   On the tenant's death during the period of the introductory tenancy, the Act provides for limited succession rights to the tenancy:

(i)   if the tenant had a spouse, then that person takes precedence over all other claims to the tenancy, as long as the tenancy is that person's only or principal home at the date of the tenant's death;[45]

---

42 Sections 127(2) and 128(1).
43 Standing Committee G, Tenth Sitting, col 364, per Mr Andrew Bennett.
44 HL Debs, Vol 573, col 354.
45 Sections 131(a) and 133(2).

(ii) if there is no spouse, then the only other category of person who would qualify is a member of the tenant's family who resided with the tenant throughout the 12 months immediately preceding the tenant's death. That person must also have occupied the property as their only or principal home at the date of the tenant's death.[46] A member of the family is defined by the Act as either the tenant's spouse or a person who lives with the tenant as husband or wife,[47] or the tenant's parent, grandparent, child, grandchild, brother, sister, uncle, aunt, nephew or niece;[48]

(iii) where there is more than one member of the family who could succeed to the tenancy, they must agree amongst themselves as to who will take on the tenancy. In default of such agreement, the landlord must select the successor.[49] Such a selection should not be arbitrary but may, for example, depend on who would best be able to meet the obligations of the tenancy;

(iv) where no such person exists and the tenancy is disposed of by will or under the intestacy rules (except as a result of a transfer on divorce or in favour of a child), then the tenancy ceases to be introductory and cannot be a secure tenancy.[50]

There can, however, be only one succession and provisions detail who else is a successor other than those included in the previous paragraph.[51] If the tenancy was taken as a joint tenancy and vested in a person by virtue of the right of survivorship,[52] the new tenant(s) will be the successor(s). If the tenancy has vested in a person on the death of the tenant (eg by way of a will), then the person who inherits the tenancy is the successor.[53]

---

46 Section 131(b).

47 This phrase is well known in social security legislation. Six factors are considered: membership of the same household; duration and stability of the relationship; financial support; sexual relationship; children; and public acknowledgement of the relationship. See A Ogus, E Barendt, and N Wikeley, *The Law of Social Security* 4th edn (Butterworths, 1995), pp 389–393.

48 Section 140; half-blood relationships, relationships by marriage, and stepchildren are included within this list. It should be remembered that a person aged under 18 cannot hold a legal estate in land and cannot therefore succeed to the tenancy, although arrangements could be made to secure this: Law of Property Act 1925, s 1(6).

49 Section 133(2)(b).

50 Section 133(3) and Sch 14, para 5. It will be a tenancy at will. This enables the landlord to gain possession from the personal representatives of the deceased introductory tenant.

51 Section 132.

52 This common law rule is that, where one of two or more joint tenants has died, the tenancy automatically vests in the remaining joint tenants, irrespective of any will. See R Megarry and H Wade, *The Law of Real Property* 5th edn (Stevens & Sons, 1984) pp 417–419.

53 Once a person has become a successor to an introductory tenancy and the tenancy subsequently becomes an assured tenancy, that person will also be considered a successor to that assured tenancy (1996 Act, Sch 14, para 1). A further succession to the assured tenancy cannot occur (Housing Act 1985, s 87).

Assignment

7.12   Introductory tenancies are, as a general rule, incapable of assignment.[54] However, there are two exceptions. First, where there has been assignment on a divorce or in favour of a child[55] and, secondly, where there has been an assignment to a person who would have been entitled to the tenancy on the death of the tenant.[56] Assignees are successors, except where the tenancy has been assigned on divorce[57] and the original tenant was *not* a successor.[58]

If the tenant was a successor to a tenancy and, within six months of that tenancy coming to an end, that person takes on a further introductory tenancy under the same landlord or of the same property, then the tenant is also a successor of the new tenancy.[59] For example, H, an introductory tenant, dies and H's spouse, W, becomes a successor to that property. That tenancy then ends for some reason and W is granted a further introductory tenancy by the same landlord. W will be a successor in the new arrangement and no further succession will be allowed.

Repairs

7.13   Section 96 of the Housing Act 1985 entitles the Secretary of State to make regulations enabling secure tenants to make repairs to their property at the expense of their landlord.[60] Section 135 of the 1996 Act enables the Secretary of State to make regulations applying any regulations made under the 1985 Act to introductory tenancies.[61]

Information and consultation

7.14   Under ss 104 and 105 of the Housing Act 1985, all secure tenants are entitled to certain information from their landlords and to be consulted on certain

---

54 Section 134(1). Any assignee does not become a secure tenant, even if assigned after the introductory period has ended (s 133(3)).

55 By virtue of s 24 of the Matrimonial Causes Act 1973, s 17 of the Matrimonial and Family Proceedings Act 1984, and Sch 1, para 1 to the Children Act 1989.

56 Section 134.

57 In accordance with s 24 of the Matrimonial Causes Act 1973 and s 17(1) of the Matrimonial and Family Proceedings Act 1984.

58 Section 132(1)(c) and (2).

59 Section 132(3).

60 As amended by s 121 of the Leasehold Reform, Housing and Urban Development Act 1993. The current regulations are the Secure Tenants of Local Housing Authorities (Right to Repair) Regulations 1994, SI 1994/133.

61 It is intended that these rights should be the same as for secure tenants (Standing Committee G, Tenth Sitting, col 378).

matters of housing management. These provisions are largely reproduced in ss 136 and 137 of the 1996 Act to the extent that they are relevant for introductory tenancies.

Information[62]

7.15 The landlord must from time to time publish information showing, in simple terms and as it considers appropriate, the effect of the express terms of the introductory tenancy, this Chapter of the Act, and the landlord's statutory repairing obligations under ss 11–16 of the Landlord and Tenant Act 1985. So far as reasonably practicable, this information must be kept up to date.[63] It should be noted that whilst an introductory tenancy can be created orally, this information must be provided to the tenant together with a written statement of the terms of the tenancy.[64] This information is to be provided to the tenant on the grant of the tenancy or as soon as practicable thereafter. Failure to perform either of these duties is clearly challengeable by way of judicial review.[65]

Consultation[66]

7.16 The landlord must consult tenants likely to be substantially affected by relevant matters of housing management. This consultation exercise requires the landlord to inform the tenant of the proposals, enable the tenants to respond within a specified period, and for those views to be taken into consideration when the landlord makes its final decision.[67] Details of the arrangements for consultation are required to be published and available for inspection or be purchased by any member of the public.[68]

'Matters of housing management' are defined as being where, in the opinion of the landlord, they relate to one or more of the following: management of dwelling-houses held by the landlord under introductory or assured tenancies; improvement[69] of those properties; maintenance of those properties; demolition of those properties; or the provision of services or amenities[70] in or to them. However, rents and charges for services and amenities are excluded from this consultation exercise.[71]

---

62 Section 136.
63 Section 136(1).
64 Section 136(2). This written statement does not need to include the obligations implied by the common law, such as the implied covenants of quiet enjoyment and non-derogation from grant.
65 See D Hoath, *Public Sector Housing Law* (Butterworths, 1989), citing *R v Hackney LBC, ex parte Fleming* (1985) *Legal Action*, 170.
66 Section 137.
67 Section 137(2).
68 Section 137(6).
69 See s 97(2) of the 1985 Act for the appropriate definition.
70 This only relates to those services and amenities provided by the landlord in their role as landlord (s 137(5)).
71 Section 137(3).

The conjunction of the word 'relevant' to the phrase 'matters of housing management', whilst new in the 1996 Act, should not alter its implementation from the 1985 Act provision as the 1996 Act provides a definition of 'relevant' in line with the 1985 Act. This is where, in the opinion of the local authority, the improvement, maintenance or demolition is a *new programme* or the landlord has instigated a *change in policy*. Furthermore, either of these must be likely to substantially affect either the introductory tenants as a whole, a distinct social group or class of them.[72] It has been held that consultation does not apply to matters which the landlord has only agreed 'in principle', nor to exploratory inquiries such as a marketing exercising.[73]

Jurisdictional issues and regulations

Jurisdiction of county court

7.17   Any dispute about introductory tenancies is a matter for the county court.[74] This, presumably, does not cover the case where an introductory tenant wishes to challenge the procedure of an internal review, which should be conducted by way of judicial review proceedings. There will be a costs penalty if proceedings are taken in the wrong court.[75]

Consequential order-making powers

7.18   There will be a need, in some cases, to amend the various pieces of legislation that refer to secure tenancies so that they also refer to introductory tenancies. This includes, for example, the Family Law Act 1996. The order-making power makes such provision.[76]

---

72 Section 137(4). Such language is, to say the least, obscure, but remains at the landlord's discretion. In particular, the use of the word 'substantial' suggests that, unless unreasonable in the *Wednesbury* sense, the landlord has the final say.
73 *Short v Tower Hamlets LBC* (1986) 18 HLR 171, 185.
74 Section 138(1).
75 Section 138(3).
76 Section 141(2)–(3).

CHAPTER 8

REPOSSESSION AND ANTI-SOCIAL BEHAVIOUR

I: Nuisance Eviction Grounds

Introduction

8.1 Whereas introductory tenancies are a completely new idea and apply only to new tenants, changes in Chapter II, Part V of the Housing Act 1996 alter traditional eviction procedures, catering for existing tenants throughout their tenancies. The changes were announced later than the introductory tenancies and without the same consultation.[1] They must be considered together with other developments such as the Noise Act 1996 and proposed legislation on molestation injunctions for 'stalking'.[2] The Government has published Guidance covering use of existing court procedures,[3] and the Woolf Report focuses on the court's handling of nuisance cases.[4] There is also important work on more effective use of councils' powers on racial harassment (which has direct relevance to general nuisance issues).[5] Other aspects of the 1996 Act are also relevant, particularly 'special control' provisions on houses in multiple occupation (Part II), the changes to assured shorthold tenancies (Part III), and the temporary housing for homeless people (Part VII).

The eviction changes operate by amending Sch 2 to the 1985 Act for secure tenancies, and Sch 2 to the 1988 Act for assured tenancies (including shortholds) from 'social' landlords.[6] All the new grounds will be subject to the test of whether it is reasonable to evict once the ground is proved, and suspended possession orders will still be available.[7] The Government rejected moves to introduce a new mandatory ground and a new set of factors to be taken into account on

---

1 *Government Gets Tough With Nuisance Neighbours*, DoE Press Notice 499, 18 October 1995.
2 *Stalking: the Solutions* (Home Office Consultation Paper LH1426A July 1996, which also summarises developments since the 1984–1985 miners' strike on torts corresponding to harassment).
3 DoE *Getting the Best out of the Court System in Possession Cases: Guidance for Local Authorities* (DoE, 1996).
4 Lord Woolf, *Access to Justice* (HMSO, 1996).
5 For example, D Forbes, *Action on Racial Harassment: Legal Remedies and Local Authorities* (Legal Action Group and London Housing Unit, 1988); Y Dhooge and J Barelli, *Racial Attacks and Harassment: The Response of Social Landlords* (HMSO, 1996).
6 Sections 144–145 and 148–149 respectively.
7 Section 84(2)(a) of the 1985 Act and s 7(4) of the 1988 Act.

reasonableness, largely on the grounds that the changes recommended by Lord Woolf and the Government's new Guidance on use of the courts should improve the situation.[8]

There is a minor separate change to Ground 5 contained in Sch 2 to the 1985 Act which allows eviction, where reasonable, for using deception to get a secure tenancy.[9] The new law extends this from statements by the tenant to statements by a third party at the tenant's instigation.

Domestic violence

8.2 A completely new discretionary ground for eviction is introduced for secure tenancies and assured tenancies with social landlords.[10] It covers cases where a violent partner has forced the other partner to leave the home and the court is satisfied that the partner who has left is unlikely to return. As originally drafted it also required under-occupation, but this was removed by agreement.[11]

Coverage

8.3 The new ground for eviction is limited by the following factors.

(i)   It applies to a couple who are married or living together as husband and wife. Section 113(1)(a) of the 1985 Act (succession to tenancy), is the closest other reference to cohabitation, and its case-law provides the clearest guidance. It does not cover same sex couples.[12] It will not cover other relationships, for example adult children abusing their parents, as the Government felt the abuser would not normally be a tenant anyway.[13]

(ii) It covers violence or threats of violence towards the leaving partner or a member of that person's family who was residing in the accommodation immediately before the partner left. The example given in debate was of a woman leaving home to protect her mother.[14] However, it would not extend to many carers.

8 Standing Committee G, Eleventh Sitting, col 412 (Mr D Curry) and HL Debs, Vol 573, col 290 (Lord Lucas).

9 Section 146 – mirroring the new ground for possession of Housing Act 1988 tenancies in s 102 of the 1996 Act (see above).

10 Section 145 (creating Ground 2A contained in Sch 2 to the 1985 Act) and s 149 (creating Ground 14A contained in Sch 2 to the 1988 Act).

11 HC Debs, Vol 276, col 1010.

12 *Harrogate Borough Council v Simpson* (1984) 17 HLR 205.

13 Standing Committee G, Tenth Sitting, col 392 (Mr D Curry).

14 Standing Committee G, Tenth Sitting, col 389 (Mr C Betts); HC Debs, Vol 276, col 1010 (Mr G Jones).

(iii) The landlord must prove the violence was the cause of the partner leaving. While local authorities are used to judging such issues on intentional homelessness, the court will need evidence of it as a fact rather than on judicial review principles.

(iv) Either or both of the partners must be a tenant. Where the leaver is the sole tenant and the couple are married, the stayer's occupation preserves security, so the landlord could not use a notice to quit to terminate the tenancy without the required grounds.

(v) The partner leaving must also be unlikely to come back. So for joint tenants it will not cover *McGrady* cases where councils agree for the leaving partner to come back to the same property with new sole tenancy in return for serving a notice to quit, which binds both joint tenants.[15]

Procedure

8.4   The landlord must serve a copy of the staying partner's notice seeking possession on a non-tenant leaving partner,[16] who may lose any ability to re-enter the property and would normally be a vital witness in proving why he or she left. Otherwise, the landlord can show it has taken all reasonable steps to try to serve the notice.[17] Alternatively, it can ask the court to accept it is just and equitable to dispense with service.[18] However, for secure tenancies, this only applies where the original notice also contains the nuisance ground and, in any case, it appears only to be an attempt to cover every conceivable situation. Where the court dispenses with notice on the partner staying, there would be no requirement to serve the leaving partner anyway.

Illegality, nuisance and witnesses

8.5   Changes are made to the discretionary eviction grounds for illegality and nuisance.[19] Many landlords were dissatisfied with the old grounds. Some had, instead, included terms in new tenancy agreements similar to or stronger than the new grounds.[20] They then used these via the eviction grounds for breach of tenancy terms,[21] or on which to found injunctions. They may not need the new

---

15 *Greenwich LBC v McGrady* (1982) 6 HLR 36; *Hammersmith and Fulham LBC v Monk* (1992) 24 HLR 203; and *Harrow LBC v Johnstone* (1996) 28 HLR 83.

16 Section 147 (inserting s 83A(2) of the 1985 Act) and s 150 (inserting s 8A(1) of the 1988 Act).

17 Ibid.

18 New s 83A(4) of the 1985 Act and s 8A(2)(b) of the 1988 Act.

19 Section 144 (inserting Ground 2 contained in Sch 2 to the 1985 Act) and s 148 (inserting Ground 14 contained in Sch 2 to the 1988 Act).

20 Or in existing council tenancies, using ss 102–103 of the Housing Act 1985.

21 Ground 1 contained in Sch 2 to the 1985 Act and Ground 12 contained in Sch 2 to the Housing Act 1988.

grounds but, none the less, may have to change their tenancies again to use the new powers of arrest.

Illegality

8.6 On illegality, the new law retains conviction for using the premises for illegal or immoral purposes, ie criminal activities and prostitution. The problem under the old law was the need to show use of the premises, not just that it happened to take place there. So the new versions add a conviction for any arrestable offence in the locality. This was said to be for problems like drug-dealing on common parts of an estate rather than using a particular tenancy.[22] The range of arrestable offences is very broad[23] and includes any offence carrying five years' or more imprisonment (eg petty shoplifting, abstracting electricity, vandalism amounting to criminal damage, possession of controlled drugs, or even bigamy[24]).[25]

Nuisance

8.7 On nuisance, the more straightforward grounds are Ground 2 contained in Sch 2 to the 1985 Act and the first part of Ground 14 contained in Sch 2 to the 1988 Act.[26]

(i)   The new versions of the grounds add persons 'visiting the dwelling-house' to both perpetrator and victim definitions. The importance of this is not necessarily that there is a big problem of visitors causing nuisance, but that the landlord may not have to prove who in the property was causing the nuisance.

(ii) The new versions also replace the concept of 'neighbourhood' with 'locality', which may still prove equally problematic. The Government said it left 'locality' undefined as 'an all-embracing term that common sense people understand' which would cover for example 'common parts of blocks of flats and other parts of estates' and parts with different landlords.[27]

Witnesses under the nuisance grounds

8.8 Fear of being identified as the complainant is a recognised problem. There are two radical changes to the nuisance grounds which reflect this concern by allowing housing staff and others like private detectives (as used in Sunderland and Salford) to give evidence of their own direct experience.[28] First, the class of

---

22 HC Debs, Vol 276, col 1009 (reason for the Opposition to withdraw amendments specifically covering drugs).

23 See Opposition concerns at HC Debs, Vol 276, Third Reading, col 1009.

24 Section 24(1)(b) of the Police and Criminal Evidence Act 1984.

25 See above on the need to show reasonableness.

26 Sections 144 and 148.

27 Standing Committee G, Tenth Sitting, cols 384–387 (Mr D Curry).

28 Standing Committee G, Twelfth Sitting, col 466: Mr Clappison emphasised the need for the officer's direct knowledge.

persons who may be affected by the nuisance or annoyance is extended to include anyone 'engaging in a lawful activity in the locality'. This will cover staff or others engaging in lawful activities of housing management or specifically surveillance work, so they will be able to give direct evidence of the effects on themselves of the behaviour. Secondly, the behaviour only has to be 'likely to' cause a nuisance. This means that no actual ill effects from the behaviour need be shown. This will allow evidence collected remotely such as by video and will counter defence arguments that officers would not be as easily affected by the behaviour as ordinary members of the public.[29] The problem with use of professional witnesses is, of course, the cost.

It is important to distinguish officers' direct evidence from cases of officers passing on tenants' allegations. Currently, such evidence is normally inadmissible as 'hearsay', and the Act does not change this. The Civil Evidence Act 1995, due to be implemented in autumn 1996, will allow hearsay more easily, but the original witness's name is still likely to have to be given. The new powers of arrest on injunctions may help to reassure witnesses whose names are given.[30]

Early notice and dispensing with notice

8.9 Local authorities have been unhappy about the four-week delay built into the Notice of Seeking Possession, and many began using injunctions to obtain immediate protection. Two changes allow for no notice to be given at the court's discretion or for shorter notice as of right.

(i)   The court can dispense with notice on secure tenancy evictions, whatever the possession ground being used, as long as it appears 'just and equitable'.[31] This levels down the position of council tenants to that already applying to assured tenants. It has effects not limited to nuisance[32] and removes certainty from tenants, because, if there is no notice, they have to wait to see whether the court will allow the case to continue. The Government justified the change on the need for extra speed in cases of a 'very serious nature' involving 'extreme physical violence and abuse'.[33] However, extra speed is given by the special notice procedure in nuisance cases,[34] so, it is submitted, it would rarely be just and equitable to dispense with even that notice. In any event, interim injunctions may be more appropriate to halt immediate violence.

---

29 Cf ss 1–3 of the Public Order Act 1986 – offences without victims as 'no person of reasonable firmness need actually be, or be likely to be, present at the scene'.

30 HL Debs, Vol 573, col 298 (Lord Lucas).

31 Section 147(1) (inserting s 83(1)(b) of the 1985 Act); s 147(3) amends Ground 16 contained in Sch 2 to the 1985 Act in consequence of this.

32 On dispensing with notice in nuisance cases, see *Kelsey Housing Association Ltd v King* (1995) 28 HLR 270.

33 HL Debs, Vol 573, cols 295–296 (Lord Lucas).

34 See (ii) below.

(ii)   The other change, for both assured and secure tenancies, is to allow special notice that proceedings can be started immediately for evictions under the nuisance grounds when used alone or with other grounds.[35] For assured tenancies, this applies to private as well as social landlords and makes the notice practically redundant for the tenant. For secure tenancies, the eviction order must not be sooner than four weeks from the notice.

II: Injunctions and Powers of Arrest

Introduction

8.10   The effectiveness of an injunction is enormously enhanced by a power for the police to stop someone breaching it by arresting them, otherwise the applicant has to apply afterwards to have the person made to attend court. These powers are now available on two types of housing injunctions,[36] but they are at the court's discretion which is modelled on s 47(3) of the Family Law Act 1996.[37] The Government, in oppposing calls for a requirement on the court to grant the powers, quoted concerns that 'vulnerable tenants or members of minority groups could fall foul of an inappropriate use of the new, stronger powers'.[38] However, courts may be swayed by case-law on the previous domestic violence discretionary powers which limited them to the most unusual or persistent cases and to preventing violence rather than molestation.[39]

Common criteria

8.11   The new injunctions and powers of arrest can only be granted where the court is of the opinion that:

(i)   violence has been used or threatened.[40] This requires witnesses of at least an actual threat of violence to someone, unlike the eviction grounds,[41] although the actual threat can have been against the landlord's staff or other professional witnesses.[42] Liaison with police will still be essential and good practice to ensure that, rather than waiting for an injunction with a power of

---

35 Section 147 (inserting s 83(2) of the 1985 Act) and s 151 (amending s 8 of the 1988 Act).
36 Sections 152(6) and 153.
37 Whereas s 47(2) of that Act has a requirement on the court to grant a power of arrest.
38 Standing Committee G, Eleventh Sitting, col 418 (Mr Gwilym Jones).
39 For example, *Lewis v Lewis* [1978] Fam 60.
40 Sections 152(3)(a) and 153(6)(a).
41 See above at para **8.8**.
42 Sections 152(1)(a), (3)(a) and 153(6)(a).

arrest, the police act on the wide range of threats for which they can arrest immediately without warrant;[43]

(ii) there is 'significant risk of harm'.[44] There appears to be a mismatch in that s 158(2)[45] goes to the trouble of defining when 'harm' is 'significant' to a child even though 'significant harm' does not feature in this Chapter of the Act. The version in s 47(3)(b) of the Family Law Act 1996, used as the model, was 'risk of significant harm', which clearly has different implications.

Limitations of the new provisions[46]

8.12 The new provisions have the following limitations:

(a) neither section applies to private landlords;

(b) the sections do not provide for undertakings, so applicants wanting powers of arrest need to say so early to minimise legal aid delays and avoid inappropriate undertakings;

(c) the sections do not change the rule that injunctions are not available against children aged under 18 or people without sufficient mental capacity.[47]

New anti-social behaviour injunction

8.13 There is a new ground for broad injunctions against anti-social behaviour.[48] Powers of arrest can also be granted ancillary to these injunctions.[49] Only the local authority can apply to the court,[50] although the injunction and power of arrest can be granted against anyone,[51] not just their tenants, for the benefit of any victim in the 'locality' of authority-tenanted premises.[52] Injunctions could therefore be granted for the benefit of private tenants or owners in that locality, catering for diversity of tenure on estates.

These injunctions do not rely on any crime, tort or breach of contract.[53] The behaviour which the injunction prohibits is very similar to the nuisance and illegal

---

43 For example ss 2–5 of the Public Order Act 1986 and breach of the peace.

44 Sections 152(3)(b) and 153(6)(b).

45 Imported from s 31(10) of the Children Act 1989.

46 The Government said these changes were 'first fruits' on which they invited anyone to offer further solutions later: HL Debs, Vol 573, col 300 (Lord Lucas), and HL Debs, Vol 574, cols 426–428.

47 *Wookey v Wookey* [1991] 2 FLR 319.

48 See s 152 generally and subss (1) and (4) for the scope of the injunction.

49 Section 152(6). These can also be granted ex parte, see s 154.

50 Section 152(1).

51 There had been problems over the use of s 222 of the Local Government Act 1972 for this in Coventry which were extensively referred to in debate: Standing Committee G, Eleventh Sitting, col 432 (Mr N Raynsford).

52 Section 152(1)(a) and (2).

53 This avoids one of the problems when using s 222 of the Local Government Act 1972.

user eviction grounds.[54] In addition, people can also be barred from entering local authority residential premises or being found in the locality.[55] This was, presumably, meant to cover burglary as in some previous local authority injunction cases, but there is nothing on the face of the Act[56] to say that it cannot cover a council tenant's own home, or even an owner-occupier on a local authority estate.[57] It would then be like an interim possession order.[58]

Local authorities will still be able to use s 222 of the Local Government Act 1972 where the problem is not on a local authority estate, although with no powers of arrest and with the other limitations which caused problems before. This may be important in racial harassment cases where discrimination by landlords has forced people to buy cheap, poor-quality housing.

Power of arrest for breach of tenancy agreement

8.14   The power of arrest can also be attached to injunctions against breaches of tenancy agreement clauses involving specified behaviour, modelled on the eviction grounds for nuisance, illegal or immoral purposes.[59] Some landlords will have to introduce nuisance clauses to enable them to use injunctions. Even those who have already done so may need to amend them to match this power closely enough to unlock its full potential.

This power is only available for social landlords acting in that capacity against their tenants,[60] although it also covers tenants allowing certain behaviour by visitors or other residents.[61] The power must be needed immediately and can only be granted when the injunction is given, not later.[62]

Power of arrest on an ex parte application

8.15   The court must consider all the circumstances in deciding whether to add either power of arrest to an ex parte injunction.[63] Specifically, it must consider whether the applicant would be deterred or prevented from asking for the power

---

54 Section 152(1)(a) and (b): see above for discussion.

55 Section 152(1)(c).

56 There is no clear statement in the debate to use under *Pepper (Inspector of Taxes) v Hart and Related Appeals* [1993] 1 All ER 42.

57 It is likely that the court's discretion could be used by the defence, on lines similar to the developing administrative law doctrine of proportionality.

58 Cf alleged squatters, s 76 of the Criminal Justice and Public Order Act 1994.

59 Section 153(5).

60 Local authority, HAT, RSL or charitable housing trust (s 153(2)).

61 Section 153(5)(c).

62 Contrast s 153(6)(b) with s 152(3) and (6).

63 Section 154(1).

of arrest if they had to wait to ask for it (normally until the on notice hearing).[64] This would most usefully cover cases where threats to witnesses may make them drop their evidence if the power of arrest is not there from the start. It must also consider whether: (i) the person is aware of the proceedings but is evading service, and (ii) the applicant or person to be protected would be seriously prejudiced in waiting for substituted service.[65]

Arrest, remand, medical reports

8.16 There is extensive detail in ss 155–157 of and Sch 15 to the Act on the procedure for arrest, remand and medical reports. It is almost entirely modelled on the equivalent provisions for domestic violence, now contained in ss 47–49 of and Sch 5 to the Family Law Act 1996. That Act, in turn, modelled its remand provisions on magistrates' powers in civil cases under ss 128–129 of the Magistrates' Courts Act 1980. So, although the concept is new to housing law, it has a long pedigree elsewhere.[66]

Broadly, the police can arrest someone without a warrant on the reasonable suspicion of breaching the injunction, and must then bring them before the court within 24 hours.[67] The court can then either deal with the case or, if an adjournment is needed, it can remand on bail or in custody using the same powers as those now available in family cases. This includes remand for medical reports or reports on the person's mental condition.[68] The court can impose requirements on bail when granted or later, to stop the person interfering with witnesses or otherwise obstructing the course of justice.[69] Similar provisions elsewhere are used for orders not to communicate with witnesses or go on to estates, to ensure victims' evidence can be given safely. Time periods, variations, extensions and discharge are governed by s 157, including specific provision for the common practice on domestic violence of granting the power for a shorter period than the injunction.

The novel aspect is the duty on the police to inform the applicant landlord or the council that the person has been arrested.[70] This will give more chance for the applicant's witnesses to be ready at the hearing following the arrest, to cut out one of the common causes of adjournments, delays and poor evidence. Further, if the court could have given a power of arrest but did not, or limited it to parts of the injunction, the position is still not as weak as an ordinary injunction, as on

---

64 Section 154(1)(a).

65 Section 154(1)(b).

66 See for example R Bird, *Domestic Violence – The New Law* (Jordans, 1996).

67 Section 155.

68 Section 156 (with the same powers as the Crown Court under s 35 of the Mental Health Act 1983).

69 Section 155(7).

70 Section 155(1).

application on oath after a breach the court can give a warrant to arrest the person to be brought before the court.[71]

---

71 Section 155(3)–(5) (modelled on magistrates' courts' powers on domestic violence).

PART VI

CHAPTER 9

ALLOCATION OF HOUSING ACCOMMODATION

Introduction

9.1   Parts VI and VII of the Housing Act 1996 create an entirely new scheme of accessing accommodation through local housing authorities. They were initially mooted by the Government in a White Paper in 1994,[1] the Housing White Paper in 1995,[2] and a further Consultation Paper in January 1996.[3] The ideology of Part VI is that housing should go to those with the greatest long-term need from a single housing register. Homelessness, whilst being a symptom of such long-term housing need, is not a cause of it. The provisions relating to homelessness are in Part VII; Part VI concerns allocation.

The new allocation scheme has been devised for a number of reasons.[4] First, it is thought that the former scheme, established under the 1985 Act (although largely derived from principles devised in 1935), was outdated because it only catered for the physical dimensions of property, and not the socio-economic characteristics of potential tenants. Secondly, it was widely perceived as unfair that homeless people were able to 'jump the housing queue'. Thirdly, although not explicit, the 1985 scheme and its forebears were so loosely drafted that local authorities could effectively allocate accommodation however they wished. Although common practice, there was no provision even that expressly required local authorities to have housing registers.[5]

The Government's approach and ideological position are highly controversial. They sprang, initially, from a speech to the Conservative Party Conference by Sir George Young, the former Housing Minister, amid the rhetoric of the *Back to Basics* campaign of 1993. The current Housing Minister has expressly distanced himself from this rhetoric. Nonetheless, there continue to be comments and statements of principle which appear to favour married couples over the unmarried and single parent families. Certain statements have also been made

---

1 *Access to Local Authority and Housing Association Tenancies* (HMSO, 1994).

2 *Our Future Homes* (HMSO, 1995), Ch 6.

3 *Allocation of Housing Accommodation by Local Authorities: Consultation Paper Linked to the Housing Bill* (DoE, 1996).

4 As detailed in the above documents. See also D Cowan and J Fionda, 'Back to Basics: The Government's Homelessness Proposals' (1994) *Modern Law Review*, 610.

5 Government-sponsored research covered all three points: P Prescott-Clarke, S Clemens, A Park, *Routes into Local Authority Housing* (HMSO, 1994).

that homeless families with enough or 'nearly enough' priority on the housing register will be entitled to be allocated accommodation in this way.

General principles of the new housing register

9.2 The scheme of Part VI is that, generally, the allocation of local authority housing can only be through a housing register, which will effectively be a register of housing need in that area. Certain people are or will not be entitled to appear on the register, such as certain asylum seekers and those not entitled to housing benefit. There are also exceptions for those currently holding certain tenancies granted by local authorities and RSLs. When allocating accommodation from the housing register, the local authority must give reasonable preference to certain people. These groups reflect not only the physical condition of the property but also certain social, economic and other welfare characteristics. The Secretary of State retains powers to add to, subtract from, or fundamentally alter these priorities. RSLs – covered in Part I of the Act – are under certain duties to co-operate with the local authority.

Bearing in mind that it represents such a fundamental reorganisation of policy and legislative scheme, Part VI is quite short.[6] However, the Government retains enormous powers of regulation and will provide Guidance.

The housing register

9.3 Local housing authorities come under a duty to set up and maintain a housing register, although it is entirely within the authority's discretion how such a register is to be kept.[7] The Act exhorts local authorities, without providing any duty to do so, to keep the register alongside other purposes (such as a register of housing need in the area, which might reflect the need of those not entitled to be on the housing register).[8] Alternatively, joint housing registers with other landlords can be established under this subsection. Local authorities, should they so wish, can have a housing register which entitles access not only to its own properties but also to those managed by an RSL or even private sector landlords. If local authorities adopt either course, they must have a way of distinguishing their housing register from other lists.[9] For example, if an authority has a common housing register with a housing association and prospective tenants can be on either or both lists, then the authority must be able to distinguish which

---

6 Additionally, Sch 16, paras 2–9, tighten the language of Sch 1 to the 1985 Act.
7 Section 162(1) and (2).
8 Section 162(3).
9 Ibid.

people are on which list. This can be done through a fairly simple computer program.[10] Joint housing registers are already fairly common.

Housing registers can be in any form whatsoever. Most registers will be computerised, because this is the most convenient medium, particularly in those authorities with larger housing registers. Such registers can also be networked between authorities and those with whom they are shared and/or between a central register and decentralised offices. Nevertheless, in contrast to the practice of many authorities, the Act entitles the authority to have only one register.[11]

This will be particularly convenient where the authority has voluntarily transferred its own housing stock, or a substantial proportion of it, to housing associations or where the authority has tendered its housing management to another body. The obligation to set up and maintain the register rests with the authority and not with any other organisation. Nonetheless, other organisations are not disentitled from managing the register and, as long as the authority has overall control, the day-to-day management of the register could be, it is submitted, contracted out.[12] Certainly, the Government has favoured such an interpretation.

Information on the register and access to it

Information

9.4   The Secretary of State retains the power to prescribe by regulation the relevant information that authorities must keep on the register.[13] Other than what is prescribed, the authority can keep whatever other information it wishes on the register.[14] The regulations will enable authorities to keep information about the applicant and other members of that household because they refer to 'other relevant matters'.[15] The detail that might be expected relates to marital status; children; whether the person may be unwell and require additional help. In response to questioning, the Housing Minister in the House of Lords also accepted that some property crimes might also be relevant.[16] Informed speculation suggests that the information may also reflect any involvement with social services, possibly any offence of paedophilia, and also the ethnic origin of prospective tenants.

---

10 Currently, 77 per cent of housing registers are computerised: Prescott-Clarke et al (above) para 3.4.

11 Section 162(1) uses the word 'register' in the singular.

12 In the similar context of a homelessness service, see, for confirmation of this view, *R v Hertsmere DC, ex parte Woolgar* (1995) 27 HLR 703; cf *R v West Dorset DC, ex parte Gerrard* (1994) 26 HLR 150.

13 Section 162(4).

14 Section 162(5).

15 Section 162(4).

16 HL Debs, Vol 574, col 517.

Access

9.5   The person who appears on the authority's housing register is entitled to see and receive free of charge their entry on the register, as well as such general information enabling an assessment to be made of the likely period before an offer of accommodation will be made.[17] The latter duty is, in fact, hedged around: it is not a duty to provide *accurate* information (although this might be implied by a general common law duty); nor to provide the possible period (as the duty is only to provide information enabling an assessment to be made).

Much more difficult questions surround the confidentiality of the information on the register. The Act prescribes that information kept on the register 'shall not be divulged to any other member of the public'.[18] In both Houses of Parliament, Opposition Members were assured that a person acting as an agent for the person appearing on the register would be entitled to see that entry, although this is not entirely clear from this subsection. There should, no doubt, be safeguards from abuse.[19] Commercial companies are clearly excluded from accessing this information. However, official bodies within the local authority and outside it may well be able to access this information in their official capacity.[20] This was seen as necessary to enable a social services authority to access the information in drawing up a community care plan for that individual (or their family) and should, more generally, aid co-operation between authorities. Whether or not the police, for example, would be entitled to access the information is open to some doubt. However, it seems that, as long as they were acting in their official capacity, this would be possible.

Who may appear on the housing register?

9.6   The housing register is open to all who apply to appear on it, provided that it appears to the authority that the individual is a qualifying person.[21] An application would seem to be required, although the form and content of such an application could, no doubt, be done or created orally. If there is no application, the authority has discretion to put the person on the register.[22] In any case, the authority must notify a person that they are on the register.[23] Such a notification is not required in writing. This power will be particularly important to those

---

17 Section 166(1). Section 106 of the 1985 Act does not apply to this duty (1996 Act, Sch 16, para 1).
18 Section 166(3).
19 These will reflect the Data Protection Act 1984 and the Access to Personal Files (Housing) Regulations 1989, SI 1989/503.
20 Guidance to be issued will consider how to validate when a person is acting in their official capacity (HL Debs, Vol 573, col 366).
21 Section 163(1).
22 Section 163(2).
23 Section 163(3).

applying as homeless under Part VII. As the housing register is the only route into permanent accommodation, a homeless applicant should routinely also be placed on the housing register. That would be good practice.

Who is a qualifying person?

9.7

(i)   Qualifying persons only are entitled to allocations under Part VI.

(ii)   The Act specifies that any person subject to immigration control under the Asylum and Immigration Act 1996 is not a qualifying person, unless the Secretary of State specifies otherwise in regulations.[24] This subsection had to be changed at a late stage in the Bill's Parliamentary passage as a result of a ruling that certain housing benefit regulations were ultra vires. The disabling arm of these regulations more generally will cover those groups in the Asylum and Immigration Act 1996 who are not entitled to public housing, certain EU nationals and those failing a habitual residence test (and, thus, not entitled to housing benefit). These groups are discussed in Part VII. The only difference between the disentitlement under Part VII and Part VI is that under Part VI even asylum seekers, who are entitled to benefits, will not be entitled to appear on the register as qualifying persons. This is because, at that point, the Government believe that 'we do not know whether they will have a long-term need'.[25] However, where a person's claim to asylum or indefinite leave to remain is accepted, then that person becomes a qualifying person (subject to (iii) below).[26] Guidance expected on such regulations will closely mirror that already available under the homelessness legislation, which was drawn up in consultation with the Commission for Racial Equality.[27]

(iii) The Secretary of State has taken other powers to prescribe other persons who do or do not qualify to appear on the register.[28] On a positive note, the Government has accepted that every person aged over 18, who is accepted for the full housing duty under Part VII (that is, for a two-year minimum period) will be entitled to appear on the register of the authority which accepts that responsibility. 'That would discourage authorities from "exporting" families [to another authority] towards whom they owed a homelessness duty.'[29] The Government also announced that they were considering extending the right to all persons aged over 18 who satisfy

---

24 Section 161(2).

25 HL Debs, Vol 573, col 338.

26 See *Allocation of Housing Accommodation by Local Authorities* (DoE, 1996), paras 12–13 for discussion; Standing Committee G, Sixteenth Sitting, cols 621–622.

27 See DoE *Homelessness Code of Practice for Local Authorities*, amended 3rd edn (HMSO, 1995).

28 Section 161(3).

29 HL Debs, Vol 573, col 333. It appears that the Housing Minister's undertaking to consider whether any person who has a local connection under Part VII and young single people should appear on the list have been answered in the negative and such matters will be left to the local authority (Standing Committee G, Sixteenth Sitting, col 623).

certain minimum tests relating to residence and previous behaviour as a tenant.[30]

(iv) Local authorities retain a discretion outside that exercised by the Secretary of State to decide what classes of persons are or are not qualifying persons. The Government has made it clear that any local authority abusing this power to limit the people who may appear on the register will be subject to adverse provisions in subsequent regulations.[31] Before making any decisions on this, it would be good practice if the authority were to consult its partners (if any) in the allocation scheme and other relevant, affected bodies such as the social services department. Such matters will be covered in Guidance. Current usual conditions relate to residence in the area for a specified period,[32] some age requirements, favouring married couples over single couples. All of these will, no doubt, continue to be valid preconditions, reflecting the authorities' 'wish for a certain amount of protection'.[33]

Some authorities refuse to enter on the register those persons who have been in arrears of rent for certain periods of time or have caused nuisance or harassment in their area. Whilst such persons may be found intentionally homeless and this may affect their priority on any allocation scheme,[34] that person's entitlement to appear on the register is a different question. It is certainly clear that local authorities are not entitled to have any rigid policy on the matter.[35] Recently, it has been held that such policies are lawful, as long as they provide for a right of appeal. This had to be balanced with the duty to give reasonable preference to certain applicants.[36] Another option, which does not have such Draconian effects, is to take this into consideration when attaching priority to individual cases.

(v) If a person is not disqualified from appearing on the register, then that person is a qualified person. It can readily be appreciated from the above that not every person will be entitled to appear on the register.

Amending and/or removing a register entry

9.8   The authority has a power to amend the register in such circumstances as they think fit, although they must notify the applicant if they do so.[37] In similar

---

30 Ibid.

31 HL Debs, Vol 573, col 345. In addition, the Government has said that local authorities will not be able to favour those born in their own area (HL Debs, Vol 574, col 45).

32 Bearing in mind the likely content of regulations, it would be as well for local authorities to ensure that their residence requirements mirror the local connection provisions.

33 This is particularly so in rural communities (HL Debs, Vol 573, col 346).

34 See, for example, *R v Canterbury CC, ex parte Gillespie* (1986) 19 HLR 7; *R v Tower Hamlets LBC, ex parte Khalique* (1994) 26 HLR 517.

35 *British Oxygen Company Ltd v Board of Trade* [1971] AC 610.

36 *R v Wolverhampton MBC, ex parte Waters* (1996) *The Times*, 11 June. This decision is not without its difficulties and, it is submitted, is vulnerable to challenge in higher tribunals.

37 Section 163(4).

circumstances, the authority may remove a person's name from the register.[38] The Act prescribes two cases where the authority must remove a person's details from the register: on a request from the person or if the person was never, or has ceased to be, a qualifying person.[39] Amendment and removal can take place on the unilateral say-so of the authority. Before removing a person's name from the register, the authority must comply with regulations from the Secretary of State.

Challenging decisions

Notification

9.9   Where an applicant's name is not entered on the register or their name is removed from the register (unless requested), the authority is required to notify the applicant of its decision to so remove it.[40] This notice must also inform the applicant of their right to a review as well as the fact that the review must be requested within 21 days (unless the authority allows for a longer period).[41] This notice must be in writing and, if not received by the person, it is treated as having been received if the authority keep a copy at its offices for a reasonable period.[42]

Internal review

9.10   There can be only one review of the decision,[43] after which the applicant will have to challenge the decision on review through judicial review proceedings. The Secretary of State is given a power to make regulations concerning the procedure of the internal review.[44] In particular, such regulations might concern the appropriate seniority of the person who is to conduct the review, and the appropriateness of an oral hearing;[45] the regulations may also provide a time within which the review must be completed.[46] Decisions must be notified to the applicant in writing.[47] Reasons must be given where the decision is unfavourable to the applicant.[48] This framework is identical to that which is required under the introductory tenancy regime and the same considerations will apply.

---

38 Section 163(6).
39 Section 163(5), although there will be requirements in regulations, see HL Debs, Vol 573, col 362.
40 Section 164(1).
41 Section 164(2)–(3).
42 Section 164(6).
43 Section 164(4).
44 Section 165(1).
45 Section 165(2).
46 Section 166(5).
47 Section 166(6). The letter is taken as being received by the applicant if the authority keeps it at its offices for a reasonable period.
48 Section 165(4).

The allocations scheme

Allocations

9.11	Local authorities are only permitted to allocate accommodation to qualified persons who appear on the register.[49] Unqualified persons are not entitled to take accommodation 'jointly' with a qualified person.[50] However, accommodation of larger proportion could be offered to the qualifying person on the basis that there will be more than that person occupying the property.

An authority allocates accommodation whenever it selects a person to be a secure or introductory tenant;[51] nominates a person to be such a tenant of accommodation held by another (such as an HAT); or nominates a person to be an assured tenant of an RSL.[52]

Schemes and procedures

9.12	All authorities are required to have a scheme and a procedure for determining allocations to accommodation. Procedure includes not only all the aspects of the allocation process but also the name or description of responsible decision-makers.[53] This wider definition of procedure was added by the Government so that it could specify in regulations that Welsh Councillors' involvement in the allocation process could be regulated.[54] No allocation can be made except in accordance with this scheme.[55]

The regulation-making power also empowers the Secretary of State to prescribe how the allocation scheme should be framed.[56] Other than those regulations, the authority is free to decide its own scheme's principles.[57] This will entitle authorities to operate points-based schemes, where individuals are granted a set number of points which determines where they will appear on the register. At

---

49 Section 161(1).

50 Section 161(4) and (5). It is assumed that 'jointly' means a joint tenancy, although at a stretch it may also include a tenancy in common in equity. The wording of subs 5 is obscure but it is assumed that it refers to those people who, say, meet the Government's qualifications but do not meet those of the local authority but their cohabitee does.

51 This includes the situation where the person is already occupying the property on an insecure basis and subsequently the authority offers a secure tenancy of that property (s 159(3)). This would cover, for example, unauthorised occupation of property, and the authority subsequently grants a secure tenancy of that property to the unauthorised occupant. Until that subsequent grant, no allocation is made.

52 Section 159(2). This applies equally to enforceable and unenforceable arrangements between these different landlords and also to single or multiple unit schemes (s 159(4)).

53 Section 167(1).

54 Standing Committee G, Seventeenth Sitting, col 648; HL Debs, Vol 573, col 394. This is to avoid such Councillors being involved in allocations in their own wards. Consideration is currently being given to including English authorities in these regulations.

55 Section 167(8).

56 Section 167(5).

57 Section 167(6).

present, 80 per cent of authorities have such schemes. Other authorities have, for example, a date-based scheme, on which priorities are determined on the basis of the application date.[58] Although the requirement is that there should be only one register, there seems to be no prescription as to whether there can be distinctive lists within an overall structure. So, for example, an authority might keep lists reflecting those categories to which priority is given as well as a more general list reflecting all those people on the register. However, tenant transfers and other modes of transfer are excluded from the operation of the scheme altogether (see below).

Reasonable preference

9.13 Section 167(2) sets out the categories of persons entitled to reasonable preference on any housing register. The phrase reasonable preference is taken directly from the Housing Act 1985, s 22,[59] and the case-law amplifying the phrase (such that it is) will therefore continue to apply.

The earliest cases suggest that allocations are entirely within the gift of local authorities and the courts should not intervene.[60] Whilst the principles of judicial review and the legislative scheme have moved on since then, the courts often remain unwilling to intervene because of concerns about the prolific use of judicial review.[61] Nevertheless, the following principles can be divined from the cases:

(i) 'reasonable' connotes some type of preferred treatment. 'To inflate the unpreferred to a highly preferred status is entirely outwith the statutory function. To deflate the preferred might be "reasonable", so long as there is some degree of preferential treatment';[62]

(ii) allocation schemes must take into account the overriding principles of public law which demand that authorities only consider the relevant factors.[63] Policies cannot be operated too rigidly so that exceptions can be admitted.[64] Policies must be operated fairly within the scheme;[65]

---

58 See Prescott-Clarke et al, *Routes into Local Authority Housing* (HMSO, 1994), para 3.7.4. Note that the Audit Commission have strongly suggested that date-based schemes are inefficient: *Developing Local Authority Housing Strategies* (HMSO, 1992).

59 It was derived from the Housing Act 1935, s 51.

60 *Shelley v London County Council* [1949] AC 56, 66.

61 See, for example, *R v Newham LBC, ex parte Watkins* (1994) 26 HLR 434, 450–1; *R v Brent LBC, ex parte Enekeme* (unreported) (1996); *R v Lambeth LBC, ex parte Njomo* (unreported, 22 March 1996), QBD.

62 *R v Newham LBC, ex parte Watkins* (1994) 26 HLR 434, 450.

63 *R v Tower Hamlets LBC, ex parte Spencer* (unreported, 5 February 1996), QBD (further medical assessment required but decision made before completed; allocation invalid).

64 See, for example, *R v Bristol CC, ex parte Johns* (1992) 25 HLR 249.

65 *R v Port Talbot BC, ex parte Jones* (1988) 20 HLR 265 (allocation to Councillor in order to better fight an election campaign).

(iii)   within each category of persons to whom the authority must give reasonable preference, authorities are entitled to give greater priority to one group over another;[66]

(iv)   authorities are entitled to refuse to allocate reasonable preference to those who have rent arrears from previous properties.[67] However, such policies must not be overly rigid in application; that is, they must admit of exceptions.[68] Authorities should be aware that, in trying to be exhaustive, they do not miss out any exceptions which should be considered. For example, where rent arrears are legitimate because of poor housing benefit administration or where there is a possibility of a set-off due to disrepair. Such cases require to be individually evaluated outside many policies;[69]

(v)   where there are other methods of collecting a debt (seemingly other than rent arrears) or otherwise penalising the person, it may be unreasonable to further penalise that person through the housing register;[70]

(vi)   groups of people such as owner-occupiers and those who have previously bought local authority housing are as entitled to be on a housing register as anybody else;[71]

(vii)   schemes must be run on the same principles throughout all the authority's offices, however decentralised. They must also be run in accordance with their obligations under the Race Relations Act 1971;[72]

(viii)   it may well be that the allocation scheme can be separated from the target setting for allocation. So, for example, securing priority through one category to which reasonable preference is guaranteed by the legislation does not guarantee an allocation. This may be because the authority quite reasonably decides to allocate no accommodation at all to this category. There is no conclusive answer to this question yet.[73]

---

66 *R v Brent LBC, ex parte Enekeme* (1996) *The Times*, 11 April (greater priority given to those decanted from a large estate than to others in the same preference group).

67 *R v Lambeth LBC, ex parte Njomo* (unreported, 22 March 1996), QBD.

68 See, for example, *R v Canterbury CC, ex parte Gillespie* (1986) 19 HLR 7; *R v Islington LBC, ex parte Aldabbagh* (1995) 27 HLR 271.

69 *R v Lambeth LBC, ex parte Njomo* (above).

70 *R v Forest Heath DC, ex parte West and Lucas* (1991) 24 HLR 85 (non-payment of community charge, which had other statutory means of collection, eg distress); *R v Tower Hamlets LBC, ex parte Khalique* (1994) 26 HLR 517 (rent arrears could be taken into account when considering applicant under homelessness legislation by finding the applicant intentionally homeless) as explained in *R v Islington LBC, ex parte Aldabbagh* (1995) 27 HLR 271 and *R v Lambeth LBC, ex parte Njomo* (unreported, 22 March 1996), QBD. The latter case may still apply, even though the homeless have lost their reasonable preference through the housing register directly because they may be considered on the housing register indirectly (see below).

71 *R v Sutton LBC, ex parte Alger* (unreported, 1992) Legal Action June 13; Commission for Local Administration (colloquially known as the Local Ombudsman) Investigation 91/C/0403, ibid; *R v Bristol CC, ex parte Johns* (1992) 25 HLR 249.

72 *R v Tower Hamlets LBC, ex parte Mohib Ali* (1993) 25 HLR 218.

73 See *R v Brent LBC, ex parte Enekeme* (1996) *The Times*, 11 April.

Categories to which reasonable preference is to be accorded

9.14 In the run-up to the Act, concern had been expressed about certain comments in the White Paper and the Consultation Paper on allocations. For example, 'Allocation schemes should reflect the underlying values of our society. They should balance specific housing needs against the need to support married couples who take a responsible approach to family life, so that tomorrow's generation grows up in a stable environment.'[74] Such comments, on one view, have probably not found themselves into the substance of the Act.[75]

The list of groups that the Act does define corresponds to the Government's idea of housing need.[76] The notion of 'need' being relatively flexible, as well as ideologically formulated, who is favoured is highly contentious.[77] Broadly, they divide into two general categories: types and tenure of accommodation; social and economic need. Crucially to the scheme, the categories are cumulative so that applicants can fit into more than one category and thereby gain greater priority.

Those statutorily homeless under Part VII

9.15 Under the 1985 Act, homeless persons, to whom the local authority owed certain duties, were entitled to reasonable preference on the housing register. The central precept of the 1996 Act is that those people will lose that preference as a class. However, those people will be able to fit into any of the other categories listed in the 1996 Act. Whilst this represents a major substantive change in the primary legislation, it may well be that it represents little change in practice. For example, local authorities will be free, if they wish, to give greater priority to homeless persons in any of the categories than to others in that same category.[78]

Furthermore, as the Government have pointed out, there is sufficient discretion within the scheme so that an authority may treat some cases as exceptional and so place particular persons at the top of the list, depending on the circumstances of the case. This is the infamous 'nearly enough priority' problem. In the Second Reading Debate in the House of Commons, the Secretary of State suggested that homeless people with 'priority or nearly enough priority' could be allocated accommodation through the housing register ahead of others and so 'jump the

---

74 *Our Future Homes* (HMSO, 1995), p 36.

75 However, within any of the preference groups, it is open to the authority to give greater preference to married couples.

76 The Government conceded that they would specify the categories in primary legislation and introduced them at Report Stage in the House of Commons (HC Debs, Vol 276, col 1013).

77 Nevertheless, they closely correspond to a Labour amendment (except that Labour would retain the priority to homeless families) (Standing Committee G, Seventeenth Sitting, cols 648–649).

78 *R v Brent LBC, ex parte Enekeme* (unreported) (1996).

queue'.[79] For a long time, the crucial issue of how that could be done went unanswered. However, in the House of Lords Committee, the Minister said that authorities had sufficient discretion to do so 'sympathetically on an exceptional basis'.[80] As only a 'reasonable preference' is required to be given to the categories and authorities are given considerable discretion in relation to the operation of the scheme, this does seem possible.

It remains to be seen how much the practice of allocation will change in this respect.

Categories to which reasonable preference is to be given

9.16   The following categories of people are to be given reasonable preference.

(i) *People occupying insanitary or overcrowded housing or otherwise living in unsatisfactory housing conditions.*[81] This is a conjunction of two categories which existed under the 1985 Act. 'Overcrowding' is statutorily defined in ss 324–326 of the 1985 Act. Essentially, a property is overcrowded when the number of rooms or the space of the property are insufficient to meet the needs of the number of persons sleeping in the property. For example, if a male and a female, who are not living together as husband and wife, occupy the same bedroom, this will fall within the definition of overcrowding.[82] As regards the other categories, a high degree of doubt exists as to their meaning. They are:

> 'elastic linguistically, such that any precise definition is not feasible ... No doubt an experienced housing officer can judge whether such conditions pertain, given a high degree of flexibility in applying general standards of sanitation, ... and satisfactory living standards ... Thus any interpretation of the provisions of section 22 [of the 1985 Act] calls for an ample margin of variation from some norm of housing in a civilised society and an appreciation of the local conditions. They import also factors which are derivative of social services rather than strictly housing policies.'[83]

The Government has stated that this category should cover those 'disabled person[s] who occupied inaccessible or unsuitable housing'. Guidance will reflect this and draw authorities' attention to their responsibilities in this regard. This group will also gain priority under (v) below.[84] Equally, it would appear that those who meet the criterion of homelessness, because they have no accommodation which they could reasonably be expected to continue to occupy, would fall within this paragraph. However, if housed in accommodation which conforms to

---

79 HC Debs, Vol 270, col 652.
80 HL Debs, Vol 573, cols 329–330, referring to it as 'the layered protocol'.
81 Section 167(2)(a).
82 Section 325(1); subs (2) contains two exceptions to this principle.
83 *R v Newham LBC, ex parte Watkins* (1994) 26 HLR 434, 448. The statutory definition of premises that are unfit for habitation (1985 Act, s 604) is not wholly irrelevant, although the wording is different.
84 HL Debs, Vol 573, cols 366–370.

the authority's standards, for however short a period, then they would not fall within this category from that time. The housing register will require updating to reflect this at appropriate moments (although, in some cases, this will be administratively inconvenient).

(ii) *People occupying accommodation which is temporary or occupied on insecure terms.*[85] In one sense, all accommodation is temporary because, at any moment, a person might have to leave it. Such a reading would, undoubtedly, be too wide. However, at the other end of the spectrum, clearly those occupying insecure licences (eg living with a friend) or insecure tenancies would qualify. It is suggested that a person who has an assured tenancy, will not qualify under this paragraph. More difficult questions will arise with assured shorthold tenancies. These are temporary and short term but, it is suggested, that they would receive less priority under this paragraph until the tenant(s) has been given a notice to quit or is subject to possession proceedings. It is clear, and the Government has accepted this, that a person to whom the authority has accepted a full housing duty under Part VII (the homelessness provisions) for the two-year period, will fit within this paragraph.[86]

The Government's view, in its Consultation Paper, was that this paragraph will cover those persons:

> 'where it is known that the present tenure is about to end, for example where a household is required to leave tied accommodation. Local authorities will also be able to give preference to applicants where it is uncertain whether the present accommodation will continue. It will be open to authorities to apply the test more broadly, but on a graduated basis; for instance, they might give limited preference to someone living in an assured shorthold tenancy and a higher weighting to anyone whose lack of security is more acute.'[87]

(iii) *Families with dependent children.*[88] It is unclear whether the word 'family' should be taken to mean the nuclear or two-parent family on the one hand, or whether it should also include lone-parent families on the other. It is submitted that the latter is the better interpretation so as to account also for, for example, where a grandparent resides with the lone parent and child. Sir Louis Blom-Cooper, sitting as Deputy High Court Judge, has argued that ' ... a local authority, in applying the provisions of section 22 [of the 1985 Act], is bound to perform its duties within the context of its overall public law duties, and not those that are directed exclusively to its duties under the housing legislation.'[89] One such other obligation is the duty on social services departments to provide

---

85 Section 167(2)(b).
86 Standing Committee G, Seventeenth Sitting, col 671.
87 *Allocation of Housing Accommodation by Local Authorities* (DoE, 1996), para 28.
88 Section 167(2)(c).
89 *R v Newham LBC, ex parte Watkins* (1994) 26 HLR 434, 451. Reference was also made to 'the pressing social problems of child welfare and the impact which poor housing has on juvenile delinquency', ibid.

accommodation to children in need; in so doing, the housing department is under a duty to co-operate unless it is incompatible with their own statutory or other duties and obligations and does not unduly prejudice the discharge of those functions.[90] Such an interpretation is not without its difficulties because Part VII refers to priority need being given to *a person* with whom dependent children reside. As that is specific and this paragraph not so, it may be that an interpretation could veer to the alternative conclusion. Furthermore, other paragraphs in this subsection refer to 'households' or 'people' and so the draftsman has used a particular word here to connote a particular meaning. On the other hand, it would seem wrong to allow reasonable preference to a single person who is pregnant (see (iv) below) but not to a single person who has a child.

The phrase 'dependent children' is well known under the homelessness legislation. The House of Lords described the Code of Guidance under the homelessness provisions of the 1985 Act as sensible in this respect.[91] The Guidance suggested that children were dependent until the age of 16; between 16 and 18, they were dependent if in full-time education or training or are unable to support themselves and living at home.[92] It has been held that a 16-year-old on a youth training scheme is in gainful employment and therefore not dependent, although the court did accept that some 16- or 17-year-olds, who were not financially dependent, could none the less be dependent within the 1985 Act.[93] However, one judge suggested that a 16- or 17-year-old who is able to work but chooses not to seek it would not be dependent.[94] An unborn child is not a dependant.[95]

(iv) *Households consisting of or including someone who is expecting a child*.[96] It seems clear that a 'household' can consist of one person.[97] The Government would like to see that 'Consideration should also be given to those who have delayed starting a family because of the inadequacies of their accommodation.'[98]

---

90 Children Act 1989, ss 17(10), 20(1), 27. One argument is that, in unitary authorities where housing and social services departments come within the same administrative structure, the Children Act is drafted so that the housing department must make the relevant assessments and, where necessary, provide accommodation (see Children Act 1989, s 106 (definition of local authority)). It may well be that this will be a fruitful challenge in such authorities in the future.

91 *R v Bexley LBC, ex parte B; Oldham MBC, ex parte G* [1993] 2 All ER 65, 69.

92 Homelessness Code of Guidance, para 6.3.

93 *R v Kensington and Chelsea RBC, ex parte Amarfio* (1995) 27 HLR 543.

94 Ibid, 547 per Evans LJ.

95 *R v Newham LBC, ex parte Dada* (1995) 27 HLR 502.

96 Section 167(2)(d).

97 At least that interpretation has been accepted by the Government because 'otherwise, a single person would never be housed ...' (HL Debs, Vol 573, col 398).

98 *Allocation of Housing Accommodation by Local Authorities* (DoE, 1996) para 29.

(v) *Households consisting of or including someone with a particular need for settled accommodation on medical or welfare grounds.*[99] The phrase 'particular need' is obscure. Such obscurity is, no doubt, welcomed by the Government and authorities so that greater priority may be accorded to those who exhibit greater need within the authority's definition. It may well be that it will be interpreted, similarly to the concept of vulnerability in s 189(1)(c), as those who have difficulty in finding and keeping settled accommodation on medical or welfare grounds. 'Particular' may involve the local authority in a comparative exercise. On this basis the question is, does this person have a greater need for settled accommodation, on medical or welfare grounds, than others in the queue? Perhaps the better interpretation is that the circumstances of medical or welfare grounds *create* the particular need.

It is unfortunate that the concept of 'settled accommodation' appears in the 1996 Act, just as its usage in relation to the homelessness legislation has been cast with doubt.[100] Ackner LJ has suggested the following in relation to the homelessness provisions of the 1985 Act:

> 'What amounts to a "settled residence" is a question of fact and degree depending upon the circumstances of each individual case. I can see no reason why the good sense of the local authority cannot be relied upon for making the right decision.'[101]

It is clear that temporary accommodation can be settled, although probably not hostel provision.[102] Guidance will reflect the need to consider any children's schooling within the notion of whether accommodation is settled.[103]

The phrase 'medical or welfare' grounds is equally obscure. Most local authorities currently have a system of ensuring requisite priority is to be given on medical grounds.[104] However, it appears that any form of medical problem should be considered and accorded requisite priority under this paragraph, as long as it inhibits the person in seeking out settled accommodation. A welfare ground could stretch from receipt of welfare benefits to psychiatric assessment.

Nevertheless, in the midst of this obscurity, one matter is entirely clear. This category reflects the Government's desire to ensure that all those persons who are within the most vulnerable sections of the community are adequately catered for in an allocations scheme. Such characteristics include, for example, 'old age,

---

99 Section 167(2)(e).

100 See *R v Brent LBC, ex parte Awua* (1995) 27 HLR 453.

101 *Din v Wandsworth LBC* (unreported 1981), CA.

102 See *R v Rushcliffe BC, ex parte Summerson and Bailey* (1992) 25 HLR 577; *R v Brent LBC, ex parte Macwan* (1994) 26 HLR 528. More generally, see C Hunter and S McGrath, *Homeless Persons*, 4th edn and supp (LAG, 1992/1995), paras 6.47–6.61.

103 HL Debs, Vol 573, col 329.

104 It is unlawful for an authority to rely solely on medical advice. The final decision is for the authority to make (*R v Lambeth LBC, ex parte Carroll* (1988) 20 HLR 142).

physical or learning disability, severe mental illness or degenerative disease'.[105] Such people are to be given *additional* preference if they *cannot reasonably be expected to find settled accommodation for themselves in the foreseeable future.*[106] 'Authorities will need to consider whether the applicant requires specially adapted housing, the opportunities that the applicant has to remain in his or her present accommodation, and whether more suitable alternatives exist (such as private or residential care).'[107] In addition, authorities will need to consider how far that person is able to find accommodation.

This reflects the ideology of community care as well as a greater appreciation of the housing needs and problems of this group, in part caused by the lack of interaction between the National Health Service and Community Care Act 1990 and the Housing Act 1985. The 1990 Act requires a co-ordinated approach between, among others, the social services and housing departments in assessment. The Government has already said that they would not expect housing departments to carry out any such assessments in isolation and that any assessment is best shared with social services, health or other agencies. Guidance will be issued on this point, indicating good practice.[108] It may well be that such good practice will indicate that, in some cases, housing authorities should ensure that a care plan is in place before it provides any accommodation.[109] However, nowhere on the face of the 1996 Act is there a duty on social services or health departments to co-operate with any request made by the housing department for an assessment. Considerable problems remain on issues such as confidentiality of material between departments.

Further problems will arise if the person has left accommodation in circumstances in which they could be found intentionally homeless (eg as a result of rent arrears or disturbance). Such a person will still be entitled to the additional priority and authorities should be aware that disentitling such a person from this priority will be in breach of this obligation. This might be described as storing up problems for the future but, as the legislation stands, is an undeniable implication from it, which schemes should reflect.

(vi) *Households whose social or economic circumstances are such that they have difficulty in securing settled accommodation.*[110] Once again, obscure terminology makes any definition somewhat difficult and undesirable. There appears to be a considerable overlap with the preceding category. For example, the Government have indicated that those on low incomes would clearly come within this category; but they would also fall within the preceding category under the

---

105 *Allocation of Housing Accommodation by Local Authorities* (DoE, 1996) para 36.
106 Section 167(2).
107 *Allocation of Housing Accommodation by Local Authorities* (DoE, 1996) para 38.
108 HL Debs, Vol 573, col 353.
109 Ibid, col 354.
110 Section 167(2)(f).

'welfare grounds' criterion as long as their circumstances fit with the other requirements. Social and medical circumstances often also overlap. The Government have suggested, in line with their belief that accommodation should be allocated to those with long-term need, that 'immediate circumstances and [. . .] longer term economic prospects' should be considered.[111]

Children not included

9.17 Direct inclusion into the reasonable preference categories is not given to those under 18 years of age. This is because youth 'is not in itself an indication of a need for an independent tenancy'. Furthermore, problems exist in granting tenancies to minors as they cannot be held responsible for their debts and have no capacity to enter contracts except for necessities.[112] However, such people will qualify for short-term accommodation under Part VII unless they do not fit within the relevant criteria. In addition, there are certain housing obligations in the Children Act 1989.[113]

Challenging a scheme

9.18 Challenges to schemes under the old legislation were few and far between, although they have become more frequent of late. It is likely that such frequency will be enhanced because this is the only route into long-term local authority housing; the wording is vague and obscure; and the scheme still allows certain groups priority over others so that expectations may be dashed. There are two possible major routes to challenge authorities' allocation schemes – through the courts in judicial review proceedings or the Commission for Local Administration. In addition, it is anticipated that Guidance will exhort local authorities to have internal review or appeal mechanisms in place.

Type of accommodation to be offered

9.19 There is no required standard of accommodation to be offered in the legislation. Therefore, this returns us to the familiar comments of Lord Brightman in *R v Hillingdon LBC, ex parte Puhlhofer*:

'The word "appropriate" or "reasonable" is not to be imported [into the definition of accommodation]. Nor is accommodation not accommodation because it might be unfit for habitation . . . or might involve overcrowding . . .

---

111 *Allocation of Housing Accommodation by Local Authorities* (DoE, 1996), para 31.
112 R Goff and G Jones *The Law of Restitution*, 4th edn (Sweet & Maxwell, 1993), ch 23 'Contracts Affected by Incapacity'. The same is true of many of those covered by (v) above.
113 HL Debs, Vol 573, cols 372–374. See also, Children Act 1989, ss 17(10), 21, 27; *R v Northavon DC, ex parte Smith* [1994] 3 All ER 313; *R v Tower Hamlets LBC, ex parte Byas* (1993) 2 FLR 605; *R v Bexley LBC, ex parte Bentum; R v Oldham MBC, ex parte Garlick* [1993] 2 All ER 65.

What is to be regarded as accommodation is a question of fact to be decided by the authority. There are no rules. Clearly some places in which a person might choose or be constrained to live could not properly be regarded as accommodation at all; it would be a misuse of language to describe Diogenes as having occupied accommodation ...'[114]

It may well be, on the other hand, that as some of the categories consider the necessity for 'settled accommodation', one could argue that such a criterion should also apply to the accommodation offered by the authority. Such an argument would have the merit of (a) consistency; (b) better reflecting the needs of the applicant; and (c) being more in tune with the Government's stated objective of ensuring that allocations reflect *long-term* need. In addition, suitable accommodation will be required in relation to homeless applicants under Part VII, to whom the main housing duty is owed, as a result of s 193(7)(b).

Finally, there is no requirement as to the number of offers that authorities must make in order to fulfil their duties. Consequently, it appears that authorities can retain a one-offer policy in full discharge of their duties.

Consultation

9.20   Before adopting or altering a scheme reflecting a major change of policy, authorities must send copies of the new draft or alterations to any RSL with which the authority has nomination rights and afford a reasonable opportunity for such bodies to comment upon them.[115] The legislation does not define 'a major change of policy' nor the time period of 'a reasonable opportunity'.[116] The former, no doubt, should be related to the effect any change will have upon the RSL; and, in the same vein, the latter should be related to the complexity of any change. The alteration only covers a policy change and, therefore, not the procedure which implements the allocations scheme. So, for example, it would cover any or most changes to priority categories but not the selectors.

Regulations and Guidance

Powers of the Secretary of State

9.21   By virtue of s 167(3)–(5), the Secretary of State retains extremely wide powers to regulate the preferential groups, other factors that are not to be taken into account, and the procedures to be followed. Any regulations must be made by Statutory Instrument, although different Parliamentary procedures are specified for regulations made under each subsection. Each regulation-making

---

114 [1986] 1 AC 454, 517. There are, however, some basic requirements. For example, accommodation would not include a refuge.
115 Section 167(7).
116 For similar wording, however, see ss 106 et seq of the 1985 Act and s 137 of the 1996 Act.

power is wide enough to include 'such incidental, supplementary and transitional provisions as appear to the Secretary of State appropriate' and can make different provision for different areas.[117]

(i) The Secretary of State retains powers to add further groups to whom a reasonable preference, or additional preference, is to be given.[118] In addition, a Henry VIII clause empowers the Secretary of State to amend or repeal any of the reasonable preference or additional preference categories.[119] Any regulations must be laid before and approved by an affirmative resolution of both Houses of Parliament.[120] The reason why these powers have been retained is, apparently, because certain conditions of housing need may change or other conditions may become apparent. These powers ensure that the Secretary of State can keep the legislation 'up to date as regards changing demographic and social conditions without the need for primary legislation'.[121]

(ii) The Secretary of State retains powers to specify, by regulation, factors which authorities will not be entitled to take into account in their schemes.[122] This power is subject to the negative resolution procedure of either House of Parliament.[123] This power will ensure Ministers can provide a quick response to prevent authorities from operating discriminatory schemes 'for example, by giving excessive priority to children of their own tenants or by refusing to give proper consideration to applications from single people'.[124]

(iii) The procedure of schemes must be framed in accordance with principles prescribed by the Secretary of State in regulations.[125] Procedure bears its wider meaning to include all aspects of the decision-making process including who are the responsible decision-makers.[126] One use of this power will be to restrict the involvement of elected officials in the allocation process.[127]

Guidance

9.22 The Secretary of State is empowered to issue Guidance which will cover any or all authorities and to which those authorities 'shall have regard'.[128] Authorities may, therefore, disregard the Code, but only if they have first

---

117 Section 172(4).
118 Section 167(3)(a).
119 Section 167(3)(b).
120 Section 172(2).
121 HL Debs, Vol 573, col 393.
122 Section 167(4). This will include inadequate criteria such as the place of birth of the applicant (HL Debs, Vol 574, col 45).
123 Section 172(3).
124 HL Debs, Vol 573, col 393.
125 Section 167(5).
126 Section 167(1).
127 HL Debs, Vol 573, col 394.
128 Section 169. For similar wording, see s 74(1) of the 1985 Act and explanatory case-law.

considered its provisions.[129] In this sense, it is exhortatory. Decisions will also be quashed if the authority only considers earlier drafts of the Guidance. The Government is committed to specifying the following additional considerations in Guidance:

(i)   good practice in the periodic updating of registers, by, for example, asking applicants to inform the authority once a year of their continued interest in appearing on the register;[130]

(ii) co-operation with other agencies, such as social services and health departments in line with the obligations under the community care legislation and the Children Act 1989. This will also cover aspects such as joint assessments.[131] The Government wishes authorities to deal appropriately with levels of individual difficulty as opposed to single group categorisation;[132]

(iii) local authorities should maintain lists of properties appropriate for special needs groups;[133]

(iv) Guidance will draw authorities' attention to their responsibilities towards 'people with both physical disabilities and other forms of incapacity'.[134]

Exemptions from the allocation scheme

9.23   Certain allocations are excluded from the operation of the above provisions. The first tranche relates to those persons who are already secure or assured tenants of property allocated by the authority, as well as assured tenants holding from an RSL.[135] This includes the situation where two or more persons wish an allocation of accommodation and one or more of them is such a person.[136]

This provision ensures that transfers of authority property, housing mobility schemes (the 'HOMES' scheme is the best known of these), and exchanges of property are outside the remit of Part VI.[137] Such moves can be within the authority or to another authority. This places them within the more general housing management duty.[138] Under this general duty, the authority is entitled to

---

129 *De Falco v Crawley BC* [1980] QB 460.
130 Standing Committee G, Sixteenth Sitting, cols 635–638.
131 Ibid, cols 639–640; HL Debs, Vol 573, cols 353–354, 357.
132 Ibid, col 642.
133 Ibid, Seventeeth Sitting, col 675.
134 HL Debs, Vol 573, col 369.
135 Section 159(5).
136 Section 159(6). This does not apply to any of the others who is not a qualifying person (s 159(6)(b)).
137 Standing Committee G, Sixteenth Sitting, cols 603, 609.
138 Section 21 of the 1985 Act. It may well have been that the case-law had reached this position anyway (*R v Islington LBC, ex parte Aldabbagh* (1995) 27 HLR 271).

take any considerations into account, such as rent arrears, the tenant's behaviour and other relevant considerations.[139]

Succession and other consequential provisions

9.24 Where a person succeeds to a secure or introductory tenancy, or is assigned such a tenancy (within the parameters of the legislation), under an order on divorce or in child proceedings,[140] such matters are excluded from the operation of Part VI. In addition, where an introductory tenancy ceases to be introductory and thereby becomes a secure tenancy, it is outside the allocation provisions.[141]

Regulation powers

9.25 The Secretary of State is empowered to make regulations excluding other matters from the operation of Part VI.[142] In particular, such regulations can relate to specified descriptions of persons, accommodation, or proportion of accommodation of such a description.[143] The Government will make regulations under this subsection entitling authorities, should it so wish, to allocate accommodation to other statutory[144] and voluntary agencies. This will reflect the need to avoid temporary accommodation 'silting up' and will, however, be tightly controlled.[145] The Government is also considering using these powers to make provision for authorities to accept referrals from social services departments[146] and so that carers can be allocated without going through the allocations process.

Information about the allocation scheme

9.26 Authorities must publish a summary of their scheme and provide free copies to anyone who so requests.[147] The complete scheme must be published at the authority's principal office and copies, for a reasonable fee, must be provided.[148] If an authority does not publish its complete scheme, or publication

---

139 *R v Islington LBC, ex parte Aldabbagh* (1995) 27 HLR 271, 281.
140 Respectively the Matrimonial Causes Act 1973, s 24; Matrimonial and Family Proceedings Act 1983, s 17; or Children Act 1989, Sch 1, para 1.
141 Section 160(2)–(3).
142 Section 160(4).
143 Section 160(5).
144 This will be with particular reference to authorities' obligations under the Children Act 1989 and the community care legislation, such as they exist.
145 Standing Committee G, Sixteenth Sitting, cols 609–610; HL Debs, Vol 573, col 323. 'Silting up' is a process which occurs when there is insufficient permanent accommodation available to enable persons to move from their temporary accommodation.
146 HL Debs, Vol 574, col 40.
147 Section 168(1). Section 106 of the 1985 Act does not apply to this duty (1996 Act, Sch 16, para 1).
148 Section 168(2).

does not reflect the whole scheme, there is some doubt about the lawfulness of the scheme itself. Sedley J has suggested that:

> 'The whole point of publication is that applicants and their advisers should know the framework within which they should approach the council and in turn expect the council to deal with them. A council which is applying rules known to nobody but itself is breaking a very fundamental aspect of the law, and therefore may be acting ultra vires if it operates rules of which it has failed to publish a summary pursuant to section 106.'[149]

Where the authority makes an alteration to their scheme 'reflecting a major change of policy', the authority must notify every person on their housing register with an explanation in general terms of its effect. Such notification must occur within a reasonable time.

Co-operation with RSLs

9.27 RSLs are under a duty to co-operate with the local housing authority where the latter requests an allocation to a person with priority on the register. The RSL must co-operate 'to such extent as is reasonable in the circumstances'.[150] Bearing in mind the limited accommodation available to local authorities in some areas, this section is bound to be a cause of future disharmony between these organisations. Judicial proceedings may well be an unsatisfactory method of achieving this co-operation.[151] The following factors among others, it is submitted, will be relevant: the availability of accommodation to the RSL; the number of people waiting for such accommodation on the RSL's own list; the type of accommodation requested (eg easy access accommodation or supported housing not readily available to local authorities); the area of accommodation requested.

Offences

9.28 If a person knowingly or recklessly makes a false statement, an offence is committed and is punishable by way of a fine at level 5 on the standard scale. A similar offence and punishment occur where a person knowingly withholds information which the authority has reasonably required under this Part.

---

149 *R v Tower Hamlets LBC, ex parte Khalique* (1993) 26 HLR 517, 526.
150 Section 170.
151 *R v Northavon DC, ex parte Smith* (1994) 26 HLR 659, 665–666.

PART VII

CHAPTER 10

HOMELESSNESS

I: Introduction

Background

10.1 Part VII of the Housing Act 1996 contains the new provisions governing local authorities' duties to certain homeless persons.[1] The Government's Consultation Paper was issued in January 1994[2] and the reforms were again mooted in *Our Future Homes*.[3] Although similar concepts are used, Part VII differs substantially from its forebears: Housing (Homeless Persons) Act 1977 and the Housing Act 1985, Part III. Part VII proved controversial both in public and Parliamentary debate.

At the heart of Part VII is the Government's belief that allocation of housing accommodation should be through a single housing register. The Government's concern has been that, under the old law, homeless people were able to 'jump the queue' so as to place themselves at the top of the housing register waiting for a diminishing supply of accommodation. This Part effectively emasculates the old law in order to give effect to this overriding policy aim.

Part VII: The general picture

The old law

10.2 The Housing Act 1985, Part III, required local housing authorities to make enquiries into whether an applicant was homeless, in priority need, and whether the homelessness was caused intentionally. If the applicant passed all the relevant tests, then the authority was required to provide accommodation of indefinite duration ('the full housing duty'). In addition, in certain circumstances, an authority could refer an applicant to another authority, with whom that applicant had a local connection, which was required to complete the provision duty.

---

1 Like other parts of the 1996 Act, this Part does not affect Scotland, where the Housing (Scotland) Act 1987 makes provision for homeless persons.
2 *Access to Local Authority and Housing Association Tenancies* (HMSO, 1994).
3 *Our Future Homes* (HMSO, 1995), ch 6.

Structural and substantive changes in Part VII

10.3　The following list shows the structural and substantive changes in Part VII:

(i)　certain categories of person become ineligible for assistance;[4]

(ii)　domestic violence is given a different definition;[5]

(iii)　housing authorities will be required to set up or have set up advice and information services for the prevention of homelessness;[6]

(iv)　the full housing duty is to provide accommodation for a minimum period of two years. Housing authorities are given a power to continue providing accommodation over and above that period in certain circumstances;[7]

(v)　limited duties only arise if there is other suitable accommodation available in the area.[8] Powers of authorities to place applicants in accommodation outside their area are curtailed to a certain extent;[9]

(vi)　applicants are given the right to request a review of their decision in certain circumstances;[10]

(vii)　there is a right of appeal to a county court on a point of law.[11]

Although it is likely that much of the earlier case-law will still apply, these changes have significantly altered the legislative landscape.[12] In addition, some reorganisation of the way in which homelessness services were provided by housing authorities under the 1985 Act is bound to result to give effect to the advisory service which the Act requires.

10.4　The Act does not assist with the legal problems which arise when a housing authority contracts out its enquiry duties.[13]

---

4 Section 185.

5 Sections 176–178.

6 Section 179.

7 Sections 193–194, 206–207.

8 Section 197.

9 Section 208.

10 Section 202.

11 Section 204.

12 It is not possible to provide full details of the old law here. Readers are recommended the following additional texts: C Hunter and S McGrath *Homeless Persons* (Legal Action, 1992; amendments, 1995); P Robson and M Poustie *Homeless People and the Law*, 3rd edn (Butterworths, 1996). In the text below, concentration is upon the more recent cases with which these books were unable to deal.

13 Conflicting first instance decisions exist on this point: *R v West Dorset DC, ex parte Gerrard* (1994) 27 HLR 150 [unlawful]; cf *R v Hertsmere DC, ex parte Woolgar* (1995) 27 HLR 703 [lawful, provided the actual decision-making is by the local authority]. The weight of Guidance and Government policy is in favour of the latter decision.

II: The housing advice service

Advice

10.5   Local housing authorities come under a duty to provide free advice about homelessness and its prevention to any person in their district.[14] Guidance, to which authorities shall have regard,[15] will be issued detailing good practice and which services might be covered.[16] It is anticipated that this service will have a pivotal role in the homelessness responsibilities.

This is a limited duty at first sight. However, if one were to construe homelessness and its prevention more widely, it would cover all the possible causes of homelessness such as domestic violence, rent or mortgage arrears, racial or other forms of harassment, and family problems. The Code of Guidance under the 1985 Act considered that such problems (including finding accommodation in the area, legal rights in the private sector, advice on welfare benefits) were covered under the banner of advice.[17]

The duty is, nevertheless, restricted to the provision of advice, the extent of which is left to the authority's discretion. There is no requirement for the authority to keep an up-to-date list of available accommodation in their area (due to administrative inconvenience).[18] However, this would be good practice in the light of the duty to consider the availability of alternative accommodation before providing some assistance under this Part.[19] Equally, there is no provision for publicising the service nor for its independence from the local authority. No doubt, Guidance will deal with these points.

Tortious duty

10.6   It is possible that a duty of care in the tort of negligence will arise if incorrect or self-serving information is provided. Under the 1985 Act, it was held that policy considerations negated the extension of a duty of care to such services.[20] The Court of Appeal, however, suggested that liability might have arisen if the authority had been directly responsible for giving advice which

---

14 There is no requirement for actual residence in that district or for the applicant to have any connection with that district whatever.

15 Section 182(1).

16 Section 182; Standing Committee G, Nineteenth Sitting, col 727. The Guidance will also be issued to social services departments.

17 Code of Guidance, ch 14.

18 In some areas, however, this will be good practice, which Guidance will reflect (Standing Committee G, Twenty-Second Sitting, col 847).

19 Section 197.

20 *Ephraim v Newham LBC* (1992) 25 HLR 207.

endangered a family. This position might change as a result of the specific instruction to set up an advice service in the 1996 Act. In addition, if self-serving advice is provided, this may well give rise to rigorous procedural questioning on judicial review.

Grants, loans and other assistance

10.7 Local authorities are empowered to provide the following.[21]

(i) Financial assistance by way of grant or loan.
(ii) Permission to use the authority's premises. This would enable local authorities, for example, to set up night shelters or refuges.
(iii) Furniture or other goods either themselves or through gifts and loans for this purpose. 'Other goods' could, for example, mean cookers and televisions. Presumably, this phrase should be read as if it were *sui generis* with 'furniture' so that it will not relate to, for example, the provision of gas and electricity services.
(iv) The services of the authority's staff.[22] This could be used to enable an advocacy service to be administered. Such services could extend from representation in mortgage or rented accommodation possession actions, through to representation in homelessness appeals. There is much potential in this provision.
(v) The same powers can be used by the Secretary of State or housing authority to fund or provide assistance to voluntary organisations which are non-profit-making.[23]

These discretionary powers are so wide as to make them almost unchallengeable were an authority not to provide them at all. Whilst any general determination by the authority that it will not provide any or all of these services will almost certainly be unlawful, so long as it occasionally considers whether to provide the services, it should be protected in judicial review proceedings.

Conditions of assistance

10.8 The donor of the assistance has a general discretion to prescribe terms and conditions of the assistance.[24] Be that as it may, certain undertakings must be

---

21 Section 179(2).
22 Section 179(3).
23 Section 180. This is in similar terms to s 73 of the 1985 Act, and appears to be wide enough to include housing associations and local housing companies: Hunter and McGrath (above), para 11.12.
24 Section 181(2).

given by the donee:[25] to use the assistance for a specified purpose and to provide such information as to its use as may reasonably be required. The donor may require this information by written notice and the donee must provide it within 21 days beginning with service of that notice.[26] In addition, the donee must keep proper accounts (which may be subject to audit), indications of how the assistance has been used, and to submit accounts and records to the donor.[27]

Restitution

10.9   There is provision for restitution where the undertakings (to use the assistance for a specified purpose and to provide information) do not appear to have been kept. A notice must be served specifying the amount recoverable and the basis upon which that has been calculated. Only the amount of the assistance is recoverable under the statute[28] (although interest may well be recoverable by virtue of the common law of restitution).[29] It must appear to the donor that the donee has broken the undertaking. The donor is then under a duty to take all reasonable steps to recover the amount of the assistance.[30]

III: Enquiry duties

Is the person eligible for assistance?

Persons from abroad ineligible

10.10   Certain persons are ineligible for all forms of assistance under Part VII. These are those persons subject to immigration control under the Asylum and Immigration Act 1996 (unless the Secretary of State gives entitlement in regulations)[31] as well as other groups of persons from abroad whom the Secretary of State specifies in regulations are to be ineligible.[32] The intention is to bring entitlement under Part VII into line with entitlement to housing benefit. At a late stage in the Parliamentary passage of the Bill, the drafting of the clauses had to be changed as a result of a Court of Appeal judgment.[33]

The Secretary of State has signalled that the following categories of persons will be specified in regulations as entitled to assistance under Part VII: (a) refugees;

---

25 Section 181(3).
26 Ibid.
27 Section 181(4).
28 Section 181(5) and (6).
29 *Woolwich Equitable Building Society v IRC* [1992] 3 All ER 737.
30 Section 181(5).
31 Section 185(2).
32 Section 185(3).
33 *R v Secretary of State for Social Security, ex parte Joint Council for the Welfare of Immigrants* (1996) 146 NLJ 985 (housing benefit regulations disentitling asylum seekers unlawful).

(b) persons granted exceptional leave to remain or having indefinite leave to remain; (c) asylum seekers and their dependants whose asylum claim has not been rejected and who either applied for asylum at the port on arrival, or applied for asylum within three months of a declaration by the Home Secretary that their country of origin has undergone an upheaval.[34] Those in category (c) will, however, be subject to more limited obligations.[35]

Those ineligible will, therefore, include the following persons or groups of persons: (a) illegal entrants;[36] (b) those overstaying their visa requirements or only given temporary admission to the UK; (c) EU nationals in breach of residence directives;[37] (d) those whose visa gives them no recourse to public funds; (e) those not habitually resident in the UK;[38] (f) asylum seekers not entitled to housing benefit, ie those who did not apply for asylum at port of entry or have been refused asylum (even where an appeal has been lodged).[39]

Two difficult problems

10.11 These new sections effectively require local authority housing officers to act as immigration officers. This raises two difficult problems (at least). First, immigration legislation and subordinate legislation are notoriously impenetrable so that, together with the new obligations under Part VII, local authority housing officers will be hard-pressed to appreciate all the implications. The new Code of Guidance will retain and modify the model screening process which was in operation in the old Code but difficult issues remain.[40] Secondly, authorities should be aware of the difficult line to be drawn between these new duties and that contained in s 71 of the Race Relations Act 1976, under which they have a duty to exercise their functions with due regard to the elimination of unlawful racial discrimination and to promote equal opportunities and good race relations.

---

34 HL Debs, Vol 574, cols 103–104.
35 Sections 186–187 (see below).
36 These include those who enter the country clandestinely; as a result of false or deceitful statements about the availability of accommodation in this country; and where the immigration authorities decide that the person is an illegal entrant. Such persons were already ineligible, see *R v Secretary of State for the Environment, ex parte Tower Hamlets LBC* [1993] QB 632, and the Code of Guidance had been redrafted to give effect to this.
37 Cf *R v Westminster CC, ex parte Tristan-Garcia and Castelli* (1996) *The Times*, 27 February, CA, (lawful entrants, who subsequently could have been required to leave the country, although nothing had been done to remove them – entitled to assistance).
38 Considered below.
39 Standing Committee G, Nineteenth Sitting, col 740; HL Debs, Vol 573, col 429; Social Security (Persons from Abroad) Miscellaneous Regulations 1996, SI 1996/30 (although held unlawful, the changes to the legislation mean that they contain the relevant affected groups).
40 See, for example, the length of the judgments in the *Castelli* case above.

Habitual residence

10.12 The habitual residence test was described by Mr David Curry, the Housing Minister, as follows: 'The test, which looks at a person's settled pattern of residence over the last few years, his future intentions, and the focus of his main interests and ties, applies equally to British citizens, European Union citizens and settled immigrants'.[41] It derives from social security law (effective since 1992) and is notoriously difficult to define.[42] The leading social security textbook says:

> ' "Habitually" implies that the residence should be adopted both voluntarily and for settled purposes, for example education, business employment or health, but it does not require an intention to live in a place permanently or indefinitely.'[43]

The following is some further guidance from an Income Support Commissioner's decision: (a) the applicant should have been in the UK for an appreciable period of time, usually about three months;[44] and (b) the applicant's residence here must have been financially viable.[45] The test remains highly controversial and challenges to its compatibility with EU law are proceeding.[46]

Other asylum seekers and their dependants ineligible

10.13 The next tranche of persons ineligible are asylum seekers or their dependants, not caught by the above provisions, but who have accommodation, however temporary, which is available for their occupation.[47] The rest of the section defines when, for the section's own purposes and any resulting obligations, a person is an asylum seeker and whom their dependants are. A person remains an asylum seeker[48] from the time when the claim is recorded by the Secretary of State until the time that the claim is determined[49] or abandoned.

---

41 Standing Committee G, Nineteenth Sitting, col 740.

42 Social Security Contributions and Benefits Act 1992, ss 124(1) and 134(1).

43 A Ogus, E Barendt and N Wikeley *The Law of Social Security*, 4th edn (Butterworths, 1995), p 401, citing *Shah v Barnet LBC* [1983] 2 AC 309, 342, per Lord Scarman.

44 Subsequently, a further Commissioner has suggested that guidelines as to the relevant period are unhelpful: CIS/2778/95. However, it appears (albeit doubtfully) that a person cannot be habitually resident on the first day of their arrival: CIS/2326/95 and CIS/1067/95. See generally on this (1996) *Legal Action*, August 12.

45 CIS/1067/95 (*82/95): (1996) *Legal Action*, February 14.

46 See (1996) *Legal Action*, August 12.

47 Section 186(1). This is a repeat of the provisions contained in the housing provisions of the Asylum and Immigration Appeals Act 1993 which are repealed in this Act: Sch 19.

48 A claim for asylum is one that is made under the Geneva Convention relating to the Status of Refugees and its Protocol (s 186(5)).

49 Where the result of an application is that the person is given 'exceptional leave to remain' in the UK, then that person is entitled to assistance (HL Debs, Vol 573, col 433).

A person is a dependant of an asylum seeker[50] during the same period as the person upon whom dependence is premised or when the dependant is recorded by the Secretary of State as ceasing to be an asylum seeker.[51]

Administrative procedures

10.14 The administrative procedures repeat the relevant provisions of the Asylum and Immigration Appeals Act 1993 and give statutory form to the old Code of Guidance and form contained therein.[52] Basically, the local authority sends a form to, or telephones, the Immigration and Nationality Department ('IND'). Two issues require consideration: (a) whether the person is or has become an asylum seeker or their dependant; and (b) whether such a person is eligible for assistance as a person from abroad.[53] The latter then respond in writing.[54] The IND must also notify the authority of any changes in status of the person.[55]

Possible duties under the Children Act 1989 and National Health Service and Community Care Act 1990

10.15 Advisers should be aware that, if a person is ineligible for assistance under Part VII, such a person should be able to access accommodation through the social services department under the Children Act 1989[56] or Ministerial Guidance given under the National Health Service and Community Care Act 1990,[57] provided the applicant fulfils the various criteria under those provisions.

Who is an applicant?

10.16 Case-law under the 1985 Act also suggests that certain other people are incapable of being applicants.[58] This embraces those who are incapable of 'comprehending or evaluating' an offer of accommodation. This was held by the House of Lords in two separate appeals relating to: (a) a 23-year-old who lacked hearing, education and speech and communicated with the outside world by sign language which only her family could understand; and (b) two four-year-old children who attempted to apply.[59] It is clear, however, that a person can apply

---

50 A person who is the spouse or child of an asylum seeker who has no right of abode nor indefinite leave to enter or remain in the UK (s 186(4)).
51 Section 186(3).
52 Section 187 and see Code of Guidance, ch 16; Annex 6.
53 Section 187(1).
54 Section 187(2).
55 Section 187(3).
56 Children Act 1989, ss 17(10), 20(1).
57 DoH LAC 93/10.
58 Section 62 of the 1985 Act; s 183 of the 1996. The latter defines an 'applicant' as a person making an application.
59 *R v Tower Hamlets LBC, ex parte Begum* and *R v Bexley LBC, ex parte B; Oldham MBC, ex parte G* [1993] 2 All ER 65.

even though another member of the family has also applied. Each member of a family is entitled to separate consideration.[60]

Extended definition of applicant

10.17 Throughout the Act, the word 'applicant' bears an extended meaning. This includes those who normally reside with the applicant as family members or any other person who might reasonably be expected to reside with the applicant.[61] Ultimately, the decision rests with the authority. However, it clearly includes dependent children or grandchildren; married and cohabiting couples. On the other hand, in certain circumstances, an extended family may be split up.[62] However, the purpose of the homelessness legislation – to keep families together – must always be remembered. In addition, the definition was specifically widened to include carers.[63]

Appropriate enquiries

10.18 If the person is an applicant who may be homeless or threatened with homelessness, the local authority then comes under a duty to make the appropriate enquiries as to eligibility (see above) and as to the scope of the duties that it might be under.[64] Local authorities are under a duty to provide a reasonable level of service delivery to enable them to meet the needs of their area. In some authorities this will mean that they should be able to take homelessness applications 24 hours a day.[65] The Housing Minister has said that he will strengthen the Code of Guidance so that authorities will be more strongly exhorted to provide a 24-hour service.[66] In addition, the authority may also consider whether the applicant has a local connection with that authority. Local authorities are not entitled, at this preliminary stage, to refer the applicant to another authority but must conduct the enquiry procedure themselves.

---

60 *R v North Devon DC, ex parte Lewis* [1981] 1 WLR 328.

61 Section 176. This does not include unborn children (*R v Newham LBC, ex parte Dada* (1995) 27 HLR 502).

62 *R v Lambeth LBC, ex parte Ly* (1986) 19 HLR 51.

63 HL Debs, Vol 574, cols 62–64; see also *R v Southwark LBC, ex parte Ryder* (1996) 28 HLR 56.

64 Section 184(1).

65 *R v Camden LBC, ex parte Gillan* (1989) 21 HLR 114.

66 Standing Committee G, Nineteenth Sitting, col 749. See also *R v Camden LBC, ex parte Gillan* (1989) 21 HLR 114.

Is the applicant homeless?

General rule

10.19   An applicant is homeless if there is no accommodation available for the applicant in the UK or elsewhere in which the applicant has an interest, a licence to occupy, or occupies by virtue of any enactment or rule of law allowing the applicant to remain there.[67] The phrase 'or elsewhere' is new in the 1996 Act. It has been added so that local authorities may consider whether the applicant has property anywhere in the world, which might be available. Under the 1985 Act, authorities were only able to consider accommodation in England, Wales or Scotland so that, if a person had accommodation, say, in Canada, they would be homeless in this country if they had no accommodation here.[68] Often, however, a finding of intentional homelessness would result in these circumstances. This corrects that loophole so that, in future, such a person will not be homeless. In *R v Brent LBC, ex parte Awua*, the House of Lords held that 'accommodation' did not mean or refer to a settled home.[69]

Specific examples

10.20   The applicant is specifically deemed homeless when: (a) they are unable to enter the property; or (b) the property is 'a moveable structure, vehicle or vessel' which cannot be lawfully placed anywhere.[70] The former is to benefit the illegally evicted. The latter is particularly crucial after the Criminal Justice and Public Order Act 1994, which repealed the Caravan Sites Act 1968, so that there is now no duty on local authorities to provide sites for travellers' caravans.

Reasonableness criterion

10.21   In addition, accommodation is not available for the applicant unless it would be reasonable for the applicant to continue to occupy it.[71] Authorities retain the power to continue to consider their general housing circumstances when assessing whether it would be reasonable to continue to occupy accommodation.[72] In practice, most authorities usually exercise this power.[73]

It is up to the housing authority to determine whether it remains reasonable to continue to occupy accommodation. In certain hard-pressed areas, this can be difficult to establish. Simply because a house is unfit for human habitation does

---

67 Section 175(1).
68 See *Defalco v Crawley BC* [1980] QB 460.
69 (1995) 27 HLR 453.
70 Section 175(2).
71 Section 175(3).
72 Section 177(2).
73 This power is difficult to use when considering an application from a person who might be referred to another authority (see below).

not necessarily make it unreasonable to remain there.[74] The Code of Guidance suggested the following factors as relevant in determining reasonableness: physical conditions; overcrowding; type of accommodation; violence or threats of violence from outside the home (as to which, see para. **10.22**); cost; and security of tenure.[75] In *Awua*, Lord Hoffmann further suggested that the physical conditions of the accommodation must be related to the time in which the applicant had lived there.[76]

Against the Code of Guidance, judicial opinion has suggested that it is reasonable for an applicant to remain in occupation of property and await the outcome of any possession action, even if (it seems) the applicant has little chance of winning such an action.[77] The Housing Minister signalled in Standing Committee that he would tighten up the Code of Guidance so that, in many cases, this should not occur.[78] However, local authorities need only have regard to the Code, although it may be persuasive in court proceedings.

Domestic violence

10.22 A substantial proportion of the pre-1996 homelessness case-load involved applicants who claimed that they were at risk of domestic violence. Such applicants are automatically homeless. Many authorities required applicants at least to consider the availability of civil remedies such as injunctions, ouster or exclusion orders before accepting an application from such a person.[79] This was and remains a highly dubious practice for two reasons: the subsection is not based on this premise; and the effectiveness of such remedies is open to doubt in many cases.

The Act makes almost entirely new provision for domestic violence. Accommodation is deemed unreasonable for occupation to continue where this will lead to domestic violence against the applicant, a person who normally resides with the applicant or any other person who might reasonably be expected to reside with

---

74 See, for example, *R v South Herefordshire DC, ex parte Miles* (1983) 17 HLR 82 (occupation of a rat-infested hut 20' by 20' with no services, borderline case for family with two children); *R v Kensington and Chelsea RBC, ex parte Ben-el-Mabraick* (1995) 27 HLR 564 (two adults and young child occupying cramped rooms on the top floor of an HMO in breach of fire regulations not homeless).

75 Code of Guidance, para 5.8.

76 'A local housing authority could take the view that a family ... put into a single cramped and squalid bedroom, can be expected to make do for a temporary period. On the other hand, there will come a time at which it is no longer reasonable to expect them to continue to occupy such accommodation. At this point they come back within the definition of homelessness ...' ([1996] 1 AC 55, 68).

77 *R v Croydon LBC, ex parte Jarvis* (1993) 26 HLR 194.

78 Standing Committee G, Eighteenth Sitting, col 719.

79 There is plenty of excellent work in this area – see, especially, E Malos and G Hague *Domestic Violence and Housing: Local Authority Responses to Women and Children Escaping Violence in the Home* (University of Bristol, 1993).

the applicant.[80] This is similar to the extended definition of applicant considered above.

Violence or threats of violence are included. However, neither is given a definition. Local authorities are known to require different gradients of violence in this extended sense.

Whilst the phrase 'domestic violence' is used, this is defined by reference to the relationship between the perpetrator and applicant, as opposed to a residence-based test. So, the perpetrator must be 'associated' with the applicant.[81] The following are included:[82] (a) persons who were married to or divorced from the applicant; (b) cohabitants and former cohabitants;[83] (c) those who live or have lived in the same household as the applicant; (d) relatives[84] of the applicant; (e) a person who has agreed to marry the applicant; (f) in relation to a child, each person who is a parent or has or had parental responsibility for the child; (g) certain persons in relation to an adopted child.[85]

Violence or threats of violence from other persons is *not*, therefore, covered by the subsection. An applicant in this position is thrown back upon the reasonableness criterion, unless that person is unable to gain entry to the accommodation.[86] All forms of racial, sexual, or religious harassment or abuse should be considered.[87] It may well be that authorities could or should require the applicant, in these circumstances, to apply for civil remedies.

Disregard of ineligible persons from abroad

10.23 When considering whether an applicant is homeless, no regard is to be given to a person from abroad who is ineligible.[88]

Regulation-making power

10.24 The final significant addition to the definition of homelessness is a general order-making power vested in the Secretary of State.[89] The Housing Minister has so far indicated two possible circumstances in which such an order-making power would be used: where housing benefit would not cover all

---

80 Section 177(1).

81 Ibid.

82 Section 178(1). These are borrowed directly from the Family Law Act 1996.

83 This only covers where persons were living together as husband and wife. It, therefore, does not include single-sex cohabitants, who presumably are included in the next category.

84 There is a precise definition of relative in s 178(3).

85 Section 178(2).

86 *R v Broxbourne BC, ex parte Willmoth* (1989) 21 HLR 415.

87 See Code of Guidance, para 5.8(d).

88 Section 185(4)(a).

89 Section 177(3).

the rent on a property; and 'to clarify the law if a court decision calls into question the meaning of a particular provision and the general understanding of how the system is supposed to operate'.[90] In addition, the Government have said that they may well address affordability, on a wider scale, in an order under this section.[91]

Is the applicant threatened with homelessness?

10.25   An applicant is threatened with homelessness if it is likely that the applicant will become homeless within 28 days.[92] A person from abroad who is ineligible shall be disregarded in determining whether an applicant is threatened with homelessness.[93]

Interim duty to accommodate

10.26   There is an interim duty to ensure that accommodation is available for the applicant if the authority 'have reason to believe' that the applicant is homeless or threatened with homelessness, eligible for assistance, and has a priority need.[94] This duty arises before the authority undertakes the full enquiry and, therefore, is irrespective of the local connection provisions.[95] This duty ceases when the authority has notified the applicant of its decision even if the applicant intends to appeal against that decision (although there is a power to continue the provision until such a review has taken place).[96] This duty is not subject to the 'alternative accommodation' provision by virtue of which the housing authority is absolved from its duties where there is other suitable accommodation available in the district (see below).[97]

Suitability

10.27   It seems that this interim duty is to provide suitable accommodation. The definition of suitability is considered below.

---

90 Standing Committee G, Eighteenth Sitting, col 720; Nineteenth Sitting, col 721. The constitutional implications of the latter are potentially staggering.
91 HL Debs, Vol 573, col 411.
92 Section 175(4).
93 Section 185(4)(a).
94 Section 188(1).
95 Section 188(2).
96 Section 188(3).
97 Section 197(6).

Does the applicant have a priority need?

10.28   Priority need arises in four circumstances.[98] These are entirely the same as under the old law. The Secretary of State retains a power to add or subtract categories from the list, after appropriate consultation and positive resolution of both Houses of Parliament.[99] This power has never been used and the Housing Minister said in Standing Committee that 'a clear case' would need to be made out for inclusion. There would also be a need to consider the relationship between any amendment and the Code of Guidance.[100]

(i) *A pregnant woman or a person with whom she resides or might reasonably be expected to reside.*[101] The residence test is worded slightly differently from the extended definition of applicant, although, practically, it is likely to be interpreted in a similar vein.

(ii) *A person with whom dependent children reside or might reasonably be expected to reside.*[102] It should be noted that the Children Act 1989 has enabled parents to share residence of their children without necessarily living together or a court order detailing this. Often, such matters are dealt with by the parents without court intervention. In such circumstances, it is entirely possible for a child to reside with both parents. Difficult questions subsequently result.

Dependency is a difficult concept. The House of Lords described the Code of Guidance under the 1985 Act as sensible in this respect.[103] It suggested that children were dependent until the age of 16; between 16 and 18, they were dependent if in full-time education or training or are unable to support themselves and live at home.[104] It has been held that a 16-year-old on a youth training scheme is in gainful employment and therefore not dependent, although the court did accept that some 16- or 17-year-olds, who were not financially dependent, could nonetheless be dependent.[105] Moreover, one judge suggested that a 16- or 17-year-old who is able to work but chooses not to seek it would not be dependent.[106]

(iii) *A person who is vulnerable as a result of old age, mental illness or handicap or physical disability or other special reason, or with whom such a person resides or might reasonably be expected to reside.*[107] Undoubtedly, this is the most difficult category because of its flexibility. It has, however, been qualified by judicial decision.

---

98 Section 189.
99 Section 189(2)–(4).
100 Standing Committee G, Twentieth Sitting, cols 759–760.
101 Section 189(1)(a).
102 Section 189(1)(b).
103 *R v Bexley LBC, ex parte B; Oldham MBC, ex parte G* [1993] 2 All ER 65, 69.
104 Code of Guidance, para 6.3.
105 *R v Kensington and Chelsea RBC, ex parte Amarfio* (1995) 27 HLR 543.
106 Ibid, 547 per Evans LJ.
107 Section 189(1)(c).

Authorities must ask themselves if the applicant is vulnerable and, secondly, whether that vulnerability is caused by any of the catalogue provided. Vulnerability on its own is insufficient.[108] Vulnerability is defined as being 'less able to fend for oneself so that injury or detriment will result where a less vulnerable person will be able to cope without harmful effects' and relates to the finding and keeping of accommodation.[109] The authority needs to compare the applicant's vulnerability with that of a supposed ordinary homeless person. Authorities must not only consider medical factors but also social factors.

Old age is a question of fact. There can be no age above which a person is considered 'old', although those over 60 are, the Code suggests, automatically 'old'.[110] Mental illness, handicap or physical disability are separate concepts which remain undefined. Housing authorities have experienced particular problems with community care.[111] It has been suggested that, if the applicant has a social worker or care manager, it is up to the applicant to request the housing authority to contact that person.[112] The Code of Guidance exhorted housing authorities to keep in close contact with relevant agencies.[113]

The Court of Appeal has recently delivered an important judgment on the meaning of 'other special reasons'.[114] The following are the salient points of the judgment:

(i) The 'other special reason' category is not to be treated as *eiusdem generis* with the other categories of vulnerable persons. 'This [is] a free standing category which, although it ha[s] to be construed in its context, [is] not restricted by any notions of physical or mental weakness other than that which [is] inherent in the word "vulnerable" itself.' A combination of different circumstances could be a 'reason'.

(ii) 'Special' indicates that the difficulties must be 'of an unusual degree of gravity', and such as to distinguish the applicant from others. So, it seems that some type of comparative process is required.

(iii) A careful examination of the applicant's circumstances is required.

It seems acceptable for some young people to fall within this criterion as well as single persons suffering domestic violence, racial or sexual harassment. All were covered by the old Code of Guidance and it would be sensible if this were to

---

108 *R v Waveney DC, ex parte Bowers* (1982) 4 HLR 118.

109 *R v Waveney DC, ex parte Bowers*; glossed in *R v Lambeth LBC, ex parte Carroll* (1987) 20 HLR 142 and *R v Reigate and Banstead BC, ex parte Di Domenico* (1987) 20 HLR 153.

110 Code of Guidance, para 6.9.

111 See D Cowan 'Accommodating Community Care' (1995) *Journal of Law and Society* 212, p 212.

112 *R v Wirrall MBC, ex parte Bell* (1995) 27 HLR 234, 242.

113 Code of Guidance, para 6.11.

114 *R v Kensington and Chelsea RBC, ex parte Kihara; Hammersmith and Fulham LBC, ex parte Ilunga-Ilunga; Westminster City Council, ex parte Pavlov; Islington LBC, ex parte Araya* (1996) *The Times*, 10 July.

continue. Difficult problems occur as to whether a person who is HIV+ falls within this criterion. It is suggested that such persons fall within this criterion irrespective of whether their status is symptomatic or not. Almost certainly, this will be challenged at some point in the future. Many authorities have lists of those illnesses or ailments which trigger this category of priority need. Such lists are acceptable as long as the authority does not overly rely on them and keeps its ears open.

It is to be deprecated that the Government has not taken this opportunity to bring the legislation into line with the provisions of the Children Act 1989, ss 20(1) and 27, as well as the NHS and Community Care Act 1990. These Acts have caused real problems in terms of the interaction between social services and housing authorities. Recent case-law has done nothing to assist in this respect.[115] The Government has, throughout the Parliamentary passage of the Bill, insisted that Guidance is the appropriate way to sort out these problems. The previous edition of the Code, which made only passing reference to these Acts will be updated and will pay greater attention to their implications.[116] It remains unlikely to sort out the confusion that exists in practice.

(iv) *A person who is homeless or threatened with homelessness as a result of an emergency such as fire, flood or other disaster.*[117] The words 'emergency' and 'disaster' are conjunctive so that an emergency must also be a disaster. Emergency is interpreted as meaning some *sudden* emergency.[118] Furthermore, it appears that fire or flood are mere examples of the type of emergency and disaster which must 'consist of physical damage to the accommodation of the applicant which have made that accommodation uninhabitable'.[119]

Disregard of ineligible persons from abroad

10.29   When considering whether an applicant is in priority need, no regard is to be given to a person from abroad who is ineligible.[120]

Is the applicant intentionally homeless?

10.30   The intentionality provision was added to the original homelessness legislation to meet the demands of certain MPs, who argued that the Act would be a charter for the 'self-induced' homeless, who would seek to take advantage of the legislation. Originally described as 'gobbledegook', it has become the most

---

115 See *R v Northavon DC, ex parte Smith* [1994] 2 AC 402.
116 HL Debs, Vol 574, col 121, for example.
117 Section 189(1)(d).
118 *R v Walsall MBC, ex parte Price* (1996) *Legal Action*, June 13.
119 *R v Bristol CC, ex parte Bradic* (1995) 27 HLR 584, 590 (illegal eviction not within this category).
120 Section 185(4)(b).

widely litigated part of the homelessness legislation. Housing authorities have found it increasingly difficult to interpret. The new provision has been beefed up.

Five questions relating to whether a person is intentionally homeless

10.31   When considering whether a person is intentionally homeless, the housing authority must satisfy itself of five basic questions:

(a)   Has there been a deliberate act or failure to do something?

(b)   Was the loss of accommodation a consequence of that act or omission?

(c)   Has the applicant ceased to occupy accommodation (as opposed to not accepting the accommodation)?

(d)   Was that accommodation available for the applicant's occupation?

(e)   Would it have been reasonable for the applicant to continue to occupy that accommodation?

Deliberate acts and failures to act

10.32   Difficult problems arise when a person has not met their rent or mortgage payments. If their accommodation is lost for this reason, they may be found intentionally homeless. Authorities must consider whether the failure to pay was caused due to inadequate resources or whether welfare benefits covered the rent or mortgage.[121] In addition, if the applicant is unable to feed their family or 'fund the necessities of life', it would not be reasonable to continue to occupy accommodation.[122] Such questions are for the local authority and not the court.[123] A deliberate omission might result from a failure to access civil remedies to protect the applicant. However, the current Code of Guidance suggests that authorities should not make such a leap of logic in the case of violence from within or outside the home.[124] The Minister has undertaken that the revised Code of Guidance will refer to the fact that a person incapable of managing their own affairs should not be regarded as capable of a deliberate act.[125] It is clear that a person can be found intentionally homeless, even when that person is in priority need as a result of 'vulnerability . . . due to mental illness'.[126]

The old Code gives details of certain acts which can be regarded as deliberate: selling a home where there was no risk of losing it; wilful and persistent refusal to pay rent; neglect of their own affairs after having received advice; voluntarily leaving accommodation in this country or abroad; anti-social behaviour; voluntary resignation from job with tied accommodation.[127]

---

121 *R v Wandsworth LBC, ex parte Hawthorne* (1995) 27 HLR 59.

122 *R v Islington LBC, ex parte Bibi* (1996) *The Times*, 10 July.

123 *R v Brent LBC, ex parte Grossett* (1996) 28 HLR 9.

124 Code of Guidance, para 7.11(b).

125 HL Debs, Vol 574, col 120; see also Standing Committee G, Twentieth Sitting, col 766.

126 *R v Wirrall MBC, ex parte Bell* (above). The Code of Guidance will be beefed up to take account of housing authorities' obligations under community care.

127 Code of Guidance, para 7.7.

Good faith

Acts or omissions in good faith, where the applicant is unaware of any relevant fact, is not deliberate.[128] Examples include lack of awareness of welfare benefits or civil remedies.

Causation

10.33   The authority must be satisfied that the deliberate act caused the loss of accommodation. It was, at one time, believed that the housing authority would need to look back and consider the reasons why the applicant left their 'last settled accommodation'. In *R v Brent LBC, ex parte Awua*,[128a] the House of Lords held that the distinction between a settled and temporary residence was only relevant when considering '... what will break the causal link between departure from accommodation which it would have been reasonable to continue to occupy and homelessness separated from that departure by a period or periods of accommodation elsewhere'.[129] For example, if an applicant gave up long-term accommodation intentionally in favour of a holiday let, which then expired, that intentional reason would persist through the duration of the holiday let.[130] The House reserved the question as to whether the occupation of a settled residence was the sole and exclusive method by which such a causal link could be broken.

Ceasing to occupy

10.34   The accommodation must have already been occupied by the applicant. This had caused difficulties under the 1985 Act because a person who had refused accommodation offered by the authority under its full housing duty, could not have been said to have occupied that accommodation at all. Consequently, no finding of intentionality could result (although authorities, with a policy of offering only one property could be said to have discharged their duty if that accommodation was suitable).[131] However, the 1996 Act makes it clear that, in these circumstances, any duty to the applicant effectively ends.[132]

Further, under the 1996 Act, if the applicant is directed to accommodation in the private sector under the 'suitable alternative accommodation' provision (see below), and fails to take on that property 'in circumstances in which it was reasonably to be expected that [the applicant] would do so', on any further application under Part VII the applicant will be treated as intentionally homeless, unless there has been a period of accommodation to break this chain of causation.[133] It would not be reasonable to expect the applicant to take on

---

128 Section 191(2).
128a (1995) 27 HLR 453.
129 (1995) 27 HLR 453, 461.
130 See, for example, *Dyson v Kerrier DC* [1980] 1 WLR 1205.
131 *R v Westminster CC, ex parte Chambers* (1982) 16 HLR 14.
132 Section 193(5) and (7) (see below).
133 Section 191(4).

accommodation beyond the applicant's means or which did not meet the applicant's requirements or where the landlord refuses to offer the property to the applicant after their first meeting. It would be reasonable, in most other circumstances, for the applicant to accept such property.

Available for occupation

10.35 This must be interpreted in relation to the extended definition of 'applicant'.

Reasonable to continue to occupy

10.36 The law here was covered in the section on homelessness. There is no reason to expect that the law will be applied any differently as the phrases used are the same. Reasonableness, once again, is related to the authority's general housing circumstances.[134]

Collusion

10.37 The Government has added one further circumstance in which a person might be found intentionally homeless. This has been added as a result of concerns that potential applicants have been colluding with family or friends so that they leave the latter accommodation in order to take advantage of the 1985 Act. If a person enters into an arrangement – binding or not – requiring the applicant to leave accommodation which it would have been reasonable to continue to occupy and the purpose of this arrangement is to enable that person to take advantage of the Act, then a finding of intentional homelessness will result unless there are other reasons for the homelessness.[135]

In Standing Committee, the Housing Minister said that 'The Government do not believe that there is a massive or intractable problem . . . local authorities can probably sort out problems almost intuitively. . . . We do not intend to impose a new draconian power but local authorities may need a little extra support to sort out problems . . .'[136] Concerns were also expressed that this might force potential applicants to go back to a violent situation or unsuitable accommodation. However, the Minister did not believe that the clause covered such situations.

It seems likely then that the Guidance issued under the 1996 Act will take a more humane approach than the clause initially seems to adopt. It should be noted that a return to the former practice of requiring the family of home leavers and others to apply to the courts for possession orders will continue to be bad practice even if prima facie the clause allows such policies to recur. Proof of such arrangements

---

134 This is presumably the case, even though, unlike the 1985 Act, there is no specific addition to the section on intentional homelessness, enabling an authority to do so. See, however, s 176 (2).

135 Section 191(4).

136 Standing Committee G, Twentieth Sitting, col 768.

will also be a difficult problem for housing authorities, especially as the courts tend to believe that a finding of intentional homelessness is a last resort.[137]

Is the applicant threatened with homelessness intentionally?

10.38   If the applicant is threatened with homelessness and in priority need, the authority must then consider whether the applicant is threatened with home-lessness intentionally. The wording is similar to the intentional homelessness provision except that the tenses are changed and the causation part slightly modified. Exactly the same set of questions, therefore, need to be asked. The same additions to the 1985 Act apply as above.[138]

Applicant's right to a decision letter

10.39   The applicant is entitled to be notified of the authority's decision on their case.[139] If the applicant is subject to an adverse decision , the applicant is entitled to be told: (a) the reasons for the decision;[140] (b) the right to request a review of the decision;[141] and (c) the time within which a request for a review must be made.[142] In addition, where the authority intends to refer the applicant to another authority under the local connection provisions, the authority must inform the applicant of that intention.[143] This notification must be in writing and sent to the applicant or made available for a reasonable period at the authority's office for collection by the applicant.[144]

Whilst it remains unclear as to whether reasons are required to establish whether accommodation is suitable or not, it is clear that reasons are required to establish adverse decisions on whether an applicant is homeless, in priority need, and intentional homelessness.[145] In addition, applicants are entitled to be given reasons when the local authority is going to use the local connection provisions. Once reasons have been given, local authorities are not entitled to fundamentally alter them in judicial proceedings by way of affidavit evidence. However, in such proceedings, they are entitled to elucidate upon them.[146] Once

---

137 See, for example, *R v Brent LBC, ex parte Awua* (1994) 26 HLR 539, 549 per Henry LJ.
138 Section 196.
139 Section 185(3).
140 Ibid.
141 Section 185(5).
142 Ibid.
143 Section 185(4).
144 Section 165(6).
145 As to the scope of this duty to give reasons, see *R v Islington LBC, ex parte Hinds* (1996) 28 HLR 302.
146 *R v Westminster CC, ex parte Ermakov* (1995) *The Times*, 20 November.

a decision letter has been issued, local authorities are not entitled to reopen their enquiries.[147]

IV: Duties to applicants

Duties to applicants who are homeless, eligible for assistance, but not in priority need and not intentionally homeless

10.40   This duty comprises a duty to provide advice and such assistance as the authority considers appropriate in the circumstances in any attempts the applicant makes to secure accommodation.[148] Such advice and assistance could, for example, comprise the giving of a loan or grant to pay a rent deposit or bond.[149] This duty is *not* subject to the alternative accommodation provision.

Duties to applicants who are threatened with homelessness, eligible for assistance, but not in priority need

10.41   The same duties apply as above, except that authorities must assist in any attempts the applicant makes to ensure that accommodation does not cease to be available for occupation.[150]

Duties to applicants who are homeless, eligible for assistance, in priority need, but intentionally homeless

10.42   In addition to the duty to provide advice and assistance as above, the authority comes under a duty to secure that accommodation becomes available for the applicant (in the extended sense). This accommodation is only for such period as the authority considers will give the applicant a reasonable opportunity to secure other accommodation.[151] Unfortunately, the uncertainties as to when

---

147 *R v Lambeth LBC, ex parte Miah* (1995) 27 HLR 21; *R v Southwark LBC, ex parte Dagou* (1996) 28 HLR 72.
148 Section 190(3).
149 Section 180(2).
150 Section 195(5)(a).
151 Section 190(2).

this duty begins, have not been cleared up.[152] Such accommodation must be 'suitable'.[153]

Duties to applicants who are threatened with homelessness, eligible for assistance, in priority need, but threatened with homelessness intentionally

10.43   The duty is to provide the applicant with advice and such assistance as the authority considers appropriate in any attempts the applicant makes to secure that the accommodation currently held is not lost.[154] This more limited duty reflects the fact that, at this stage, the applicant has not lost the accommodation in which they are living at the time of the application.

Duties to applicants who are homeless, eligible for assistance, in priority need, and not intentionally homeless

10.44   The Act refers to the accommodation duties to such applicants as 'the main housing duty'.[155] However, before entering upon this obligation, (a) the local authority is entitled to make further enquiry as to whether it is entitled to refer the applicant to another authority; and (b) the authority is under a duty to consider whether suitable alternative accommodation is available in its district.

(a) Further enquiries: local connection

10.45   The authority has a discretion to make further enquiries as to whether the applicant has a *local connection* with that authority. If no local connection exists with that authority, but one does exist with another authority, then the first authority is entitled to refer the applicant to the second authority to be housed. The local connection provision was originally inserted in the homelessness legislation to meet the criticism that there would be an influx of people to desirable areas who required housing and to whom the authority owed duties.

---

152 For three different views, see *De Falco v Crawley BC* [1980] QB 460.
153 Section 210.
154 Section 195(5)(b).
155 Section 200(1)(b).

Local connection defined

10.46　A local connection arises in the following circumstances:

(i)　*Because he is, or in the past was, normally resident there, and that residence is or was of his own choice.*[156] The local connection provisions have been subject to a voluntary agreement between housing authorities for some time now and such arrangements will continue. The arrangement is annexed to the Code of Guidance.[157] It suggests that, for the residence category to operate, a person must have lived in the district for six months in the previous 12 months or not less than three years in the previous five-year period.[158]

(ii)　*Because he is employed there.*[159] This is usually taken to mean permanent employment, although this differs throughout the country.[160] One can imagine an area such as Westminster, where a significant number of people work but few reside, adopting a harsher interpretation.

(iii)　*Because of family associations.*[161] This has been the subject of two important recent cases. In *Khan*,[161a] the High Court held that 'What matters, at the end of the day, is not the relatives' connection with [the authority], but the duration and extent of the applicant's connection with [the authority] through their relatives formerly and now living in the [authority]'. In the second judgment, it was held that family associations also do not extend beyond parents, adult children, brothers or sisters. Cousins are not included. Furthermore, if a family association was too weak, it could not count as a 'special circumstance' under subparagraph (d).[162]

(iv)　*Because of special circumstances.*[163] This is something of a catch-all and its ambit is uncertain. It is clear that membership of a place of worship, such as a mosque or synagogue, in a particular area does not constitute a special circumstance.[164] However, if there was a religious denomination with only one place of worship, then this might fall within this subparagraph. Difficult questions arise where a person is receiving treatment in a particular hospital or outpatient service. In these circumstances, authorities should bear in

---

156 Section 199(1)(a).

157 Code of Guidance, Annex 2.

158 Code of Guidance, Annex 2, para 2.5(i). Apparently, 97 per cent of housing authorities accept this proposition: DoE, *Evaluation of the 1991 Homelessness Code of Guidance* (HMSO, 1996). However, rigid adherence to this criterion is unlawful. Authorities must consider all the circumstances of the applicant's case.

159 Section 199(1)(b). The Secretary of State retains an order-making power to specify circumstances in which a person is not to be treated as being employed in a particular area (s 199(5)(a)).

160 Code of Guidance, Annex 2, para 2.5(ii).

161 Section 199(1)(c).

161a *R v Slough BC, ex parte Khan* (1995) 27 HLR 492.

162 *R v Hammersmith and Fulham LBC, ex parte Avdic* (1996) *The Times*, 11 June.

163 Section 199(1)(d).

164 *R v Westminster CC, ex parte Benniche* (1996) *The Times*, 15 April.

mind the availability and quality of the treatment in the authority with which the applicant does have a local connection.

Each of these is disjunctive so that one (or more) of these categories on its own provides the local connection.[165] It is possible for an applicant to have a local connection with more than one authority. In such a case, the authorities cannot refer the obligation between them. Equally, it is possible for an applicant to have a local connection nowhere, in which case the authority to whom an application is made must accept the responsibility.[166]

Membership of the regular armed forces (including Queen Alexandra's Royal Naval Nursing Service) and those detained in an area (eg prisoners or those detained under Mental Health Act 1983 powers) have no local connection with the authority in which they are serving their time.[167] The Secretary of State retains an order-making power to add circumstances in which residence is not to be treated as of a person's choice.[168]

Using local connection to refer the applicant to another authority

10.47   The direct consequence of an authority's finding that an applicant has no local connection with it but does have such a connection with another authority, is that the first authority ('the notifying authority') may refer the applicant to that other authority ('the notified authority') as long as certain conditions are satisfied.[169] A referral can only be made if the applicant is homeless, in priority need, and not intentionally homeless.[170] Where a referral is made, the notified authority is under a duty to perform the duty.[171] Consequently, the Court of Appeal has held that 'good administration and comity between local authorities' require the notifying authority to take into account the housing conditions in both areas in order to consider whether 'the public interest' requires the notifying authority to perform the duty.[172] There is no need for the notifying authority to consider whether other suitable accommodation is available before making a referral.[173]

---

165 Authorities need to consider all categories in relation to each applicant (*R v Slough BC, ex parte Khan* (1995) 27 HLR 492).

166 No doubt, most such people would have been weeded out by this stage as a result of the eligibility sections.

167 Section 199(2)–(4).

168 Section 199(5)(b).

169 Section 198(1).

170 As the opening words of s 198 emphasise.

171 Disputes often arise between authorities as to the scope of the referral provision. Arbitration is the appropriate method of resolution of such disputes under the authorities' agreement. Research on such arbitrations can be found in R Thornton, 'Who Houses? Homelessness, Local Connection and Inter-Authority Referrals under Section 67 of the Housing Act 1985' [now section 198 of the 1996 Act] (1994) *Journal of Social Welfare and Family Law* 19.

172 *R v Newham LBC, ex parte Tower Hamlets LBC* [1992] 2 All ER 767, 783.

173 Section 198(1).

Conditions for referral

10.48 The notifying authority, before a referral is made, must ensure that the conditions for referral are met. These are that: (a) the applicant must have no local connection with the notifying authority; (b) the applicant must have a local connection with the receiving authority; and (c) the applicant (together with those that might reasonably be expected to reside with the applicant) will not run the risk of domestic violence in the receiving authority.[174]

In some areas, an authority might exercise its full housing duty to the applicant by placing the applicant in accommodation in a different authority. This is particularly true of some London boroughs which 'export' applicants in this way. If this happens, and the applicant then applies under Part VII to the nearest authority, then the conditions for referral are met as long as 'the previous application was within such period as may be prescribed of the present application'.[175] This wording leaves a lot to be desired but seems to give the Secretary of State the power to prescribe a time-limit.[176] The Housing Minister has said that he will consult authorities as to the length of this period and then introduce regulations.[177]

Running the risk of domestic violence

10.49 An applicant runs the risk of violence, or threats of violence which are likely to be carried out, from a person with whom they are associated (see above).[178] This is a significant change from the 1985 Act because it represents an attempt to bring each enquiry under Part VII into line so as to provide a consolidated definition of domestic violence.

Alternative dispute resolution

10.50 All disputes under this section are to be decided by agreement by the local authorities and the joint procedures provide for arbitration panels.[179]

Duties to applicant who is referred

10.51 A new, exhaustive section details the duties of the respective authorities to an applicant in the following circumstances:

---

174 Section 198(2).
175 Section 198(3)(b).
176 The subsection was amended at Report Stage in the House of Lords (HL Debs, Vol 574, col 129) 'for clarification'!
177 There is, as yet, no indication as to the length of this period: Standing Committee G, Twenty-First Sitting, 26 March 1996, col 811.
178 Section 198(3).
179 Section 198(5).

(i) *Notifying authority's duties.* Where the notifying authority informs[180] the applicant of its intention to make a referral in their case, all that authority's accommodation duties cease. However, the authority must continue to provide accommodation until the applicant is notified that the conditions for referral are satisfied.[181] The applicant is entitled to notification of the authority's decision as to whether the conditions have been met. In addition, the applicant must be notified of the right to request a review as well as the time within which the applicant may request a review of that decision.[182] If the authority decides that the conditions have not been met, then it is responsible for complying with the relevant duties.[183]

(ii) *Notified authority's duties.* Where the conditions for referral are met, the notified authority becomes subject to all the duties, including considering whether alternative accommodation is available in its area.[184]

Scotland

10.52   As the 1996 Act does not apply to Scotland, the above applies when applications are referred to and from Scottish authorities.[185]

(b) Further enquiries: suitable alternative accommodation

10.53   All authorities must ask themselves a preliminary question before they fulfil the main housing duty: is other suitable accommodation available for occupation by the applicant in the district?[186] If the answer to that question is affirmative, then the only duty incumbent upon the authority is to furnish the applicant with advice and such assistance as the authority considers is reasonably required to enable the applicant to secure such accommodation.[187] The accommodation duty completely ceases if the applicant does not take reasonable steps to secure the accommodation.[188] It is the authority's decision as to what constitutes 'reasonable steps'.

---

180 All notifications to the applicant under s 200 are required to be in writing and, if not received
  by the applicant, will be treated as being received if kept at the notifying authority's offices
  (s 200(6)).
181 Section 200(1).
182 Section 200(2). All duties cease on notification, even if the applicant requests a review,
  although there is power for their continuance (s 200(5)).
183 Section 200(3).
184 Section 200(4).
185 Section 201.
186 Section 197(1).
187 Section 197(2).
188 Section 197(3).

Considerable concern was expressed throughout the Parliamentary debates that local authorities could circumvent their housing duties by simply handing applicants, to whom such duties are owed, lists of accommodation agencies operating in the area or lists of available accommodation. Whilst the Government believes that applicants should have some responsibility for securing their own accommodation, it specifically amended the clause to ensure that the requisite advice and assistance did not fall below an appropriate level.[189] Whilst the list approach remains within the letter of the Act, it is not within its spirit. However, local authorities will be expected to have relationships with private landlords operating in their area. Finally, 'the duty must be interpreted actively, not merely in a "this is what we can get away with" sense'.[190] Guidance will be issued to make this plain and its operation will be monitored.

A further issue is that no time-limits are specified as to the duration of this suitable accommodation. Indeed, it could be argued that the minimum assured shorthold tenancy will be appropriate. It will, no doubt, be possible to argue that applicants, to whom the full housing duty is owed, must be guaranteed a minimum period of two years by way of parity with s 193 (which creates such a minimum period). However, those putting forward this argument will have to contend with the fact that s 193 is made expressly subject to this section. Furthermore, there is no time-limit given within the definition of 'suitability', although this word does imply that, for certain persons, an assured shorthold tenancy for, say, a minimum period will not be suitable.

Two further safeguards

10.54 In deciding the scope of its duty under this section as well as what constitutes 'reasonable steps', the authority must have regard to the characteristics and personal circumstances of the applicant, the state of the local housing market and the type of accommodation available.[191] For example, if the applicant requires adapted accommodation which is unavailable in the private sector, then the authority should not exercise its duty under this section. Secondly, accommodation is not available if the assistance required to secure it goes beyond what the authority considers is reasonable in the circumstances.[192]

(c) The main housing duty

10.55 Where the alternative accommodation provision is inoperable for some reason, local authorities come under a duty to provide suitable accommodation

---

189 HL Debs, Vol 574, col 94.
190 Standing Committee G, Twenty-First Sitting, cols 799–802.
191 Section 197(4).
192 Section 197(5).

for a minimum period of two years to applicants, who are homeless, in priority need, and not intentionally homeless.[193] There is a power to extend this in certain circumstances.[194]

Commencement of the main housing duty

10.56   The period begins with the date of: (a) the authority's notification of its decision, if the applicant was already occupying temporary accommodation; (b) notification that the conditions for referral under the local connection provisions were not met; (c) in all other cases, when the authority provides the accommodation.[195]

Cessation of the main housing duty

10.57   In the following circumstances, the full housing duty ceases to be owed to certain applicants, even though they may fulfil the criteria required.

(i)   Where a person has been offered suitable accommodation but turns it down after being told of the consequences of such a refusal. The authority must also notify the applicant that it regards itself as having discharged its duty to the applicant.[196] This puts into statutory form the policy of many authorities under the 1985 Act, which only made one offer of accommodation. The courts accepted that this policy was unchallengeable under the 1985 Act. Authorities wishing to make more than one offer may still continue to do so.

(ii)   Where an applicant, who has been informed of the possible consequences, refuses an offer of accommodation from the housing register before the end of the main housing duty. At that stage, the main housing duty will cease provided the authority is satisfied that the offer was suitable and it was reasonable for the applicant to accept it, and it notifies the applicant of this within 21 days.[197] Whether there is a substantial difference between 'reasonableness' on the one hand and 'suitability' on the other is open to doubt.[198] It will be unreasonable for the applicant to reject this offer even if the applicant has other accommodation obligations, which can be brought to an end by the time of the grant under Part VI.[199]

(iii)   If the applicant ceases to be eligible for assistance under Part VII, then the duty also ceases.[200]

---

193 Section 193(3).
194 Section 194.
195 Section 193(4).
196 Section 193(5).
197 Section 193(7).
198 See, for example, *R v Tower Hamlets LBC, ex parte Macwan* (1994) 26 HLR 528, 534.
199 Section 193(8).
200 Section 193(6)(a).

(iv) If the applicant becomes intentionally homeless from this accommodation, similarly no further duties are owed.[201] So, for example, if the applicant fails to pay the rent in this accommodation for no good reason, no further duties will be owed.

(v) If the applicant voluntarily ceases to occupy the property as his only or principal home, then the duties also cease.[202] The 'only or principal home' test is well known within the case-law on security of tenure and has a long history. There are two elements to consider: an intention to return to the property, and some physical sign that the applicant will return to it.[203]

(vi) When the applicant takes up accommodation offered under Part VI.[204]

It seems clear from these exceptions that the local authority will have a continuing duty to make enquiries, throughout the two-year period, in order to consider whether the applicant remains eligible.

Power to continue providing accommodation

10.58 There is a power for the local authority to continue providing accommodation, after the end of the two-year period, for further periods of two years at a time.[205] Towards the end[206] of the two-year period, the authority must conduct further enquiries appropriate to determine that the likely situation at the end of the two-year period will be that: (a) the applicant still has a priority need; (b) there is no other suitable accommodation available in their area; and (c) the applicant wishes the authority to continue to provide accommodation.[207] This will involve hypothetical enquiries by the local authority as to the 'likely situation'. Furthermore, the authority must satisfy itself that none of the events, which lead to the authority ceasing to come under the duty, has occurred (other than the applicant refusing a single offer of accommodation).[208]

If the authority does continue to provide accommodation, it may cease to do so at any time, as long as it notifies the applicant of the day on which it proposes to cease to provide the accommodation and the action it intends to take, if any.[209]

---

201 Section 193(6)(b).
202 Section 193(6)(c).
203 *Brown v Brash* [1948] 2 KB 247; *Crawley BC v Sawyer* (1988) 20 HLR 98.
204 Section 193(6)(d).
205 Section 194(1) and (2).
206 This date is unspecified.
207 Section 194(2).
208 Section 194(3).
209 Section 194(6). The day specified must be a certain period, to be prescribed, after the notice is given.

Duties to applicants who are threatened with homelessness, eligible for assistance, in priority need, and not threatened with homelessness intentionally

10.59   The duties are the same as above, except that the authority must also take all reasonable steps to ensure that the accommodation does not cease to be available for the applicant (except where the authority, by virtue of a contract, rule of law, or enactment is itself seeking possession of the applicant's property).[210]

Meaning of accommodation

10.60   In order to fulfil the main housing duty, the duty to provide interim accommodation pending enquiries, and the duty to provide accommodation to an intentionally homeless applicant, the accommodation provided must be suitable.[211] The Act prescribes a number of different accommodation sources that can be used: (a) the authority itself; (b) some other person; or (c) by providing advice and assistance to enable the applicant to secure such accommodation.[212] The latter does not include the provision of accommodation but local authorities must ensure that the applicant will be able to find and keep suitable accommodation. The Act also gives the authority power to make reasonable charges for the accommodation.[213]

Provision from authority's own stock

10.61   If the authority decides to provide accommodation itself, it may do so only for two in any three years, irrespective of the number of applications made by the applicant.[214] The aim of this provision 'is to preserve the principle of a single route into long-term social housing'.[215] There are two exceptions from this rule: (a) hostel accommodation;[216] and (b) accommodation leased to the authority.[217] The leased accommodation provision ties in with Sch 1, para 6 to the 1985 Act so that it will not be capable of becoming a secure tenancy. This

---

210 Section 195(2)–(4).
211 Section 206(1).
212 Ibid.
213 Section 206(2).
214 Section 207(1). Indeed, this also applies if a person with whom the applicant resides or might reasonably be expected to reside makes an application (s 207(3)).
215 HL Debs, Vol 574, col 133.
216 As defined in s 622 of the 1985 Act: '(a) residential accommodation otherwise than in separate and self-contained sets of premises, and (b) either board or facilities for the preparation of food adequate to the needs of those persons, or both'.
217 Section 207(1)(a) and (b).

accommodation is defined as: (a) accommodation leased for the purposes of providing temporary accommodation with vacant possession at the end of the term; (b) the lessor is not within the landlord condition for secure tenancies (1985 Act, s 80); and (c) the authority has no interest in the property except under the lease or by way of a mortgage.[218]

However, the Secretary of State may exclude or modify the two-in-three rule by direction if it appears that the authority will be unable reasonably to discharge its functions.[219] This direction only has effect as regards specified groups of applicants and only extends the period for one further year (so that it becomes a three-in-four-year rule).[220] Two possible examples of categories provided by the Secretary of State are large families or those requiring specially adapted housing.[221] If an authority frames its allocation scheme incorrectly, the Government has signalled its intention not to use the power to, so to speak, bail the authority out.[222] The authority is required to be proactive in that it must itself apply to the Secretary of State to make such a direction. However, any waiver may be subject to conditions, such as the authority reviewing its allocation priorities.[223]

Out-of-area placements

10.62 Authorities are exhorted by the Act to secure accommodation in their own areas, so far as reasonably practicable.[224] If they provide accommodation in another area, they must notify the local authority in that other area within 14 days of the provision of the accommodation, giving various information.[225]

Arrangements with private landlords

10.63 Where the applicant is housed with a private landlord,[226] any interim housing duty cannot create an assured tenancy for one year, unless the tenant is served with a notice stating that the tenancy is intended to be an assured shorthold or an assured tenancy other than an assured shorthold.[227]

Suitability

10.64 Accommodation provided or found by the authority must be suitable for the applicant. This is the local authority's decision but it must have regard to

---

218 Section 207(2).
219 Section 207(4).
220 Section 207(5).
221 HL Debs, Vol 574, col 134.
222 HL Debs, Vol 574, col 138.
223 Section 207(6); HL Debs, Vol 574, col 134.
224 Section 208(1).
225 Section 208(2)–(4).
226 Defined as a person not within s 80(1) of the 1985 Act (landlord condition).
227 Section 209(2).

Parts IX, X and XI of the 1985 Act (slum clearance; overcrowding; houses in multiple occupation).[228] A considerable volume of case-law has been generated as to what constitutes suitable accommodation, even though it is a decision for the local authority.

The following matters must be taken into consideration: suitability applies not only to the applicant but also to anyone who resides with, or might reasonably be expected to reside with, the applicant; all relevant information, including social and medical reports must be taken into consideration and form part of a composite assessment.[229] Leggatt LJ has suggested that '... suitability imports questions of fact and degree, and is dependent upon all the circumstances of the case, including the size, composition and health of the applicant's household, and the applicant's preferences as to area and type of accommodation, as well as the availability of housing and the pressures upon the local housing authority from competing applicants'.[230] To this, one can also add time-limits, subject of course to the new minimum period in the full housing duty.[231]

Reasons

10.65   Recent judicial decisions have also considered the scope of the reasons required to justify whether accommodation is suitable under the provisions of the 1985 Act.[232] In addition, there is a developing judicial trend to require some bodies to provide reasons for their decisions.[233] In *R v Kensington and Chelsea RBC, ex parte Grillo*, the Court of Appeal held that authorities were not required to give reasons as to whether accommodation provided was 'suitable'. Neill LJ said that '... the courts should be careful not to impose legal duties on housing authorities where Parliament has chosen not to do so unless the exceptional facts of a particular case justify the interference of a court'.[234] It seems that the addition of a right of review by the authority on questions of suitability will not place this in the category of an exceptional case.

Regulations and Guidance

10.66   The Secretary of State is given a wide order power to specify circumstances when accommodation is or is not suitable, as well as matters to be taken into account or disregarded in such an assessment.[235] The Government will not

---

228 Section 210(1).

229 *R v Brent LBC, ex parte Omar* (1991) 23 HLR 446; *R v Lewisham LBC, ex parte Dolan* (1993) 25 HLR 68.

230 *R v Brent LBC, ex parte Macwan* (1994) 26 HLR 528, 534.

231 *R v Brent LBC, ex parte Awua* (1994) 26 HLR 539. This part of the decision will remain important when considering the temporary accommodation granted to an intentionally homeless applicant.

232 1985 Act, s 64.

233 *R v Home Secretary, ex parte Doody* [1994] 1 AC 1.

234 (1996) 28 HLR 94, 106.

235 Section 210(2).

be too prescriptive in its use of this power because that 'could reduce the number of houses available for those families who are homeless or about to become homeless'.[236] Whilst, at the time of writing, the Government is unclear as to how this power should be exercised, it has indicated its willingness to consider general issues of affordability.[237] For example, property with a rent too high for a person on housing benefit will not be suitable and, if a person had to leave such a property, that person would not be intentionally homeless.

Guidance will also be more forthcoming on the issue of suitability than has been the case until now. The following are specific matters that the Government is committed to including in its Guidance: accommodation should, wherever possible and necessary, be within easy reach of schools; accommodation offered should not be a manifestly hard-to-let property;[238] it must meet the needs of disabled people (and the Government is committed to using its order-making power if authorities do not so provide);[239] authorities must take account of the state and fitness of repair of the property; whilst accommodation subject to a repair notice might be suitable in some circumstances, this will not be so in general;[240] authorities should co-operate with social services on questions of suitability to enable any care needs to be met.[241]

Challenging the decision of a local authority

Internal review

10.67 For the first time, the homelessness legislation provides aggrieved applicants with a right to have the decision reviewed by the authority. The following matters can be subject to a review:[242]

(a) the applicant's eligibility for assistance under ss 185–186;
(b) any decision as to what duty is owed under ss 190–193 and 195–197 (duties to persons found to be homeless or threatened with homelessness);[243]
(c) any decision by an authority to notify another authority of a referral of the applicant under s 198(1);
(d) any decision as to whether the local connection referral conditions are met under s 198(5);

---

236 HL Debs, Vol 573, col 874.
237 Ibid, cols 878–879.
238 Ibid, col 416.
239 Ibid, cols 825–826.
240 Ibid, col 875.
241 Ibid, col 875.
242 Section 202(1).
243 Sections 191 and 196 are the intentional homelessness provisions. As s 202(1) gives a right of review only as regards the duties owed by the authority, this does not appear to cover the substantive question of whether an applicant is threatened with homelessness intentionally or intentionally homeless.

(e)   any decision as to the duties owed to an applicant whose case is considered for referral or referred under the local connection provisions in s 200(3) or (4);

(f)   any issue as to the suitability of accommodation in paras (b) or (e) above.

The applicant is only entitled to one internal review, after which alternative means of redress must be sought.[244]

Procedure

10.68   The time-limit within which the applicant must exercise the right to have their case reviewed is within 21 days of notification of the decision.[245] On receipt of that request, the authority or authorities (where there is a local connection issue) must conduct the review.[246] No time-limits are specified within which the review must be conducted, although the Secretary of State retains the power to specify this in regulations.[247] The Secretary of State has taken power to specify the procedure which must be followed in enforceable regulations.[248] These regulations can require the review decision to be made by a person of appropriate seniority who was not involved in the original decision and the circumstances in which an oral hearing is required as well as issues of representation at the oral hearing.[249] The applicant is entitled to be informed of the decision of the review. Where the decision of the review body is adverse to the applicant, the applicant must be informed of the reasons for that decision.[250] The notification must also inform the applicant of the right to appeal to the county court on a point of law as well as the time within which such an appeal can be made (see para **10.69**).[251]

Although this is a major advance on the 1985 Act, the importance of this is, in fact, limited. The right is only to a review and not to an appeal. The difference is slight but significant. Additionally, it seems that there is no right to have a substantive decision on the 'key concepts' (homelessness, priority need, and intentional homelessness) reviewed.

Appeals to the county court

10.69   If the applicant is dissatisfied with the decision of the review or does not receive notification of that decision within the appropriate time, the applicant may appeal to the county court on a point of law.[252] The appeal must be brought

---

244 Section 202(4).
245 Section 181(3).
246 Section 202(4).
247 Section 203(7).
248 Section 203(1).
249 Section 203(2).
250 Section 203(3)–(4). Notification must be sent to the applicant and treated as if it has been received if then made available at the authority's office (s 203(8)).
251 Section 203(5). If these matters are not stated in the notice, the notice is deemed not to have been given (s 203(6)).
252 Section 204(1).

within 21 days of notification of the decision and the court can make an order confirming, quashing or varying the decision.[253] The authority is given a power to continue providing accommodation until the appeal is determined.[254]

What is a 'point of law'?

10.70 Although this is a term regularly used now in statutes, there is still no conclusive answer as to how to distinguish between a point of law and a point of fact. The leading textbook on administrative law makes the following point: 'The truth is, however, that there can hardly be a subject on which the courts act with such total lack of consistency as the difference between fact and law.'[255] This complexity is such that reference can only be made to other texts.[256]

Judicial review

10.71 All other issues are subject to judicial review proceedings.

Commission for Local Administration

10.72 The Commission for Local Administration – colloquially known as the Local Government Ombudsman – has shown itself willing to consider homelessness issues. The Commission considers whether an action or omission has caused maladministration due to injustice.

V: Other provisions

Protection of property

10.73 Where the authority has become subject to an accommodation duty towards an applicant[257] or is referring (or is considering referring) the applicant to another area under the local connection provisions, the authority may come under a duty to protect the possessions of the applicant (whether or not it is still subject to that duty).[258] If it has not become subject to any such duty, it retains a discretion to take any steps it considers reasonable for that purpose.[259]

---

253 Section 204(2) and (3).
254 Section 204(4).
255 H Wade and C Forsyth, *Administrative Law* 7th edn (Oxford, 1994), p 948.
256 Ibid, pp 946–952.
257 References to the applicant here relate also to any person who might reasonably be expected to reside with the applicant (ss 211(5) and 212(6)).
258 Section 211(2).
259 Section 211(3).

The duty arises where the authority has reason to believe that there is a danger of loss or damage to the applicant's personal property[260] because of the applicant's inability to protect or deal with it and no other suitable arrangements have been made.[261] The scope of the duty is to take reasonable steps to prevent the loss of the property or prevent or mitigate damage to it.[262] The authority retains a power to enter premises (subject to certain restrictions) and deal with the property in any way including storage.[263] In addition, it can refuse to take any action except upon conditions.[264] The applicant may request the authority to move the property to a nominated location. The authority may do this if it appears to it to be a reasonable request. When this is done, the authority ceases to be under any obligation.[265] Authorities which do not return the applicant's property on request, become insurers of it.[266]

The duty ends when there is no longer any danger of loss or damage, although the property may be kept in store after that point. The authority must notify the applicant that it has ceased to be subject to the duty or ceased to have power by delivering such notification to the applicant or by leaving or sending the notification to the applicant's last known address.[267]

Criminal liability

10.74 An applicant who makes certain statements 'knowingly or recklessly' which are false or knowingly withholds information reasonably required, is subject to criminal liability if they are intended to induce the authority to believe that the applicant is entitled to any of the duties under Part VII.[268] Furthermore, an authority must explain to the applicant, in language which the applicant is able to understand, that the applicant is under a duty to notify the authority of any change of circumstances. If the applicant does not do this, then, unless the explanation was not given or there is some other reasonable excuse, the applicant commits an offence.[269] These offences are subject to heavy fines at level 5 on the standard scale.[270]

---

260 It has been suggested that this duty does not extend to business equipment (*R v Chiltern DC, ex parte Roberts* (1990) 23 HLR 387).
261 The duty ceases if the authority have no reason to believe that these conditions are still in operation (s 212(3)).
262 Section 211(2).
263 Section 212(1).
264 Section 211(4).
265 Section 212(2).
266 *Mitchell v Ealing LBC* [1979] QB 1 (bailment at will ends at that point).
267 Section 212(4) and (5).
268 Section 214(1).
269 Section 214(2) and (3).
270 Section 214(4).

Co-operation with other authorities

10.75   Whilst the duty to make enquiries remains with the authority to which an application is made, that authority is entitled to call on other bodies for assistance.[271] These other bodies 'shall co-operate in rendering such assistance in the discharge of the functions to which the request relates as is reasonable in the circumstances'.[272] This is a very limited power because of the restrictions placed on it. Stronger powers under the Children Act 1989, s 27, have been held to impose no real justiciable obligations. The House of Lords suggested that 'Judicial review is not the way to obtain co-operation. The court cannot decide what form co-operation should take'.[273] Furthermore, as Hoffmann LJ remarked under the same provision in relation to a unitary authority 'You cannot ask yourself for help', so that this provision presumably has no effect between departments in such authorities.[274] Nevertheless, the corresponding provision in the 1985 Act was used, with some success, to refer applicants back to social security departments, which had referred them in the first place. This use is highly questionable.

Regulations and orders

10.76   The Secretary of State retains substantial regulatory powers, by way of Statutory Instrument.[275]

---

271 These other bodies are other housing authorities, a New Town Corporation, an RSL (under
   Part I of the Act), housing action trust, and other Scottish authorities.
272 Section 213(1).
273 *R v Northavon DC, ex parte Smith* [1994] 3 All ER 313, 320.
274 *R v Tower Hamlets LBC, ex parte Byas* [1993] 2 FLR 605.
275 Section 215.

PART VIII

CHAPTER 11

SUPPLEMENTARY PROVISIONS

Introduction

11.1 As is usual with most Acts of Parliament, the final Part contains miscellaneous, general and supplementary provisions. These provisions tie up loose ends and uncertainties in earlier legislation. In addition, they occasionally contain provisions which do not fit elsewhere but which attempt to provide solutions to unforeseen problems created by earlier legislation. This is their only coherence. These provisions are occasionally tremendously complex.

The 1996 Act is no exception. There are remedies for two particular problems in the text of the Act[1] – large service charges for those who bought leases from local authorities, and compulsory purchase powers of Crown land; and several in Sch 18 – broadly relating to housing management, housing finance, bringing housing law into line with family and matrimonial law, and other housing provisions. In addition, there is provision made for the administration of the Act within the Common Council of the City of London.

Service charges

11.2 Local authorities are empowered under earlier legislation to sell their accommodation to their tenants, with a discount depending upon how long the tenant has occupied the property. Some properties, particularly flats, were sold on long leaseholds with the local authority retaining the freehold together with general repairing obligations and the ability to reclaim their outlay through a service charge. The size of some of the service charges levied has been a cause of some concern and media publicity, particularly as some of the tenants were unaware at the time of their purchase of the repairs that the authority would undertake. In addition, local authorities often gain grants centrally for the work but are, nevertheless, forced to charge the leaseholders for the full cost of the work.

The solution to this problem is to give the Secretary of State power to give directions to social landlords[2] concerning service charges in respect of repairs, maintenance or improvement. A service charge is defined as an amount directly

---

1 Sections 219–221.

2 Defined as a local authority, New Town Corporation, Development Board for Rural Wales, Housing Corporation, a housing trust which is a charity, or an RSL (s 219(4)).

or indirectly payable by a tenant in relation to repairs, maintenance and improvement which varies according to the costs of the works.[3]

These directions require or permit the landlord to reduce or waive their service charge when relevant assistance[4] has been given by the Secretary of State or in such other circumstances as the Secretary of State specifies.[5] Any direction may relate to past service charges or works, although not for central assistance applied for before the date on which the direction was given.[6] The directions have a corresponding effect in relation to charges already demanded and paid so as to require their non-enforcement or a refund.[7]

Scope of the directions

11.3   The power is extremely wide, enabling the Secretary of State to make different provisions for different areas, landlords and properties.[8] They can specify the reduction or provide for its determination in a specified manner as well as any relevant criteria.[9] There is a duty to publish any direction in such manner as is appropriate to bring it to the attention of the landlords concerned.[10]

Secretary of State's intention

11.4   In the House of Commons Standing Committee, the Under Secretary of State made the following comment:

> 'We intend to issue directions as soon as possible after the primary legislation comes into force. They will give landlords discretion to reduce charges on categories of current and past schemes that have received specific additional assistance from the Government under estate action, city challenge and the single regeneration budget challenge fund. We also intend to issue directions that will require or allow landlords to reduce charges on schemes where specific additional funding is applied for. Again that will be from the date of the direction and for a variety of schemes. We will also issue directions that will give landlords the freedom to reduce charges on, for instance, particularly high-cost schemes, irrespective of whether they receive specific additional funding.
>
> The directions will set out the circumstances in which charges can be reduced. Charges might need to be above a certain level, although we would consider applications even where the circumstances are not met. We are also

---

3 Section 220(5). This includes overheads (s 220(7)).
4 Defined as a grant or other financial assistance, although the Secretary of State may further describe it in the direction as well as which properties are relevant (s 219(5)).
5 Section 219(1).
6 Section 219(2).
7 Section 219(3).
8 Section 220(1).
9 Section 220(2)–(3).
10 Section 220(4).

considering setting criteria that landlords should take into account in deciding whether and by how much to reduce charges.'[11]

Extension of compulsory purchase powers

11.5   Section 220 extends certain powers of compulsory purchase over interests in Crown land that are held otherwise than by the Crown, provided the requisite consent is granted.[12]

Housing management

Common Council of the City of London

11.6   The Council does not have the standard powers of a local authority and therefore required provision to set up committees of persons to regulate and manage their obligations under the Act. They are granted a discretionary power enabling them to do so subject to certain conditions.[13]

Tenant's choice repealed

11.7   Under the Housing Act 1988, Part IV, tenants of local authority properties were given the right to choose a different landlord. This was known as 'tenant's choice'. Since that time, just under 1,000 tenants have chosen a different landlord. That part of the legislation is therefore repealed.[14] The Housing Minister described tenant's choice as 'silly, ineffective, adversarial, lengthy and costly'.[15] This repeal extends to Scotland.[16]

Encouraging local authority tenants to move

11.8   Local housing authorities are given a discretion to make a payment to their tenants or licensees to assist or encourage them to move to other accommodation owned by them, any other local housing authority, or by an RSL.[17] The property occupied by the tenant must be within the authority's housing revenue account.[18]

---

11 Standing Committee G, Twenty-Sixth Sitting, cols 1064–5.

12 There are definitions of Crown land (s 221(3)) and as to whom or which body should give the consent (s 221(4)–(5)).

13 Section 224.

14 Schedule 18, para 1.

15 Standing Committee G, Twenty-Sixth Sitting, col 1041.

16 Section 231(4)(a).

17 Schedule 18, para 2.

18 See s 74(1) of the Local Government and Housing Act 1989. Such properties include all those allocated through the waiting list, for example.

These payments are meant to be made with a view to rationalising the use of the authority's own accommodation, for example by moving people from properties which are too large for them.

Further provision for consultation with tenants

11.9 Compulsory competitive tendering, a process by which local authorities are required to offer some of their services to tender, has been in operation for a number of years and is just being completed in relation to housing management. Although the private sector is able to tender, it appears that most tenders have been won 'in-house' (or, by the authority, itself). Whenever it is proposed to contract out the functions, local authorities are under a statutory duty to consult their tenants.[19] The 1996 Act corrects a potential anomaly so that the Secretary of State is entitled to make regulations ensuring that local authorities consult, or consider representations from, their tenants where the authority retains its housing management for itself.[20] Whilst the terms of the regulation-making power are wide, examples are provided in the new section of the width of the new power; that is, the regulations might cover the type of matters on which authorities are required to consult or consider tenants' representations as well as the method by which the authority is to undertake the consultation or consider the representations.[21]

Housing finance

Leaseholders and the housing revenue account

11.10 As suggested above, considerable concern had been aroused by the large amounts of service charges which local authorities charge long leaseholders of properties bought from the authorities. The 1996 Act makes further provision for this problem.[22] The Secretary of State is entitled to give directions to housing authorities as to the items or amounts which are to be regarded as referable to a property within the housing revenue account, where one or more has been sold and common parts remain in the ownership of the authority.[23] This might be regarded as authorised manipulation of accounts and will take effect from 1 April 1997.[24]

---

19 Housing Act 1985, ss 27A and 27AA.
20 Schedule 18, para 3(2), inserting s 27BA of the Housing Act 1985. Other provisions of the 1985 Act are amended to give effect to this inclusion (para 3(4) and (6)). Introductory tenants and secure tenants are given the same right to consultation (s 27BA(8)–(9)).
21 Section 27BA(2) and (3), respectively. Section 27BA(4)–(5) gives further examples although nothing is to affect the generality of the power (s 27BA(6)).
22 Schedule 18, para 4, inserting s 78A of the Local Government and Housing Act 1989.
23 Schedule 18, para 4(1).
24 Schedule 18, para 4(2).

Accounting for compulsory competitive tendering

11.11   There is provision clarifying the way in which authorities account for work for which they have successfully bid through compulsory competitive tendering.[25] This entitles the Secretary of State to issue directions ensuring that the authority debits the amount of the successful tender from the housing revenue account, as opposed to the actual amount spent, as well as crediting the account with any excess.[26] Once again, this has effect from 1 April 1997.

Final decisions on housing revenue account subsidy

11.12   Also inserted into the Local Government and Housing Act 1989 is provision to ensure that decisions of the Secretary of State, as regards Central Government subsidy for the authority's housing revenue account, are final once notified to the authority.[27] Not only is the Secretary of State's decision final, but also the new section provides that this determination cannot be questioned in any court of law.[28] Nevertheless, the courts will consider whether any determination is ultra vires (or, beyond the powers of the Secretary of State) because the determination was outside the jurisdiction of the Secretary of State or on a misconstruction by the Secretary of State of the jurisdiction.[29] Other powers of the Secretary of State in the new section are the ability, irrespective of other common law means (such as through the law of restitution) to recover overpayments with interest.[30] This new section applies to authorities in England from 1 April 1996 and to authorities in Wales by way of Statutory Instrument commencement.[31]

Payment of agricultural grant for agricultural housing

11.13   Schedule 15 to the 1985 Act enabled the Treasury to make grants in respect of agricultural housing. These small grants (approximately £10)[32] cost a large amount to process. These grants, on satisfaction of certain conditions, can now be made by local housing authorities.[33]

---

25 Schedule 18, para 4(1), inserting s 78B of the Local Government and Housing Act 1989.

26 Section 78B(2).

27 Schedule 18, para 5(1), inserting s 80A of the Local Government and Housing Act 1989.

28 Section 80A(2).

29 See *Anisminic Ltd v Foreign Compensation Commission* [1969] 2 AC 147; *Pearlman v Harrow School Governors* [1979] QB 56; *Re Racal Communications Ltd* [1981] AC 374.

30 Section 80A(4).

31 Schedule 18, para 5(2).

32 Their orginal derivation is from s 46 of the Housing (Financial Provisions) Act 1958, which may explain the small amount.

33 Schedule 18, para 6, amending Sch 15 to the 1985 Act.

Property orders in family and matrimonial proceedings

General

11.14 Throughout the debates on the 1996 Act, considerable concern was expressed that housing legislation had failed to take into account legislation relating to family law, such as the Matrimonial Causes Act 1973 (and its amendments); the Inheritance (Provision for Family and Dependants) Act 1975; the Matrimonial and Family Proceedings Act 1984; and the Children Act 1989. Part III of Sch 18 to the 1996 Act introduced by the Government at Report Stage in the House of Lords, is a complicated attempt to remedy this deficiency.

Specific

11.15 The following provisions (together with brief explanation) are amended to take into account parts of some or all of these Acts:

(i)   Housing Act 1985, s 39: exempted disposals from the right to buy;[34]

(ii)   Housing Act 1985, s 88(2): cases were secure tenant is a successor;[35]

(iii)   Housing Act 1985, s 89(3): succession to periodic tenancy;[36]

(iv)   Housing Act 1985, s 90(3): cases where term certain ceases to be secure;[37]

(v)   Housing Act 1985, s 91(3): cases where assignment of secure tenancy permitted;[38]

(vi)   Housing Act 1985, s 99B(2): persons qualifying for compensation for improvements;[39]

(vii)   Housing Act 1985, s 101(3): rent not to be increased on account of tenant's improvements;[40]

(viii) Housing Act 1985, s 160: disposals exempted from right to buy;[41]

(ix)   Housing Act 1985, s 171B(4)(b): extent of preserved right to buy for qualifying successors of tenant;[42]

(x)   Housing Act 1985, Sch 6A, para 1(2): disposals excluded from obligation to redeem landlord's share;[43]

---

34 Schedule 18, para 8.

35 Schedule 18, para 9.

36 Schedule 18, para 10. This enables the landlord to gain possession from the personal representatives of the secure tenant, where there is no successor. It mirrors provision made in s 133(3) in respect of introductory tenants.

37 Schedule 18, para 11.

38 Schedule 18, para 12.

39 Schedule 18, para 13.

40 Schedule 18, para 14.

41 Schedule 18, para 15.

42 Schedule 18, para 16.

43 Schedule 18, para 17.

(xi) Landlord and Tenant Act 1987, s 4(2): disposals excluded from right of first refusal;[44]

(xii) Housing Act 1988, Sch 11, para 4: disposals excluded from repayment of discount on disposal.[45]

Other housing provisions

Exercise of powers by Greater London authorities outside Greater London

11.16 Section 16 of the 1985 Act disallowed Greater London housing authorities the power to exercise their powers outside Greater London, unless the Secretary of State's consent had already been granted. This section is abolished.[46]

Resale of property bought under the right to buy

11.17 Section 133 of the Housing Act 1988 enabled the Secretary of State to give consent to any subsequent disposal of a property bought under the right to buy. This is widened so as to entitle the Secretary of State to give general or particular consent in relation to any original disposals prior to the coming into force of this paragraph.[47] It also narrows the consultation process required before the subsequent disposal.[48]

Abolition of requirement of Treasury consent in certain cases

11.18 The requirement to receive Treasury consent or approval to certain matters is abolished.[49]

Limits on duty to consult tenants on disposal of property to private sector landlord

11.19 Local housing authorities are required to consult their tenants before they dispose of any of their property to the private sector, subject to secure tenancies.[50] This requirement is excluded where the authority has acquired the property by compulsory purchase order, which states that the property is being

---

44 Schedule 18, para 18.

45 Schedule 18, para 19.

46 Schedule 18, para 20.

47 Schedule 18, para 21(2) and (3), inserting s 133(1A) and (2A) of the Housing Act 1988 respectively.

48 Schedule 18, para 21(4), inserting s 133(5A) of the Housing Act 1988.

49 Schedule 18, para 22. The Housing Minister commented that 'this is one of the rare occasions on which we are getting some freedom from Treasury constraints' (Standing Committee G, Twenty-Sixth Sitting, col 1038).

50 Housing Act 1985, s 106A.

acquired for disposal to an RSL, and it has been done within a year of the order.[51]

Clarification of compulsory purchase powers

11.20   Authorities may compulsorily purchase land[52] and the 1996 Act ensures that land includes 'facilities which serve a beneficial purpose in connection with the requirements of persons for whom housing accommodation is provided.'[53] The definition of a 'beneficial purpose' is left unclarified but includes, for example, conveniences such as toilets and possibly playgrounds.

Clarification of Housing Action Trusts' Powers

11.21   Under the Housing Act 1988, HATs were given certain powers.[54] It was unclear whether they could exercise their powers outside their designated areas. The 1988 Act is amended to allow HATs to achieve their objects or exercise their powers in their area, even if they benefit people outside that area or improve the social conditions or general environment outside their area.[55]

Extension of preserved right to buy

11.22   Where an authority transfers stock to a different sector, the tenant retains their right to buy the property (if it existed in the first place). This is known as the preserved right to buy.[56] The 1996 Act extends this right to those in whom the assured tenancy vested, such as a widowed spouse, even though their children had that right.[57]

Deregulation of local authority assistance with mortgages

11.23   The 1996 Act removes restrictions on the ability of local authorities to assist people in obtaining mortgages.[58]

---

51 Schedule 18, para 23, inserting s 106A(3) of the Housing Act 1985.
52 Housing Act 1985, s 17.
53 Schedule 18, para 24(1).
54 Section 63.
55 Schedule 18, para 25(1)(b), inserting s 63(2A) of the Housing Act 1988.
56 See ss 171A–H of the Housing Act 1985.
57 Schedule 18, para 26, as explained in Standing Committee G, Twenty-Sixth Sitting, col 1043.
58 Schedule 18, para 27, as explained in Standing Committee G, Twenty-Sixth Sitting, col 1044.
     See also DoE *Deregulating Local Government – The First Steps* (DoE, 1995).

APPENDIX

HOUSING ACT 1996
(1996 c. 52)

ARRANGEMENT OF SECTIONS

PART I
SOCIAL RENTED SECTOR

CHAPTER I
REGISTERED SOCIAL LANDLORDS

Registration

Regulation of registered social landlords

CHAPTER II
DISPOSAL OF LAND AND RELATED MATTERS

Power of registered social landlord to dispose of land

Control by Corporation of land transactions

CHAPTER V
MISCELLANEOUS AND GENERAL PROVISIONS

Housing complaints

Orders and determinations

Minor and consequential amendments

Interpretation

PART II
HOUSES IN MULTIPLE OCCUPATION

Registration schemes

PART III
LANDLORD AND TENANT

CHAPTER I
TENANTS' RIGHTS

Forfeiture

Service charges

Appointment of manager

Right of first refusal

General legal advice

PART IV
HOUSING BENEFIT AND RELATED MATTERS

PART V
CONDUCT OF TENANTS

CHAPTER I
INTRODUCTORY TENANCIES

General provisions

Proceedings for possession

Succession on death of tenant

Assignment

Repairs

Provision of information and consultation

CHAPTER II
REPOSSESSION, ETC.: SECURE AND ASSURED TENANCIES

Secure tenancies

Assured tenancies

CHAPTER III
INJUNCTIONS AGAINST ANTI-SOCIAL BEHAVIOUR

PART VI
ALLOCATION OF HOUSING ACCOMMODATION

Introductory

The housing register

PART VII
HOMELESSNESS

Homelessness and threatened homelessness

General functions in relation to homelessness or threatened homelessness

Application for assistance in case of homelessness or threatened homelessness

Eligibility for assistance

Interim duty to accommodate

Duties to persons found to be homeless or threatened with homelessness

PART VIII
MISCELLANEOUS AND GENERAL PROVISIONS

Miscellaneous

An Act to make provision about housing, including provision about the social rented sector, houses in multiple occupation, landlord and tenant matters, the administration of housing benefit, the conduct of tenants, the allocation of housing accommodation by local housing authorities and homelessness; and for connected purposes.   [24th July 1996]

PART I
SOCIAL RENTED SECTOR

CHAPTER I
REGISTERED SOCIAL LANDLORDS

Registration

1 The register of social landlords

(1) The Corporation shall maintain a register of social landlords which shall be open to inspection at all reasonable times at the head office of the Corporation.

(2) On the commencement of this section every housing association which immediately before commencement was registered in the register kept by the Corporation under Part I of the Housing Associations Act 1985 shall be registered as a social landlord.

2 Eligibility for registration

(1) A body is eligible for registration as a social landlord if it is—

(a) a registered charity which is a housing association,

(b) a society registered under the Industrial and Provident Societies Act 1965 which satisfies the conditions in subsection (2), or

(c) a company registered under the Companies Act 1985 which satisfies those conditions.

(2) The conditions are that the body is non-profit-making and is established for the purpose of, or has among its objects or powers, the provision, construction, improvement or management of—

(a) houses to be kept available for letting,

(b) houses for occupation by members of the body, where the rules of the body restrict membership to persons entitled or prospectively entitled (as tenants or otherwise) to occupy a house provided or managed by the body, or

(c) hostels,

and that any additional purposes or objects are among those specified in subsection (4).

(3) For the purposes of this section a body is non-profit-making if—

(a) it does not trade for profit, or

(b) its constitution or rules prohibit the issue of capital with interest or dividend exceeding the rate prescribed by the Treasury for the purposes of section 1(1)(b) of the Housing Associations Act 1985.

(4) The permissible additional purposes or objects are—

(a) providing land, amenities or services, or providing, constructing, repairing or improving buildings, for its residents, either exclusively or together with other persons;

(b) acquiring, or repairing and improving, or creating by the conversion of houses or other property, houses to be disposed of on sale, on lease or on shared ownership terms;

(c) constructing houses to be disposed of on shared ownership terms;

(d) managing houses held on leases or other lettings (not being houses within subsection (2)(a) or (b)) or blocks of flats;

(e) providing services of any description for owners or occupiers of houses in arranging or carrying out works of maintenance, repair or improvement, or encouraging or facilitating the carrying out of such works;

(f) encouraging and giving advice on the forming of housing associations or providing services for, and giving advice on the running of, such associations and other voluntary organisations concerned with housing, or matters connected with housing.

(5) A body is not ineligible for registration as a social landlord by reason only that its powers include power—

(a) to acquire commercial premises or businesses as an incidental part of a project or series of projects undertaken for purposes or objects falling within subsection (2) or (4);

(b) to repair, improve or convert commercial premises acquired as mentioned in paragraph (a) or to carry on for a limited period any business so acquired;

(c) to repair or improve houses, or buildings in which houses are situated, after a disposal of the houses by the body by way of sale or lease or on shared ownership terms.

(6) In this section—

'block of flats' means a building containing two or more flats which are held on leases or other lettings and which are occupied or intended to be occupied wholly or mainly for residential purposes;

'disposed of on shared ownership terms' means disposed of on a lease—

(a) granted on a payment of a premium calculated by reference to a percentage of the value of the house or of the cost of providing it, or

(b) under which the tenant (or his personal representatives) will or may be entitled to a sum calculated by reference directly or indirectly to the value of the house;

'letting' includes the grant of a licence to occupy;

'residents', in relation to a body, means persons occupying a house or hostel provided or managed by the body; and

'voluntary organisation' means an organisation whose activities are not carried on for profit.

(7) The Secretary of State may by order specify permissible purposes, objects or powers additional to those specified in subsections (4) and (5).

The order may (without prejudice to the inclusion of other incidental or supplementary provisions) contain such provision as the Secretary of State thinks fit with respect to the priority of mortgages entered into in pursuance of any additional purposes, objects or powers.

(8) An order under subsection (7) shall be made by statutory instrument which shall be subject to annulment in pursuance of a resolution of either House of Parliament.

3 Registration

(1) The Corporation may register as a social landlord any body which is eligible for such registration.

(2) An application for registration shall be made in such manner, and shall be accompanied by such fee (if any), as the Corporation may determine.

(3) As soon as may be after registering a body as a social landlord the Corporation shall give notice of the registration—

(a) in the case of a registered charity, to the Charity Commissioners,

(b) in the case of an industrial and provident society, to the appropriate registrar, and

(c) in the case of a company registered under the Companies Act 1985 (including such a company which is also a registered charity), to the registrar of companies,

who shall record the registration.

(4) A body which at any time is, or was, registered as a social landlord shall, for all purposes other than rectification of the register, be conclusively presumed to be, or to have been, at that time a body eligible for registration as a social landlord.

4 Removal from the register

(1) A body which has been registered as a social landlord shall not be removed from the register except in accordance with this section.

(2) If it appears to the Corporation that a body which is on the register of social landlords—

(a) is no longer a body eligible for such registration, or
(b) has ceased to exist or does not operate,

the Corporation shall, after giving the body at least 14 days' notice, remove it from the register.

(3) In the case of a body which appears to the Corporation to have ceased to exist or not to operate, notice under subsection (2) shall be deemed to be given to the body if it is served at the address last known to the Corporation to be the principal place of business of the body.

(4) A body which is registered as a social landlord may request the Corporation to remove it from the register and the Corporation may do so, subject to the following provisions.

(5) Before removing a body from the register of social landlords under subsection (4) the Corporation shall consult the local authorities in whose area the body operates; and the Corporation shall also inform those authorities of its decision.

(6) As soon as may be after removing a body from the register of social landlords the Corporation shall give notice of the removal—

(a) in the case of a registered charity, to the Charity Commissioners,
(b) in the case of an industrial and provident society, to the appropriate registrar, and
(c) in the case of a company registered under the Companies Act 1985 (including such a company which is also a registered charity), to the registrar of companies,

who shall record the removal.

5 Criteria for registration or removal from register

(1) The Corporation shall establish (and may from time to time vary) criteria which should be satisfied by a body seeking registration as a social landlord; and in deciding whether to register a body the Corporation shall have regard to whether those criteria are met.

(2) The Corporation shall establish (and may from time to time vary) criteria which should be satisfied where such a body seeks to be removed from the register of social landlords; and in deciding whether to remove a body from the register the Corporation shall have regard to whether those criteria are met.

(3) Before establishing or varying any such criteria the Corporation shall consult such bodies representative of registered social landlords, and such bodies representative of local authorities, as it thinks fit.

(4) The Corporation shall publish the criteria for registration and the criteria for removal from the register in such manner as the Corporation considers appropriate for bringing the criteria to the notice of bodies representative of registered social landlords and bodies representative of local authorities.

6 Appeal against decision on removal

(1) A body which is aggrieved by a decision of the Corporation—

    (a) not to register it as a social landlord, or

    (b) to remove or not to remove it from the register of social landlords,

may appeal against the decision to the High Court.

(2) If an appeal is brought against a decision relating to the removal of a body from the register, the Corporation shall not remove the body from the register until the appeal has been finally determined or is withdrawn.

(3) As soon as may be after an appeal is brought against a decision relating to the removal of a body from the register, the Corporation shall give notice of the appeal—

    (a) in the case of a registered charity, to the Charity Commissioners,

    (b) in the case of an industrial and provident society, to the appropriate registrar, and

    (c) in the case of a company registered under the Companies Act 1985 (including such a company which is also a registered charity), to the registrar of companies.

Regulation of registered social landlords

7 Regulation of registered social landlords

Schedule 1 has effect for the regulation of registered social landlords.

Part I relates to the control of payments to members and similar matters.

Part II relates to the constitution, change of rules, amalgamation or dissolution of a registered social landlord.

Part III relates to accounts and audit.

Part IV relates to inquiries into the affairs of a registered social landlord.

CHAPTER II
DISPOSAL OF LAND AND RELATED MATTERS

Power of registered social landlord to dispose of land

8 Power of registered social landlord to dispose of land

(1) A registered social landlord has power by virtue of this section and not otherwise to dispose, in such manner as it thinks fit, of land held by it.

(2) Section 39 of the Settled Land Act 1925 (disposal of land by trustees) does not apply to the disposal of land by a registered social landlord; and accordingly the disposal need not be for the best consideration in money that can reasonably be obtained.

Nothing in this subsection shall be taken to authorise any action on the part of a charity which would conflict with the trusts of the charity.

(3) This section has effect subject to section 9 (control by Corporation of land transactions).

Control by Corporation of land transactions

9 Consent required for disposal of land by registered social landlord

(1) The consent of the Corporation, given by order under the seal of the Corporation, is required for any disposal of land by a registered social landlord under section 8.

(2) The consent of the Corporation may be so given—

    (a) generally to all registered social landlords or to a particular landlord or description of landlords;

    (b) in relation to particular land or in relation to a particular description of land,

and may be given subject to conditions.

(3) Before giving any consent other than a consent in relation to a particular landlord or particular land, the Corporation shall consult such bodies representative of registered social landlords as it thinks fit.

(4) A disposal of a house by a registered social landlord made without the consent required by this section is void unless—

    (a) the disposal is to an individual (or to two or more individuals),

    (b) the disposal does not extend to any other house, and

    (c) the landlord reasonably believes that the individual or individuals intend to use the house as their principal dwelling.

(5) Any other disposal by a registered social landlord which requires consent under this section is valid in favour of a person claiming under the landlord notwithstanding that that consent has not been given; and a person dealing with a registered social landlord, or with a person claiming under such a landlord, shall not be concerned to see or inquire whether any such consent has been given.

(6) Where at the time of its removal from the register of social landlords a body owns land, this section continues to apply to that land after the removal as if the body concerned continued to be a registered social landlord.

(7) For the purposes of this section 'disposal' means sale, lease, mortgage, charge or any other disposition.

(8) This section has effect subject to section 10 (lettings and other disposals not requiring consent of Corporation).

10 Lettings and other disposals not requiring consent of Corporation

(1) A letting by a registered social landlord does not require consent under section 9 if it is—

    (a) a letting of land under an assured tenancy or an assured agricultural occupancy, or what would be an assured tenancy or an assured agricultural occupancy but for any of paragraphs 4 to 8, or paragraph 12(1)(h), of Schedule 1 to the Housing Act 1988, or

    (b) a letting of land under a secure tenancy or what would be a secure tenancy but for any of paragraphs 2 to 12 of Schedule 1 to the Housing Act 1985.

(2) Consent under section 9 is not required in the case of a disposal to which section 81 or 133 of the Housing Act 1988 applies (certain disposals for which the consent of the Secretary of State is required).

(3) Consent under section 9 is not required for a disposal under Part V of the Housing Act 1985 (the right to buy) or under the right conferred by section 16 below (the right to acquire).

11 Covenant for repayment of discount on disposal

(1) Where on a disposal of a house by a registered social landlord, in accordance with a consent given by the Corporation under section 9, a discount has been given to the purchaser, and the consent does not provide otherwise, the conveyance, grant or assignment shall contain a covenant binding on the purchaser and his successors in title to the following effect.

(2) The covenant shall be to pay to the landlord on demand, if within a period of three years there is a relevant disposal which is not an exempted disposal (but if there is more than one such disposal then only on the first of them), an amount equal to the discount reduced by one-third for each complete year which has elapsed after the conveyance, grant or assignment and before the further disposal.

(3) The liability that may arise under the covenant is a charge on the house, taking effect as if it had been created by deed expressed to be by way of legal mortgage.

(4) A charge taking effect by virtue of this section is a land charge for the purposes of section 59 of the Land Registration Act 1925 notwithstanding subsection (5) of that section (exclusion of mortgages), and subsection (2) of that section applies accordingly with respect to its protection and realisation.

(5) Where there is a relevant disposal which is an exempted disposal by virtue of section 15(4)(d) or (e) (compulsory disposal or disposal of yard, garden, etc.)—

    (a) the covenant required by this section is not binding on the person to whom the disposal is made or any successor in title of his, and

    (b) the covenant and the charge taking effect by virtue of this section ceases to apply in relation to the property disposed of.

12 Priority of charge for repayment of discount

(1) The charge taking effect by virtue of section 11 (charge for repayment of discount) has priority immediately after any legal charge securing an amount—

    (a) left outstanding by the purchaser, or

    (b) advanced to him by an approved lending institution for the purpose of enabling him to acquire the interest disposed of on the first disposal,

subject to the following provisions.

(2) An advance which is made for a purpose other than that mentioned in subsection (1)(b) and which is secured by a legal charge having priority to the charge taking effect by virtue of section 11, and any further advance which is so secured, shall rank in priority to that charge if, and only if, the registered social landlord by notice served on the institution concerned gives consent.

The landlord shall give consent if the purpose of the advance or further advance is an approved purpose.

(3) The registered social landlord may at any time by notice served on an approved lending institution postpone the charge taking effect by virtue of section 11 to an advance or further advance which—

(a) is made to the purchaser by that institution, and

(b) is secured by a legal charge not having priority to that charge;

and the landlord shall serve such a notice if the purpose of the advance or further advance is an approved purpose.

(4) The covenant required by section 11 does not, by virtue of its binding successors in title of the purchaser, bind a person exercising rights under a charge having priority over the charge taking effect by virtue of that section, or a person deriving title under him.

A provision of the conveyance, grant or assignment, or of a collateral agreement, is void in so far as it purports to authorise a forfeiture, or to impose a penalty or disability, in the event of any such person failing to comply with that covenant.

(5) In this section 'approved lending institution' means—

(a) a building society, bank, insurance company or friendly society,

(b) the Corporation, or

(c) any body specified, or of a class or description specified, in an order made under section 156 of the Housing Act 1985 (which makes corresponding provision in relation to disposals in pursuance of the right to buy).

(6) The following are 'approved purposes' for the purposes of this section—

(a) to enable the purchaser to defray, or to defray on his behalf, any of the following—

(i) the cost of any works to the house,

(ii) any service charge payable in respect of the house for works, whether or not to the house, and

(iii) any service charge or other amount payable in respect of the house for insurance, whether or not of the house, and

(b) to enable the purchaser to discharge, or to discharge on his behalf, any of the following—

(i) so much as is still outstanding of any advance or further advance which ranks in priority to the charge taking effect by virtue of section 11,

(ii) any arrears of interest on such an advance or further advance, and

(iii) any costs and expenses incurred in enforcing payment of any such interest, or repayment (in whole or in part) of any such advance or further advance.

In this subsection 'service charge' has the meaning given by section 621A of the Housing Act 1985.

(7) Where different parts of an advance or further advance are made for different purposes, each of those parts shall be regarded as a separate advance or further advance for the purposes of this section.

13 Restriction on disposal of houses in National Parks, etc.

(1) On the disposal by a registered social landlord, in accordance with a consent given by the Corporation under section 9, of a house situated in—

(a) a National Park,

(b) an area designated under section 87 of the National Parks and Access to the Countryside Act 1949 as an area of outstanding natural beauty, or

(c) an area designated as a rural area by order under section 157 of the Housing Act 1985, the conveyance, grant or assignment may (unless it contains a condition of a kind mentioned in section 33(2)(b) or (c) of the Housing Act 1985 (right of pre-emption or restriction on assignment)) contain a covenant to the following effect limiting the freedom of the purchaser (including any successor in title of his and any person deriving title under him or such a successor) to dispose of the house.

(2) The limitation is that until such time (if any) as may be notified in writing by the registered social landlord to the purchaser or a successor in title of his, there will be no relevant disposal which is not an exempted disposal without the written consent of the landlord.

(3) That consent shall not be withheld if the person to whom the disposal is made (or, if it is made to more than one person, at least one of them) has, throughout the period of three years immediately preceding the application for consent—

(a) had his place of work in a region designated by order under section 157(3) of the Housing Act 1985 which, or part of which, is comprised in the National Park or area concerned, or

(b) had his only or principal home in such a region,

or if he has had the one in part or parts of that period and the other in the remainder.

The region need not have been the same throughout the period.

(4) A disposal in breach of such a covenant as is mentioned above is void.

(5) The limitation imposed by such a covenant is a local land charge and, if the land is registered under the Land Registration Act 1925, the Chief Land Registrar shall enter the appropriate restriction on the register of title as if an application to that effect had been made under section 58 of that Act.

(6) In this section 'purchaser' means the person acquiring the interest disposed of by the first disposal.

(7) Where there is a relevant disposal which is an exempted disposal by virtue of section 15(4)(d) or (e) (compulsory disposal or disposal of yard, garden, etc.), any such covenant as is mentioned in this section ceases to apply in relation to the property disposed of.

14 Treatment of options

(1) For the purposes of sections 9 to 13 the grant of an option enabling a person to call for a relevant disposal which is not an exempted disposal shall be treated as such a disposal made to him.

(2) For the purposes of section 13(2) (requirement of consent to disposal of house in National Park, etc.) consent to such a grant shall be treated as consent to a disposal made in pursuance of the option.

15 Relevant and exempted disposals

(1) In sections 11 to 14 the expression 'relevant disposal which is not an exempted disposal' shall be construed as follows.

(2) A disposal, whether of the whole or part of the house, is a relevant disposal if it is—

(a) a conveyance of the freehold or an assignment of the lease, or

   (b) the grant of a lease or sub-lease (other than a mortgage term) for a term of more than 21 years otherwise than at a rack-rent.

(3) For the purposes of subsection (2)(b) it shall be assumed—

   (a) that any option to renew or extend a lease or sub-lease, whether or not forming part of a series of options, is exercised, and

   (b) that any option to terminate a lease or sub-lease is not exercised.

(4) A disposal is an exempted disposal if—

   (a) it is a disposal of the whole of the house and a conveyance of the freehold or an assignment of the lease and the person or each of the persons to whom it is made is a qualifying person (as defined in subsection (5));

   (b) it is a vesting of the whole of the house in a person taking under a will or on an intestacy;

   (c) it is a disposal of the whole of the house in pursuance of any such order as is mentioned in subsection (6);

   (d) it is a compulsory disposal (as defined in subsection (7));

   (e) the property disposed of is a yard, garden, outhouses or appurtenances belonging to a house or usually enjoyed with it.

(5) For the purposes of subsection (4)(a) a person is a qualifying person in relation to a disposal if—

   (a) he is the person or one of the persons by whom the disposal is made,

   (b) he is the spouse or a former spouse of that person or one of those persons, or

   (c) he is a member of the family of that person or one of those persons and has resided with him throughout the period of twelve months ending with the disposal.

(6) The orders referred to in subsection (4)(c) are orders under—

   (a) section 24 or 24A of the Matrimonial Causes Act 1973 (property adjustment orders or orders for the sale of property in connection with matrimonial proceedings);

   (b) section 2 of the Inheritance (Provision for Family and Dependants) Act 1975 (orders as to financial provision to be made from estate);

   (c) section 17 of the Matrimonial and Family Proceedings Act 1984 (property adjustment orders or orders for the sale of property after overseas divorce, etc.); or

   (d) paragraph 1 of Schedule 1 to the Children Act 1989 (orders for financial relief against parents).

(7) For the purposes of subsection (4)(d) a compulsory disposal is a disposal of property which is acquired compulsorily, or is acquired by a person who has made or would have made, or for whom another person has made or would have made, a compulsory purchase order authorising its compulsory purchase for the purposes for which it is acquired.

Right of tenant to acquire dwelling

16 Right of tenant to acquire dwelling

(1) A tenant of a registered social landlord has the right to acquire the dwelling of which he is a tenant if—

   (a) he is a tenant under an assured tenancy, other than an assured shorthold tenancy or a long tenancy, or under a secure tenancy,

(b) the dwelling was provided with public money and has remained in the social rented sector, and

(c) he satisfies any further qualifying conditions applicable under Part V of the Housing Act 1985 (the right to buy) as it applies in relation to the right conferred by this section.

(2) For this purpose a dwelling shall be regarded as provided with public money if—

(a) it was provided or acquired wholly or in part by means of a grant under section 18 (social housing grant),

(b) it was provided or acquired wholly or in part by applying or appropriating sums standing in the disposal proceeds fund of a registered social landlord (see section 25), or

(c) it was acquired by a registered social landlord after the commencement of this paragraph on a disposal by a public sector landlord at a time when it was capable of being let as a separate dwelling.

(3) A dwelling shall be regarded for the purposes of this section as having remained within the social rented sector if, since it was so provided or acquired—

(a) the person holding the freehold interest in the dwelling has been either a registered social landlord or a public sector landlord; and

(b) any person holding an interest as lessee (otherwise than as mortgagee) in the dwelling has been—

   (i) an individual holding otherwise than under a long tenancy; or

   (ii) a registered social landlord or a public sector landlord.

(4) A dwelling shall be regarded for the purposes of this section as provided by means of a grant under section 18 (social housing grant) if, and only if, the Corporation when making the grant notified the recipient that the dwelling was to be so regarded.

The Corporation shall before making the grant inform the applicant that it proposes to give such a notice and allow him an opportunity to withdraw his application within a specified time.

17 Right of tenant to acquire dwelling: supplementary provisions

(1) The Secretary of State may by order—

(a) specify the amount or rate of discount to be given on the exercise of the right conferred by section 16; and

(b) designate rural areas in relation to dwellings in which the right conferred by that section does not arise.

(2) The provisions of Part V of the Housing Act 1985 apply in relation to the right to acquire under section 16—

(a) subject to any order under subsection (1) above, and

(b) subject to such other exceptions, adaptations and other modifications as may be specified by regulations made by the Secretary of State.

(3) The regulations may provide—

(a) that the powers of the Secretary of State under sections 164 to 170 of that Act (powers to intervene, give directions or assist) do not apply,

(b) that paragraphs 1 and 3 (exceptions for charities and certain housing associations), and paragraph 11 (right of appeal to Secretary of State), of Schedule 5 to that Act do not apply,

(c) that the provisions of Part V of that Act relating to the right to acquire on rent to mortgage terms do not apply,

(d) that the provisions of that Part relating to restrictions on disposals in National Parks, etc. do not apply, and

(e) that the provisions of that Part relating to the preserved right to buy do not apply.

Nothing in this subsection affects the generality of the power conferred by subsection (2).

(4) The specified exceptions, adaptations and other modifications shall take the form of textual amendments of the provisions of Part V of that Act as they apply in relation to the right to buy under that Part; and the first regulations, and any subsequent consolidating regulations, shall set out the provisions of Part V as they so apply.

(5) An order or regulations under this section—

(a) may make different provision for different cases or classes of case including different areas, and

(b) may contain such incidental, supplementary and transitional provisions as the Secretary of State considers appropriate.

(6) Before making an order which would have the effect that an area ceased to be designated under subsection (1)(b), the Secretary of State shall consult—

(a) the local housing authority or authorities in whose district the area or any part of it is situated or, if the order is general in its effect, local housing authorities in general, and

(b) such bodies appearing to him to be representative of registered social landlords as he considers appropriate.

(7) An order or regulations under this section shall be made by statutory instrument which shall be subject to annulment in pursuance of a resolution of either House of Parliament.

CHAPTER III
GRANTS AND OTHER FINANCIAL MATTERS

Grants and other financial assistance

18 Social housing grants

(1) The Corporation may make grants to registered social landlords in respect of expenditure incurred or to be incurred by them in connection with their housing activities.

(2) The Corporation, acting in accordance with such principles as it may from time to time determine, shall specify in relation to grants under this section—

(a) the procedure to be followed in relation to applications for grant,

(b) the circumstances in which grant is or is not to be payable,

(c) the method for calculating, and any limitations on, the amount of grant, and

(d) the manner in which, and time or times at which, grant is to be paid.

(3) In making a grant under this section, the Corporation may provide that the grant is conditional on compliance by the landlord with such conditions as the Corporation may specify.

(4) The Corporation may, with the agreement of a local housing authority, appoint the authority to act as its agent in connection with the assessment and payment of grant under this section.

(5) The appointment shall be on such terms as the Corporation may, with the approval of the Secretary of State given with the consent of the Treasury, specify; and the authority shall act in accordance with those terms.

(6) Where—

    (a) a grant under this section is payable to a registered social landlord, and

    (b) at any time property to which the grant relates becomes vested in, or is leased for a term of years to, or reverts to, another registered social landlord, or trustees for another such landlord,

this section (including this subsection) shall have effect after that time as if the grant, or such proportion of it as is specified or determined under subsection (7), were payable to the other landlord.

(7) The proportion mentioned in subsection (6) is that which, in the circumstances of the particular case—

    (a) the Corporation, acting in accordance with such principles as it may from time to time determine, may specify as being appropriate, or

    (b) the Corporation may determine to be appropriate.

(8) Where one of the landlords mentioned in subsection (6) is registered by the Housing Corporation and another is registered by Housing for Wales, the determination mentioned in subsection (7) shall be such as shall be agreed between the two Corporations.

19 Land subject to housing management agreement

A registered social landlord is not entitled to a grant under section 18 (social housing grant) in respect of land comprised in a management agreement within the meaning of the Housing Act 1985 (see sections 27(2) and 27B(4) of that Act: delegation of housing management functions by certain authorities).

20 Purchase grant where right to acquire exercised

(1) The Corporation shall make grants to registered social landlords in respect of discounts given by them to persons exercising the right to acquire conferred by section 16.

(2) The amount of the grant for any year shall be the aggregate value of the discounts given in that year.

(3) The Corporation, acting in accordance with such principles as it may from time to time determine, shall specify in relation to grants under this section—

    (a) the procedure to be followed in relation to applications for grant,

(b) the manner in which, and time or times at which, grant is to be paid.

(4) In making a grant the Corporation may provide that the grant is conditional on compliance by the registered social landlord with such conditions as the Corporation may specify.

21 Purchase grant in respect of other disposals

(1) The Corporation may make grants to registered social landlords in respect of discounts on disposals by them of dwellings to tenants otherwise than in pursuance of the right conferred by section 16.

(2) The Corporation shall make such a grant if the tenant was entitled to exercise the right conferred by section 16 in relation to another dwelling of the landlord's.

The amount of the grant in such a case shall not exceed the amount of the discount to which the tenant would have been entitled in respect of the other dwelling.

(3) The Corporation, acting in accordance with such principles as it may from time to time determine, shall specify in relation to grants under this section—

  (a) the procedure to be followed in relation to applications for grant;
  (b) the circumstances in which grant is or is not to be payable;
  (c) the method for calculating, and any limitations on, the amount of grant; and
  (d) the manner in which, and time or times at which, grant is to be paid.

(4) In making a grant under this section, the Corporation may provide that the grant is conditional on compliance by the registered social landlord with such conditions as the Corporation may specify.

22 Assistance from local authorities

(1) A local authority may promote—

  (a) the formation of bodies to act as registered social landlords, and
  (b) the extension of the objects or activities of registered social landlords.

(2) A local authority may for the assistance of any registered social landlord subscribe for share or loan capital of the landlord.

(3) A local authority may for the assistance of a registered social landlord—

  (a) make grants or loans to the landlord, or
  (b) guarantee or join in guaranteeing the payment of the principal of, and interest on, money borrowed by the landlord (including money borrowed by the issue of loan capital) or of interest on share capital issued by the landlord.

(4) A local housing authority may sell or supply under a hire-purchase agreement furniture to the occupants of houses provided by a registered social landlord, and may buy furniture for that purpose.

In this subsection 'hire-purchase agreement' means a hire-purchase agreement or conditional sale agreement within the meaning of the Consumer Credit Act 1974.

23 Loans by Public Works Loans Commissioners

(1) The Public Works Loans Commissioners may lend money to a registered social landlord—

(a) for the purpose of constructing or improving, or facilitating or encouraging the construction or improvement, of dwellings,

(b) for the purchase of dwellings which the landlord desires to purchase with a view to their improvement, and

(c) for the purchase and development of land.

(2) A loan for any of those purposes, and interest on the loan, shall be secured by a mortgage of—

(a) the land in respect of which that purpose is to be carried out, and

(b) such other lands (if any) as may be offered as security for the loan;

and the money lent shall not exceed three-quarters (or, if the payment of the principal of, and interest on, the loan is guaranteed by a local authority, nine-tenths) of the value, to be ascertained to the satisfaction of the Public Works Commissioners, of the estate or interest in the land proposed to be so mortgaged.

(3) Loans may be made by instalments as the building of dwellings or other work on the land mortgaged under subsection (2) progresses (so, however, that the total amount lent does not at any time exceed the amount specified in that subsection); and a mortgage may accordingly be made to secure such loans to be so made.

(4) If the loan exceeds two-thirds of the value referred to in subsection (2), and is not guaranteed as to principal and interest by a local authority, the Public Works Loans Commissioners shall require, in addition to such a mortgage as is mentioned in that subsection, such further security as they think fit.

(5) Subject to subsection (6), the period for repayment of a loan under this section shall not exceed 40 years, and no money shall be lent on mortgage of any land unless the estate proposed to be mortgaged is either an estate in fee simple absolute in possession or an estate for a term of years absolute of which not less than 50 years are unexpired at the date of the loan.

(6) Where a loan under this section is made for the purpose of carrying out a scheme for the provision of houses approved by the Secretary of State, the maximum period for the repayment of the loan is 50 instead of 40 years, and money may be lent on the mortgage of an estate for a term of years absolute of which a period of not less than ten years in excess of the period fixed for the repayment of the sums advanced remains unexpired at the date of the loan.

Treatment of disposal proceeds

24 The disposal proceeds fund

(1) A registered social landlord shall show separately in its accounts for any period ending after the coming into force of this section its net disposal proceeds.

(2) The net disposal proceeds of a registered social landlord are—

(a) the net proceeds of sale received by it in respect of any disposal of land to a tenant—

    (i) in pursuance of the right conferred by section 16 (right of tenant to acquire dwelling), or

    (ii) in respect of which a grant was made under section 21 (purchase grant in respect of other disposals);

(b) payments of grant received by it under section 20 or 21 (purchase grant);

(c) where any such grant has been paid to it, any repayments of discount in respect of which the grant was given; and

(d) such other proceeds of sale or payments of grant (if any) as the Corporation may from time to time determine.

(3) The net proceeds of sale means the proceeds of sale less an amount calculated in accordance with a determination by the Corporation.

(4) The disposal proceeds shall be shown in a fund to be known as a disposal proceeds fund.

(5) The method of constituting the fund and showing it in the landlord's accounts shall be as required by determination of the Corporation under paragraph 16 of Schedule 1 (general requirements as to accounts).

(6) Interest shall be added to the fund in accordance with a determination made by the Corporation.

(7) Where this section applies in relation to the proceeds of sale arising on a disposal, section 27 below (recovery, etc. of social housing grants) and section 52 of the Housing Act 1988 (recovery, etc. of grants under that Act and earlier enactments) do not apply.

25 Application or appropriation of disposal proceeds

(1) The sums standing in the disposal proceeds account of a registered social landlord ('disposal proceeds') may only be applied or appropriated by it for such purposes and in such manner as the Corporation may determine.

(2) If any disposal proceeds are not applied or appropriated as mentioned in subsection (1) within such time as is specified by determination of the Corporation, the Corporation may direct that the whole or part of them shall be paid to it.

26 Disposal proceeds: power to require information

(1) The Corporation may give notice—

(a) to all registered social landlords,

(b) to registered social landlords of a particular description, or

(c) to particular registered social landlords,

requiring them to furnish it with such information as it may reasonably require in connection with the exercise of its functions under sections 24 and 25 (treatment of disposal proceeds).

(2) A notice under subsection (1)(a) or (b) may be given by publication in such manner as the Corporation considers appropriate for bringing it to the attention of the landlords concerned.

Recovery, etc. of social housing grants

27 Recovery, etc. of social housing grants

(1) Where a registered social landlord has received a grant under section 18 (social housing grant), the following powers are exercisable in such events as the Corporation may from time to time determine.

(2) The Corporation may, acting in accordance with such principles as it has determined—

(a) reduce any grant payable by it, or suspend or cancel any instalment of any such grant, or

(b) direct the registered social landlord to apply or appropriate for such purposes as the Corporation may specify, or to pay to the Corporation, such amount as the Corporation may specify.

(3) A direction by the Corporation under subsection (2)(b) may require the application, appropriation or payment of an amount with interest.

(4) Any such direction shall specify—

(a) the rate or rates of interest (whether fixed or variable) which is or are applicable,

(b) the date from which interest is payable, and

(c) any provision for suspended or reduced interest which is applicable.

The date from which interest is payable must not be earlier than the date of the event giving rise to the exercise of the Corporation's powers under this section.

(5) In subsection (4)(c)—

(a) provision for suspended interest means provision to the effect that if the principal amount is applied, appropriated or paid before a date specified in the direction, no interest will be payable for any period after the date of the direction; and

(b) provision for reduced interest means provision to the effect that if the principal amount is so applied, appropriated or paid, any interest payable will be payable at a rate or rates lower than the rate or rates which would otherwise be applicable.

(6) Where—

(a) a registered social landlord has received a payment in respect of a grant under section 18, and

(b) at any time property to which the grant relates becomes vested in, or is leased for a term of years to, or reverts to, some other registered social landlord,

this section (including this subsection) shall have effect in relation to periods after that time as if the grant, or such proportion of it as may be determined by the Corporation to be appropriate, had been made to that other registered social landlord.

(7) The matters specified in a direction under subsection (4)(a) to (c), and the proportion mentioned in subsection (6), shall be—

(a) such as the Corporation, acting in accordance with such principles as it may from time to time determine, may specify as being appropriate, or

(b) such as the Corporation may determine to be appropriate in the particular case.

Grants, etc. under earlier enactments

28 Grants under ss 50 to 55 of the Housing Act 1988

(1) No application for a grant under section 50 of the Housing Act 1988 (housing association grant) may be made after the commencement of this subsection.

(2) No application for a grant under section 51 of that Act (revenue deficit grant) may be made after the commencement of this subsection except by an association which had such

a deficit as is mentioned in that section for any of the years beginning 1st April 1994, 1st April 1995 or 1st April 1996.

(3) Section 52 of that Act (recovery, etc. of grants) is amended as follows—

 (a) in subsection (2)(c), for 'to pay to it' substitute 'to apply or appropriate for such purposes as the Corporation may specify, or to pay to the Corporation,';
 (b) in the closing words of subsection (2), for the words from 'requiring' to 'interest on that amount' substitute 'may require the application, appropriation or payment of an amount with interest';
 (c) in subsection (7), for the words from 'requiring' to 'to the Corporation' substitute 'requiring the application, appropriation or payment of an amount with interest';
 (d) in subsection (8)(a), for the words from 'the amount' to 'is paid' substitute 'the principal amount is applied, appropriated or paid';
 (e) in subsection (8)(b), for 'that amount is so paid' substitute 'the principal amount is so applied, appropriated or paid'.

(4) In section 53 of that Act (determinations by Corporation), for subsection (2) (requirement of approval of Secretary of State and, in the case of a general determination, consent of the Treasury) substitute—

'(2) The Corporation shall not make a general determination under the foregoing provisions of this Part except with the approval of the Secretary of State.'.

(5) In section 55(1) of that Act (surplus rental income: cases in which section applies), omit paragraph (a).

(6) Any reference in sections 50 to 55 of that Act to registration as a housing association shall be construed after the commencement of section 1 of this Act (the register of social landlords) as a reference to registration as a social landlord.

29 Commutation of payments of special residual subsidy

(1) The Secretary of State may, after consultation with a housing association, determine to commute any payments of special residual subsidy payable to the association under paragraph 2 of Part I of Schedule 5 to the Housing Associations Act 1985 for the financial year 1998–99 and subsequent years.

(2) Where the Secretary of State makes such a determination the payments of special residual subsidy payable to a housing association shall be commuted into a single sum calculated in such manner, and payable on such date, as the Secretary of State may consider appropriate.

(3) If after a commuted payment has been made to a housing association it appears to the Secretary of State that the payment was smaller or greater than it should have been, the Secretary of State may make a further payment to the association or require the association to repay to him such sum as he may direct.

(4) The Secretary of State may delegate to the Housing Corporation, to such extent and subject to such conditions as he may specify, any of his functions under this section and, where he does so, references to him in this section shall be construed accordingly.

CHAPTER IV
GENERAL POWERS OF THE CORPORATION

Information

30 General power to obtain information

(1) The Corporation may for any purpose connected with the discharge of any of its functions in relation to registered social landlords serve a notice on a person requiring him—

(a) to give to the Corporation, at a time and place and in the form and manner specified in the notice, such information relating to the affairs of a registered social landlord as may be specified or described in the notice, or

(b) to produce to the Corporation or a person authorised by the Corporation, at a time and place specified in the notice, any documents relating to the affairs of the registered social landlord which are specified or described in the notice and are in his custody or under his control.

(2) A notice under this section may be served on—

(a) a registered social landlord,

(b) any person who is, or has been, an officer, member, employee or agent of a registered social landlord,

(c) a subsidiary or associate of a registered social landlord,

(d) any person who is, or has been, an officer, member, employee or agent of a subsidiary or associate of a registered social landlord, or

(e) any other person whom the Corporation has reason to believe is or may be in possession of relevant information.

In this section 'agent' includes banker, solicitor and auditor.

(3) No notice shall be served on a person within paragraphs (b) to (e) of subsection (2) unless—

(a) a notice has been served on the registered social landlord and has not been complied with, or

(b) the Corporation believes that the information or documents in question are not in the possession of the landlord.

(4) Nothing in this section authorises the Corporation to require—

(a) the disclosure of anything which a person would be entitled to refuse to disclose on grounds of legal professional privilege in proceedings in the High Court, or

(b) the disclosure by a banker of anything in breach of any duty of confidentiality owed by him to a person other than a registered social landlord or a subsidiary or associate of a registered social landlord.

(5) A notice under this section shall be given under the seal of the Corporation.

(6) References in this section to a document are to anything in which information of any description is recorded; and in relation to a document in which information is recorded otherwise than in legible form, references to producing it are to producing it in legible form.

(7) Where by virtue of this section documents are produced to any person, he may take copies of or make extracts from them.

31 Enforcement of notice to provide information, etc.

(1) A person who without reasonable excuse fails to do anything required of him by a notice under section 30 commits an offence and is liable on summary conviction to a fine not exceeding level 5 on the standard scale.

(2) A person who intentionally alters, suppresses or destroys a document which he has been required by a notice under section 30 to produce commits an offence and is liable—

(a) on summary conviction, to a fine not exceeding the statutory maximum,

(b) on conviction on indictment, to a fine.

(3) Proceedings for an offence under subsection (1) or (2) may be brought only by or with the consent of the Corporation or the Director of Public Prosecutions.

(4) If a person makes default in complying with a notice under section 30, the High Court may, on the application of the Corporation, make such order as the court thinks fit for requiring the default to be made good.

Any such order may provide that all the costs or expenses of and incidental to the application shall be borne by the person in default or by any officers of a body who are responsible for its default.

32 Disclosure of information to the Corporation

(1) A body or person to whom this section applies may, subject to the following provisions, disclose to the Corporation, for the purpose of enabling the Corporation to discharge any of its functions relating to registered social landlords, any information received by that body or person under or for the purposes of any enactment.

(2) This section applies to the following bodies and persons—

(a) any government department (including a Northern Ireland department);

(b) any local authority;

(c) any constable; and

(d) any other body or person discharging functions of a public nature (including a body or person discharging regulatory functions in relation to any description of activities).

(3) This section has effect subject to any express restriction on disclosure imposed by or under any other enactment.

(4) Nothing in this section shall be construed as affecting any power of disclosure exercisable apart from this section.

33 Disclosure of information by the Corporation

(1) The Corporation may disclose to a body or person to whom this section applies any information received by it relating to a registered social landlord—

(a) for any purpose connected with the discharge of the functions of the Corporation in relation to such landlords, or

(b) for the purpose of enabling or assisting that body or person to discharge any of its or his functions.

(2) This section applies to the following bodies and persons—

(a) any government department (including a Northern Ireland department);

(b) any local authority;

(c) any constable; and

(d) any other body or person discharging functions of a public nature (including a body or person discharging regulatory functions in relation to any description of activities).

Paragraph (d) extends to any such body or person in a country or territory outside the United Kingdom.

(3) Where any information disclosed to the Corporation under section 32 is so disclosed subject to any express restriction on the further disclosure of the information, the Corporation's power of disclosure under this section is exercisable subject to that restriction.

A person who discloses information in contravention of any such restriction commits an offence and is liable on summary conviction to a fine not exceeding level 3 on the standard scale.

(4) Any information disclosed by the Corporation under this section may be subject by the Corporation to any express restriction on the further disclosure of the information.

(5) A person who discloses information in contravention of any such restriction commits an offence and is liable on summary conviction to a fine not exceeding level 3 on the standard scale.

Proceedings for such an offence may be brought only by or with the consent of the Corporation or the Director of Public Prosecutions.

(6) Nothing in this section shall be construed as affecting any power of disclosure exercisable apart from this section.

Standards of performance

34 Standards of performance

The Corporation may, after consultation with persons or bodies appearing to it to be representative of registered social landlords, from time to time—

(a) determine such standards of performance in connection with the provision of housing as, in its opinion, ought to be achieved by such landlords, and

(b) arrange for the publication, in such form and in such manner as it considers appropriate, of the standards so determined.

35 Information as to levels of performance

(1) The Corporation shall from time to time collect information as to the levels of performance achieved by registered social landlords in connection with the provision of housing.

(2) On or before such date in each year as may be specified in a direction given by the Corporation, each registered social landlord shall provide the Corporation, as respects each standard determined under section 34, with such information as to the level of performance achieved by him as may be so specified.

(3) A registered social landlord who without reasonable excuse fails to do anything required of him by a direction under subsection (2) commits an offence and is liable on summary conviction to a fine not exceeding level 5 on the standard scale.

Proceedings for such an offence may be brought only by or with the consent of the Corporation or the Director of Public Prosecutions.

(4) The Corporation shall at least once in every year arrange for the publication, in such form and in such manner as it considers appropriate, of such of the information collected by or provided to it under this section as appears to it expedient to give to tenants or potential tenants of registered social landlords.

(5) In arranging for the publication of any such information the Corporation shall have regard to the need for excluding, so far as that is practicable—

(a) any matter which relates to the affairs of an individual, where publication of that matter would or might, in the opinion of the Corporation, seriously and prejudicially affect the interests of that individual; and

(b) any matter which relates specifically to the affairs of a particular body of persons, whether corporate or unincorporate, where publication of that matter would or might, in the opinion of the Corporation, seriously and prejudicially affect the interests of that body.

Housing management

36 Issue of guidance by the Corporation

(1) The Corporation may issue guidance with respect to the management of housing accommodation by registered social landlords.

(2) Guidance under this section may, in particular, be issued with respect to—

(a) the housing demands for which provision should be made and the means of meeting those demands;

(b) the allocation of housing accommodation between individuals;

(c) the terms of tenancies and the principles upon which levels of rent should be determined;

(d) standards of maintenance and repair and the means of achieving those standards;

(e) the services to be provided to tenants;

(f) the procedures to be adopted to deal with complaints by tenants against a landlord;

(g) consultation and communication with tenants;

(h) the devolution to tenants of decisions concerning the management of housing accommodation.

(3) Before issuing any guidance under this section the Corporation shall—

(a) consult such bodies appearing to it to be representative of registered social landlords as it considers appropriate, and

(b) submit a draft of the proposed guidance to the Secretary of State for his approval.

(4) If the Secretary of State gives his approval to the draft submitted to him, the Corporation shall issue the guidance in such manner as the Corporation considers appropriate for bringing it to the notice of the landlords concerned.

(5) Guidance issued under this section may be revised or withdrawn; and subsections (3) and (4) apply in relation to the revision of guidance as in relation to its issue.

(6) Guidance under this section may make different provision in relation to different cases and, in particular, in relation to different areas, different descriptions of housing accommodation and different descriptions of registered social landlord.

(7) In considering whether action needs to be taken to secure the proper management of the affairs of a registered social landlord or whether there has been mismanagement, the Corporation may have regard (among other matters) to the extent to which any guidance under this section is being or has been followed.

37 Powers of entry

(1) This section applies where it appears to the Corporation that a registered social landlord may be failing to maintain or repair any premises in accordance with guidance issued under section 36.

(2) A person authorised by the Corporation may at any reasonable time, on giving not less than 28 days' notice of his intention to the landlord concerned, enter any such premises for the purpose of survey and examination.

(3) Where such notice is given to the landlord, the landlord shall give the occupier or occupiers of the premises not less than seven days' notice of the proposed survey and examination.

A landlord who fails to do so commits an offence and is liable on summary conviction to a fine not exceeding level 3 on the standard scale.

(4) Proceedings for an offence under subsection (3) may be brought only by or with the consent of the Corporation or the Director of Public Prosecutions.

(5) An authorisation for the purposes of this section shall be in writing stating the particular purpose or purposes for which the entry is authorised and shall, if so required, be produced for inspection by the occupier or anyone acting on his behalf.

(6) The Corporation shall give a copy of any survey carried out in exercise of the powers conferred by this section to the landlord concerned.

(7) The Corporation may require the landlord concerned to pay to it such amount as the Corporation may determine towards the costs of carrying out any survey under this section.

38 Penalty for obstruction of person exercising power of entry

(1) It is an offence for a registered social landlord or any of its officers or employees to obstruct a person authorised under section 37 (powers of entry) to enter premises in the performance of anything which he is authorised by that section to do.

(2) A person who commits such an offence is liable on summary conviction to a fine not exceeding level 3 on the standard scale.

(3) Proceedings for such an offence may be brought only by or with the consent of the Corporation or the Director of Public Prosecutions.

Insolvency, etc. of registered social landlord

39 Insolvency, etc. of registered social landlord: scheme of provisions

(1) The following sections make provision—

- (a) for notice to be given to the Corporation of any proposal to take certain steps in relation to a registered social landlord (section 40), and for further notice to be given when any such step is taken (section 41),
- (b) for a moratorium on the disposal of land, and certain other assets, held by the registered social landlord (sections 42 and 43),
- (c) for proposals by the Corporation as to the future ownership and management of the land held by the landlord (section 44), which are binding if agreed (section 45),
- (d) for the appointment of a manager to implement agreed proposals (section 46) and as to the powers of such a manager (sections 47 and 48),
- (e) for the giving of assistance by the Corporation (section 49), and
- (f) for application to the court to secure compliance with the agreed proposals (section 50).

(2) In those sections—

'disposal' means sale, lease, mortgage, charge or any other disposition, and includes the grant of an option;

'secured creditor' means a creditor who holds a mortgage or charge (including a floating charge) over land held by the landlord or any existing or future interest of the landlord in rents or other receipts from land; and

'security' means any mortgage, charge or other security.

(3) The Secretary of State may make provision by order defining for the purposes of those sections what is meant by a step to enforce security over land.

Any such order shall be made by statutory instrument which shall be subject to annulment in pursuance of a resolution of either House of Parliament.

40 Initial notice to be given to the Corporation

(1) Notice must be given to the Corporation before any of the steps mentioned below is taken in relation to a registered social landlord.

The person by whom the notice must be given is indicated in the second column.

(2) Where the registered social landlord is an industrial and provident society, the steps and the person by whom notice must be given are—

Any step to enforce any security over land held by the landlord.	The person proposing to take the step.
Presenting a petition for the winding up of the landlord.	The petitioner.
Passing a resolution for the winding up of the landlord.	The landlord.

(3) Where the registered social landlord is a company registered under the Companies Act 1985 (including a registered charity), the steps and the person by whom notice must be given are—

Any step to enforce any security over land held by the landlord.	The person proposing to take the step.
Applying for an administration order.	The applicant.
Presenting a petition for the winding up of the landlord.	The petitioner.
Passing a resolution for the winding up of the landlord.	The landlord.

(4) Where the registered social landlord is a registered charity (other than a company registered under the Companies Act 1985), the steps and the person by whom notice must be given are—

Any step to enforce any security over land held by the landlord.	The person proposing to take the step.

(5) Notice need not be given under this section in relation to a resolution for voluntary winding up where the consent of the Corporation is required (see paragraphs 12(4) and 13(6) of Schedule 1).

(6) Any step purportedly taken without the requisite notice being given under this section is ineffective.

41 Further notice to be given to the Corporation

(1) Notice must be given to the Corporation as soon as may be after any of the steps mentioned below is taken in relation to a registered social landlord.

The person by whom the notice must be given is indicated in the second column.

(2) Where the registered social landlord is an industrial and provident society, the steps and the person by whom notice must be given are—

The taking of a step to enforce any security over land held by the landlord.	The person taking the step.
The making of an order for the winding up of the landlord.	The petitioner.
The passing of a resolution for the winding up of the landlord.	The landlord.

(3) Where the registered social landlord is a company registered under the Companies Act 1985 (including a registered charity), the steps and the person by whom notice must be given are—

The taking of a step to enforce any security over land held by the landlord.	The person taking the step.
The making of an administration order.	The person who applied for the order.
The making of an order for the winding up of the landlord.	The petitioner.
The passing of a resolution for the winding up of the landlord.	The landlord.

(4) Where the registered social landlord is a registered charity (other than a company

registered under the Companies Act 1985), the steps and the person by whom notice must be given are—

The taking of a step to enforce any security over land held by the land-lord.	The person taking the step.

(5) Failure to give notice under this section does not affect the validity of any step taken; but the period of 28 days mentioned in section 43(1) (period after which moratorium on disposal of land, etc. ends) does not begin to run until any requisite notice has been given under this section.

42 Moratorium on disposal of land, etc.

(1) Where any of the steps mentioned in section 41 is taken in relation to a registered social landlord, there is a moratorium on the disposal of land held by the landlord.

(2) During the moratorium the consent of the Corporation under this section is required (except as mentioned below) for any disposal of land held by the landlord, whether by the landlord itself or any person having a power of disposal in relation to the land.

Consent under this section may be given in advance and may be given subject to conditions.

(3) Consent is not required under this section for any such disposal as is mentioned in section 10(1), (2) or (3) (lettings and other disposals not requiring consent under section 9).

(4) A disposal made without the consent required by this section is void.

(5) Nothing in this section prevents a liquidator from disclaiming any land held by the landlord as onerous property.

(6) The provisions of this section apply in relation to any existing or future interest of the landlord in rent or other receipts arising from land as they apply to an interest in land.

43 Period of moratorium

(1) The moratorium in consequence of the taking of any step as mentioned in section 41—

- (a) begins when the step is taken, and
- (b) ends at the end of the period of 28 days beginning with the day on which notice of its having been taken was given to the Corporation under that section,

subject to the following provisions.

(2) The taking of any further step as mentioned in section 41 at a time when a moratorium is already in force does not start a further moratorium or affect the duration of the existing one.

(3) A moratorium may be extended from time to time with the consent of all the landlord's secured creditors.

Notice of any such extension shall be given by the Corporation to—

- (a) the landlord, and
- (b) any liquidator, administrative receiver, receiver or administrator appointed in respect of the landlord or any land held by it.

(4) If during a moratorium the Corporation considers that the proper management of the landlord's land can be secured without making proposals under section 44 (proposals as to ownership and management of landlord's land), the Corporation may direct that the moratorium shall cease to have effect.

Before making any such direction the Corporation shall consult the person who took the step which brought about the moratorium.

(5) When a moratorium comes to an end, or ceases to have effect under subsection (4), the Corporation shall give notice of that fact to the landlord and the landlord's secured creditors.

(6) When a moratorium comes to an end (but not when it ceases to have effect under subsection (4)), the following provisions of this section apply.

The Corporation's notice shall, in such a case, inform the landlord and the landlord's secured creditors of the effect of those provisions.

(7) If any further step as mentioned in section 41 is taken within the period of three years after the end of the original period of the moratorium, the moratorium may be renewed with the consent of all the landlord's secured creditors (which may be given before or after the step is taken).

Notice of any such renewal shall be given by the Corporation to the persons to whom notice of an extension is required to be given under subsection (3).

(8) If a moratorium ends without any proposals being agreed, then, for a period of three years the taking of any further step as mentioned in section 41 does not start a further moratorium except with the consent of the landlord's secured creditors as mentioned in subsection (7) above.

44 Proposals as to ownership and management of landlord's land

(1) During the moratorium (see sections 42 and 43) the Corporation may make proposals as to the future ownership and management of the land held by the registered social landlord, designed to secure the continued proper management of the landlord's land by a registered social landlord.

(2) In drawing up its proposals the Corporation—

   (a) shall consult the landlord and, so far as is practicable, its tenants, and
   (b) shall have regard to the interests of all the landlord's creditors, both secured and unsecured.

(3) The Corporation shall also consult—

   (a) where the landlord is an industrial and provident society, the appropriate registrar, and
   (b) where the landlord is a registered charity, the Charity Commissioners.

(4) No proposals shall be made under which—

   (a) a preferential debt of the landlord is to be paid otherwise than in priority to debts which are not preferential debts, or
   (b) a preferential creditor is to be paid a smaller proportion of his preferential debt than another preferential creditor, except with the concurrence of the creditor concerned.

In this subsection references to preferential debts and preferential creditors have the same meaning as in the Insolvency Act 1986.

(5) So far as practicable no proposals shall be made which have the effect that unsecured creditors of the landlord are in a worse position than they would otherwise be.

(6) Where the landlord is a charity the proposals shall not require the landlord to act outside the terms of its trusts, and any disposal of housing accommodation occupied under a tenancy or licence from the landlord must be to another charity whose objects appear to the Corporation to be, as nearly as practicable, akin to those of the landlord.

(7) The Corporation shall serve a copy of its proposals on—

    (a) the landlord and its officers,

    (b) the secured creditors of the landlord, and

    (c) any liquidator, administrator, administrative receiver or receiver appointed in respect of the landlord or its land;

and it shall make such arrangements as it considers appropriate to see that the members, tenants and unsecured creditors of the landlord are informed of the proposals.

45 Effect of agreed proposals

(1) The following provisions apply if proposals made by the Corporation under section 44 are agreed, with or without modifications, by all the secured creditors of the registered social landlord.

(2) Once agreed the proposals are binding on the Corporation, the landlord, all the landlord's creditors (whether secured or unsecured) and any liquidator, administrator, administrative receiver or receiver appointed in respect of the landlord or its land.

(3) It is the duty of—

    (a) the members of the committee where the landlord is an industrial and provident society,

    (b) the directors where the landlord is a company registered under the Companies Act 1985 (including a company which is a registered charity), and

    (c) the trustees where the landlord is a charitable trust,

to co-operate in the implementation of the proposals.

This does not mean that they have to do anything contrary to any fiduciary or other duty owed by them.

(4) The Corporation shall serve a copy of the agreed proposals on—

    (a) the landlord and its officers,

    (b) the secured creditors of the landlord, and

    (c) any liquidator, administrator, administrative receiver or receiver appointed in respect of the landlord or its land, and

    (d) where the landlord is an industrial and provident society or registered charity, the appropriate registrar or the Charity Commissioners, as the case may be;

and it shall make such arrangements as it considers appropriate to see that the members, tenants and unsecured creditors of the landlord are informed of the proposals.

(5) The proposals may subsequently be amended with the consent of the Corporation and all the landlord's secured creditors.

Section 44(2) to (7) and subsections (2) to (4) above apply in relation to the amended proposals as in relation to the original proposals.

46 Appointment of manager to implement agreed proposals

(1) Where proposals agreed as mentioned in section 45 so provide, the Corporation may by order under its seal appoint a manager to implement the proposals or such of them as are specified in the order.

(2) If the landlord is a registered charity, the Corporation shall give notice to the Charity Commissioners of the appointment.

(3) Where proposals make provision for the appointment of a manager, they shall also provide for the payment of his reasonable remuneration and expenses.

(4) The Corporation may give the manager directions in relation to the carrying out of his functions.

(5) The manager may apply to the High Court for directions in relation to any particular matter arising in connection with the carrying out of his functions.

A direction of the court supersedes any direction of the Corporation in respect of the same matter.

(6) If a vacancy occurs by death, resignation or otherwise in the office of manager, the Corporation may by further order under its seal fill the vacancy.

47 Powers of the manager

(1) An order under section 46(1) shall confer on the manager power generally to do all such things as are necessary for carrying out his functions.

(2) The order may include the following specific powers—

1. Power to take possession of the land held by the landlord and for that purpose to take any legal proceedings which seem to him expedient.

2. Power to sell or otherwise dispose of the land by public auction or private contract.

3. Power to raise or borrow money and for that purpose to grant security over the land.

4. Power to appoint a solicitor or accountant or other professionally qualified person to assist him in the performance of his functions.

5. Power to bring or defend legal proceedings relating to the land in the name and on behalf of the landlord.

6. Power to refer to arbitration any question affecting the land.

7. Power to effect and maintain insurance in respect of the land.

8. Power where the landlord is a body corporate to use the seal of the body corporate for purposes relating to the land.

9. Power to do all acts and to execute in the name and on behalf of the landlord any deed, receipt or other document relating to the land.

10. Power to appoint an agent to do anything which he is unable to do for himself or which can more conveniently be done by an agent, and power to employ and dismiss any employees.

11. Power to do all such things (including the carrying out of works) as may be necessary in connection with the management or transfer of the land.

12. Power to make any payment which is necessary or incidental to the performance of his functions.

13. Power to carry on the business of the landlord so far as relating to the management or transfer of the land.

14. Power to grant or accept a surrender of a lease or tenancy of any of the land, and to take a lease or tenancy of any property required or convenient for the landlord's housing activities.

15. Power to make any arrangement or compromise on behalf of the landlord in relation to the management or transfer of the land.

16. Power to do all other things incidental to the exercise of any of the above powers.

(3) In carrying out his functions the manager acts as the landlord's agent and he is not personally liable on a contract which he enters into as manager.

(4) A person dealing with the manager in good faith and for value is not concerned to inquire whether the manager is acting within his powers.

(5) The manager shall, so far as practicable, consult the landlord's tenants about any exercise of his powers which is likely to affect them and inform them about any such exercise of his powers.

48 Powers of the manager: transfer of engagements

(1) An order under section 46(1) may, where the landlord is an industrial and provident society, give the manager power to make and execute on behalf of the society an instrument transferring the engagements of the society.

(2) Any such instrument has the same effect as a transfer of engagements under section 51 or 52 of the Industrial and Provident Societies Act 1965 (transfer of engagements by special resolution to another society or a company).

In particular, its effect is subject to section 54 of that Act (saving for rights of creditors).

(3) A copy of the instrument, signed by the manager, shall be sent to the appropriate registrar and registered by him; and until that copy is so registered the instrument shall not take effect.

(4) It is the duty of the manager to send a copy for registration within 14 days from the day on which the instrument is executed; but this does not invalidate registration after that time.

49 Assistance by the Corporation

(1) The Corporation may give such assistance as it thinks fit—

    (a) to the landlord, for the purpose of preserving the position pending the making of and agreement to proposals;

    (b) to the landlord or a manager appointed under section 46, for the purpose of carrying out any agreed proposals.

(2) The Corporation may, in particular—

    (a) lend staff;

    (b) pay or secure payment of the manager's reasonable remuneration and expenses;

    (c) give such financial assistance as appears to the Corporation to be appropriate.

(3) The following forms of assistance require the consent of the Secretary of State—

    (a) making grants or loans;

    (b) agreeing to indemnify the manager in respect of liabilities incurred or loss or damage sustained by him in connection with his functions;

    (c) paying or guaranteeing the repayment of the principal of, the payment of interest on and the discharge of any other financial obligation in connection with any sum borrowed (before or after the making of the order) and secured on any land disposed of.

50 Application to court to secure compliance with agreed proposals

(1) The landlord or any creditor of the landlord may apply to the High Court on the ground that an action of the manager appointed under section 46 is not in accordance with the agreed proposals.

On such an application the court may confirm, reverse or modify any act or decision of the manager, give him directions or make such other order as it thinks fit.

(2) The Corporation or any other person bound by agreed proposals may apply to the High Court on the ground that any action, or proposed action, by another person bound by the proposals is not in accordance with those proposals.

On such an application the court may—

    (a) declare any such action to be ineffective, and

    (b) grant such relief by way of injunction, damages or otherwise as appears to the court appropriate.

CHAPTER V

MISCELLANEOUS AND GENERAL PROVISIONS

Housing complaints

51 Schemes for investigation of complaints

(1) The provisions of Schedule 2 have effect for the purpose of enabling tenants and other individuals to have complaints against social landlords investigated by a housing ombudsman in accordance with a scheme approved by the Secretary of State.

(2) For the purposes of that Schedule a 'social landlord' means—

    (a) a registered social landlord;

    (b) a transferee of housing pursuant to a qualifying disposal under section 135 of the Leasehold Reform, Housing and Urban Development Act 1993;

    (c) a body which has acquired dwellings under Part IV of the Housing Act 1988 (change of landlord: secure tenants); or

    (d) any other body which was at any time registered with the Corporation and which owns or manages publicly-funded dwellings.

(3) In subsection (2)(d) a 'publicly-funded dwelling' means a dwelling which was—

  (a) provided by means of a grant under—
      section 18 of this Act (social housing grant), or
      section 50 of the Housing Act 1988, section 41 of the Housing Associations Act
      1985, or section 29 or 29A of the Housing Act 1974 (housing association grant);
      or

  (b) acquired on a disposal by a public sector landlord.

(4) The Secretary of State may by order add to or amend the descriptions of landlords who are to be treated as social landlords for the purposes of Schedule 2.

(5) Before making any such order the Secretary of State shall consult such persons as he considers appropriate.

(6) Any such order shall be made by statutory instrument which shall be subject to annulment in pursuance of a resolution of either House of Parliament.

Orders and determinations

52 General provisions as to orders

(1) The following provisions apply to any power of the Secretary of State under this Part to make an order.

(2) An order may make different provision for different cases or descriptions of case.

This includes power to make different provision for different bodies or descriptions of body, different provision for different housing activities and different provision for different areas.

(3) An order may contain such supplementary, incidental, consequential or transitional provisions and savings as the Secretary of State considers appropriate.

53 General provisions as to determinations

(1) The following provisions apply to determinations of the Corporation or the Secretary of State under this Part.

(2) A determination may make different provision for different cases or descriptions of case.

This includes power to make—

  (a) different provision for different registered social landlords or descriptions of
      registered social landlord, and
  (b) different provision for different housing activities and different provision for
      different areas;

and for the purposes of paragraph (b) descriptions may be framed by reference to any matters whatever, including in particular, in the case of housing activities, the manner in which they are financed.

(3) In this Part a general determination means a determination which does not relate solely to a particular case.

(4) Before making a general determination, the Corporation or the Secretary of State shall consult such bodies appearing to them to be representative of registered social landlords as they consider appropriate.

(5) After making a general determination, the Corporation or the Secretary of State shall publish the determination in such manner as they consider appropriate for bringing the determination to the notice of the landlords concerned.

54 Determinations of the Corporation requiring approval

The Corporation shall not make—

(a) a general determination under paragraph 16 of Schedule 1 (accounting and audit requirements for registered social landlords) or section 18 (social housing grant), or

(b) any determination under section 27 (recovery, etc. of social housing grants),

except with the approval of the Secretary of State.

Minor and consequential amendments

55 Minor and consequential amendments: Part I

(1) The enactments mentioned in Schedule 3 have effect with the minor amendments specified there.

(2) The Secretary of State may by order make such amendments or repeals of any enactment as appear to him necessary or expedient in consequence of the provisions of this Part.

(3) Any such order shall be made by statutory instrument which shall be subject to annulment in pursuance of a resolution of either House of Parliament.

Interpretation

56 Meaning of 'the Corporation'

(1) In this Part 'the Corporation' means the Housing Corporation or Housing for Wales, as follows.

(2) In relation to a registered social landlord, or a body applying for such registration, which is—

(a) a registered charity which has its address for the purposes of registration by the Charity Commissioners in Wales,

(b) an industrial and provident society which has its registered office for the purposes of the Industrial and Provident Societies Act 1965 in Wales, or

(c) a company registered under the Companies Act 1985 which has its registered office for the purposes of that Act in Wales,

'the Corporation' means Housing for Wales.

(3) In relation to any other registered social landlord or body applying for such registration, 'the Corporation' means the Housing Corporation.

(4) Nothing in this Part shall be construed as requiring the Housing Corporation and Housing for Wales to establish the same criteria for registration as a social landlord, or

otherwise to act on the same principles in respect of any matter in relation to which they have functions under this Part.

57 Definitions relating to industrial and provident societies

(1) In this Part, in relation to an industrial and provident society—

'appropriate registrar' has the same meaning as in the Industrial and Provident Societies Act 1965 (where it is defined in section 73(1)(c) by reference to the situation of the society's registered office);

'committee' means the committee of management or other directing body of the society; and

'co-opted member', in relation to the committee, includes any person co-opted to serve on the committee, whether he is a member of the society or not.

(2) Any reference in this Part to a member of the committee of an industrial and provident society includes a co-opted member.

58 Definitions relating to charities

(1) In this Part—

(a) 'charity' and 'trusts', in relation to a charity, have the same meaning as in the Charities Act 1993, and 'trustee' means a charitable trustee within the meaning of that Act; and

(b) 'registered charity' means a charity which is registered under section 3 of that Act and is not an exempt charity within the meaning of that Act.

(2) References in this Part to a company registered under the Companies Act 1985 do not include a company which is a registered charity, except where otherwise provided.

59 Meaning of 'officer' of registered social landlord

(1) References in this Part to an officer of a registered social landlord are—

(a) in the case of a registered charity which is not a company registered under the Companies Act 1985, to any trustee, secretary or treasurer of the charity;

(b) in the case of an industrial and provident society, to any officer of the society as defined in section 74 of the Industrial and Provident Societies Act 1965; and

(c) in the case of a company registered under the Companies Act 1985 (including such a company which is also a registered charity), to any director or other officer of the company within the meaning of that Act.

(2) Any such reference includes, in the case of an industrial and provident society, a co-opted member of the committee of the society.

60 Meaning of 'subsidiary'

(1) In this Part 'subsidiary', in relation to a registered social landlord, means a company with respect to which one of the following conditions is fulfilled—

(a) the landlord is a member of the company and controls the composition of the board of directors;

(b) the landlord holds more than half in nominal value of the company's equity share capital; or

(c) the company is a subsidiary, within the meaning of the Companies Act 1985 or the Friendly and Industrial and Provident Societies Act 1968, of another company which, by virtue of paragraph (a) or paragraph (b), is itself a subsidiary of the landlord.

(2) For the purposes of subsection (1)(a), the composition of a company's board of directors shall be deemed to be controlled by a registered social landlord if, but only if, the landlord, by the exercise of some power exercisable by him without the consent or concurrence of any other person, can appoint or remove the holders of all or a majority of the directorships.

(3) In relation to a company which is an industrial and provident society—

(a) any reference in this section to the board of directors is a reference to the committee of management of the society; and

(b) the reference in subsection (2) to the holders of all or a majority of the directorships is a reference—

(i) to all or a majority of the members of the committee, or

(ii) if the landlord is himself a member of the committee, such number as together with him would constitute a majority.

(4) In the case of a registered social landlord which is a body of trustees, references in this section to the landlord are to the trustees acting as such.

61 Meaning of 'associate'

(1) In this Part 'associate', in relation to a registered social landlord, means—

(a) any body of which the landlord is a subsidiary, and

(b) any other subsidiary of such a body.

(2) In this section 'subsidiary' has the same meaning as in the Companies Act 1985 or the Friendly and Industrial and Provident Societies Act 1968 or, in the case of a body which is itself a registered social landlord, has the meaning given by section 60.

62 Members of a person's family: Part I

(1) A person is a member of another's family within the meaning of this Part if—

(a) he is the spouse of that person, or he and that person live together as husband and wife, or

(b) he is that person's parent, grandparent, child, grandchild, brother, sister, uncle, aunt, nephew or niece.

(2) For the purpose of subsection (1)(b)—

(a) a relationship by marriage shall be treated as a relationship by blood,

(b) a relationship of the half-blood shall be treated as a relationship of the whole blood, and

(c) the stepchild of a person shall be treated as his child.

63 Minor definitions: Part I

(1) In this Part—

'dwelling' means a building or part of a building occupied or intended to be occupied as a separate dwelling, together with any yard, garden, outhouses and appurtenances belonging to it or usually enjoyed with it;

'fully mutual', in relation to a housing association, and 'co-operative housing association' have the same meaning as in the Housing Associations Act 1985 (see section 1(2) of that Act);

'hostel' means a building in which is provided for persons generally or for a class or classes of persons—

(a) residential accommodation otherwise than in separate and self-contained premises, and
(b) either board or facilities for the preparation of food adequate to the needs of those persons, or both;

'house' includes—

(a) any part of a building occupied or intended to be occupied as a separate dwelling, and
(b) any yard, garden, outhouses and appurtenances belonging to it or usually enjoyed with it;

'housing accommodation' includes flats, lodging-houses and hostels;

'housing activities' means, in relation to a registered social landlord, all its activities in pursuance of the purposes, objects and powers mentioned in or specified under section 2;

'information' includes accounts, estimates and returns;

'local authority' has the same meaning as in the Housing Associations Act 1985;

'long tenancy' has the same meaning as in Part V of the Housing Act 1985;

'modifications' includes additions, alterations and omissions and cognate expressions shall be construed accordingly;

'notice' means notice in writing;

'public sector landlord' means any of the authorities or bodies within section 80(1) of the Housing Act 1985 (the landlord condition for secure tenancies);

'registrar of companies' has the same meaning as in the Companies Act 1985;

'statutory tenancy' has the same meaning as in the Housing Act 1985.

(2) References in this Part to the provision of a dwelling or house include the provision of a dwelling or house—

(a) by erecting the dwelling or house, or converting a building into dwellings or a house, or

(b) by altering, enlarging, repairing or improving an existing dwelling or house;

and references to a dwelling or house provided by means of a grant or other financial assistance are to its being so provided directly or indirectly.

64 Index of defined expressions: Part I

The following Table shows provisions defining or otherwise explaining expressions used in this Part (other than provisions defining or explaining an expression used in the same section)—

appointed person (in relation to inquiry into affairs of registered social landlord)	paragraph 20 of Schedule 1
appropriate registrar (in relation to an industrial and provident society)	section 57(1)
associate (in relation to a registered social landlord)	section 61(1)
assured tenancy	section 230
assured agricultural occupancy	section 230
assured shorthold tenancy	section 230
charity	section 58(1)(a)
committee member (in relation to an industrial and provident society)	section 57(2)
company registered under the Companies Act 1985	section 58(2)
co-operative housing association	section 63
co-opted member (of committee of industrial and provident society)	section 57(1)
the Corporation	section 56
disposal proceeds fund	section 24
dwelling	section 63
enactment	section 230
fully mutual housing association	section 63
hostel	section 63
house	section 63
housing accommodation	section 63
housing activities	section 63
housing association	section 230
industrial and provident society	section 2(1)(b)
information	section 63
lease	section 229
local authority	section 63
long tenancy	section 63
member of family	section 62
modifications	section 63
notice	section 63
officer of registered social landlord	section 59

provision (in relation to dwelling or house)	section 63(2)
public sector landlord	section 63
register, registered and registration (in relation to social landlords)	section 1
registered charity	section 58(1)(b)
registrar of companies	section 63
relevant disposal which is not an exempted disposal (in sections 11 to 14)	section 15
secure tenancy	section 230
social housing grant	section 18(1)
statutory tenancy	section 63
subsidiary (in relation to a registered social landlord)	section 60(1)
trustee and trusts (in relation to a charity)	section 58(1)(a)

PART II
HOUSES IN MULTIPLE OCCUPATION

Registration schemes

65 Making and approval of registration schemes

(1) In Part XI of the Housing Act 1985 (houses in multiple occupation), for section 346 (registration schemes) substitute—

'346 Registration schemes

(1) A local housing authority may make a registration scheme authorising the authority to compile and maintain a register for their district of houses in multiple occupation.

(2) A registration scheme need not be for the whole of the authority's district and need not apply to every description of house in multiple occupation.

(3) A registration scheme may vary or revoke a previous registration scheme; and the local housing authority may at any time by order revoke a registration scheme.

346A Contents of registration scheme

(1) A registration scheme shall make it the duty of such person as may be specified by the scheme to register a house to which the scheme applies and to renew the registration as and when required by the scheme.

(2) A registration scheme shall provide that registration under the scheme—

    (a) shall be for a period of five years from the date of first registration, and

    (b) may on application be renewed, subject to such conditions as are specified in the scheme, for further periods of five years at a time.

(3) A registration scheme may—

    (a) specify the particulars to be inserted in the register,

    (b) make it the duty of such persons as may be specified by the scheme to give the authority as regards a house all or any of the particulars specified in the scheme,

    (c) make it the duty of such persons as may be specified by the scheme to notify the authority of any change which makes it necessary to alter the particulars inserted in the register as regards a house.

(4) A registration scheme shall, subject to subsection (5)—

    (a) require the payment on first registration of a reasonable fee of an amount determined by the local housing authority, and

    (b) require the payment on any renewal of registration of half the fee which would then have been payable on a first registration of the house.

(5) The Secretary of State may by order make provision as to the fee payable on registration—

    (a) specifying the maximum permissible fee (whether by specifying an amount or a method for calculating an amount), and

    (b) specifying cases in which no fee is payable.

(6) An order under subsection (5)—

    (a) may make different provision with respect to different cases or descriptions of case (including different provision for different areas), and

    (b) shall be made by statutory instrument which shall be subject to annulment in pursuance of a resolution of either House of Parliament.

346B Model schemes and confirmation of schemes

(1) The Secretary of State may prepare model registration schemes.

(2) Model registration schemes may be prepared with or without control provisions (see section 347) or special control provisions (see section 348B); and different model schemes may be prepared for different descriptions of authorities and for different areas.

(3) A registration scheme which conforms to a model scheme—

    (a) does not require confirmation by the Secretary of State, and

    (b) comes into force on such date (at least one month after the making of the scheme) as may be specified in the scheme.

(4) Any other registration scheme does not come into force unless and until confirmed by the Secretary of State.

(5) The Secretary of State may if he thinks fit confirm such a scheme with or without modifications.

(6) A scheme requiring confirmation shall not come into force before it has been confirmed but, subject to that, comes into force on such date as may be specified in the scheme or, if no date is specified, one month after it is confirmed.'.

(2) In section 351(1) of the Housing Act 1985 (proof of matters relating to registration scheme), in paragraph (c) at the beginning insert 'that the scheme did not require confirmation by the Secretary of State or'.

66 Registration schemes: control provisions

In Part XI of the Housing Act 1985 (houses in multiple occupation), for sections 347 and 348 (registration schemes: control provisions) substitute—

'347 Control provisions

(1) A registration scheme may contain control provisions, that is to say, provisions for preventing multiple occupation of a house unless—

- (a) the house is registered, and
- (b) the number of households or persons occupying it does not exceed the number registered for it.

(2) Control provisions may prohibit persons from permitting others to take up residence in a house or part of a house but shall not prohibit a person from taking up or remaining in residence in the house.

(3) Control provisions shall not prevent the occupation of a house by a greater number of households or persons than the number registered for it if all of those households or persons have been in occupation of the house without interruption since before the number was first registered.

348 Control provisions: decisions on applications and appeals

(1) Control provisions may enable the local housing authority, on an application for first registration of a house or a renewal or variation of registration—

- (a) to refuse the application on the ground that the house is unsuitable and incapable of being made suitable for such occupation as would be permitted if the application were granted;
- (b) to refuse the application on the ground that the person having control of the house or the person intended to be the person managing the house is not a fit and proper person;
- (c) to require as a condition of granting the application that such works as will make the house suitable for such occupation as would be permitted if the application were granted are executed within such time as the authority may determine;
- (d) to impose such conditions relating to the management of the house during the period of registration as the authority may determine.

(2) Control provisions shall provide that the local housing authority shall give an applicant a written statement of their reasons where they—

- (a) refuse to grant his application for first registration or for a renewal or variation of registration,
- (b) require the execution of works as a condition of granting such an application, or
- (c) impose conditions relating to the management of the house.

(3) Where the local housing authority—

- (a) notify an applicant that they refuse to grant his application for first registration or for the renewal or variation of a registration,
- (b) notify an applicant that they require the execution of works as a condition of granting such an application,

(c) notify an applicant that they intend to impose conditions relating to the management of the house, or

(d) do not within five weeks of receiving the application, or such longer period as may be agreed in writing between the authority and the applicant, register the house or vary or renew the registration in accordance with the application,

the applicant may, within 21 days of being so notified or of the end of the period mentioned in paragraph (d), or such longer period as the authority may in writing allow, appeal to the county court.

(4) On appeal the court may confirm, reverse or vary the decision of the authority.

(5) Where the decision of the authority was a refusal—

(a) to grant an application for first registration of a house, or

(b) for the renewal or variation of the registration,

the court may direct the authority to grant the application as made or as varied in such manner as the court may direct.

(6) For the purposes of subsections (4)and (5) an appeal under subsection (3)(d) shall be treated as an appeal against a decision of the authority to refuse the application.

(7) Where the decision of the authority was to impose conditions relating to the management of the house, the court may direct the authority to grant the application without imposing the conditions or to impose the conditions as varied in such manner as the court may direct.

348A Control provisions: other decisions and appeals

(1) Control provisions may enable the local housing authority at any time during a period of registration (whether or not an application has been made—

(a) to alter the number of households or persons for which a house is registered or revoke the registration on the ground that the house is unsuitable and incapable of being made suitable for such occupation as is permitted by virtue of the registration; or

(b) to alter the number of households or persons for which a house is registered or revoke the registration unless such works are executed within a specified time as will make the house in question suitable for such occupation as is permitted by virtue of the registration.

(2) Control provisions which confer on a local housing authority any such power as is mentioned in subsection (1) shall provide that the authority shall, in deciding whether to exercise the power, apply the same standards in relation to the circumstances existing at the time of the decision as were applied at the beginning of the period of registration.

(3) Control provisions may enable the local housing authority to revoke a registration if they consider that—

(a) the person having control of the house or the person managing it is not a fit and proper person, or

(b) there has been a breach of conditions relating to the management of the house.

(4) Control provisions shall also provide that the local housing authority shall—

(a) notify the person having control of a house and the person managing it of any decision by the authority to exercise a power mentioned in subsection (1) or (3) in relation to the house, and

(b) at the same time give them a written statement of the authority's reasons.

(5) A person who has been so notified may within 21 days of being so notified, or such longer period as the authority may in writing allow, appeal to the county court.

(6) On appeal the court may confirm, reverse or vary the decision of the authority.'.

67 Registration schemes: special control provisions

(1) In Part XI of the Housing Act 1985 (houses in multiple occupation), after section 348A (as inserted by section 66 above) insert—

'348B Special control provisions

(1) A registration scheme which contains control provisions may also contain special control provisions, that is, provisions for preventing houses in multiple occupation, by reason of their existence or the behaviour of their residents, from adversely affecting the amenity or character of the area in which they are situated.

(2) Special control provisions may provide for the refusal or revocation of registration, for reducing the number of households or persons for which a house is registered and for imposing conditions of registration.

(3) The conditions of registration may include conditions relating to the management of the house or the behaviour of its occupants.

(4) Special control provisions may authorise the revocation of registration in the case of—

(a) occupation of the house by more households or persons than the registration permits, or

(b) a breach of any condition imposed in pursuance of the special control provisions,

which is due to a relevant management failure.

(5) Special control provisions shall not authorise the refusal of—

(a) an application for first registration of a house which has been in operation as a house in multiple occupation since before the introduction by the local housing authority of a registration scheme with special control provisions, or

(b) any application for renewal of registration of a house previously registered under such a scheme,

unless there has been a relevant management failure.

(6) Special control provisions may provide that in any other case where an application is made for first registration of a house the local housing authority may take into account the number of houses in multiple occupation in the vicinity in deciding whether to permit or refuse registration.

348C Special control provisions: general provisions as to decisions and appeals

(1) Special control provisions shall provide that the local housing authority shall give a written statement of their reasons to the applicant where they refuse to grant his application for first registration, or for a renewal or variation of a registration, or impose conditions of registration on such an application.

(2) Special control provisions shall provide that the authority shall give written notice to the person having control of the house and the person managing it of any decision by the authority—

  (a) to vary the conditions of registration (otherwise than on an application to which subsection (1) applies), or
  (b) to revoke the registration of the house,

and at the same time give them a written statement of the authority's reasons.

(3) Where in accordance with special control provisions the local housing authority—

  (a) notify an applicant that they refuse to grant his application for first registration or for the renewal or variation of a registration,
  (b) notify such an applicant of the imposition of conditions of registration, or
  (c) give notice to the person having control or the person managing the house of any such decision as is mentioned in subsection (2),

that person may, within 21 days of being so notified, or such longer period as the authority may in writing allow, appeal to the county court.

(4) If on appeal it appears to the court—

  (a) that there has been any informality, defect or error in, or in connection with, the authority's decision, or
  (b) that the authority acted unreasonably,

the court may reverse or vary the decision of the authority.

(5) In so far as an appeal is based on the ground mentioned in subsection (4)(a), the court shall dismiss the appeal if it is satisfied that the informality, defect or error was not a material one.

(6) Where the decision of the authority was a refusal—

  (a) to grant an application for first registration of a house, or
  (b) for the renewal or variation of the registration,

the court may direct the authority to grant the application as made or as varied in such manner as the court may direct.

(7) Where the decision of the authority was to impose conditions of registration, the court may direct the authority to grant the application without imposing the conditions or to impose the conditions as varied in such manner as the court may direct.

348D Special control provisions: occupancy directions

(1) Special control provisions may provide that where the local housing authority decide that the registration of a house should be revoked the authority may direct that the level of occupation of the house be reduced, within such period of not less than 28 days as they may direct, to a level such that the registration scheme does not apply.

Such a direction is referred to in this Part as an "occupancy direction".

(2) Special control provisions shall provide that the authority shall only make an occupancy direction if it appears to the authority that there has been a relevant management failure resulting in a serious adverse effect on the amenity or character of the area in which the house is situated.

(3) In considering whether to make an occupancy direction the authority shall take into account the interests of the occupants of the house and the person having control of the house as well as the interests of local residents and businesses.

(4) Special control provisions may require the person having control of the house, and the person managing it, to take all reasonably practicable steps to comply with an occupancy direction.

(5) Nothing in Part I of the Housing Act 1988 prevents possession being obtained by any person in order to comply with an occupancy direction.

(6) Nothing in this section affects any liability in respect of any other contravention or failure to comply with control provisions or special control provisions.

348E Special control provisions: decisions and appeals relating to occupancy directions

(1) Special control provisions shall provide that where the local housing authority make an occupancy direction in respect of a house they shall give written notice of the direction to the person having control of the house and the person managing it and at the same time give them a written statement of the authority's reasons.

(2) A person aggrieved by an occupancy direction may, within 21 days after the date of the service of notice as mentioned in subsection (1), appeal to the county court.

(3) If on appeal it appears to the court—

>   (a)   that there has been any informality, defect or error in, or in connection with, the authority's decision, or
>   (b)   that the authority acted unreasonably,

the court may make such order either confirming, quashing or varying the notice as it thinks fit.

(4) In so far as an appeal is based on the ground mentioned in subsection (3)(a), the court shall dismiss the appeal if it is satisfied that the informality, defect or error was not a material one.

(5) If an appeal is brought the direction does not become operative until—

>   (a)   a decision on the appeal confirming the direction (with or without variation) is given and the period within which an appeal to the Court of Appeal may be brought expires without any such appeal having been brought, or
>   (b)   if a further appeal to the Court of Appeal is brought, a decision on that appeal is given confirming the direction (with or without variation).

(6) For this purpose the withdrawal of an appeal has the same effect as a decision confirming the direction or decision appealed against.

348F Special control provisions: "relevant management failure"

A "relevant management failure" for the purposes of sections 348B to 348E (special control provisions) means a failure on the part of the person having control of, or the person managing, a house in multiple occupation to take such steps as are reasonably practicable to prevent the existence of the house or the behaviour of its residents from adversely affecting the amenity or character of the area in which the house is situated, or to reduce any such adverse effect.'.

(2) In section 400 of the Housing Act 1985 (index of defined expressions: Part XI), at the appropriate places insert—

'occupancy direction (in connection with special control provisions)	section 348D
relevant management failure (for purposes of sections 348B to 348E)	section 348F
special control provisions	section 348B'.

68 Offences in connection with registration schemes

(1) In Part XI of the Housing Act 1985, after section 348F (as inserted by section 67 above) insert—

'348G Offences in connection with registration schemes

(1) A person who contravenes or fails to comply with a provision of a registration scheme commits an offence.

(2) A person who commits an offence under this section consisting of a contravention of so much of control provisions as relates—

    (a) to occupation to a greater extent than permitted under those provisions of a house which is not registered, or

    (b) to occupation of a house which is registered by more households or persons than the registration permits,

is liable on summary conviction to a fine not exceeding level 5 on the standard scale.

(3) A person who commits an offence under this section consisting of a contravention of so much of special control provisions as requires all reasonably practicable steps to be taken to comply with an occupancy direction is liable on summary conviction to a fine not exceeding level 5 on the standard scale.

(4) A person who commits any other offence under this section is liable on summary conviction to a fine not exceeding level 4 on the standard scale.'.

(2) In section 395(2) of the Housing Act 1985 (power of entry to ascertain if offence being committed), for 'section 346(6)' substitute 'section 348G'.

69 Information requirements in connection with registration schemes

(1) In Part XI of the Housing Act 1985 (houses in multiple occupation), for section 349 (steps required to inform public about registration schemes) substitute—

'349 Steps required to inform public about schemes

(1) Where a local housing authority intend to make a registration scheme which does not require confirmation by the Secretary of State, they shall publish notice of their intention at least one month before the scheme is made.

As soon as the scheme is made, the local housing authority shall publish a notice stating—

(a) that a registration scheme which does not require confirmation has been made, and

(b) the date on which the scheme is to come into force.

(2) Where a local housing authority intend to submit to the Secretary of State a registration scheme which requires his confirmation, they shall publish notice of their intention at least one month before the scheme is submitted.

As soon as the scheme is confirmed, the local housing authority shall publish a notice stating—

(a) that a registration scheme has been confirmed, and

(b) the date on which the scheme is to come into force.

(3) A notice under subsection (1) or (2) of the authority's intention to make a scheme or submit a scheme for confirmation shall—

(a) describe any steps which will have to be taken under the scheme by those concerned with registrable houses (other than steps which have only to be taken after a notice from the authority), and

(b) name a place where a copy of the scheme may be seen at all reasonable hours.

(4) After publication of notice under subsection (1) or (2) that a registration scheme has been made or confirmed, and for as long as the scheme is in force, the local housing authority—

(a) shall keep a copy of the scheme, and of the register, available for public inspection at the offices of the authority free of charge at all reasonable hours, and

(b) on request, and on payment of such reasonable fee as the authority may require, shall supply a copy of the scheme or the register, or of any entry in the register, to any person.

(5) If the local housing authority revoke a registration scheme by order they shall publish notice of the order.

(6) In this section "publish" means publish in one or more newspapers circulating in the district of the local housing authority concerned.'.

(2) In section 350(1) of the Housing Act 1985 (power to require information for purposes of scheme) for the words 'a person' substitute 'the person having control of the house or the person managing the house or any person'.

70 Existing registration schemes

(1) The amendments made by sections 65 to 69 do not apply to registration schemes in force immediately before the coming into force of those sections.

(2) The unamended provisions of Part XI of the Housing Act 1985 continue to apply to such schemes, subject as follows.

(3) Any such scheme may be revoked—

(a) by a new scheme complying with the provisions of that Part as amended, or

(b) by order of the local housing authority.

(4) If not so revoked any such scheme shall cease to have effect at the end of the period of two years beginning with the date on which the amendments come into force.

Other amendments of Part XI of the Housing Act 1985

71 Restriction on notices requiring execution of works

(1) In section 352 of the Housing Act 1985 (power to require execution of works to render premises fit for number of occupants), at end insert—

'(7) Where a local housing authority serve a notice under this section in respect of any of the requirements specified in subsection (1A), and the works specified in the notice are carried out, whether by the person on whom the notice was served or by the local housing authority under section 375, the authority shall not, within the period of five years from the service of the notice, serve another notice under this section in respect of the same requirement unless they consider that there has been a change of circumstances in relation to the premises.

(8) Such a change may, in particular, relate to the condition of the premises or the availability or use of the facilities mentioned in subsection (1A).'.

(2) The above amendment does not apply in relation to a notice served under section 352 of the Housing Act 1985 before this section comes into force.

72 Recovery of expenses of notice requiring execution of works

(1) After section 352 of the Housing Act 1985 insert—

'352A Recovery of expenses of notice under s 352

(1) A local housing authority may, as a means of recovering certain administrative and other expenses incurred by them in serving a notice under section 352, make such reasonable charge as they consider appropriate.

(2) The expenses are the expenses incurred in—

    (a) determining whether to serve a notice under that section,
    (b) identifying the works to be specified in the notice, and
    (c) serving the notice.

(3) The amount of the charge shall not exceed such amount as is specified by order of the Secretary of State.

(4) A charge under this section may be recovered by the authority from any person on whom the notice under section 352 is served.

(5) The provisions of Schedule 10 apply to the recovery by the authority of a charge under this section as they apply to the recovery of expenses incurred by the authority under section 375 (expenses of carrying out works required by notice).

(6) An order under this section—

    (a) may make different provision with respect to different cases or descriptions of case (including different provision for different areas), and

(b)   shall be made by statutory instrument which shall be subject to annulment in pursuance of a resolution of either House of Parliament.

(7) This section has effect subject to any order under section 353(6) (power of court on appeal against s 352 notice).'.

(2) In section 353 of that Act (appeal against notice under section 352), after subsection (5) insert—

'(6) Where the court allows an appeal under this section or makes an order under subsection (5), it may make such order as it thinks fit reducing, quashing or requiring the repayment of any charge under section 352A made in respect of the notice to which the appeal relates.'.

(3) The above amendments do not apply in relation to a notice served under section 352 of the Housing Act 1985 before this section comes into force.

73 Duty to keep premises fit for number of occupants

(1) After section 353 of the Housing Act 1985 insert—

'353A Duty to keep premises fit for number of occupants

(1) It is the duty of the person having control of a house in multiple occupation, and of the person managing it, to take such steps as are reasonably practicable to prevent the occurrence of a state of affairs calling for the service of a notice or further notice under section 352 (notice requiring execution of works to render house fit for number of occupants).

(2) A breach of that duty is actionable in damages at the suit of any tenant or other occupant of the premises, or any other person who suffers loss, damage or personal injury in consequence of the breach.

(3) A person who fails to comply with the duty imposed on him by subsection (1) commits a summary offence and is liable on conviction to a fine not exceeding level 5 on the standard scale.'.

(2) In section 395(2) of the Housing Act 1985 (power of entry to ascertain whether offence being committed), after the entry for section 346(6) insert—

'section 353A (failure to keep premises fit for number of occupants),'.

74 Section 354 direction to be local land charge

In section 354 of the Housing Act 1985 (power to limit number of occupants of house), at the end insert—

'(8) A direction under this section is a local land charge.'.

75 Means of escape from fire

(1) Section 365 of the Housing Act 1985 (means of escape from fire: general provisions as to exercise of powers) is amended as follows.

(2) In subsection (1)(b) (ground for exercise of additional powers) after 'paragraph (d)' insert 'or (e)'.

(3) For subsection (3) (consultation requirements) substitute—

'(3) The local housing authority shall consult with the fire authority concerned before exercising any of the powers mentioned in subsection (2)—

(a) where they are under a duty to exercise those powers, or
(b) where they are not under such a duty but may exercise those powers and the house is of such description or is occupied in such manner as the Secretary of State may specify by order for the purposes of this subsection.'.

(4) In subsection (4) (orders) for 'or (2A)' substitute ', (2A) or (3)'.

(5) In subsection (5) (other powers unaffected) omit 'and (e)'.

76 Works notices: improvement of enforcement procedures

After section 377 of the Housing Act 1985 insert—

'377A Works notices: improvement of enforcement procedures

(1) The Secretary of State may by order provide that a local housing authority shall act as specified in the order before serving a works notice.

In this section a "works notice" means a notice under section 352 or 372 (notices requiring the execution of works).

(2) An order under this section may provide that the authority—

(a) shall as soon as practicable give to the person on whom the works notice is to be served a written notice which satisfies the requirements of subsection (3); and
(b) shall not serve the works notice until after the end of such period beginning with the giving of a notice which satisfies the requirements of subsection (3) as may be determined by or under the order.

(3) A notice satisfies the requirements of this subsection if it—

(a) states the works which in the authority's opinion should be undertaken, and explains why and within what period;
(b) explains the grounds on which it appears to the authority that the works notice might be served;
(c) states the type of works notice which is to be served, the consequences of serving it and whether there is a right to make representations before, or a right of appeal against, the serving of it.

(4) An order under this section may also provide that, before the authority serves the works notice on any person, they—

(a) shall give to that person a written notice stating—
   (i) that they are considering serving the works notice and the reasons why they are considering serving the notice; and
   (ii) that the person may, within a period specified in the written notice, make written representations to them or, if the person so requests, make oral representations to them in the presence of a person determined by or under the order; and

(b) shall consider any representations which are duly made and not withdrawn.

(5) An order under this section may in particular—

    (a) make provision as to the consequences of any failure to comply with a provision made by the order;

    (b) contain such consequential, incidental, supplementary or transitional provisions and savings as the Secretary of State considers appropriate (including provisions modifying enactments relating to the periods within which proceedings must be brought).

(6) An order under this section—

    (a) may make different provision with respect to different cases or descriptions of case (including different provision for different areas), and

    (b) shall be made by statutory instrument which shall be subject to annulment in pursuance of a resolution of either House of Parliament.

(7) Nothing in any order under this section shall—

    (a) preclude a local housing authority from serving a works notice on any person, or from requiring any person to take immediate remedial action to avoid a works notice being served on him, in any case where it appears to them to be necessary to serve such a notice or impose such a requirement; or

    (b) require such an authority to disclose any information the disclosure of which would be contrary to the public interest.'.

77 Codes of practice

After section 395 of the Housing Act 1985 insert—

'395A Codes of practice

(1) The Secretary of State may by order—

    (a) approve any code of practice (whether prepared by him or another person) which, in his opinion, gives suitable guidance to any person in relation to any matter arising under this Part;

    (b) approve any modification of such a code; or

    (c) withdraw such a code or modification.

(2) The Secretary of State shall only approve a code of practice or a modification of a code if he is satisfied that—

    (a) the code or modification has been published (whether by him or by another person) in such manner as he considers appropriate for the purpose of bringing the code or modification to the notice of those likely to be affected by it; or

    (b) arrangements have been made for the code or modification to be so published.

(3) The Secretary of State may approve—

    (a) more than one code of practice in relation to the same matter;

    (b) a code of practice which makes different provision with respect to different cases or descriptions of case (including different provision for different areas).

(4) A failure to comply with a code of practice for the time being approved under this section shall not of itself render a person liable to any civil or criminal proceedings; but in any civil or criminal proceedings—

(a) any code of practice approved under this section shall be admissible in evidence, and

(b) any provision of any such code which appears to the court to be relevant to any question arising in the proceedings shall be taken into account in determining that question.

(5) An order under this section shall be made by statutory instrument which shall be subject to annulment in pursuance of a resolution of either House of Parliament.

(6) In this section references to a code of practice include references to a part of a code of practice.'.

78 Increase of fines, etc.

(1) In section 350(2) of the Housing Act 1985 (information in relation to registration schemes)—

(a) in paragraph (a) (failure to give information) for 'level 2' substitute 'level 3', and

(b) in paragraph (b) (mis-statement) for 'level 3' substitute 'level 5'.

(2) In section 355(2) of that Act (failure to comply with occupancy restrictions) for 'level 4' substitute 'level 5'.

(3) In section 356(2) of that Act (information in relation to occupation of house) for 'level 2' substitute 'level 3'.

(4) In section 364(2) of that Act (information in relation to overcrowding) for 'level 2 on the standard scale' substitute ', in the case of such failure, level 3 on the standard scale and, in the case of furnishing such a statement, level 5 on the standard scale'.

(5) In section 368(3) of that Act (use of house in contravention of undertaking) omit from 'and if' to the end.

(6) In section 369(5) of that Act (failure to comply with management code) for 'level 3' substitute 'level 5'.

(7) In section 376(1) and (2) of that Act (penalties for failures to execute works) for 'level 4' substitute in each case 'level 5'.

(8) In section 377(3) of that Act (failure to permit execution of works) for the words from 'level 3' to the end substitute 'level 5 on the standard scale'.

(9) In section 387(5) of that Act (failure to permit carrying out of works) for the words from 'level 3' to the end substitute 'level 5 on the standard scale'.

(10) In section 396(2) of that Act (penalty for obstruction) for the words 'level 3' substitute 'level 4'.

79 Minor amendments

(1) In section 355(1) of the Housing Act 1985 (effect of direction limiting number of occupants) for the words from 'the number' to the end substitute 'any individual to take up residence in that house or part unless the number of individuals or households then occupying the house or part would not exceed the limit specified in the direction.'.

(2) In section 398 of the Housing Act 1985 for subsection (6) (meaning of 'person managing') substitute—

'(6) "Person managing"—

    (a) means the person who, being an owner or lessee of the premises—

        (i) receives, directly or through an agent or trustee, rents or other payments from persons who are tenants of parts of the premises, or who are lodgers, or

        (ii) would so receive those rents or other payments but for having entered into an arrangement (whether in pursuance of a court order or otherwise) with another person who is not an owner or lessee of the premises by virtue of which that other person receives the rents or other payments, and

    (b) includes, where those rents or other payments are received through another person as agent or trustee, that other person.'.

(3) In Part IV of Schedule 13 to the Housing Act 1985 (control order followed by compulsory purchase order), in paragraph 22 (application of provisions where compulsory purchase order is made within 28 days of a control order), for '28 days' substitute 'eight weeks'.

Common lodging houses

80 Repeal of Part XII of the Housing Act 1985

(1) Part XII of the Housing Act 1985 (common lodging houses) is hereby repealed.

(2) In consequence of the above repeal—

    (a) in section 619(2) of the Housing Act 1985, for 'The other provisions of this Act' substitute 'The provisions of Parts I to XI and XIII to XVIII of this Act'; and

    (b) in section 65(2)(a) of the Housing Act 1988, for 'XII' substitute 'XI'.

(3) The Secretary of State may by order make such consequential amendments or repeals in any local Act as he considers necessary or expedient.

Any such order shall be made by statutory instrument which shall be subject to annulment in pursuance of a resolution of either House of Parliament.

PART III
LANDLORD AND TENANT

CHAPTER I
TENANTS' RIGHTS

Forfeiture

81 Restriction on termination of tenancy for failure to pay service charge

(1) A landlord may not, in relation to premises let as a dwelling, exercise a right of re-entry or forfeiture for failure to pay a service charge unless the amount of the service charge—

    (a) is agreed or admitted by the tenant, or

    (b) has been the subject of determination by a court or by an arbitral tribunal in proceedings pursuant to an arbitration agreement (within the meaning of Part I of the Arbitration Act 1996).

(2) Where the amount is the subject of determination, the landlord may not exercise any such right of re-entry or forfeiture until after the end of the period of 14 days beginning with the day after that on which the decision of the court or arbitral tribunal is given.

(3) For the purposes of this section the amount of a service charge shall be taken to be determined when the decision of the court or arbitral tribunal is given, notwithstanding the possibility of an appeal or other legal challenge to the decision.

(4) The reference in subsection (1) to premises let as a dwelling does not include premises let on—

(a) a tenancy to which Part II of the Landlord and Tenant Act 1954 applies (business tenancies),

(b) a tenancy of an agricultural holding within the meaning of the Agricultural Holdings Act 1986 in relation to which that Act applies, or

(c) a farm business tenancy within the meaning of the Agricultural Tenancies Act 1995.

(5) In this section 'service charge' means a service charge within the meaning of section 18(1) of the Landlord and Tenant Act 1985, other than one excluded from that section by section 27 of that Act (rent of dwelling registered and not entered as variable).

(6) Nothing in this section affects the exercise of a right of re-entry or forfeiture on other grounds.

82 Notice under s 146 of the Law of Property Act 1925

(1) Nothing in section 81 (restriction on termination of tenancy for failure to pay service charge) affects the power of a landlord to serve a notice under section 146(1) of the Law of Property Act 1925 (restrictions on and relief against forfeiture: notice of breach of covenant or condition).

(2) But such a notice in respect of premises let as a dwelling and failure to pay a service charge is ineffective unless it complies with the following requirements.

(3) It must state that section 81 applies and set out the effect of subsection (1) of that section.

The Secretary of State may by regulations prescribe a form of words to be used for that purpose.

(4) The information or words required must be in characters not less conspicuous than those used in the notice—

(a) to indicate that the tenancy may be forfeited, or

(b) to specify the breach complained of

whichever is the more conspicuous.

(5) In this section 'premises let as a dwelling' and 'service charge' have the same meaning as in section 81.

(6) Regulations under this section—

(a) shall be made by statutory instrument, and

(b) may make different provision for different cases or classes of case including different areas.

Service charges

83 Determination of reasonableness of service charges

(1) In section 19 of the Landlord and Tenant Act 1985 (limitation of service charges: reasonableness), after subsection (2) insert—

'(2A) A tenant by whom, or a landlord to whom, a service charge is alleged to be payable may apply to a leasehold valuation tribunal for a determination—

   (a) whether costs incurred for services, repairs, maintenance, insurance or management were reasonably incurred,

   (b) whether services or works for which costs were incurred are of a reasonable standard, or

   (c) whether an amount payable before costs are incurred is reasonable.

(2B) An application may also be made to a leasehold valuation tribunal by a tenant by whom, or landlord to whom, a service charge may be payable for a determination—

   (a) whether if costs were incurred for services, repairs, maintenance, insurance or management of any specified description they would be reasonable,

   (b) whether services provided or works carried out to a particular specification would be of a reasonable standard, or

   (c) what amount payable before costs are incurred would be reasonable.

(2C) No application under subsection (2A) or (2B) may be made in respect of a matter which—

   (a) has been agreed or admitted by the tenant,

   (b) under an arbitration agreement to which the tenant is a party is to be referred to arbitration, or

   (c) has been the subject of determination by a court or arbitral tribunal.'.

(2) In the Schedule to the Landlord and Tenant Act 1985, for paragraph 8 (right to challenge landlord's choice of insurers) substitute—

'8(1) This paragraph applies where a tenancy of a dwelling requires the tenant to insure the dwelling with an insurer nominated by the landlord.

(2) The tenant or landlord may apply to a county court or leasehold valuation tribunal for a determination whether—

   (a) the insurance which is available from the nominated insurer for insuring the tenant's dwelling is unsatisfactory in any respect, or

   (b) the premiums payable in respect of any such insurance are excessive.

(3) No such application may be made in respect of a matter which—

   (a) has been agreed or admitted by the tenant,

   (b) under an arbitration agreement to which the tenant is a party is to be referred to arbitration, or

   (c) has been the subject of determination by a court or arbitral tribunal.

(4) On an application under this paragraph the court or tribunal may make—

   (a) an order requiring the landlord to nominate such other insurer as is specified in the order, or

   (b) an order requiring him to nominate another insurer who satisfies such requirements in relation to the insurance of the dwelling as are specified in the order.

(5) Any such order of a leasehold valuation tribunal may, with the leave of the court, be enforced in the same way as an order of a county court to the same effect.

(6) An agreement by the tenant of a dwelling (other than an arbitration agreement) is void in so far as it purports to provide for a determination in a particular manner, or on particular evidence, of any question which may be the subject of an application under this paragraph.'.

(3) In the Landlord and Tenant Act 1985 before section 32 under the heading '*Supplementary provisions*' insert—

'31A Jurisdiction of leasehold valuation tribunal

(1) The jurisdiction conferred by this Act on a leasehold valuation tribunal is exercisable by a rent assessment committee constituted in accordance with Schedule 10 to the Rent Act 1977 which when so constituted for the purposes of exercising any such jurisdiction shall be known as a leasehold valuation tribunal.

(2) The power to make regulations under section 74(1)(b) of the Rent Act 1977 (procedure of rent assessment committees) extends to prescribing the procedure to be followed in connection with any proceedings before a leasehold valuation tribunal under this Act.

(3) Such regulations may, in particular, make provision—

    (a) for securing consistency where numerous applications under this Act are or may be brought in respect of the same or substantially the same matters; and

    (b) empowering a leasehold valuation tribunal to dismiss an application, in whole or in part, on the ground that it is frivolous or vexatious or otherwise an abuse of the process of the tribunal.

(4) No costs incurred by a party in connection with proceedings under this Act before a leasehold valuation tribunal shall be recoverable by order of any court.

(5) Paragraphs 2, 3 and 7 of Schedule 22 to the Housing Act 1980 (supplementary provisions relating to leasehold valuation tribunals: appeals and provision of information) apply to a leasehold valuation tribunal constituted for the purposes of this section.

(6) No appeal shall lie to the Lands Tribunal from a decision of a leasehold valuation tribunal under this Act without the leave of the leasehold valuation tribunal concerned or the Lands Tribunal.

(7) On any such appeal—

    (a) the Lands Tribunal may exercise any power available to the leasehold valuation tribunal in relation to the original matter, and

    (b) an order of the Lands Tribunal may be enforced in the same way as an order of the leasehold valuation tribunal.

31B Leasehold valuation tribunal: applications and fees

(1) The Secretary of State may make provision by order as to the form of, or the particulars to be contained in, an application made to a leasehold valuation tribunal under this Act.

(2) The Secretary of State may make provision by order—

    (a) requiring the payment of fees in respect of any such application, or in respect of any proceedings before, a leasehold valuation tribunal under this Act; and

(b) empowering a leasehold valuation tribunal to require a party to proceedings before it to reimburse any other party the whole or part of any fees paid by him.

(3) The fees payable shall be such as may be specified in or determined in accordance with the order subject to this limit, that the fees payable in respect of any one application or reference by the court together with any proceedings before the tribunal arising out of that application or reference shall not exceed £500 or such other amount as may be specified by order of the Secretary of State.

(4) An order under this section may make different provision for different cases or classes of case or for different areas.

(5) An order may in particular—

(a) make different provision in relation to proceedings transferred to the tribunal from that applicable where an application was made to the tribunal, and
(b) provide for the reduction or waiver of fees by reference to the financial resources of the party by whom they are to be paid or met.

(6) In the latter case the order may apply, subject to such modifications as may be specified in the order, any other statutory means-testing regime as it has effect from time to time.

(7) An order under this section shall be made by statutory instrument.

(8) No order altering the limit under subsection (3) shall be made unless a draft of the order has been laid before and approved by a resolution of each House of Parliament.

(9) Any other order under this section, unless it contains only such provision as is mentioned in subsection (1), shall be subject to annulment in pursuance of a resolution of either House of Parliament.

31C Transfer of cases from county court

(1) Where in any proceedings before a court there falls for determination a question falling within the jurisdiction of a leasehold valuation tribunal under this Act, the court—

(a) may by order transfer to such a tribunal so much of the proceedings as relate to the determination of that question, and
(b) may then dispose of all or any remaining proceedings, or adjourn the disposal of all or any of such proceedings, pending the determination of that question by the tribunal, as it thinks fit.

(2) When the tribunal has determined the question, the court may give effect to the determination in an order of the court.

(3) Any such order shall be treated as a determination by the court for the purposes of section 81 of the Housing Act 1996 (restriction on termination of tenancy for failure to pay service charge).

(4) Rules of court may prescribe the procedure to be followed in the court in connection with or in consequence of a transfer under this section.'.

(4) For section 20C of the Landlord and Tenant Act 1985 (limitation of service charges: costs of court proceedings) substitute—

'20C Limitation of service charges: costs of proceedings

(1) A tenant may make an application for an order that all or any of the costs incurred, or to be incurred, by the landlord in connection with proceedings before a court or leasehold valuation tribunal, or the Lands Tribunal, or in connection with arbitration proceedings, are not to be regarded as relevant costs to be taken into account in determining the amount of any service charge payable by the tenant or any other person or persons specified in the application.

(2) The application shall be made—

(a) in the case of court proceedings; to the court before which the proceedings are taking place or, if the application is made after the proceedings are concluded, to a county court;

(b) in the case of proceedings before a leasehold valuation tribunal, to the tribunal before which the proceedings are taking place or, if the application is made after the proceedings are concluded, to any leasehold valuation tribunal;

(c) in the case of proceedings before the Lands Tribunal, to the tribunal;

(d) in the case of arbitration proceedings, to the arbitral tribunal or, if the application is made after the proceedings are concluded, to a county court.

(3) The court or tribunal to which the application is made may make such order on the application as it considers just and equitable in the circumstances.'.

(5) In section 38 of the Landlord and Tenant Act 1985 (minor definitions), at the appropriate place insert—

' "arbitration agreement", "arbitration proceedings" and "arbitral tribunal" have the same meaning as in Part I of the Arbitration Act 1996;'.

(6) In section 39 of that Act (index of defined expressions), at the appropriate place insert—

"arbitration agreement, arbitration   section 38"
    proceedings and arbitral tribunal

84 Right to appoint surveyor to advise on matters relating to service charges

(1) A recognised tenants' association may appoint a surveyor for the purposes of this section to advise on any matters relating to, or which may give rise to, service charges payable to a landlord by one or more members of the association.

The provisions of Schedule 4 have effect for conferring on a surveyor so appointed rights of access to documents and premises.

(2) A person shall not be so appointed unless he is a qualified surveyor.

For this purpose 'qualified surveyor' has the same meaning as in section 78(4)(a) of the Leasehold Reform, Housing and Urban Development Act 1993 (persons qualified for appointment to carry out management audit).

(3) The appointment shall take effect for the purposes of this section upon notice in writing being given to the landlord by the association stating the name and address of the surveyor, the duration of his appointment and the matters in respect of which he is appointed.

(4) An appointment shall cease to have effect for the purposes of this section if the association gives notice in writing to the landlord to that effect or if the association ceases to exist.

(5) A notice is duly given under this section to a landlord of any tenants if it is given to a person who receives on behalf of the landlord the rent payable by those tenants; and a person to whom such a notice is so given shall forward it as soon as may be to the landlord.

(6) In this section—

'recognised tenants' association' has the same meaning as in the provisions of the Landlord and Tenant Act 1985 relating to service charges (see section 29 of that Act); and

'service charge' means a service charge within the meaning of section 18(1) of that Act, other than one excluded from that section by section 27 of that Act (rent of dwelling registered and not entered as variable).

Appointment of manager

85 Appointment of manager by the court

(1) Section 24 of the Landlord and Tenant Act 1987 (appointment of manager by the court) is amended as follows.

(2) In subsection (2) (circumstances in which order may be made), in paragraph (a) (breach of obligation by landlord), omit sub-paragraph (ii) (requirement that circumstances likely to continue).

(3) In that subsection, after paragraph (a), and before the word 'or' following that paragraph, insert—

'(ab) where the court is satisfied—

  (i) that unreasonable service charges have been made, or are proposed or likely to be made, and
  (ii) that it is just and convenient to make the order in all the circumstances of the case;

(ac) where the court is satisfied—

  (i) that the landlord has failed to comply with any relevant provision of a code of practice approved by the Secretary of State under section 87 of the Leasehold Reform, Housing and Urban Development Act 1993 (codes of management practice), and
  (ii) that it is just and convenient to make the order in all the circumstances of the case;'.

(4) After that subsection insert—

'(2A) For the purposes of subsection (2)(ab) a service charge shall be taken to be unreasonable—

  (a) if the amount is unreasonable having regard to the items for which it is payable,
  (b) if the items for which it is payable are of an unnecessarily high standard, or
  (c) if the items for which it is payable are of an insufficient standard with the result that additional service charges are or may be incurred.

In that provision and this subsection "service charge" means a service charge within the meaning of section 18(1) of the Landlord and Tenant Act 1985, other than one excluded from that section by section 27 of that Act (rent of dwelling registered and not entered as variable).'.

(5) The above amendments apply to applications for an order under section 24 of the Landlord and Tenant Act 1987 which are made after this section comes into force.

In relation to any such application the reference in the inserted subsection (2)(ab) to service charges which have been made includes services charges made before that date.

(6) After subsection (9) insert—

'(9A) The court shall not vary or discharge an order under subsection (9) on a landlord's application unless it is satisfied—

(a) that the variation or discharge of the order will not result in a recurrence of the circumstances which led to the order being made, and

(b) that it is just and convenient in all the circumstances of the case to vary or discharge the order.'.

86 Appointment of manager: transfer of jurisdiction to leasehold valuation tribunal

(1) Part II of the Landlord and Tenant Act 1987 (appointment of managers by the court) is amended as follows for the purpose of transferring to a leasehold valuation tribunal the jurisdiction of the court under that Part.

(2) In the following contexts for 'the court', in the first (or only) place where it occurs, substitute 'a leasehold valuation tribunal': section 21(1), section 22(2)(b), section 22(3), section 23(1), section 24(1), (2), (9) and (10); and in every other context in those sections, except section 21(6), for 'the court' substitute 'the tribunal'.

(3) In section 21(6) (exclusion of application under inherent jurisdiction of court) for 'any jurisdiction existing apart from this Act' substitute 'any jurisdiction'.

(4) In section 23(2)—

(a) for 'Rules of court' substitute 'Procedure regulations', and

(b) in paragraph (a), for 'rules' substitute 'regulations'.

(5) After section 24 insert—

'24A Jurisdiction of leasehold valuation tribunal

(1) The jurisdiction conferred by this Part on a leasehold valuation tribunal is exercisable by a rent assessment committee constituted in accordance with Schedule 10 to the Rent Act 1977 which when so constituted for the purposes of exercising any such jurisdiction shall be known as a leasehold valuation tribunal.

(2) The power to make regulations under section 74(1)(b) of the Rent Act 1977 (procedure of rent assessment committees) extends to prescribing the procedure to be followed in connection with any proceedings before a leasehold valuation tribunal under this Part.

Such regulations are referred to in this Part as 'procedure regulations'.

(3) Procedure regulations may, in particular, make provision—

(a) for securing consistency where numerous applications under this Part are or may be brought in respect of the same or substantially the same matters; and

(b) empowering a leasehold valuation tribunal to dismiss an application, in whole or in part, on the ground that it is frivolous or vexatious or otherwise an abuse of the process of the tribunal.

(4) Any order made by a leasehold valuation tribunal under this Part may, with the leave of the court, be enforced in the same way as an order of the county court.

(5) No costs incurred by a party in connection with proceedings under this Part before a leasehold valuation tribunal shall be recoverable by order of any court.

(6) Paragraphs 2, 3 and 7 of Schedule 22 to the Housing Act 1980 (supplementary provisions relating to leasehold valuation tribunals: appeals and provision of information) apply to a leasehold valuation tribunal constituted for the purposes of this section.

(7) No appeal shall lie to the Lands Tribunal from a decision of a leasehold valuation tribunal under this Part without the leave of the leasehold valuation tribunal concerned or the Lands Tribunal.

(8) On an appeal to the Lands Tribunal from a decision of a leasehold valuation tribunal under this Part—

(a) the Lands Tribunal may exercise any power available to the leasehold valuation tribunal in relation to the original matter, and

(b) an order of the Lands Tribunal may be enforced in the same way as an order of the leasehold valuation tribunal.

24B Leasehold valuation tribunal: applications and fees

(1) The Secretary of State may make provision by order as to the form of, or the particulars to be contained in, an application made to a leasehold valuation tribunal under this Part.

(2) The Secretary of State may make provision by order—

(a) requiring the payment of fees in respect of any such application, or in respect of any proceedings before, a leasehold valuation tribunal under this Part; and

(b) empowering a leasehold valuation tribunal to require a party to proceedings before it to reimburse any other party the whole or part of any fees paid by him.

(3) The fees payable shall be such as may be specified in or determined in accordance with the order subject to this limit, that the fees payable in respect of any one application or reference by the court together with any proceedings before the tribunal arising out of that application or reference shall not exceed £500 or such other amount as may be specified by order of the Secretary of State.

(4) An order under this section may make different provision for different cases or classes of case or for different areas.

(5) An order may, in particular, provide for the reduction or waiver of fees by reference to the financial resources of the party by whom they are to be paid or met.

Any such order may apply, subject to such modifications as may be specified in the order, any other statutory means-testing regime as it has effect from time to time.

(6) An order under this section shall be made by statutory instrument.

(7) No order altering the limit under subsection (3) shall be made unless a draft of the order has been laid before and approved by a resolution of each House of Parliament.

(8) Any other order under this section, unless it contains only such provision as is mentioned in subsection (1), shall be subject to annulment in pursuance of a resolution of either House of Parliament.'.

(6) In section 52 of the Landlord and Tenant Act 1987 (jurisdiction of county courts), in subsection (2)(a) for 'Parts I to IV' substitute 'Parts I, III and IV'.

87 Text of Part II of the Landlord and Tenant Act 1987, as amended

The text of Part II of the Landlord and Tenant Act 1987 as amended by this Act is set out in Schedule 5.

88 Period after which acquisition order may be made

In Part III of the Landlord and Tenant Act 1987 (compulsory acquisition by tenants of their landlord's interest), in section 29(3) (conditions for making acquisition orders: period since appointment of manager under Part II) for 'three years' substitute 'two years'.

Right of first refusal

89 Application of right of first refusal in relation to contracts

(1) After section 4 of the Landlord and Tenant Act 1987 (relevant disposals) insert—

'4A Application of provisions to contracts

(1) The provisions of this Part apply to a contract to create or transfer an estate or interest in land, whether conditional or unconditional and whether or not enforceable by specific performance, as they apply in relation to a disposal consisting of the creation or transfer of such an estate or interest.

As they so apply—

    (a) references to a disposal of any description shall be construed as references to a contract to make such a disposal;

    (b) references to making a disposal of any description shall be construed as references to entering into a contract to make such a disposal; and

    (c) references to the transferee under the disposal shall be construed as references to the other party to the contract and include a reference to any other person to whom an estate or interest is to be granted or transferred in pursuance of the contract.

(2) The provisions of this Part apply to an assignment of rights under such a contract as is mentioned in subsection (1) as they apply in relation to a disposal consisting of the transfer of an estate or interest in land.

As they so apply—

    (a) references to a disposal of any description shall be construed as references to an assignment of rights under a contract to make such a disposal;

    (b) references to making a disposal of any description shall be construed as references to making an assignment of rights under a contract to make such a disposal;

(c)   references to the landlord shall be construed as references to the assignor; and

(d)   references to the transferee under the disposal shall be construed as references to the assignee of such rights.

(3) The provisions of this Part apply to a contract to make such an assignment as is mentioned in subsection (2) as they apply (in accordance with subsection (1)) to a contract to create or transfer an estate or interest in land.

(4) Nothing in this section affects the operation of the provisions of this Part relating to options or rights of pre-emption.'.

(2) In section 4(2) of the Landlord and Tenant Act 1987 (relevant disposals: excluded disposals), for paragraph (i) (certain disposals in pursuance of existing obligations) substitute—

'(i)   a disposal in pursuance of a contract, option or right of pre-emption binding on the landlord (except as provided by section 3D (application of sections 11 to 17 to disposal in pursuance of option or right of pre-emption));'.

(3) In section 20(1) (interpretation), in the definition of 'disposal' for 'has the meaning given by section 4(3)' substitute 'shall be construed in accordance with section 4(3) and section 4A (application of provisions to contracts)'.

90 Notice required to be given by landlord making disposal

(1) In section 4(2) of the Landlord and Tenant Act 1987 (disposals which are not relevant disposals for the purposes of Part I of that Act), for paragraph (l) substitute—

'(l)   a disposal by a body corporate to a company which has been an associated company of that body for at least two years.'.

(2) The above amendment does not apply to a disposal made in pursuance of an obligation entered into before the commencement of this section.

91 Offence of failure to comply with requirements of Part I

(1) After section 10 of the Landlord and Tenant Act 1987 insert—

'10A Offence of failure to comply with requirements of Part I

(1) A landlord commits an offence if, without reasonable excuse, he makes a relevant disposal affecting premises to which this Part applies—

(a)   without having first complied with the requirements of section 5 as regards the service of notices on the qualifying tenants of flats contained in the premises, or

(b)   in contravention of any prohibition or restriction imposed by sections 6 to 10.

(2) A person guilty of an offence under this section is liable on summary conviction to a fine not exceeding level 5 on the standard scale.

(3) Where an offence under this section committed by a body corporate is proved—

(a)   to have been committed with the consent or connivance of a director, manager, secretary or other similar officer of the body corporate, or a person purporting to act in such a capacity, or

(b)   to be due to any neglect on the part of such an officer or person, he, as well as the body corporate, is guilty of the offence and liable to be proceeded against and punished accordingly.

Where the affairs of a body corporate are managed by its members, the above provision applies in relation to the acts and defaults of a member in connection with his functions of management as if he were a director of the body corporate.

(4) Proceedings for an offence under this section may be brought by a local housing authority (within the meaning of section 1 of the Housing Act 1985).

(5) Nothing in this section affects the validity of the disposal.'.

(2) The above amendment does not apply to a disposal made in pursuance of an obligation entered into before the commencement of this section.

92 Procedure for exercise of rights of first refusal

(1) Part I of the Landlord and Tenant Act 1987 (tenants' rights of first refusal) is amended in accordance with Schedule 6.

(2) The amendments restate the principal provisions of that Part so as to—

(a) simplify the procedures for the exercise of the rights conferred on tenants, and
(b) apply those procedures in relation to contracts and certain special cases.

(3) In Schedule 6—

Part I sets out provisions replacing sections 5 to 10 of the Act (rights of first refusal),
Part II sets out provisions replacing sections 11 to 15 of the Act (enforcement by tenants of rights against purchaser),
Part III sets out provisions replacing sections 16 and 17 of the Act (enforcement of rights against subsequent purchasers and termination of rights), and
Part IV contains consequential amendments.

93 Duty of new landlord to inform tenant of rights

(1) In the Landlord and Tenant Act 1985, after section 3 (duty to inform tenant of assignment of landlord's interest) insert—

'3A Duty to inform tenant of possible right to acquire landlord's interest

(1) Where a new landlord is required by section 3(1) to give notice to a tenant of an assignment to him, then if—

(a) the tenant is a qualifying tenant within the meaning of Part I of the Landlord and Tenant Act 1987 (tenants' rights of first refusal), and
(b) the assignment was a relevant disposal within the meaning of that Part affecting premises to which at the time of the disposal that Part applied,

the landlord shall give also notice in writing to the tenant to the following effect.

(2) The notice shall state—

(a) that the disposal to the landlord was one to which Part I of the Landlord and Tenant Act 1987 applied;
(b) that the tenant (together with other qualifying tenants) may have the right under that Part—

    (i) to obtain information about the disposal, and

    (ii) to acquire the landlord's interest in the whole or part of the premises in which the tenant's flat is situated; and

  (c) the time within which any such right must be exercised, and the fact that the time would run from the date of receipt of notice under this section by the requisite majority of qualifying tenants (within the meaning of that Part).

(3) A person who is required to give notice under this section and who fails, without reasonable excuse, to do so within the time allowed for giving notice under section 3(1) commits a summary offence and is liable on conviction to a fine not exceeding level 4 on the standard scale.'.

(2) In section 32(1) of the Landlord and Tenant Act 1985 (provisions not applying to tenancies within Part II of the Landlord and Tenant Act 1954), for 'sections 1 to 3' substitute 'sections 1 to 3A'.

General legal advice

94 Provision of general legal advice about residential tenancies

(1) The Secretary of State may give financial assistance to any person in relation to the provision by that person of general advice about—

  (a) any aspect of the law of landlord and tenant, so far as relating to residential tenancies, or

  (b) Chapter IV of Part I of the Leasehold Reform, Housing and Urban Development Act 1993 (estate management schemes in connection with enfranchisement).

(2) Financial assistance under this section may be given in such form and on such terms as the Secretary of State considers appropriate.

(3) The terms on which financial assistance under this section may be given may, in particular, include provision as to the circumstances in which the assistance must be repaid or otherwise made good to the Secretary of State and the manner in which that is to be done.

Supplementary

95 Jurisdiction of county courts

(1) Any jurisdiction expressed by a provision to which this section applies to be conferred on the court shall be exercised by a county court.

(2) There shall also be brought in a county court any proceedings for determining any question arising under or by virtue of any provision to which this section applies.

(3) Where, however, other proceedings are properly brought in the High Court, that court has jurisdiction to hear and determine proceedings to which subsection (1) or (2) applies which are joined with those proceedings.

(4) Where proceedings are brought in a county court by virtue of subsection (1) or (2), that court has jurisdiction to hear and determine other proceedings joined with those proceedings despite the fact that they would otherwise be outside its jurisdiction.

(5) The provisions to which this section applies are—

(a) section 81 (restriction on termination of tenancy for failure to pay service charge), and

(b) section 84 (right to appoint surveyor to advise on matters relating to service charges) and Schedule 4 (rights exercisable by surveyor appointed by tenants' association).

CHAPTER II
ASSURED TENANCIES

Assured shorthold tenancies

96 Tenancies which are assured shorthold tenancies

(1) In Chapter II of Part I of the Housing Act 1988 (assured shorthold tenancies) there shall be inserted at the beginning—

'19A Assured shorthold tenancies: post-Housing Act 1996 tenancies

An assured tenancy which—

(a) is entered into on or after the day on which section 96 of the Housing Act 1996 comes into force (otherwise than pursuant to a contract made before that day), or

(b) comes into being by virtue of section 5 above on the coming to an end of an assured tenancy within paragraph (a) above,

is an assured shorthold tenancy unless it falls within any paragraph in Schedule 2A to this Act.'.

(2) After Schedule 2 to that Act there shall be inserted the Schedule set out in Schedule 7 to this Act.

97 Duty of landlord to provide statement of terms of assured shorthold tenancy

After section 20 of the Housing Act 1988 there shall be inserted—

'20A Post-Housing Act 1996 tenancies: duty of landlord to provide statement as to terms of tenancy

(1) Subject to subsection (3) below, a tenant under an assured shorthold tenancy to which section 19A above applies may, by notice in writing, require the landlord under that tenancy to provide him with a written statement of any term of the tenancy which—

(a) falls within subsection (2) below, and

(b) is not evidenced in writing.

(2) The following terms of a tenancy fall within this subsection, namely—

(a) the date on which the tenancy began or, if it is a statutory periodic tenancy or a tenancy to which section 39(7) below applies, the date on which the tenancy came into being,

(b) the rent payable under the tenancy and the dates on which that rent is payable,

(c) any term providing for a review of the rent payable under the tenancy, and

(d) in the case of a fixed term tenancy, the length of the fixed term.

(3) No notice may be given under subsection (1) above in relation to a term of the tenancy if—

(a) the landlord under the tenancy has provided a statement of that term in response to an earlier notice under that subsection given by the tenant under the tenancy, and

(b) the term has not been varied since the provision of the statement referred to in paragraph (a) above.

(4) A landlord who fails, without reasonable excuse, to comply with a notice under subsection (1) above within the period of 28 days beginning with the date on which he received the notice is liable on summary conviction to a fine not exceeding level 4 on the standard scale.

(5) A statement provided for the purposes of subsection (1) above shall not be regarded as conclusive evidence of what was agreed by the parties to the tenancy in question.

(6) Where—

(a) a term of a statutory periodic tenancy is one which has effect by virtue of section 5(3)(e) above, or

(b) a term of a tenancy to which subsection (7) of section 39 below applies is one which has effect by virtue of subsection (6)(e) of that section,

subsection (1) above shall have effect in relation to it as if paragraph (b) related to the term of the tenancy from which it derives.

(7) In subsections (1) and (3) above—

(a) references to the tenant under the tenancy shall, in the case of joint tenants, be taken to be references to any of the tenants, and

(b) references to the landlord under the tenancy shall, in the case of joint landlords, be taken to be references to any of the landlords.'.

98 Form of notices under s 21 of the Housing Act 1988

(1) Section 21 of the Housing Act 1988 (recovery of possession on expiry or termination of assured shorthold tenancy) shall be amended as follows.

(2) In subsection (1)(b) (which requires the landlord under a fixed term tenancy to give two months' notice to recover possession), after 'notice' there shall be inserted 'in writing'.

(3) In subsection (4)(a) (corresponding provision for periodic tenancies), after 'notice', where it first occurs, there shall be inserted 'in writing'.

99 Restriction on recovery of possession on expiry or termination

In section 21 of the Housing Act 1988 there shall be inserted at the end—

'(5) Where an order for possession under subsection (1) or (4) above is made in relation to a dwelling-house let on a tenancy to which section 19A above applies, the order may not be made so as to take effect earlier than—

(a) in the case of a tenancy which is not a replacement tenancy, six months after the beginning of the tenancy, and

(b) in the case of a replacement tenancy, six months after the beginning of the original tenancy.

(6) In subsection (5)(b) above, the reference to the original tenancy is—

(a) where the replacement tenancy came into being on the coming to an end of a tenancy which was not a replacement tenancy, to the immediately preceding tenancy, and

(b) where there have been successive replacement tenancies, to the tenancy immediately preceding the first in the succession of replacement tenancies.

(7) For the purposes of this section, a replacement tenancy is a tenancy—

(a) which comes into being on the coming to an end of an assured shorthold tenancy, and

(b) under which, on its coming into being—

(i) the landlord and tenant are the same as under the earlier tenancy as at its coming to an end, and

(ii) the premises let are the same or substantially the same as those let under the earlier tenancy as at that time.'.

100 Applications for determination of rent: time limit

(1) Section 22 of the Housing Act 1988 (reference of excessive rents to rent assessment committee) shall be amended as follows.

(2) In subsection (2) (circumstances in which no application under the section may be made) after paragraph (a) there shall be inserted—

'(aa) the tenancy is one to which section 19A above applies and more than six months have elapsed since the beginning of the tenancy or, in the case of a replacement tenancy, since the beginning of the original tenancy; or'.

(3) At the end there shall be inserted—

'(6) In subsection (2)(aa) above, the references to the original tenancy and to a replacement tenancy shall be construed in accordance with subsections (6) and (7) respectively of section 21 above.'.

Grounds for possession

101 Mandatory possession for non-payment of rent: reduction in arrears required

In Part I of Schedule 2 to the Housing Act 1988 (grounds on which court must order possession) in Ground 8 (rent unpaid for certain periods)—

(a) in paragraph (a) (rent payable weekly or fortnightly) for 'thirteen weeks' there shall be substituted 'eight weeks', and

(b) in paragraph (b) (rent payable monthly) for 'three months' there shall be substituted 'two months'.

102 Recovery of possession where grant induced by false statement

In Part II of Schedule 2 to the Housing Act 1988 (grounds on which court may order possession) there shall be inserted at the end—

'Ground 17

The tenant is the person, or one of the persons, to whom the tenancy was granted and the landlord was induced to grant the tenancy by a false statement made knowingly or recklessly by—

(a) the tenant, or
(b) a person acting at the tenant's instigation.'.

Assured agricultural occupancies

103 Assured agricultural occupancies: exclusion of tenancies of agricultural holdings and farm business tenancies

(1) Section 24 of the Housing Act 1988 (assured agricultural occupancies) shall be amended as follows.

(2) In subsection (2)(b) (under which a tenancy is an assured agricultural occupancy if it would be an assured tenancy, but for paragraph 7 of Schedule 1 to that Act) there shall be inserted at the end 'and is not an excepted tenancy'.

(3) After subsection (2) there shall be inserted—

'(2A) For the purposes of subsection (2)(b) above, a tenancy is an excepted tenancy if it is—

(a) a tenancy of an agricultural holding within the meaning of the Agricultural Holdings Act 1986 in relation to which that Act applies, or
(b) a farm business tenancy within the meaning of the Agricultural Tenancies Act 1995.'.

Consequential amendments

104 Consequential amendments: assured tenancies

The enactments mentioned in Schedule 8 have effect with the amendments specified there which are consequential on the provisions of this Chapter.

CHAPTER III
LEASEHOLD REFORM

Scope of rights

105 Low rent test: nil rateable values

(1) In section 4(1) of the Leasehold Reform Act 1967 (meaning of 'low rent')—

(a) in paragraph (i) (cases where rent limit of two-thirds of rateable value on later of appropriate day and first day of term applies), for the words from 'or (where' to 'that date' there shall be substituted ', or on or after 1st April 1990 in pursuance of a contract made before that date, and the property had a rateable value other than nil at the date of the commencement of the tenancy or else at any time before 1st April 1990,',

(b) in paragraph (ii) (other cases), for the words from 'is entered' to '1990),' there shall be substituted 'does not fall within paragraph (i) above,', and

(c) in paragraph (a) (definition of 'appropriate day' by reference to section 25(3) of the Rent Act 1977), there shall be inserted at the end 'if the reference in paragraph (a) of that provision to a rateable value were to a rateable value other than nil'.

(2) In section 4A of the Leasehold Reform Act 1967 (alternative rent limits for the purposes of section 1A(2) of that Act)—

(a) in subsection (1)(b) (cases where rent limit of two-thirds of rateable value on the relevant date applies), for sub-paragraph (ii) there shall be substituted—

'(ii) the property had a rateable value other than nil at the date of commencement of the tenancy or else at any time before 1st April 1990,', and

(b) in subsection (2), for paragraph (b) there shall be substituted—

'(b) "the relevant date" means the date of the commencement of the tenancy or, if the property did not have a rateable value, or had a rateable value of nil, on that date, the date on which it first had a rateable value other than nil;'.

(3) In section 8 of the Leasehold Reform, Housing and Urban Development Act 1993 (leases at a low rent)—

(a) in subsection (1)(b) (cases where rent limit of two-thirds of rateable value on the appropriate date applies), for sub-paragraph (ii) there shall be substituted—

'(ii) the flat had a rateable value other than nil at the date of the commencement of the lease or else at any time before 1st April 1990,', and

(b) in subsection (2), for paragraph (b) there shall be substituted—

'(b) "the appropriate date" means the date of commencement of the lease or, if the flat in question did not have a rateable value, or had a rateable value of nil, on that date, the date on which the flat first had a rateable value other than nil;'.

106 Low rent test: extension of rights

Schedule 9 (which makes provision for conferring an additional right to enfranchisement in relation to tenancies which fail the low rent test and for introducing an alternative to the low rent test in the case of the right to collective enfranchisement and the right to a new lease) shall have effect.

107 Collective enfranchisement: multiple freeholders

(1) In section 3 of the Leasehold Reform, Housing and Urban Development Act 1993 (premises in respect of which the right to collective enfranchisement is exercisable), in subsection (1)(a), the words 'and the freehold of the whole of the building or of that part of the building is owned by the same person' shall be omitted.

(2) In section 4 of that Act (premises excluded from the right to collective enfranchisement), after subsection (3) there shall be inserted—

'(3A) Where different persons own the freehold of different parts of premises within subsection (1) of section 3, this Chapter does not apply to the premises if any of those parts is a self-contained part of a building for the purposes of that section.'.

(3) In section 1(3) of that Act (additional property which may be acquired by tenants exercising the right to collective enfranchisement), the words 'the freehold of it is owned by the person who owns the freehold of the relevant premises and' shall be omitted.

(4) Schedule 10 (amendments consequential on this section) shall have effect.

Valuation

108 Collective enfranchisement: removal of need for professional valuation of interests to be acquired

In section 13 of the Leasehold Reform, Housing and Urban Development Act 1993 (notice by qualifying tenants of claim to exercise right to collective enfranchisement) subsection (6) (tenants to obtain professional valuation of interests proposed to be acquired before giving notice) shall cease to have effect.

109 Collective enfranchisement: valuation principles

(1) Schedule 6 to the Leasehold Reform, Housing and Urban Development Act 1993 (purchase price payable by nominee purchaser) shall be amended as follows.

(2) In paragraph 3(1) (freeholder's interest to be valued on the basis that neither the nominee purchaser nor any participating tenant is in the market) for 'neither the nominee purchaser nor any participating tenant' there shall be substituted 'no person who falls within sub-paragraph (1A)'.

(3) After paragraph 3(1) there shall be inserted—

'(1A) A person falls within this sub-paragraph if he is—

  (a) the nominee purchaser, or
  (b) a tenant of premises contained in the specified premises, or
  (c) an owner of an interest which the nominee purchaser is to acquire in pursuance of section 2(1)(b).'.

(4) In paragraph 7 (value of intermediate leasehold interests) after sub-paragraph (1) there shall be inserted—

'(1A) In its application in accordance with sub-paragraph (1), paragraph 3(1A) shall have effect with the addition after paragraph (a) of—

"(aa) an owner of a freehold interest in the specified premises, or" '.

(5) In paragraph 11 (value of other interests) after sub-paragraph (3) there shall be inserted—

'(4) In its application in accordance with sub-paragraph (2) above, paragraph 3(1A) shall have effect with the addition after paragraph (a) of—

"(aa) an owner of a freehold interest in the specified premises, or" '.

110 New leases: valuation principles

(1) Schedule 13 to the Leasehold Reform, Housing and Urban Development Act 1993 (premium and other amounts payable by tenant on grant of new lease) shall be amended as mentioned in subsections (2) to (4) below.

(2) In paragraph 3(2) (landlord's interest to be valued on the basis that the tenant is not buying or seeking to buy) for 'the tenant not' there shall be substituted 'neither the tenant nor any owner of an intermediate leasehold interest'.

(3) In paragraph 4(3) (calculation of marriage value) for paragraph (a) (value of tenant's interest) there shall be substituted—

'(a) the value of the interest of the tenant under his existing lease shall be determined in accordance with paragraph 4A;

(aa) the value of the interest to be held by the tenant under the new lease shall be determined in accordance with paragraph 4B;',

and, in paragraph (b), for 'that sub-paragraph' there shall be substituted 'sub-paragraph (2)'.

(4) After paragraph 4 there shall be inserted—

'4A—(1) Subject to the provisions of this paragraph, the value of the interest of the tenant under the existing lease is the amount which at the valuation date that interest might be expected to realise if sold on the open market by a willing seller (with neither the landlord nor any owner of an intermediate leasehold interest buying or seeking to buy) on the following assumptions—

(a) on the assumption that the vendor is selling such interest as is held by the tenant subject to any interest inferior to the interest of the tenant;

(b) on the assumption that Chapter I and this Chapter confer no right to acquire any interest in any premises containing the tenant's flat or to acquire any new lease;

(c) on the assumption that any increase in the value of the flat which is attributable to an improvement carried out at his own expense by the tenant or by any predecessor in title is to be disregarded; and

(d) on the assumption that (subject to paragraph (b)) the vendor is selling with and subject to the rights and burdens with and subject to which any interest inferior to the existing lease of the tenant has effect.

(2) It is hereby declared that the fact that sub-paragraph (1) requires assumptions to be made in relation to particular matters does not preclude the making of assumptions as to other matters where those assumptions are appropriate for determining the amount which at the valuation date the interest of the tenant under his existing lease might be expected to realise if sold as mentioned in that sub-paragraph.

(3) In determining any such amount there shall be made such deduction (if any) in respect of any defect in title as on a sale of that interest on the open market might be expected to be allowed between a willing seller and a willing buyer.

(4) Subject to sub-paragraph (5), the value of the interest of the tenant under his existing lease shall not be increased by reason of—

(a) any transaction which—

(i) is entered into after 19th January 1996, and

(ii) involves the creation or transfer of an interest inferior to the tenant's existing lease; or

(b) any alteration after that date of the terms on which any such inferior interest is held.

(5) Sub-paragraph (4) shall not apply to any transaction which falls within paragraph (a) of that sub-paragraph if—

  (a) the transaction is entered into in pursuance of a contract entered into on or before the date mentioned in that paragraph; and

  (b) the amount of the premium payable by the tenant in respect of the grant of the new lease was determined on or before that date either by agreement or by a leasehold valuation tribunal under this Chapter.

4B—(1) Subject to the provisions of this paragraph, the value of the interest to be held by the tenant under the new lease is the amount which at the valuation date that interest (assuming it to have been granted to him at that date) might be expected to realise if sold on the open market by a willing seller (with the owner of any interest superior to the interest of the tenant not buying or seeking to buy) on the following assumptions—

  (a) on the assumption that the vendor is selling such interest as is to be held by the tenant under the new lease subject to the inferior interests to which the tenant's existing lease is subject at the valuation date;

  (b) on the assumption that Chapter I and this Chapter confer no right to acquire any interest in any premises containing the tenant's flat or to acquire any new lease;

  (c) on the assumption that there is to be disregarded any increase in the value of the flat which would fall to be disregarded under paragraph (c) of sub-paragraph (1) of paragraph 4A in valuing in accordance with that sub-paragraph the interest of the tenant under his existing lease; and

  (d) on the assumption that (subject to paragraph (b)) the vendor is selling with and subject to the rights and burdens with and subject to which any interest inferior to the tenant's existing lease at the valuation date then has effect.

(2) It is hereby declared that the fact that sub-paragraph (1) requires assumptions to be made in relation to particular matters does not preclude the making of assumptions as to other matters where those assumptions are appropriate for determining the amount which at the valuation date the interest to be held by the tenant under the new lease might be expected to realise if sold as mentioned in that sub-paragraph.

(3) In determining any such amount there shall be made such deduction (if any) in respect of any defect in title as on a sale of that interest on the open market might be expected to be allowed between a willing seller and a willing buyer.

(4) Subject to sub-paragraph (5), the value of the interest to be held by the tenant under the new lease shall not be decreased by reason of—

  (a) any transaction which—

    (i)   is entered into after 19th January 1996, and

    (ii) involves the creation or transfer of an interest inferior to the tenant's existing lease; or

  (b) any alteration after that date of the terms on which any such inferior interest is held.

(5) Sub-paragraph (4) shall not apply to any transaction which falls within paragraph (a) of that sub-paragraph if—

  (a) the transaction is entered into in pursuance of a contract entered into on or before the date mentioned in that paragraph; and

(b) the amount of the premium payable by the tenant in respect of the grant of the new lease was determined on or before that date either by agreement or by a leasehold valuation tribunal under this Chapter.'.

(5) This section applies in relation to any claim made after 19th January 1996 by the giving of notice under section 42 of the Act of 1993 unless the amount of the premium payable in pursuance of the claim has been determined, either by agreement or by a leasehold valuation tribunal under Chapter II of the Act of 1993, before the day on which this Act is passed.

Trusts

111 Satisfaction of residence condition: collective enfranchisement

(1) In section 6 of the Leasehold Reform, Housing and Urban Development Act 1993 (which provides when a qualifying tenant of a flat satisfies the residence condition) for subsection (4) there shall be substituted—

'(4) Subsection (1) shall not apply where a lease is vested in trustees (other than a sole tenant for life within the meaning of the Settled Land Act 1925), and, in that case, a qualifying tenant of a flat shall, for the purposes of this Chapter, be treated as satisfying the residence condition at any time when the condition in subsection (5) is satisfied with respect to an individual having an interest under the trust (whether or not also a trustee).

(5) That condition is that the individual has occupied the flat as his only or principal home—

(a) for the last twelve months, or
(b) for periods amounting to three years in the last ten years,

whether or not he has used the flat also for other purposes.

(6) For the purposes of subsection (5)—

(a) any reference to the flat includes a reference to part of it; and
(b) it is immaterial whether at any particular time the individual's occupation was in right of the lease by virtue of which the trustees are a qualifying tenant or in right of some other lease or otherwise.'.

(2) In section 13(3)(e)(iii) of that Act (particulars of satisfaction of residence condition to be included in the notice by which qualifying tenants exercise right to collective enfranchisement)—

(a) after 'which he' there shall be inserted ', or, where the tenant's lease is vested as mentioned in section 6(4), the individual concerned,', and
(b) for 'his', in the first place where it occurs, there shall be substituted 'the'.

112 Satisfaction of residence condition: new leases

(1) Section 39 of the Leasehold Reform, Housing and Urban Development Act 1993 (right of qualifying tenant of flat to acquire new lease) shall be amended as mentioned in subsections (2) to (4) below.

(2) In subsection (2) (circumstances in which the right conferred) for paragraph (b) (residence condition) there shall be substituted—

'(b) the condition specified in subsection (2A) or, as the case may be, (2B) is satisfied.

(2A) Where the lease by virtue of which the tenant is a qualifying tenant is vested in trustees (other than a sole tenant for life within the meaning of the Settled Land Act 1925), the condition is that an individual having an interest under the trust (whether or not also a trustee) has occupied the flat as his only or principal home—

    (a) for the last three years, or
    (b) for periods amounting to three years in the last ten years,

whether or not he has used it also for other purposes.

(2B) Where the lease by virtue of which the tenant is a qualifying tenant is not vested as mentioned in subsection (2A), the condition is that the tenant has occupied the flat as his only or principal home—

    (a) for the last three years, or
    (b) for periods amounting to three years in the last ten years,

whether or not he has used it also for other purposes.'.

(3) After subsection (4) there shall be inserted—

'(4A) For the purposes of subsection (2A)—

    (a) any reference to the flat includes a reference to part of it; and
    (b) it is immaterial whether at any particular time the individual's occupation was in right of the lease by virtue of which the trustees are a qualifying tenant or in right of some other lease or otherwise.'.

(4) In subsection (5), for '(2)(b)' there shall be substituted '(2B)'.

(5) In section 42 of that Act (notice by qualifying tenant of claim to exercise right) for subsection (4) there shall be substituted—

'(4) If the tenant's lease is vested as mentioned in section 39(2A), the reference to the tenant in subsection (3)(b)(iv) shall be read as a reference to any individual with respect to whom it is claimed the condition in section 39(2A) is satisfied.'.

113 Powers of trustees

After section 93 of the Leasehold Reform, Housing and Urban Development Act 1993 there shall be inserted—

'93A Powers of trustees in relation to rights under Chapters I and II

(1) Where trustees are a qualifying tenant of a flat for the purposes of Chapter I or II, their powers under the instrument regulating the trusts shall include power to participate in the exercise of the right to collective enfranchisement under Chapter I or, as the case may be, to exercise the right to a new lease under Chapter II.

(2) Subsection (1) shall not apply where the instrument regulating the trusts—

    (a) is made on or after the day on which section 113 of the Housing Act 1996 comes into force, and
    (b) contains an explicit direction to the contrary.

(3) The powers conferred by subsection (1) shall be exercisable with the like consent or on the like direction (if any) as may be required for the exercise of the trustees' powers (or ordinary powers) of investment.

(4) The following purposes, namely—

    (a) those authorised for the application of capital money by section 73 of the Settled Land Act 1925, or by that section as applied by section 28 of the Law of Property Act 1925 in relation to trusts for sale, and

    (b) those authorised by section 71 of the Settled Land Act 1925, or by that section as so applied, as purposes for which moneys may be raised by mortgage,

shall include the payment of any expenses incurred by a tenant for life or statutory owners or by trustees for sale, as the case may be, in or in connection with participation in the exercise of the right to collective enfranchisement under Chapter I or in or in connection with the exercise of the right to a new lease under Chapter II.'.

Miscellaneous

114 Minor amendment of section 1(1)(a) of Leasehold Reform Act 1967

In section 1 of the Leasehold Reform Act 1967 (tenants entitled to enfranchisement or extension), in subsection (1)(a)—

    (a) in sub-paragraph (i), for the words from 'or (where' to 'that date,' there shall be substituted ', or on or after 1st April 1990 in pursuance of a contract made before that date, and the house and premises had a rateable value at the date of commencement of the tenancy or else at any time before 1st April 1990,', and

    (b) in sub-paragraph (ii), for the words from 'is entered' to '1990),' there shall be substituted 'does not fall within sub-paragraph (i) above,'.

115 Power for leasehold valuation tribunal to determine amount of costs payable under Leasehold Reform Act 1967

In section 21(1) of the Leasehold Reform Act 1967 (matters to be determined by leasehold valuation tribunal), after paragraph (b) there shall be inserted—

'(ba) the amount of any costs payable under section 9(4) or 14(2);'.

116 Compensation for postponement of termination in connection with ineffective claims

Schedule 11 (which makes, in relation to claims to enfranchisement or an extended lease under Part I of the Leasehold Reform Act 1967 and claims to collective enfranchisement or a new lease under Chapter I or II of Part I of the Leasehold Reform, Housing and Urban Development Act 1993, provision for compensation of the landlord where the claim has prolonged an existing tenancy, but is ineffective) shall have effect.

117 Priority of interests on grant of new lease

After section 58 of the Leasehold Reform, Housing and Urban Development Act 1993 there shall be inserted—

'58A Priority of interests on grant of new lease

(1) Where a lease granted under section 56 takes effect subject to two or more interests to which the existing lease was subject immediately before its surrender, the interests shall have the same priority in relation to one another on the grant of the new lease as they had immediately before the surrender of the existing lease.

(2) Subsection (1) is subject to agreement to the contrary.

(3) Where a person who is entitled on the grant of a lease under section 56 to rights of occupation in relation to the flat comprised in that lease was entitled immediately before the surrender of the existing lease to rights of occupation in relation to the flat comprised in that lease, the rights to which he is entitled on the grant of the new lease shall be treated as a continuation of the rights to which he was entitled immediately before the surrender of the existing lease.

(4) In this section—

> "the existing lease", in relation to a lease granted under section 56, means the lease surrendered on the grant of the new lease, and
>
> "rights of occupation" has the same meaning as in the Matrimonial Homes Act 1983.'.

118 Estate management schemes in connection with enfranchisement by virtue of s 106

(1) Chapter IV of Part I of the 1993 Act, except section 75(1), (estate management schemes in connection with enfranchisement by virtue of that Act) shall also have effect subject to the modifications mentioned in subsections (2) to (4) below.

(2) In section 69(1) (definition of estate management schemes), for paragraphs (a) and (b) there shall be substituted—

> '(a) acquiring the landlord's interest in their house and premises ('the house') under Part I of the Leasehold Reform Act 1967 by virtue of the provisions of section 1AA of that Act (as inserted by paragraph 1 of Schedule 9 to the Housing Act 1996), or
>
> (b) acquiring the landlord's interest in any premises ('the premises') in accordance with Chapter I of this Part of this Act by virtue of the amendments of that Chapter made by paragraph 3 of Schedule 9 to the Housing Act 1996,'.

(3) In section 70 (time limit for applications for approval), for 'two years beginning with the date of the coming into force of this section' there shall be substituted 'two years beginning with the coming into force of section 118 of the Housing Act 1996'.

(4) In section 74 (effect of application for approval on claim to acquire freehold), in subsection (1)—

> (a) in paragraph (b), in sub-paragraph (i), the words from 'being' to the end shall be omitted, and
>
> (b) after that paragraph there shall be inserted 'and
>
> > (c) in the case of an application for the approval of a scheme as an estate management scheme, the scheme would extend to the house or premises if acquired in pursuance of the notice.'.

(5) Section 94(6) to (8) of the 1993 Act (estate management schemes relating to Crown land) shall also have effect with the substitution for any reference to a provision of

Chapter IV of Part I of that Act of a reference to that provision as it has effect by virtue of subsection (1) above.

(6) In section 33 of the National Heritage Act 1983 (general functions of the Historic Buildings and Monuments Commission for England), after subsection (2B) there shall be inserted—

'(2C) In subsection (2B), references to provisions of the Leasehold Reform, Housing and Urban Development Act 1993 include references to those provisions as they have effect by virtue of section 118(1) of the Housing Act 1996.'.

(7) In section 72 of the Planning (Listed Buildings and Conservation Areas) Act 1990 (general duty as respects conservation area in exercise of planning functions), at the end there shall be inserted—

'(3) In subsection (2), references to provisions of the Leasehold Reform, Housing and Urban Development Act 1993 include references to those provisions as they have effect by virtue of section 118(1) of the Housing Act 1996.'.

(8) In this section, 'the 1993 Act' means the Leasehold Reform, Housing and Urban Development Act 1993.

119 Leasehold valuation tribunals: pre-trial review

(1) Procedure regulations may make provision in relation to proceedings before a leasehold valuation tribunal—

    (a) for the holding of a pre-trial review, on the application of a party to the proceedings or of the tribunal's own motion; and

    (b) for the exercise of the functions of the tribunal in relation to, or at, a pre-trial review by a single member who is qualified to exercise them.

(2) In subsection (1) 'procedure regulations' means regulations under section 74(1)(b) of the Rent Act 1977, as that section applies in relation to leasehold valuation tribunals.

(3) For the purposes of subsection (1)(b)—

    (a) a 'member' means a member of the panel provided for in Schedule 10 to that Act, and

    (b) a member is qualified to exercise the functions referred to if he was appointed to that panel by the Lord Chancellor.

PART IV
HOUSING BENEFIT AND RELATED MATTERS

120 Payment of housing benefit to third parties

(1) In section 5 of the Social Security Administration Act 1992 (regulations about claims for and payments of benefit), after subsection (5) insert—

'(6) As it has effect in relation to housing benefit subsection (1)(p) above authorises provision requiring the making of payments of benefit to another person, on behalf of the beneficiary, in such circumstances as may be prescribed.'.

(2) The above amendment shall be deemed always to have had effect; and provision corresponding to that made by the amendment shall be deemed to have had effect at all material times in relation to corresponding earlier enactments.

121 Administration of housing benefit, etc.

Part VIII of the Social Security Administration Act 1992 (arrangements for housing benefit and council tax benefit and related subsidies) is amended in accordance with Schedule 12.

122 Functions of rent officers in connection with housing benefit and rent allowance subsidy

(1) The Secretary of State may by order require rent officers to carry out such functions as may be specified in the order in connection with housing benefit and rent allowance subsidy.

(2) Without prejudice to the generality of subsection (1), an order under this section may contain provision—

    (a) enabling a prospective landlord to apply for a determination for the purposes of any application for housing benefit which may be made by a tenant of a dwelling which he proposes to let;

    (b) as to the payment of a fee by the landlord for that determination;

    (c) requiring the landlord to give a copy of the determination to the appropriate local authority; and

    (d) enabling the appropriate local authority to seek a redetermination when a claim for housing benefit or rent allowance subsidy is made.

(3) Regulations under section 130(4) of the Social Security Contributions and Benefits Act 1992 (housing benefit: manner of determining appropriate maximum benefit) may provide for benefit to be limited by reference to determinations made by rent officers in exercise of functions conferred under this section.

(4) In relation to rent allowance subsidy, the Secretary of State may by order under section 140B of the Social Security Administration Act 1992—

    (a) provide for any calculation under subsection (2) of that section to be made,

    (b) specify any additions and deductions as are referred to in that subsection, and

    (c) exercise his discretion as to what is unreasonable for the purposes of subsection (4) of that section,

by reference to determinations made by rent officers in exercise of functions conferred on them under this section.

(5) The Secretary of State may by any such regulations or order as are mentioned in subsection (3) or (4) require a local authority in any prescribed case—

    (a) to apply to a rent officer for a determination to be made in pursuance of the functions conferred on them under this section, and

    (b) to do so within such time as may be specified in the order or regulations.

(6) An order under this section—

    (a) shall be made by statutory instrument which shall be subject to annulment in pursuance of a resolution of either House of Parliament;

    (b) may make different provision for different cases or classes of case and for different areas; and

    (c) may contain such transitional, incidental and supplementary provisions as appear to the Secretary of State to be desirable.

(7) In this section 'housing benefit' and 'rent allowance subsidy' have the same meaning as in Part VIII of the Social Security Administration Act 1992.

123 Consequential amendments: Part IV

The enactments mentioned in Schedule 13 have effect with the amendments specified there which are consequential on the provisions of this Part.

PART V
CONDUCT OF TENANTS

CHAPTER I
INTRODUCTORY TENANCIES

General provisions

124 Introductory tenancies

(1) A local housing authority or a housing action trust may elect to operate an introductory tenancy regime.

(2) When such an election is in force, every periodic tenancy of a dwelling-house entered into or adopted by the authority or trust shall, if it would otherwise be a secure tenancy, be an introductory tenancy, unless immediately before the tenancy was entered into or adopted the tenant or, in the case of joint tenants, one or more of them was—

   (a) a secure tenant of the same or another dwelling-house, or
   (b) an assured tenant of a registered social landlord (otherwise than under an assured shorthold tenancy) in respect of the same or another dwelling-house.

(3) Subsection (2) does not apply to a tenancy entered into or adopted in pursuance of a contract made before the election was made.

(4) For the purposes of this Chapter a periodic tenancy is adopted by a person if that person becomes the landlord under the tenancy, whether on a disposal or surrender of the interest of the former landlord.

(5) An election under this section may be revoked at any time, without prejudice to the making of a further election.

125 Duration of introductory tenancy

(1) A tenancy remains an introductory tenancy until the end of the trial period, unless one of the events mentioned in subsection (5) occurs before the end of that period.

(2) The 'trial period' is the period of one year beginning with—

   (a) in the case of a tenancy which was entered into by a local housing authority or housing action trust—
      (i) the date on which the tenancy was entered into, or
      (ii) if later, the date on which a tenant was first entitled to possession under the tenancy; or
   (b) in the case of a tenancy which was adopted by a local housing authority or housing action trust, the date of adoption;

subject as follows.

(3) Where the tenant under an introductory tenancy was formerly a tenant under another introductory tenancy, or held an assured shorthold tenancy from a registered social landlord, any period or periods during which he was such a tenant shall count towards the trial period, provided—

    (a) if there was one such period, it ended immediately before the date specified in subsection (2), and

    (b) if there was more than one such period, the most recent period ended immediately before that date and each period succeeded the other without interruption.

(4) Where there are joint tenants under an introductory tenancy, the reference in subsection (3) to the tenant shall be construed as referring to the joint tenant in whose case the application of that subsection produces the earliest starting date for the trial period.

(5) A tenancy ceases to be an introductory tenancy if, before the end of the trial period—

    (a) the circumstances are such that the tenancy would not otherwise be a secure tenancy,

    (b) a person or body other than a local housing authority or housing action trust becomes the landlord under the tenancy,

    (c) the election in force when the tenancy was entered into or adopted is revoked, or

    (d) the tenancy ceases to be an introductory tenancy by virtue of section 133(3) (succession).

(6) A tenancy does not come to an end merely because it ceases to be an introductory tenancy, but a tenancy which has once ceased to be an introductory tenancy cannot subsequently become an introductory tenancy.

(7) This section has effect subject to section 130 (effect of beginning proceedings for possession).

126 Licences

(1) The provisions of this Chapter apply in relation to a licence to occupy a dwelling-house (whether or not granted for a consideration) as they apply in relation to a tenancy.

(2) Subsection (1) does not apply to a licence granted as a temporary expedient to a person who entered the dwelling-house or any other land as a trespasser (whether or not, before the grant of that licence, another licence to occupy that or another dwelling-house had been granted to him).

Proceedings for possession

127 Proceedings for possession

(1) The landlord may only bring an introductory tenancy to an end by obtaining an order of the court for the possession of the dwelling-house.

(2) The court shall make such an order unless the provisions of section 128 apply.

(3) Where the court makes such an order, the tenancy comes to an end on the date on which the tenant is to give up possession in pursuance of the order.

128 Notice of proceedings for possession

(1) The court shall not entertain proceedings for the possession of a dwelling-house let under an introductory tenancy unless the landlord has served on the tenant a notice of proceedings complying with this section.

(2) The notice shall state that the court will be asked to make an order for the possession of the dwelling-house.

(3) The notice shall set out the reasons for the landlord's decision to apply for such an order.

(4) The notice shall specify a date after which proceedings for the possession of the dwelling-house may be begun.

The date so specified must not be earlier than the date on which the tenancy could, apart from this Chapter, be brought to an end by notice to quit given by the landlord on the same date as the notice of proceedings.

(5) The court shall not entertain any proceedings for possession of the dwelling-house unless they are begun after the date specified in the notice of proceedings.

(6) The notice shall inform the tenant of his right to request a review of the landlord's decision to seek an order for possession and of the time within which such a request must be made.

(7) The notice shall also inform the tenant that if he needs help or advice about the notice, and what to do about it, he should take it immediately to a Citizens' Advice Bureau, a housing aid centre, a law centre or a solicitor.

129 Review of decision to seek possession

(1) A request for review of the landlord's decision to seek an order for possession of a dwelling-house let under an introductory tenancy must be made before the end of the period of 14 days beginning with the day on which the notice of proceedings is served.

(2) On a request being duly made to it, the landlord shall review its decision.

(3) The Secretary of State may make provision by regulations as to the procedure to be followed in connection with a review under this section.

Nothing in the following provisions affects the generality of this power.

(4) Provision may be made by regulations—

   (a) requiring the decision on review to be made by a person of appropriate seniority who was not involved in the original decision, and

   (b) as to the circumstances in which the person concerned is entitled to an oral hearing, and whether and by whom he may be represented at such a hearing.

(5) The landlord shall notify the person concerned of the decision on the review.

If the decision is to confirm the original decision, the landlord shall also notify him of the reasons for the decision.

(6) The review shall be carried out and the tenant notified before the date specified in the notice of proceedings as the date after which proceedings for the possession of the dwelling-house may be begun.

130 Effect of beginning proceedings for possession

(1) This section applies where the landlord has begun proceedings for the possession of a dwelling-house let under an introductory tenancy and—

- (a) the trial period ends, or
- (b) any of the events specified in section 125(5) occurs (events on which a tenancy ceases to be an introductory tenancy).

(2) Subject to the following provisions, the tenancy remains an introductory tenancy until—

- (a) the tenancy comes to an end in pursuance of section 127(3) (that is, on the date on which the tenant is to give up possession in pursuance of an order of the court), or
- (b) the proceedings are otherwise finally determined.

(3) If any of the events specified in section 125(5)(b) to (d) occurs, the tenancy shall thereupon cease to be an introductory tenancy but—

- (a) the landlord (or, as the case may be, the new landlord) may continue the proceedings, and
- (b) if he does so, section 127(2) and (3) (termination by landlord) apply as if the tenancy had remained an introductory tenancy.

(4) Where in accordance with subsection (3) a tenancy ceases to be an introductory tenancy and becomes a secure tenancy, the tenant is not entitled to exercise the right to buy under Part V of the Housing Act 1985 unless and until the proceedings are finally determined on terms such that he is not required to give up possession of the dwelling-house.

(5) For the purposes of this section proceedings shall be treated as finally determined if they are withdrawn or any appeal is abandoned or the time for appealing expires without an appeal being brought.

Succession on death of tenant

131 Persons qualified to succeed tenant

A person is qualified to succeed the tenant under an introductory tenancy if he occupies the dwelling-house as his only or principal home at the time of the tenant's death and either—

- (a) he is the tenant's spouse, or
- (b) he is another member of the tenant's family and has resided with the tenant throughout the period of twelve months ending with the tenant's death;

unless, in either case, the tenant was himself a successor, as defined in section 132.

132 Cases where the tenant is a successor

(1) The tenant is himself a successor if—

- (a) the tenancy vested in him by virtue of section 133 (succession to introductory tenancy),
- (b) he was a joint tenant and has become the sole tenant,
- (c) he became the tenant on the tenancy being assigned to him (but subject to subsections (2) and (3)), or

(d) he became the tenant on the tenancy being vested in him on the death of the previous tenant.

(2) A tenant to whom the tenancy was assigned in pursuance of an order under section 24 of the Matrimonial Causes Act 1973 (property adjustment orders in connection with matrimonial proceedings) or section 17(1) of the Matrimonial and Family Proceedings Act 1984 (property adjustment orders after overseas divorce, etc.) is a successor only if the other party to the marriage was a successor.

(3) Where within six months of the coming to an end of an introductory tenancy ('the former tenancy') the tenant becomes a tenant under another introductory tenancy, and—

(a) the tenant was a successor in relation to the former tenancy, and
(b) under the other tenancy either the dwelling-house or the landlord, or both, are the same as under the former tenancy,

the tenant is also a successor in relation to the other tenancy unless the agreement creating that tenancy otherwise provides.

133 Succession to introductory tenancy

(1) This section applies where a tenant under an introductory tenancy dies.

(2) Where there is a person qualified to succeed the tenant, the tenancy vests by virtue of this section in that person, or if there is more than one such person in the one to be preferred in accordance with the following rules—

(a) the tenant's spouse is to be preferred to another member of the tenant's family;
(b) of two or more other members of the tenant's family such of them is to be preferred as may be agreed between them or as may, where there is no such agreement, be selected by the landlord.

(3) Where there is no person qualified to succeed the tenant, the tenancy ceases to be an introductory tenancy—

(a) when it is vested or otherwise disposed of in the course of the administration of the tenant's estate, unless the vesting or other disposal is in pursuance of an order made under—
   (i) section 24 of the Matrimonial Causes Act 1973 (property adjustment orders made in connection with matrimonial proceedings),
   (ii) section 17(1) of the Matrimonial and Family Proceedings Act 1984 (property adjustment orders after overseas divorce, etc.), or
   (iii) paragraph 1 of Schedule 1 to the Children Act 1989 (orders for financial relief against parents); or

(b) when it is known that when the tenancy is so vested or disposed of it will not be in pursuance of such an order.

Assignment

134 Assignment in general prohibited

(1) An introductory tenancy is not capable of being assigned except in the cases mentioned in subsection (2).

(2) The exceptions are—

  (a) an assignment in pursuance of an order made under—

      (i) section 24 of the Matrimonial Causes Act 1973 (property adjustment orders in connection with matrimonial proceedings),

     (ii) section 17(1) of the Matrimonial and Family Proceedings Act 1984 (property adjustment orders after overseas divorce, etc.), or

    (iii) paragraph 1 of Schedule 1 to the Children Act 1989 (orders for financial relief against parents);

  (b) an assignment to a person who would be qualified to succeed the tenant if the tenant died immediately before the assignment.

(3) Subsection (1) also applies to a tenancy which is not an introductory tenancy but would be if the tenant, or where the tenancy is a joint tenancy, at least one of the tenants, were occupying or continuing to occupy the dwelling-house as his only or principal home.

Repairs

135 Right to carry out repairs

The Secretary of State may by regulations under section 96 of the Housing Act 1985 (secure tenants: right to carry out repairs) apply to introductory tenants any provision made under that section in relation to secure tenants.

Provision of information and consultation

136 Provision of information about tenancies

(1) Every local housing authority or housing action trust which lets dwelling-houses under introductory tenancies shall from time to time publish information about its introductory tenancies, in such form as it considers best suited to explain in simple terms, and, so far as it considers it appropriate, the effect of—

  (a) the express terms of its introductory tenancies,

  (b) the provisions of this Chapter, and

  (c) the provisions of sections 11 to 16 of the Landlord and Tenant Act 1985 (landlord's repairing obligations),

and shall ensure that so far as is reasonably practicable the information so published is kept up to date.

(2) The landlord under an introductory tenancy shall supply the tenant with—

  (a) a copy of the information for introductory tenants published by it under subsection (1), and

  (b) a written statement of the terms of the tenancy, so far as they are neither expressed in the lease or written tenancy agreement (if any) nor implied by law;

and the statement required by paragraph (b) shall be supplied on the grant of the tenancy or as soon as practicable afterwards.

137 Consultation on matters of housing management

(1) This section applies in relation to every local housing authority and housing action trust which lets dwelling-houses under introductory tenancies and which is a landlord authority for the purposes of Part IV of the Housing Act 1985 (secure tenancies).

(2) The authority or trust shall maintain such arrangements as it considers appropriate to enable those of its introductory tenants who are likely to be substantially affected by a relevant matter of housing management—

(a) to be informed of the proposals of the authority or trust in respect of the matter, and

(b) to make their views known to the authority or trust within a specified period;

and the authority or trust shall, before making a decision on the matter, consider any representations made to it in accordance with those arrangements.

(3) A matter is one of housing management if, in the opinion of the authority or trust concerned, it relates to—

(a) the management, improvement, maintenance or demolition of dwelling-houses let by the authority or trust under introductory or secure tenancies, or

(b) the provision of services or amenities in connection with such dwelling-houses;

but not so far as it relates to the rent payable under an introductory or secure tenancy or to charges for services or facilities provided by the authority or trust.

(4) A matter is relevant if, in the opinion of the authority or trust concerned, it represents—

(a) a new programme of maintenance, improvement or demolition, or

(b) a change in the practice or policy of the authority or trust,

and is likely substantially to affect either its introductory tenants as a whole or a group of them who form a distinct social group or occupy dwelling-houses which constitute a distinct class (whether by reference to the kind of dwelling-house, or the housing estate or other larger area in which they are situated).

(5) In the case of a local housing authority, the reference in subsection (3) to the provision of services or amenities is a reference only to the provision of services or amenities by the authority acting in its capacity as landlord of the dwelling-houses concerned.

(6) The authority or trust shall publish details of the arrangements which it makes under this section, and a copy of the documents published under this subsection shall—

(a) be made available at its principal office for inspection at all reasonable hours, without charge, by members of the public, and

(b) be given, on payment of a reasonable fee, to any member of the public who asks for one.

Supplementary

138 Jurisdiction of county court

(1) A county court has jurisdiction to determine questions arising under this Chapter and to entertain proceedings brought under this Chapter and claims, for whatever amount, in connection with an introductory tenancy.

(2) That jurisdiction includes jurisdiction to entertain proceedings as to whether a statement supplied in pursuance of section 136(2)(b) (written statement of certain terms of tenancy) is accurate notwithstanding that no other relief is sought than a declaration.

(3) If a person takes proceedings in the High Court which, by virtue of this section, he could have taken in the county court, he is not entitled to recover any costs.

(4) The Lord Chancellor may make such rules and give such directions as he thinks fit for the purpose of giving effect to this section.

(5) The rules and directions may provide—

    (a) for the exercise by a district judge of a county court of any jurisdiction exercisable under this section, and

    (b) for the conduct of proceedings in private.

(6) The power to make rules is exercisable by statutory instrument which shall be subject to annulment in pursuance of a resolution of either House of Parliament.

139 Meaning of 'dwelling-house'

(1) For the purposes of this Chapter a dwelling-house may be a house or a part of a house.

(2) Land let together with a dwelling-house shall be treated for the purposes of this Chapter as part of the dwelling-house unless the land is agricultural land which would not be treated as part of a dwelling-house for the purposes of Part IV of the Housing Act 1985 (see section 112(2) of that Act).

140 Members of a person's family: Chapter I

(1) A person is a member of another's family within the meaning of this Chapter if—

    (a) he is the spouse of that person, or he and that person live together as husband and wife, or

    (b) he is that person's parent, grandparent, child, grandchild, brother, sister, uncle, aunt, nephew or niece.

(2) For the purpose of subsection (1)(b)—

    (a) a relationship by marriage shall be treated as a relationship by blood,

    (b) a relationship of the half-blood shall be treated as a relationship of the whole blood, and

    (c) the stepchild of a person shall be treated as his child.

141 Consequential amendments: introductory tenancies

(1) The enactments mentioned in Schedule 14 have effect with the amendments specified there which are consequential on the provisions of this Chapter.

(2) The Secretary of State may by order make such other amendments or repeals of any enactment as appear to him necessary or expedient in consequence of the provisions of this Chapter.

(3) Without prejudice to the generality of subsection (2), an order under that subsection may make such provision in relation to an enactment as the Secretary of State considers appropriate as regards its application (with or without modifications) or non-application in relation to introductory tenants or introductory tenancies.

142 Regulations and orders

Any regulations or order under this Part—

(a) may contain such incidental, supplementary or transitional provisions, or savings, as the Secretary of State thinks fit, and

(b) shall be made by statutory instrument which shall be subject to annulment in pursuance of a resolution of either House of Parliament.

143 Index of defined expressions: introductory tenancies

The following Table shows provisions defining or otherwise explaining provisions used in this Chapter (other than provisions defining or explaining an expression in the same section)—

adopt (in relation to periodic tenancy)	section 124(4)
assured tenancy and assured shorthold tenancy	section 230
dwelling-house	section 139
housing action trust	section 230
introductory tenancy and introductory tenant	section 124
local housing authority	section 230
member of family	section 140
registered social landlord	section 2
secure tenancy and secure tenant	section 230

CHAPTER II
REPOSSESSION, ETC.: SECURE AND ASSURED TENANCIES

Secure tenancies

144 Extension of ground of nuisance or annoyance to neighbours, etc.

For Ground 2 in Schedule 2 to the Housing Act 1985 (nuisance or annoyance to neighbours, etc.) substitute—

'*Ground 2*

The tenant or a person residing in or visiting the dwelling-house—

(a) has been guilty of conduct causing or likely to cause a nuisance or annoyance to a person residing, visiting or otherwise engaging in a lawful activity in the locality, or

(b) has been convicted of—

    (i)   using the dwelling-house or allowing it to be used for immoral or illegal purposes, or

    (ii) an arrestable offence committed in, or in the locality of, the dwelling-house.'.

145 New ground of domestic violence: secure tenancies

After Ground 2 in Schedule 2 to the Housing Act 1985 (as substituted by section 144) insert—

'*Ground 2A*

The dwelling-house was occupied (whether alone or with others) by a married couple or a couple living together as husband and wife and—

    (a) one or both of the partners is a tenant of the dwelling-house,

    (b) one partner has left because of violence or threats of violence by the other towards—

        (i)   that partner, or

        (ii) a member of the family of that partner who was residing with that partner immediately before the partner left, and

    (c) the court is satisfied that the partner who has left is unlikely to return.'.

146 Extension of ground that grant of tenancy induced by false statement

In Ground 5 in Schedule 2 to the Housing Act 1985 (grant of tenancy induced by false statement) for 'by the tenant' substitute 'by—

    (a) the tenant, or

    (b) a person acting at the tenant's instigation'.

147 Proceedings for possession or termination

(1) For section 83 of the Housing Act 1985 (notice of proceedings for possession or termination) substitute—

'83 Proceedings for possession or termination: notice requirements

(1) The court shall not entertain proceedings for the possession of a dwelling-house let under a secure tenancy or proceedings for the termination of a secure tenancy unless—

    (a) the landlord has served a notice on the tenant complying with the provisions of this section, or

    (b) the court considers it just and equitable to dispense with the requirement of such a notice.

(2) A notice under this section shall—

    (a) be in a form prescribed by regulations made by the Secretary of State,

    (b) specify the ground on which the court will be asked to make an order for the possession of the dwelling-house or for the termination of the tenancy, and

    (c) give particulars of that ground.

(3) Where the tenancy is a periodic tenancy and the ground or one of the grounds specified in the notice is Ground 2 in Schedule 2 (nuisance or other anti-social behaviour), the notice—

  (a) shall also—
    (i) state that proceedings for the possession of the dwelling-house may be begun immediately, and
    (ii) specify the date sought by the landlord as the date on which the tenant is to give up possession of the dwelling-house, and
  (b) ceases to be in force twelve months after the date so specified.

(4) Where the tenancy is a periodic tenancy and Ground 2 in Schedule 2 is not specified in the notice, the notice—

  (a) shall also specify the date after which proceedings for the possession of the dwelling-house may be begun, and
  (b) ceases to be in force twelve months after the date so specified.

(5) The date specified in accordance with subsection (3) or (4) must not be earlier than the date on which the tenancy could, apart from this Part, be brought to an end by notice to quit given by the landlord on the same date as the notice under this section.

(6) Where a notice under this section is served with respect to a secure tenancy for a term certain, it has effect also with respect to any periodic tenancy arising on the termination of that tenancy by virtue of section 86; and subsections (3) to (5) of this section do not apply to the notice.

(7) Regulations under this section shall be made by statutory instrument and may make different provision with respect to different cases or descriptions of case, including different provision for different areas.

83A Additional requirements in relation to certain proceedings for possession

(1) Where a notice under section 83 has been served on a tenant containing the information mentioned in subsection (3)(a) of that section, the court shall not entertain proceedings for the possession of the dwelling-house unless they are begun at a time when the notice is still in force.

(2) Where—

  (a) a notice under section 83 has been served on a tenant, and
  (b) a date after which proceedings may be begun has been specified in the notice in accordance with subsection (4)(a) of that section,

the court shall not entertain proceedings for the possession of the dwelling-house unless they are begun after the date so specified and at a time when the notice is still in force.

(3) Where—

  (a) the ground or one of the grounds specified in a notice under section 83 is Ground 2A in Schedule 2 (domestic violence), and
  (b) the partner who has left the dwelling-house as mentioned in that ground is not a tenant of the dwelling-house,

the court shall not entertain proceedings for the possession of the dwelling-house unless it is satisfied that the landlord has served a copy of the notice on the partner who has left or has taken all reasonable steps to serve a copy of the notice on that partner.

This subsection has effect subject to subsection (5).

(4) Where—

(a) Ground 2A in Schedule 2 is added to a notice under section 83 with the leave of the court after proceedings for possession are begun, and

(b) the partner who has left the dwelling-house as mentioned in that ground is not a party to the proceedings,

the court shall not continue to entertain the proceedings unless it is satisfied that the landlord has served a notice under subsection (6) on the partner who has left or has taken all reasonable steps to serve such a notice on that partner.

This subsection has effect subject to subsection (5).

(5) Where subsection (3) or (4) applies and Ground 2 in Schedule 2 (nuisance or other anti-social behaviour) is also specified in the notice under section 83, the court may dispense with the requirements as to service in relation to the partner who has left the dwelling-house if it considers it just and equitable to do so.

(6) A notice under this subsection shall—

(a) state that proceedings for the possession of the dwelling-house have begun,

(b) specify the ground or grounds on which possession is being sought, and

(c) give particulars of the ground or grounds.'.

(2) In section 84 of that Act (grounds and orders for possession), for subsection (3) substitute—

'(3) Where a notice under section 83 has been served on the tenant, the court shall not make such an order on any of those grounds above unless the ground is specified in the notice; but the grounds so specified may be altered or added to with the leave of the court.

(4) Where a date is specified in a notice under section 83 in accordance with subsection (3) of that section, the court shall not make an order which requires the tenant to give up possession of the dwelling-house in question before the date so specified.'.

(3) In Schedule 2 to that Act, in Ground 16, after 'notice of the proceedings for possession was served under section 83' insert '(or, where no such notice was served, the proceedings for possession were begun)'.

Assured tenancies

148 Extension of ground of nuisance or annoyance to adjoining occupiers etc.

For Ground 14 in Schedule 2 to the Housing Act 1988 (nuisance or annoyance to adjoining occupiers etc.) substitute—

'Ground 14

The tenant or a person residing in or visiting the dwelling-house—

(a) has been guilty of conduct causing or likely to cause a nuisance or annoyance to a person residing, visiting or otherwise engaging in a lawful activity in the locality, or

(b) has been convicted of—
    (i) using the dwelling-house or allowing it to be used for immoral or illegal purposes, or
    (ii) an arrestable offence committed in, or in the locality of, the dwelling-house.'.

149 New ground of domestic violence: assured tenancies

After Ground 14 in Schedule 2 to the Housing Act 1988 (as substituted by section 148) insert—

'Ground 14A

The dwelling-house was occupied (whether alone or with others) by a married couple or a couple living together as husband and wife and—

(a) one or both of the partners is a tenant of the dwelling-house,
(b) the landlord who is seeking possession is a registered social landlord or a charitable housing trust,
(c) one partner has left the dwelling-house because of violence or threats of violence by the other towards—
    (i) that partner, or
    (ii) a member of the family of that partner who was residing with that partner immediately before the partner left, and
(d) the court is satisfied that the partner who has left is unlikely to return.

For the purposes of this ground "registered social landlord" and "member of the family" have the same meaning as in Part I of the Housing Act 1996 and "charitable housing trust" means a housing trust, within the meaning of the Housing Associations Act 1985, which is a charity within the meaning of the Charities Act 1993.'.

150 Additional notice requirements: domestic violence

After section 8 of the Housing Act 1988 insert—

'8A Additional notice requirements: ground of domestic violence

(1) Where the ground specified in a notice under section 8 (whether with or without other grounds) is Ground 14A in Schedule 2 to this Act and the partner who has left the dwelling-house as mentioned in that ground is not a tenant of the dwelling-house, the court shall not entertain proceedings for possession of the dwelling-house unless—

(a) the landlord or, in the case of joint landlords, at least one of them has served on the partner who has left a copy of the notice or has taken all reasonable steps to serve a copy of the notice on that partner, or
(b) the court considers it just and equitable to dispense with such requirements as to service.

(2) Where Ground 14A in Schedule 2 to this Act is added to a notice under section 8 with the leave of the court after proceedings for possession are begun and the partner who has left the dwelling-house as mentioned in that ground is not a party to the proceedings, the court shall not continue to entertain the proceedings unless—

(a) the landlord or, in the case of joint landlords, at least one of them has served a notice under subsection (3) below on the partner who has left or has taken all reasonable steps to serve such a notice on that partner, or

(b) the court considers it just and equitable to dispense with the requirement of such a notice.

(3) A notice under this subsection shall—

(a) state that proceedings for the possession of the dwelling-house have begun,

(b) specify the ground or grounds on which possession is being sought, and

(c) give particulars of the ground or grounds.'.

151 Early commencement of certain proceedings for possession

(1) Section 8 of the Housing Act 1988 (notice of proceedings for possession) is amended as follows.

(2) In subsection (1)(a) for the words 'subsections (3) and (4)' substitute 'subsections (3) to (4B)'.

(3) In subsection (3)(b) for the words from 'which,' to 'of the notice' substitute 'in accordance with subsections (4) to (4B) below'.

(4) For subsection (4) substitute—

'(4) If a notice under this section specifies in accordance with subsection (3)(a) above Ground 14 in Schedule 2 to this Act (whether with or without other grounds), the date specified in the notice as mentioned in subsection (3)(b) above shall not be earlier than the date of the service of the notice.

(4A) If a notice under this section specifies in accordance with subsection (3)(a) above, any of Grounds 1, 2, 5 to 7, 9 and 16 in Schedule 2 to this Act (whether without other grounds or with any ground other than Ground 14), the date specified in the notice as mentioned in subsection (3)(b) above shall not be earlier than—

(a) two months from the date of service of the notice; and

(b) if the tenancy is a periodic tenancy, the earliest date on which, apart from section 5(1) above, the tenancy could be brought to an end by a notice to quit given by the landlord on the same date as the date of service of the notice under this section.

(4B) In any other case, the date specified in the notice as mentioned in subsection (3)(b) above shall not be earlier than the expiry of the period of two weeks from the date of the service of the notice.'.

CHAPTER III
INJUNCTIONS AGAINST ANTI-SOCIAL BEHAVIOUR

152 Power to grant injunctions against anti-social behaviour

(1) The High Court or a county court may, on an application by a local authority, grant an injunction prohibiting a person from—

(a) engaging in or threatening to engage in conduct causing or likely to cause a nuisance or annoyance to a person residing in, visiting or otherwise engaging in a lawful activity in residential premises to which this section applies or in the locality of such premises,

(b) using or threatening to use residential premises to which this section applies for immoral or illegal purposes, or

(c) entering residential premises to which this section applies or being found in the locality of any such premises.

(2) This section applies to residential premises of the following descriptions—

(a) dwelling-houses held under secure or introductory tenancies from the local authority;

(b) accommodation provided by that authority under Part VII of this Act or Part III of the Housing Act 1985 (homelessness).

(3) The court shall not grant an injunction under this section unless it is of the opinion that—

(a) the respondent has used or threatened to use violence against any person of a description mentioned in subsection (1)(a), and

(b) there is a significant risk of harm to that person or a person of a similar description if the injunction is not granted.

(4) An injunction under this section may—

(a) in the case of an injunction under subsection (1)(a) or (b), relate to particular acts or to conduct, or types of conduct, in general or to both, and

(b) in the case of an injunction under subsection (1)(c), relate to particular premises or a particular locality;

and may be made for a specified period or until varied or discharged.

(5) An injunction under this section may be varied or discharged by the court on an application by—

(a) the respondent, or

(b) the local authority which made the original application.

(6) The court may attach a power of arrest to one or more of the provisions of an injunction which it intends to grant under this section.

(7) The court may, in any case where it considers that it is just and convenient to do so, grant an injunction under this section, or vary such an injunction, even though the respondent has not been given such notice of the proceedings as would otherwise be required by rules of court.

If the court does so, it must afford the respondent an opportunity to make representations relating to the injunction or variation as soon as just and convenient at a hearing of which notice has been given to all the parties in accordance with rules of court.

(8) In this section 'local authority' has the same meaning as in the Housing Act 1985.

153 Power of arrest for breach of other injunctions against anti-social behaviour

(1) In the circumstances set out in this section, the High Court or a county court may attach a power of arrest to one or more of the provisions of an injunction which it intends to grant in relation to a breach or anticipated breach of the terms of a tenancy.

(2) The applicant is—

  (a) a local housing authority,

  (b) a housing action trust,

  (c) a registered social landlord, or

  (d) a charitable housing trust,

acting in its capacity as landlord of the premises which are subject to the tenancy.

(3) The respondent is the tenant or a joint tenant under the tenancy agreement.

(4) The tenancy is one by virtue of which—

  (a) a dwelling-house is held under an introductory, secure or assured tenancy, or

  (b) accommodation is provided under Part VII of this Act or Part III of the Housing Act 1985 (homelessness).

(5) The breach or anticipated breach of the terms of the tenancy consists of the respondent—

  (a) engaging in or threatening to engage in conduct causing or likely to cause a nuisance or annoyance to a person residing, visiting or otherwise engaging in a lawful activity in the locality,

  (b) using or threatening to use the premises for immoral or illegal purposes, or

  (c) allowing any sub-tenant or lodger of his or any other person residing (whether temporarily or otherwise) on the premises or visiting them to act as mentioned in paragraph (a) or (b).

(6) The court is of the opinion that—

  (a) the respondent or any person mentioned in subsection (5)(c) has used or threatened violence against a person residing, visiting or otherwise engaging in a lawful activity in the locality, and

  (b) there is a significant risk of harm to that person or a person of a similar description if the power of arrest is not attached to one or more provisions of the injunction immediately.

(7) Nothing in this section prevents the grant of an injunction relating to other matters, in addition to those mentioned above, in relation to which no power of arrest is attached.

154 Powers of arrest: ex-parte applications for injunctions

(1) In determining whether to exercise its power under section 152(6) or section 153 to attach a power of arrest to an injunction which it intends to grant on an ex-parte application, the High Court or a county court shall have regard to all the circumstances including—

  (a) whether it is likely that the applicant will be deterred or prevented from seeking the exercise of the power if the power is not exercised immediately, and

  (b) whether there is reason to believe that the respondent is aware of the proceedings for the injunction but is deliberately evading service and that the applicant or any person of a description mentioned in 152(1)(a) or section 153(5)(a) (as the case may be) will be seriously prejudiced if the decision as to whether to exercise the power were delayed until substituted service is effected.

(2) Where the court exercises its power as mentioned in subsection (1), it shall afford the respondent an opportunity to make representations relating to the exercise of the power as

soon as just and convenient at a hearing of which notice has been given to all the parties in accordance with rules of court.

155 Arrest and remand

(1) If a power of arrest is attached to certain provisions of an injunction by virtue of section 152(6) or section 153, a constable may arrest without warrant a person whom he has reasonable cause for suspecting to be in breach of any such provision or otherwise in contempt of court in relation to a breach of any such provision.

A constable shall after making any such arrest forthwith inform the person on whose application the injunction was granted.

(2) Where a person is arrested under subsection (1)—

(a) he shall be brought before the relevant judge within the period of 24 hours beginning at the time of his arrest, and

(b) if the matter is not then disposed of forthwith, the judge may remand him.

In reckoning for the purposes of this subsection any period of 24 hours no account shall be taken of Christmas Day, Good Friday or any Sunday.

(3) If the court has granted an injunction in circumstances such that a power of arrest could have been attached under section 152(6) or section 153 but—

(a) has not attached a power of arrest under the section in question to any provisions of the injunction, or

(b) has attached that power only to certain provisions of the injunction,

then, if at any time the applicant considers that the respondent has failed to comply with the injunction, he may apply to the relevant judge for the issue of a warrant for the arrest of the respondent.

(4) The relevant judge shall not issue a warrant on an application under subsection (3) unless—

(a) the application is substantiated on oath, and

(b) he has reasonable grounds for believing that the respondent has failed to comply with the injunction.

(5) If a person is brought before a court by virtue of a warrant issued under subsection (4) and the court does not dispose of the matter forthwith, the court may remand him.

(6) Schedule 15 (which makes provision corresponding to that applying in magistrates' courts in civil cases under sections 128 and 129 of the Magistrates' Courts Act 1980) applies in relation to the powers of the High Court and a county court to remand a person under this section.

(7) If a person remanded under this section is granted bail by virtue of subsection (6), he may be required by the relevant judge to comply, before release on bail or later, with such requirements as appear to the judge to be necessary to secure that he does not interfere with witnesses or otherwise obstruct the course of justice.

156 Remand for medical examination and report

(1) If the relevant judge has reason to consider that a medical report will be required, any power to remand a person under section 155 may be exercised for the purpose of enabling a medical examination and report to be made.

(2) If such a power is so exercised the adjournment shall not be for more than 4 weeks at a time unless the judge remands the accused in custody.

(3) If the judge so remands the accused, the adjournment shall not be for more than 3 weeks at a time.

(4) If there is reason to suspect that a person who has been arrested—

(a) under section 155(1), or
(b) under a warrant issued under section 155(4),

is suffering from mental illness or severe mental impairment, the relevant judge shall have the same power to make an order under section 35 of the Mental Health Act 1983 (remand for report on accused's mental condition) as the Crown Court has under section 35 of that Act in the case of an accused person within the meaning of that section.

157 Powers of arrest: supplementary provisions

(1) If in exercise of its power under section 152(6) or section 153 the High Court or a county court attaches a power of arrest to any provisions of an injunction, it may provide that the power of arrest is to have effect for a shorter period than the other provisions of the injunction.

(2) Any period specified for the purposes of subsection (1) may be extended by the court (on one or more occasions) on an application to vary or discharge the injunction.

(3) If a power of arrest has been attached to certain provisions of an injunction by virtue of section 152(6) or section 153, the court may vary or discharge the injunction in so far as it confers a power of arrest (whether or not any application has been made to vary or discharge any other provision of the injunction).

(4) An injunction may be varied or discharged under subsection (3) on an application by the respondent or the person on whose application the injunction was made.

158 Interpretation: Chapter III

(1) For the purposes of this Chapter—

'charitable housing trust' means a housing trust, within the meaning of the Housing Associations Act 1985, which is a charity within the meaning of the Charities Act 1993;

'child' means a person under the age of 18 years;

'harm'—

(a) in relation to a person who has reached the age of 18 years, means ill-treatment or the impairment of health, and
(b) in relation to a child, means ill-treatment or the impairment of health or development;

'health' includes physical or mental health;

'ill-treatment', in relation to a child, includes sexual abuse and forms of ill-treatment which are not physical;

'relevant judge', in relation to an injunction, means—

(a) where the injunction was granted by the High Court, a judge of that court,

(b) where the injunction was granted by a county court, a judge or district judge of that or any other county court;

'tenancy' includes a licence, and 'tenant' and 'landlord' shall be construed accordingly.

(2) Where the question of whether harm suffered by a child is significant turns on the child's health or development, his health or development shall be compared with that which could reasonably be expected of a similar child.

PART VI
ALLOCATION OF HOUSING ACCOMMODATION

Introductory

159 Allocation of housing accommodation

(1) A local housing authority shall comply with the provisions of this Part in allocating housing accommodation.

(2) For the purposes of this Part a local housing authority allocate housing accommodation when they—

(a) select a person to be a secure or introductory tenant of housing accommodation held by them,

(b) nominate a person to be a secure or introductory tenant of housing accommodation held by another person, or

(c) nominate a person to be an assured tenant of housing accommodation held by a registered social landlord.

(3) The reference in subsection (2)(a) to selecting a person to be a secure tenant includes deciding to exercise any power to notify an existing tenant or licensee that his tenancy or licence is to be a secure tenancy.

(4) The references in subsection (2)(b) and (c) to nominating a person include nominating a person in pursuance of any arrangements (whether legally enforceable or not) to require that housing accommodation, or a specified amount of housing accommodation, is made available to a person or one of a number of persons nominated by the authority.

(5) The provisions of this Part do not apply to the allocation of housing accommodation by a local housing authority to a person who is already—

(a) a secure or introductory tenant,

(b) an assured tenant (otherwise than under an assured shorthold tenancy) of housing accommodation held by a registered social landlord, or

(c) an assured tenant of housing accommodation allocated to him by a local housing authority.

(6) The provisions of this Part do not apply to the allocation of housing accommodation by a local housing authority to two or more persons jointly if—

(a) one or more of them is a person within subsection (5)(a), (b) or (c), and

(b) none of the others is excluded from being a qualifying person by section 161(2) or regulations under section 161(3).

(7) Subject to the provisions of this Part, a local housing authority may allocate housing accommodation in such manner as they consider appropriate.

160 Cases where provisions about allocation do not apply

(1) The provisions of this Part about the allocation of housing accommodation do not apply in the following cases.

(2) They do not apply where a secure tenancy—

(a) vests under section 89 of the Housing Act 1985 (succession to periodic secure tenancy on death of tenant),

(b) remains a secure tenancy by virtue of section 90 of that Act (devolution of term certain of secure tenancy on death of tenant),

(c) is assigned under section 92 of that Act (assignment of secure tenancy by way of exchange),

(d) is assigned to a person who would be qualified to succeed the secure tenant if the secure tenant died immediately before the assignment, or

(e) vests or is otherwise disposed of in pursuance of an order made under—

  (i) section 24 of the Matrimonial Causes Act 1973 (property adjustment orders in connection with matrimonial proceedings),

  (ii) section 17(1) of the Matrimonial and Family Proceedings Act 1984 (property adjustment orders after overseas divorce, etc.), or

  (iii) paragraph 1 of Schedule 1 to the Children Act 1989 (orders for financial relief against parents).

(3) They do not apply where an introductory tenancy—

(a) becomes a secure tenancy on ceasing to be an introductory tenancy,

(b) vests under section 133(2) (succession to introductory tenancy on death of tenant),

(c) is assigned to a person who would be qualified to succeed the introductory tenant if the introductory tenant died immediately before the assignment, or

(d) vests or is otherwise disposed of in pursuance of an order made under—

  (i) section 24 of the Matrimonial Causes Act 1973 (property adjustment orders in connection with matrimonial proceedings),

  (ii) section 17(1) of the Matrimonial and Family Proceedings Act 1984 (property adjustment orders after overseas divorce, etc.), or

  (iii) paragraph 1 of Schedule 1 to the Children Act 1989 (orders for financial relief against parents).

(4) They do not apply in such other cases as the Secretary of State may prescribe by regulations.

(5) The regulations may be framed so as to make the exclusion of the provisions of this Part about the allocation of housing accommodation subject to such restrictions or conditions as may be specified.

In particular, those provisions may be excluded—

(a) in relation to specified descriptions of persons, or

(b) in relation to housing accommodation of a specified description or a specified proportion of housing accommodation of any specified description.

The housing register

161 Allocation only to qualifying persons

(1) A local housing authority shall allocate housing accommodation only to persons ('qualifying persons') who are qualified to be allocated housing accommodation by that authority.

(2) A person subject to immigration control within the meaning of the Asylum and Immigration Act 1996 is not qualified to be allocated housing accommodation by any authority in England and Wales unless he is of a class prescribed by regulations made by the Secretary of State.

(3) The Secretary of State may by regulations prescribe other classes of persons who are, or are not, qualifying persons in relation to local housing authorities generally or any particular local housing authority.

(4) Subject to subsection (2) and any regulations under subsection (3) a local housing authority may decide what classes of persons are, or are not, qualifying persons.

(5) The prohibition in subsection (1) extends to the allocation of housing accommodation to two or more persons jointly if any of them is excluded from being a qualifying person by subsection (2) or regulations under subsection (3).

(6) The prohibition does not otherwise extend to the allocation of housing accommodation to two or more persons jointly if one or more of them are qualifying persons.

162 The housing register

(1) Every local housing authority shall establish and maintain a register of qualifying persons (their 'housing register').

(2) An authority's housing register may be kept in such form as the authority think fit.

(3) It may, in particular, be kept as part of a register maintained for other housing purposes or maintained in common by the authority and one or more other landlords, provided the entries constituting the authority's housing register can be distinguished.

(4) An authority's housing register shall contain such information about the persons on it and other relevant matters as the Secretary of State may prescribe by regulations.

(5) Subject to any such regulations, the authority may decide what information is to be contained in the register.

163 Operation of housing register

(1) A person shall be put on a local housing authority's housing register if he applies to be put on and it appears to the authority that he is a qualifying person.

(2) A local housing authority may put a person on their housing register without any application, if it appears to them that he is a qualifying person.

(3) When a local housing authority put a person on their housing register (on his application or otherwise), they shall notify him that they have done so.

(4) A local housing authority may amend an entry on their housing register in such circumstances as they think fit.

If they do so, they shall notify the person concerned of the amendment.

(5) A local housing authority may remove a person from their housing register in such circumstances as they think fit.

(6) They shall do so—

    (a) if it appears to them that he has never been a qualifying person or is no longer such a person, or

    (b) if he requests them to do so and he is not owed any duty under section 193 or 195(2) (main housing duties owed to persons who are homeless or threatened with homelessness).

(7) Before removing a person from the register, a local housing authority shall comply with such requirements, as to notification or otherwise, as the Secretary of State may prescribe by regulations.

164 Notification of adverse decision and right to review

(1) If a local housing authority decide—

    (a) not to put a person on their housing register who has applied to be put on, or

    (b) to remove a person from their housing register otherwise than at his request,

they shall notify him of their decision and of the reasons for it.

(2) The notice shall also inform him of his right to request a review of the decision and of the time within which such a request must be made.

(3) A request for review must be made before the end of the period of 21 days beginning with the day on which he is notified of the authority's decision and reasons, or such longer period as the authority may in writing allow.

(4) There is no right to request a review of the decision reached on an earlier review.

(5) On a request being duly made to them, the authority shall review their decision.

(6) Notice required to be given to a person under this section shall be given in writing and, if not received by him, shall be treated as having been given if it is made available at the authority's office for a reasonable period for collection by him.

165 Procedure on a review

(1) The Secretary of State may make provision by regulations as to the procedure to be followed in connection with a review under section 164.

Nothing in the following provisions affects the generality of this power.

(2) Provision may be made by regulations—

    (a) requiring the decision on review to be made by a person of appropriate seniority who was not involved in the original decision, and

    (b) as to the circumstances in which the person concerned is entitled to an oral hearing, and whether and by whom he may be represented at such a hearing.

(3) The authority shall notify the person concerned of the decision on the review.

(4) If the decision is to confirm the original decision, they shall also notify him of the reasons for the decision.

(5) Provision may be made by regulations as to the period within which the review must be carried out and notice given of the decision.

(6) Notice required to be given to a person under this section shall be given in writing and, if not received by him, shall be treated as having been given if it is made available at the authority's office for a reasonable period for collection by him.

166 Information about housing register

(1) A person on the housing register of a local housing authority is entitled—

  (a) to see the entry relating to himself and to receive a copy of it free of charge, and
  (b) to be given such general information as will enable him to assess how long it is likely to be before housing accommodation appropriate to his needs becomes available for allocation to him.

(2) The fact that a person is on an authority's housing register, and the information about him included in the register, shall not be divulged to any other member of the public.

The allocation scheme

167 Allocation in accordance with allocation scheme

(1) Every local housing authority shall have a scheme (their 'allocation scheme') for determining priorities, and as to the procedure to be followed, in allocating housing accommodation.

For this purpose 'procedure' includes all aspects of the allocation process, including the persons or descriptions of persons by whom decisions are to be taken.

(2) As regards priorities, the scheme shall be framed so as to secure that reasonable preference is given to—

  (a) people occupying insanitary or overcrowded housing or otherwise living in unsatisfactory housing conditions,
  (b) people occupying housing accommodation which is temporary or occupied on insecure terms,
  (c) families with dependent children,
  (d) households consisting of or including someone who is expecting a child,
  (e) households consisting of or including someone with a particular need for settled accommodation on medical or welfare grounds, and
  (f) households whose social or economic circumstances are such that they have difficulty in securing settled accommodation.

The scheme shall also be framed so as to secure that additional preference is given to households within paragraph (e) consisting of someone with a particular need for settled accommodation on medical or welfare grounds who cannot reasonably be expected to find settled accommodation for themselves in the foreseeable future.

(3) The Secretary of State may by regulations—

(a) specify further descriptions of people to whom preference is to be given as mentioned in subsection (2), or

(b) amend or repeal any part of subsection (2).

(4) The Secretary of State may by regulations specify factors which a local housing authority shall not take into account in allocating housing accommodation.

(5) As regards the procedure to be followed, the scheme shall be framed in accordance with such principles as the Secretary of State may prescribe by regulations.

(6) Subject to the above provisions, and to any regulations made under them, the authority may decide on what principles the scheme is to be framed.

(7) Before adopting an allocation scheme, or making an alteration to their scheme reflecting a major change of policy, a local housing authority shall—

(a) send a copy of the draft scheme, or proposed alteration, to every registered social landlord with which they have nomination arrangements (see section 159(4)), and

(b) afford those persons a reasonable opportunity to comment on the proposals.

(8) A local housing authority shall not allocate housing accommodation except in accordance with their allocation scheme.

168 Information about allocation scheme

(1) A local housing authority shall publish a summary of their allocation scheme and provide a copy of the summary free of charge to any member of the public who asks for one.

(2) The authority shall make the scheme available for inspection at their principal office and shall provide a copy of the scheme, on payment of a reasonable fee, to any member of the public who asks for one.

(3) When the authority make an alteration to their scheme reflecting a major change of policy, they shall within a reasonable period of time notify everyone on their housing register, explaining in general terms the effect of the change.

Supplementary

169 Guidance to authorities by the Secretary of State

(1) In the exercise of their functions under this Part, local housing authorities shall have regard to such guidance as may from time to time be given by the Secretary of State.

(2) The Secretary of State may give guidance generally or to specified descriptions of authorities.

170 Co-operation between registered social landlords and local housing authorities

Where a local housing authority so request, a registered social landlord shall co-operate to such extent as is reasonable in the circumstances in offering accommodation to people with priority on the authority's housing register.

171 False statements and withholding information

(1) A person commits an offence if, in connection with the exercise by a local housing authority of their functions under this Part—

(a) he knowingly or recklessly makes a statement which is false in a material particular, or

(b) he knowingly withholds information which the authority have reasonably required him to give in connection with the exercise of those functions.

(2) A person guilty of an offence under this section is liable on summary conviction to a fine not exceeding level 5 on the standard scale.

172 Regulations

(1) Regulations under this Part shall be made by statutory instrument.

(2) No regulations shall be made under section 167(3) (regulations amending provisions about priorities in allocating housing accommodation) unless a draft of the regulations has been laid before and approved by a resolution of each House of Parliament.

(3) Any other regulations under this Part shall be subject to annulment in pursuance of a resolution of either House of Parliament.

(4) Regulations under this Part may contain such incidental, supplementary and transitional provisions as appear to the Secretary of State appropriate, and may make different provision for different cases including different provision for different areas.

173 Consequential amendments: Part VI

The enactments mentioned in Schedule 16 have effect with the amendments specified there which are consequential on the provisions of this Part.

174 Index of defined expressions: Part VI

The following Table shows provisions defining or otherwise explaining expressions used in this Part (other than provisions defining or explaining an expression used in the same section)—

allocation (of housing)	section 159(2)
allocation scheme	section 167
assured tenancy	section 230
housing register	section 162
introductory tenancy and introductory tenant	sections 230 and 124
local housing authority	section 230
qualifying person (in relation to housing register)	section 161
registered social landlord	sections 230 and 2
secure tenancy and secure tenant	section 230

PART VII
HOMELESSNESS

Homelessness and threatened homelessness

175 Homelessness and threatened homelessness

(1) A person is homeless if he has no accommodation available for his occupation, in the United Kingdom or elsewhere, which he—

(a) is entitled to occupy by virtue of an interest in it or by virtue of an order of a court,

(b) has an express or implied licence to occupy, or

(c) occupies as a residence by virtue of any enactment or rule of law giving him the right to remain in occupation or restricting the right of another person to recover possession.

(2) A person is also homeless if he has accommodation but—

(a) he cannot secure entry to it, or

(b) it consists of a moveable structure, vehicle or vessel designed or adapted for human habitation and there is no place where he is entitled or permitted both to place it and to reside in it.

(3) A person shall not be treated as having accommodation unless it is accommodation which it would be reasonable for him to continue to occupy.

(4) A person is threatened with homelessness if it is likely that he will become homeless within 28 days.

176 Meaning of accommodation available for occupation

Accommodation shall be regarded as available for a person's occupation only if it is available for occupation by him together with—

(a) any other person who normally resides with him as a member of his family, or

(b) any other person who might reasonably be expected to reside with him.

References in this Part to securing that accommodation is available for a person's occupation shall be construed accordingly.

177 Whether it is reasonable to continue to occupy accommodation

(1) It is not reasonable for a person to continue to occupy accommodation if it is probable that this will lead to domestic violence against him, or against—

(a) a person who normally resides with him as a member of his family, or

(b) any other person who might reasonably be expected to reside with him.

For this purpose 'domestic violence', in relation to a person, means violence from a person with whom he is associated, or threats of violence from such a person which are likely to be carried out.

(2) In determining whether it would be, or would have been, reasonable for a person to continue to occupy accommodation, regard may be had to the general circumstances prevailing in relation to housing in the district of the local housing authority to whom he has applied for accommodation or for assistance in obtaining accommodation.

(3) The Secretary of State may by order specify—

(a) other circumstances in which it is to be regarded as reasonable or not reasonable for a person to continue to occupy accommodation, and

(b) other matters to be taken into account or disregarded in determining whether it would be, or would have been, reasonable for a person to continue to occupy accommodation.

178　Meaning of associated person

(1) For the purposes of this Part, a person is associated with another person if—

(a) they are or have been married to each other;
(b) they are cohabitants or former cohabitants;
(c) they live or have lived in the same household;
(d) they are relatives;
(e) they have agreed to marry one another (whether or not that agreement has been terminated);
(f) in relation to a child, each of them is a parent of the child or has, or has had, parental responsibility for the child.

(2) If a child has been adopted or has been freed for adoption by virtue of any of the enactments mentioned in section 16(1) of the Adoption Act 1976, two persons are also associated with each other for the purposes of this Part if—

(a) one is a natural parent of the child or a parent of such a natural parent, and
(b) the other is the child or a person—
    (i) who has become a parent of the child by virtue of an adoption order or who has applied for an adoption order, or
    (ii) with whom the child has at any time been placed for adoption.

(3) In this section—

'adoption order' has the meaning given by section 72(1) of the Adoption Act 1976;
'child' means a person under the age of 18 years;
'cohabitants' means a man and a woman who, although not married to each other, are living together as husband and wife, and 'former cohabitants' shall be construed accordingly;
'parental responsibility' has the same meaning as in the Children Act 1989; and
'relative', in relation to a person, means—

(a) the father, mother, stepfather, stepmother, son, daughter, stepson, stepdaughter, grandmother, grandfather, grandson or granddaughter of that person or of that person's spouse or former spouse, or
(b) the brother, sister, uncle, aunt, niece or nephew (whether of the full blood or of the half blood or by affinity) of that person or of that person's spouse or former spouse,

and includes, in relation to a person who is living or has lived with another person as husband and wife, a person who would fall within paragraph (a) or (b) if the parties were married to each other.

General functions in relation to homelessness or threatened homelessness

179　Duty of local housing authority to provide advisory services

(1) Every local housing authority shall secure that advice and information about homelessness, and the prevention of homelessness, is available free of charge to any person in their district.

(2) The authority may give to any person by whom such advice and information is provided on behalf of the authority assistance by way of grant or loan.

(3) A local housing authority may also assist any such person—

(a) by permitting him to use premises belonging to the authority,

(b) by making available furniture or other goods, whether by way of gift, loan or otherwise, and

(c) by making available the services of staff employed by the authority.

180 Assistance for voluntary organisations

(1) The Secretary of State or a local housing authority may give assistance by way of grant or loan to voluntary organisations concerned with homelessness or matters relating to homelessness.

(2) A local housing authority may also assist any such organisation—

(a) by permitting them to use premises belonging to the authority,

(b) by making available furniture or other goods, whether by way of gift, loan or otherwise, and

(c) by making available the services of staff employed by the authority.

(3) A 'voluntary organisation' means a body (other than a public or local authority) whose activities are not carried on for profit.

181 Terms and conditions of assistance

(1) This section has effect as to the terms and conditions on which assistance is given under section 179 or 180.

(2) Assistance shall be on such terms, and subject to such conditions, as the person giving the assistance may determine.

(3) No assistance shall be given unless the person to whom it is given undertakes—

(a) to use the money, furniture or other goods or premises for a specified purpose, and

(b) to provide such information as may reasonably be required as to the manner in which the assistance is being used.

The person giving the assistance may require such information by notice in writing, which shall be complied with within 21 days beginning with the date on which the notice is served.

(4) The conditions subject to which assistance is given shall in all cases include conditions requiring the person to whom the assistance is given—

(a) to keep proper books of account and have them audited in such manner as may be specified,

(b) to keep records indicating how he has used the money, furniture or other goods or premises, and

(c) to submit the books of account and records for inspection by the person giving the assistance.

(5) If it appears to the person giving the assistance that the person to whom it was given has failed to carry out his undertaking as to the purpose for which the assistance was to be

used, he shall take all reasonable steps to recover from that person an amount equal to the amount of the assistance.

(6) He must first serve on the person to whom the assistance was given a notice specifying the amount which in his opinion is recoverable and the basis on which that amount has been calculated.

182 Guidance by the Secretary of State

(1) In the exercise of their functions relating to homelessness and the prevention of homelessness, a local housing authority or social services authority shall have regard to such guidance as may from time to time be given by the Secretary of State.

(2) The Secretary of State may give guidance either generally or to specified descriptions of authorities.

Application for assistance in case of homelessness or threatened homelessness

183 Application for assistance

(1) The following provisions of this Part apply where a person applies to a local housing authority for accommodation, or for assistance in obtaining accommodation, and the authority have reason to believe that he is or may be homeless or threatened with homelessness.

(2) In this Part—

'applicant' means a person making such an application,

'assistance under this Part' means the benefit of any function under the following provisions of this Part relating to accommodation or assistance in obtaining accommodation, and

'eligible for assistance' means not excluded from such assistance by section 185 (persons from abroad not eligible for housing assistance) or section 186 (asylum seekers and their dependants).

(3) Nothing in this section or the following provisions of this Part affects a person's entitlement to advice and information under section 179 (duty to provide advisory services).

184 Inquiry into cases of homelessness or threatened homelessness

(1) If the local housing authority have reason to believe that an applicant may be homeless or threatened with homelessness, they shall make such inquiries as are necessary to satisfy themselves—

(a) whether he is eligible for assistance, and
(b) if so, whether any duty, and if so what duty, is owed to him under the following provisions of this Part.

(2) They may also make inquiries whether he has a local connection with the district of another local housing authority in England, Wales or Scotland.

(3) On completing their inquiries the authority shall notify the applicant of their decision and, so far as any issue is decided against his interests, inform him of the reasons for their decision.

(4) If the authority have notified or intend to notify another local housing authority under section 198 (referral of cases), they shall at the same time notify the applicant of that decision and inform him of the reasons for it.

(5) A notice under subsection (3) or (4) shall also inform the applicant of his right to request a review of the decision and of the time within which such a request must be made (see section 202).

(6) Notice required to be given to a person under this section shall be given in writing and, if not received by him, shall be treated as having been given to him if it is made available at the authority's office for a reasonable period for collection by him or on his behalf.

Eligibility for assistance

185 Persons from abroad not eligible for housing assistance

(1) A person is not eligible for assistance under this Part if he is a person from abroad who is ineligible for housing assistance.

(2) A person who is subject to immigration control within the meaning of the Asylum and Immigration Act 1996 is not eligible for housing assistance unless he is of a class prescribed by regulations made by the Secretary of State.

(3) The Secretary of State may make provision by regulations as to other descriptions of persons who are to be treated for the purposes of this Part as persons from abroad who are ineligible for housing assistance.

(4) A person from abroad who is not eligible for housing assistance shall be disregarded in determining for the purposes of this Part whether another person—

(a)   is homeless or threatened with homelessness, or
(b)   has a priority need for accommodation.

186 Asylum-seekers and their dependants

(1) An asylum-seeker, or a dependant of an asylum-seeker who is not by virtue of section 185 a person from abroad who is ineligible for housing assistance, is not eligible for assistance under this Part if he has any accommodation in the United Kingdom, however temporary, available for his occupation.

(2) For the purposes of this section a person who makes a claim for asylum—

(a)   becomes an asylum-seeker at the time when his claim is recorded by the Secretary of State as having been made, and
(b)   ceases to be an asylum-seeker at the time when his claim is recorded by the Secretary of State as having been finally determined or abandoned.

(3) For the purposes of this section a person—

(a)   becomes a dependant of an asylum-seeker at the time when he is recorded by the Secretary of State as being a dependant of the asylum-seeker, and
(b)   ceases to be a dependant of an asylum-seeker at the time when the person whose dependant he is ceases to be an asylum-seeker or, if it is earlier, at the time when he is recorded by the Secretary of State as ceasing to be a dependant of the asylum-seeker.

(4) In relation to an asylum-seeker, 'dependant' means a person—

(a) who is his spouse or a child of his under the age of eighteen, and

(b) who has neither a right of abode in the United Kingdom nor indefinite leave under the Immigration Act 1971 to enter or remain in the United Kingdom.

(5) In this section a 'claim for asylum' means a claim made by a person that it would be contrary to the United Kingdom's obligations under the Convention relating to the Status of Refugees done at Geneva on 28th July 1951 and the Protocol to that Convention for him to be removed from, or required to leave, the United Kingdom.

187 Provision of information by Secretary of State

(1) The Secretary of State shall, at the request of a local housing authority, provide the authority with such information as they may require—

(a) as to whether a person is or has become an asylum-seeker, or a dependant of an asylum-seeker, and

(b) to enable them to determine whether such a person is eligible for assistance under this Part under section 185 (persons from abroad not eligible for housing assistance).

(2) Where that information is given otherwise than in writing, the Secretary of State shall confirm it in writing if a written request is made to him by the authority.

(3) If it appears to the Secretary of State that any application, decision or other change of circumstances has affected the status of a person about whom information was previously provided by him to a local housing authority under this section, he shall inform the authority in writing of that fact, the reason for it and the date on which the previous information became inaccurate.

Interim duty to accommodate

188 Interim duty to accommodate in case of apparent priority need

(1) If the local housing authority have reason to believe that an applicant may be homeless, eligible for assistance and have a priority need, they shall secure that accommodation is available for his occupation pending a decision as to the duty (if any) owed to him under the following provisions of this Part.

(2) The duty under this section arises irrespective of any possibility of the referral of the applicant's case to another local housing authority (see sections 198 to 200).

(3) The duty ceases when the authority's decision is notified to the applicant, even if the applicant requests a review of the decision (see section 202).

The authority may continue to secure that accommodation is available for the applicant's occupation pending a decision on a review.

189 Priority need for accommodation

(1) The following have a priority need for accommodation—

(a) a pregnant woman or a person with whom she resides or might reasonably be expected to reside;

(b) a person with whom dependent children reside or might reasonably be expected to reside;

(c) a person who is vulnerable as a result of old age, mental illness or handicap or physical disability or other special reason, or with whom such a person resides or might reasonably be expected to reside;

(d) a person who is homeless or threatened with homelessness as a result of an emergency such as flood, fire or other disaster.

(2) The Secretary of State may by order—

(a) specify further descriptions of persons as having a priority need for accommodation, and

(b) amend or repeal any part of subsection (1).

(3) Before making such an order the Secretary of State shall consult such associations representing relevant authorities, and such other persons, as he considers appropriate.

(4) No such order shall be made unless a draft of it has been approved by resolution of each House of Parliament.

Duties to persons found to be homeless or threatened with homelessness

190 Duties to persons becoming homeless intentionally

(1) This section applies where the local housing authority are satisfied that an applicant is homeless and is eligible for assistance but are also satisfied that he became homeless intentionally.

(2) If the authority are satisfied that the applicant has a priority need, they shall—

(a) secure that accommodation is available for his occupation for such period as they consider will give him a reasonable opportunity of securing accommodation for his occupation, and

(b) provide him with advice and such assistance as they consider appropriate in the circumstances in any attempts he may make to secure that accommodation becomes available for his occupation.

(3) If they are not satisfied that he has a priority need, they shall provide him with advice and such assistance as they consider appropriate in the circumstances in any attempts he may make to secure that accommodation becomes available for his occupation.

191 Becoming homeless intentionally

(1) A person becomes homeless intentionally if he deliberately does or fails to do anything in consequence of which he ceases to occupy accommodation which is available for his occupation and which it would have been reasonable for him to continue to occupy.

(2) For the purposes of subsection (1) an act or omission in good faith on the part of a person who was unaware of any relevant fact shall not be treated as deliberate.

(3) A person shall be treated as becoming homeless intentionally if—

(a) he enters into an arrangement under which he is required to cease to occupy accommodation which it would have been reasonable for him to continue to occupy, and

(b) the purpose of the arrangement is to enable him to become entitled to assistance under this Part,

and there is no other good reason why he is homeless.

(4) A person who is given advice or assistance under section 197 (duty where other suitable alternative accommodation available), but fails to secure suitable accommodation in circumstances in which it was reasonably to be expected that he would do so, shall, if he makes a further application under this Part, be treated as having become homeless intentionally.

192 Duty to persons not in priority need who are not homeless intentionally

(1) This section applies where the local housing authority—

(a) are satisfied that an applicant is homeless and eligible for assistance, and
(b) are not satisfied that he became homeless intentionally,

but are not satisfied that he has a priority need.

(2) The authority shall provide the applicant with advice and such assistance as they consider appropriate in the circumstances in any attempts he may make to secure that accommodation becomes available for his occupation.

193 Duty to persons with priority need who are not homeless intentionally

(1) This section applies where the local housing authority are satisfied that an applicant is homeless, eligible for assistance and has a priority need, and are not satisfied that he became homeless intentionally.

This section has effect subject to section 197 (duty where other suitable accommodation available).

(2) Unless the authority refer the application to another local housing authority (see section 198), they shall secure that accommodation is available for occupation by the applicant.

(3) The authority are subject to the duty under this section for a period of two years ('the minimum period'), subject to the following provisions of this section.

After the end of that period the authority may continue to secure that accommodation is available for occupation by the applicant, but are not obliged to do so (see section 194).

(4) The minimum period begins with—

(a) if the applicant was occupying accommodation made available under section 188 (interim duty to accommodate), the day on which he was notified of the authority's decision that the duty under this section was owed to him;
(b) if the applicant was occupying accommodation made available to him under section 200(3) (interim duty where case considered for referral but not referred), the date on which he was notified under subsection (2) of that section of the decision that the conditions for referral were not met;
(c) in any other case, the day on which accommodation was first made available to him in pursuance of the duty under this section.

(5) The local housing authority shall cease to be subject to the duty under this section if the applicant, having been informed by the authority of the possible consequence of refusal,

refuses an offer of accommodation which the authority are satisfied is suitable for him and the authority notify him that they regard themselves as having discharged their duty under this section.

(6) The local housing authority shall cease to be subject to the duty under this section if the applicant—

(a) ceases to be eligible for assistance,
(b) becomes homeless intentionally from the accommodation made available for his occupation,
(c) accepts an offer of accommodation under Part VI (allocation of housing), or
(d) otherwise voluntarily ceases to occupy as his only or principal home the accommodation made available for his occupation.

(7) The local housing authority shall also cease to be subject to the duty under this section if—

(a) the applicant, having been informed of the possible consequence of refusal, refuses an offer of accommodation under Part VI, and
(b) the authority are satisfied that the accommodation was suitable for him and that it was reasonable for him to accept it and notify him accordingly within 21 days of the refusal.

(8) For the purposes of subsection (7) an applicant may reasonably be expected to accept an offer of accommodation under Part VI even though he is under contractual or other obligations in respect of his existing accommodation, provided he is able to bring those obligations to an end before he is required to take up the offer.

(9) A person who ceases to be owed the duty under this section may make a fresh application to the authority for accommodation or assistance in obtaining accommodation.

194 Power exercisable after minimum period of duty under s 193

(1) Where a local housing authority have been subject to the duty under section 193 in relation to a person until the end of the minimum period, they may continue to secure that accommodation is available for his occupation.

(2) They shall not do so unless they are satisfied on a review under this section that—

(a) he has a priority need,
(b) there is no other suitable accommodation available for occupation by him in their district, and
(c) he wishes the authority to continue securing that accommodation is available for his occupation;

and they shall not continue to do so for more than two years at a time unless they are satisfied on a further review under this section as to those matters.

The review shall be carried out towards the end of the minimum period, or subsequent two year period, with a view to enabling the authority to make an assessment of the likely situation at the end of that period.

(3) They shall cease to do so if events occur such that, by virtue of section 193(6) or (7), they would cease to be subject to any duty under that section.

(4) Where an authority carry out a review under this section they shall make such inquiries as they consider appropriate to determine—

(a) whether they are satisfied as to the matters mentioned in subsection (2)(a) to (c), and
(b) whether any of the events referred to in subsection (3) has occurred;

and on completing the review they shall notify the applicant of their determination and of whether they propose to exercise, or continue to exercise, their power under this section.

(5) The authority may at any time, whether in consequence of a review or otherwise, give notice to the person concerned that they propose to cease exercising their power under this section in his case.

(6) The notice must specify—

(a) the day on which they will cease exercising their power under this section, and
(b) any action that they intend to take as a result,

and must be given not less than the prescribed period before the day so specified.

195 Duties in case of threatened homelessness

(1) This section applies where the local housing authority are satisfied that an applicant is threatened with homelessness and is eligible for assistance.

(2) If the authority—

(a) are satisfied that he has a priority need, and
(b) are not satisfied that he became threatened with homelessness intentionally,

they shall take reasonable steps to secure that accommodation does not cease to be available for his occupation.

This subsection has effect subject to section 197 (duty where other suitable accommodation available).

(3) Subsection (2) does not affect any right of the authority, whether by virtue of a contract, enactment or rule of law, to secure vacant possession of any accommodation.

(4) Where in pursuance of the duty under subsection (2) the authority secure that accommodation other than that occupied by the applicant when he made his application is available for occupation by him, the provisions of section 193(3) to (9) (period for which duty owed) and section 194 (power exercisable after minimum period of duty) apply, with any necessary modifications, in relation to the duty under this section as they apply in relation to the duty under section 193.

(5) If the authority—

(a) are not satisfied that the applicant has a priority need, or

(b) are satisfied that he has a priority need but are also satisfied that he became threatened with homelessness intentionally,

they shall furnish him with advice and such assistance as they consider appropriate in the circumstances in any attempts he may make to secure that accommodation does not cease to be available for his occupation.

196 Becoming threatened with homelessness intentionally

(1) A person becomes threatened with homelessness intentionally if he deliberately does or fails to do anything the likely result of which is that he will be forced to leave accommodation which is available for his occupation and which it would have been reasonable for him to continue to occupy.

(2) For the purposes of subsection (1) an act or omission in good faith on the part of a person who was unaware of any relevant fact shall not be treated as deliberate.

(3) A person shall be treated as becoming threatened with homelessness intentionally if—

(a) he enters into an arrangement under which he is required to cease to occupy accommodation which it would have been reasonable for him to continue to occupy, and
(b) the purpose of the arrangement is to enable him to become entitled to assistance under this Part,

and there is no other good reason why he is threatened with homelessness.

(4) A person who is given advice or assistance under section 197 (duty where other suitable alternative accommodation available), but fails to secure suitable accommodation in circumstances in which it was reasonably to be expected that he would do so, shall, if he makes a further application under this Part, be treated as having become threatened with homelessness intentionally.

Duty where other suitable accommodation available

197 Duty where other suitable accommodation available

(1) This section applies if the local housing authority would be under a duty under this Part—

(a) to secure that accommodation is available for occupation by an applicant, or
(b) to secure that accommodation does not cease to be available for his occupation,

but are satisfied that other suitable accommodation is available for occupation by him in their district.

(2) In that case, their duty is to provide the applicant with such advice and assistance as the authority consider is reasonably required to enable him to secure such accommodation.

(3) The duty ceases if the applicant fails to take reasonable steps to secure such accommodation.

(4) In deciding what advice and assistance to provide under this section, and whether the applicant has taken reasonable steps, the authority shall have regard to all the circumstances including—

(a) the characteristics and personal circumstances of the applicant, and

(b) the state of the local housing market and the type of accommodation available.

(5) For the purposes of this section accommodation shall not be regarded as available for occupation by the applicant if it is available only with assistance beyond what the authority consider is reasonable in the circumstances.

(6) Subsection (1) does not apply to the duty of a local housing authority under—

section 188 (interim duty to accommodate in case of apparent priority need),
section 190(2)(a) (limited duty to person becoming homeless intentionally), or
section 200(1), (3) or (4) (interim duties where case is considered for referral or referred).

Referral to another local housing authority

198 Referral of case to another local housing authority

(1) If the local housing authority would be subject to the duty under section 193 (accommodation for those with priority need who are not homeless intentionally) but consider that the conditions are met for referral of the case to another local housing authority, they may notify that other authority of their opinion.

The authority need not consider under section 197 whether other suitable accommodation is available before proceeding under this section.

(2) The conditions for referral of the case to another authority are met if—

(a) neither the applicant nor any person who might reasonably be expected to reside with him has a local connection with the district of the authority to whom his application was made,
(b) the applicant or a person who might reasonably be expected to reside with him has a local connection with the district of that other authority, and
(c) neither the applicant nor any person who might reasonably be expected to reside with him will run the risk of domestic violence in that other district.

(3) For this purpose a person runs the risk of domestic violence—

(a) if he runs the risk of violence from a person with whom he is associated, or
(b) if he runs the risk of threats of violence from such a person which are likely to be carried out.

(4) The conditions for referral of the case to another authority are also met if—

(a) the applicant was on a previous application made to that other authority placed (in pursuance of their functions under this Part) in accommodation in the district of the authority to whom his application is now made, and
(b) the previous application was within such period as may be prescribed of the present application.

(5) The question whether the conditions for referral of a case are satisfied shall be decided by agreement between the notifying authority and the notified authority or, in default of agreement, in accordance with such arrangements as the Secretary of State may direct by order.

(6) An order may direct that the arrangements shall be—

(a) those agreed by any relevant authorities or associations of relevant authorities, or

(b) in default of such agreement, such arrangements as appear to the Secretary of State to be suitable, after consultation with such associations representing relevant authorities, and such other persons, as he thinks appropriate.

(7) No such order shall be made unless a draft of the order has been approved by a resolution of each House of Parliament.

199 Local connection

(1) A person has a local connection with the district of a local housing authority if he has a connection with it—

(a) because he is, or in the past was, normally resident there, and that residence is or was of his own choice,

(b) because he is employed there,

(c) because of family associations, or

(d) because of special circumstances.

(2) A person is not employed in a district if he is serving in the regular armed forces of the Crown.

(3) Residence in a district is not of a person's own choice if—

(a) he becomes resident there because he, or a person who might reasonably be expected to reside with him, is serving in the regular armed forces of the Crown, or

(b) he, or a person who might reasonably be expected to reside with him, becomes resident there because he is detained under the authority of an Act of Parliament.

(4) In subsections (2) and (3) 'regular armed forces of the Crown' means the Royal Navy, the regular forces as defined by section 225 of the Army Act 1955, the regular air force as defined by section 223 of the Air Force Act 1955 and Queen Alexandra's Royal Naval Nursing Service.

(5) The Secretary of State may by order specify other circumstances in which—

(a) a person is not to be treated as employed in a district, or

(b) residence in a district is not to be treated as of a person's own choice.

200 Duties to applicant whose case is considered for referral or referred

(1) Where a local housing authority notify an applicant that they intend to notify or have notified another local housing authority of their opinion that the conditions are met for the referral of his case to that other authority—

(a) they cease to be subject to any duty under section 188 (interim duty to accommodate in case of apparent priority need), and

(b) they are not subject to any duty under section 193 (the main housing duty),

but they shall secure that accommodation is available for occupation by the applicant until he is notified of the decision whether the conditions for referral of his case are met.

(2) When it has been decided whether the conditions for referral are met, the notifying authority shall notify the applicant of the decision and inform him of the reasons for it.

The notice shall also inform the applicant of his right to request a review of the decision and of the time within which such a request must be made.

(3) If it is decided that the conditions for referral are not met, the notifying authority shall secure that accommodation is available for occupation by the applicant until they have considered whether other suitable accommodation is available for his occupation in their district.

If they are satisfied that other suitable accommodation is available for his occupation in their district, section 197(2) applies; and if they are not so satisfied, they are subject to the duty under section 193 (the main housing duty).

(4) If it is decided that the conditions for referral are met, the notified authority shall secure that accommodation is available for occupation by the applicant until they have considered whether other suitable accommodation is available for his occupation in their district.

If they are satisfied that other suitable accommodation is available for his occupation in their district, section 197(2) applies; and if they are not so satisfied, they are subject to the duty under section 193 (the main housing duty).

(5) The duty under subsection (1), (3) or (4) ceases as provided in that subsection even if the applicant requests a review of the authority's decision (see section 202).

The authority may continue to secure that accommodation is available for the applicant's occupation pending the decision on a review.

(6) Notice required to be given to an applicant under this section shall be given in writing and, if not received by him, shall be treated as having been given to him if it is made available at the authority's office for a reasonable period for collection by him or on his behalf.

201 Application of referral provisions to cases arising in Scotland

Sections 198 and 200 (referral of application to another local housing authority and duties to applicant whose case is considered for referral or referred) apply—

  (a) to applications referred by a local authority in Scotland in pursuance of sections 33 and 34 of the Housing (Scotland) Act 1987, and
  (b) to persons whose applications are so transferred,

as they apply to cases arising under this Part (the reference in section 198 to this Part being construed as a reference to Part II of that Act).

Right to request review of decision

202 Right to request review of decision

(1) An applicant has the right to request a review of—

  (a) any decision of a local housing authority as to his eligibility for assistance,
  (b) any decision of a local housing authority as to what duty (if any) is owed to him under sections 190 to 193 and 195 to 197 (duties to persons found to be homeless or threatened with homelessness),
  (c) any decision of a local housing authority to notify another authority under section 198(1) (referral of cases),
  (d) any decision under section 198(5) whether the conditions are met for the referral of his case,

(e) any decision under section 200(3) or (4) (decision as to duty owed to applicant whose case is considered for referral or referred), or

(f) any decision of a local housing authority as to the suitability of accommodation offered to him in discharge of their duty under any of the provisions mentioned in paragraph (b) or (e).

(2) There is no right to request a review of the decision reached on an earlier review.

(3) A request for review must be made before the end of the period of 21 days beginning with the day on which he is notified of the authority's decision or such longer period as the authority may in writing allow.

(4) On a request being duly made to them, the authority or authorities concerned shall review their decision.

203 Procedure on a review

(1) The Secretary of State may make provision by regulations as to the procedure to be followed in connection with a review under section 202.

Nothing in the following provisions affects the generality of this power.

(2) Provision may be made by regulations—

(a) requiring the decision on review to be made by a person of appropriate seniority who was not involved in the original decision, and

(b) as to the circumstances in which the applicant is entitled to an oral hearing, and whether and by whom he may be represented at such a hearing.

(3) The authority, or as the case may be either of the authorities, concerned shall notify the applicant of the decision on the review.

(4) If the decision is—

(a) to confirm the original decision on any issue against the interests of the applicant, or

(b) to confirm a previous decision—
  (i) to notify another authority under section 198 (referral of cases), or
  (ii) that the conditions are met for the referral of his case,

they shall also notify him of the reasons for the decision.

(5) In any case they shall inform the applicant of his right to appeal to a county court on a point of law, and of the period within which such an appeal must be made (see section 204).

(6) Notice of the decision shall not be treated as given unless and until subsection (5), and where applicable subsection (4), is complied with.

(7) Provision may be made by regulations as to the period within which the review must be carried out and notice given of the decision.

(8) Notice required to be given to a person under this section shall be given in writing and, if not received by him, shall be treated as having been given if it is made available at the authority's office for a reasonable period for collection by him or on his behalf.

204 Right of appeal to county court on point of law

(1) If an applicant who has requested a review under section 202—

(a) is dissatisfied with the decision on the review, or

(b) is not notified of the decision on the review within the time prescribed under section 203,

he may appeal to the county court on any point of law arising from the decision or, as the case may be, the original decision.

(2) An appeal must be brought within 21 days of his being notified of the decision or, as the case may be, of the date on which he should have been notified of a decision on review.

(3) On appeal the court may make such order confirming, quashing or varying the decision as it thinks fit.

(4) Where the authority were under a duty under section 188, 190 or 200 to secure that accommodation is available for the applicant's occupation, they may continue to secure that accommodation is so available—

(a) during the period for appealing under this section against the authority's decision, and

(b) if an appeal is brought, until the appeal (and any further appeal) is finally determined.

Supplementary provisions

205 Discharge of functions: introductory

(1) The following sections have effect in relation to the discharge by a local housing authority of their functions under this Part to secure that accommodation is available for the occupation of a person—

section 206 (general provisions),
section 207 (provision of accommodation by authority),
section 208 (out-of-area placements),
section 209 (arrangements with private landlord).

(2) In those sections those functions are referred to as the authority's 'housing functions under this Part'.

206 Discharge of functions by local housing authorities

(1) A local housing authority may discharge their housing functions under this Part only in the following ways—

(a) by securing that suitable accommodation provided by them is available,

(b) by securing that he obtains suitable accommodation from some other person, or

(c) by giving him such advice and assistance as will secure that suitable accommodation is available from some other person.

(2) A local housing authority may require a person in relation to whom they are discharging such functions—

(a) to pay such reasonable charges as they may determine in respect of accommodation which they secure for his occupation (either by making it available themselves or otherwise), or

(b) to pay such reasonable amount as they may determine in respect of sums payable by them for accommodation made available by another person.

207 Discharge of functions: provision of accommodation by the authority

(1) A local housing authority shall not under section 206(1)(a) discharge their housing functions under this Part by providing accommodation other than—

(a) accommodation in a hostel within the meaning of section 622 of the Housing Act 1985, or

(b) accommodation leased to the authority as mentioned in subsection (2) below,

for more than two years (continuously or in aggregate) in any period of three years.

This applies irrespective of the number of applications for accommodation or assistance in obtaining accommodation made by the person concerned.

(2) The accommodation referred to in subsection (1)(b) is accommodation—

(a) leased to the authority with vacant possession for use as temporary housing accommodation on terms which include provision for the lessor to obtain vacant possession from the authority on the expiry of a specified period or when required by the lessor,

(b) the lessor of which is not an authority or body within section 80(1) of the Housing Act 1985 (the landlord condition for secure tenancies), and

(c) in which the authority have no interest other than under the lease in question or as a mortgagee.

(3) The authority shall not discharge such functions in relation to a person who—

(a) normally resides with another person as a member of his family, or

(b) might reasonably be expected to reside with another person,

in such a way that subsection (1) would be contravened if the functions were discharged in relation to that other person.

(4) The Secretary of State may, on the application of a local housing authority, by direction exclude or modify the operation of subsection (1) in relation to that authority if it appears to him that the authority will not otherwise be able reasonably to discharge their housing functions under this Part.

(5) Any such direction shall have effect only—

(a) with respect to applicants of a description specified in the direction, and

(b) for a period specified in the direction, which shall not exceed one year,

and may be expressed to have effect subject to any conditions specified in the direction.

(6) Where the Secretary of State gives or has given a direction under subsection (4), he may give the authority such directions as he considers appropriate as to the discharge of

their housing functions under this Part in cases affected by the direction having or ceasing to have effect.

208 Discharge of functions: out-of-area placements

(1) So far as reasonably practicable a local housing authority shall in discharging their housing functions under this Part secure that accommodation is available for the occupation of the applicant in their district.

(2) If they secure that accommodation is available for the occupation of the applicant outside their district, they shall give notice to the local housing authority in whose district the accommodation is situated.

(3) The notice shall state—

(a) the name of the applicant,
(b) the number and description of other persons who normally reside with him as a member of his family or might reasonably be expected to reside with him,
(c) the address of the accommodation,
(d) the date on which the accommodation was made available to him, and
(e) which function under this Part the authority was discharging in securing that the accommodation is available for his occupation.

(4) The notice must be in writing, and must be given before the end of the period of 14 days beginning with the day on which the accommodation was made available to the applicant.

209 Discharge of functions: arrangements with private landlord

(1) This section applies where in pursuance of any of their housing functions under this Part a local housing authority make the arrangements with a private landlord to provide accommodation.

For this purpose a 'private landlord' means a landlord who is not within section 80(1) of the Housing Act 1985 (the landlord condition for secure tenancies).

(2) If the housing function arises under section 188, 190, 200, or 204(4) (interim duties), a tenancy granted in pursuance of the arrangements to a person specified by the authority cannot be an assured tenancy before the end of the period of twelve months beginning with—

(a) the date on which the applicant was notified of the authority's decision under section 184(3) or 198(5), or
(b) if there is a review of that decision under section 202 or an appeal to the court under section 204, the date on which he is notified of the decision on review or the appeal is finally determined,

unless, before or during that period, the tenant is notified by the landlord (or, in the cases of joint landlords, at least one of them) that the tenancy is to be regarded as an assured shorthold tenancy or an assured tenancy other than an assured shorthold tenancy.

A registered social landlord cannot serve such a notice making such a tenancy an assured tenancy other than an assured shorthold tenancy.

(3) Where in any other case a tenancy is granted in pursuance of the arrangements by a registered social landlord to a person specified by the authority—

(a) the tenancy cannot be an assured tenancy unless it is an assured shorthold tenancy, and

(b) the landlord cannot convert the tenancy to an assured tenancy unless the accommodation is allocated to the tenant under Part VI.

210 Suitability of accommodation

(1) In determining for the purposes of this Part whether accommodation is suitable for a person, the local housing authority shall have regard to Parts IX, X and XI of the Housing Act 1985 (slum clearance; overcrowding; houses in multiple occupation).

(2) The Secretary of State may by order specify—

(a) circumstances in which accommodation is or is not to be regarded as suitable for a person, and

(b) matters to be taken into account or disregarded in determining whether accommodation is suitable for a person.

211 Protection of property of homeless persons and persons threatened with homelessness

(1) This section applies where a local housing authority have reason to believe that—

(a) there is danger of loss of, or damage to, any personal property of an applicant by reason of his inability to protect it or deal with it, and

(b) no other suitable arrangements have been or are being made.

(2) If the authority have become subject to a duty towards the applicant under—

section 188 (interim duty to accommodate),

section 190, 193 or 195 (duties to persons found to be homeless or threatened with homelessness), or

section 200 (duties to applicant whose case is considered for referral or referred),

then, whether or not they are still subject to such a duty, they shall take reasonable steps to prevent the loss of the property or prevent or mitigate damage to it.

(3) If they have not become subject to such a duty, they may take any steps they consider reasonable for that purpose.

(4) The authority may decline to take action under this section except upon such conditions as they consider appropriate in the particular case, which may include conditions as to—

(a) the making and recovery by the authority of reasonable charges for the action taken, or

(b) the disposal by the authority, in such circumstances as may be specified, of property in relation to which they have taken action.

(5) References in this section to personal property of the applicant include personal property of any person who might reasonably be expected to reside with him.

(6) Section 212 contains provisions supplementing this section.

212 Protection of property: supplementary provisions

(1) The authority may for the purposes of section 211 (protection of property of homeless persons or persons threatened with homelessness)—

(a) enter, at all reasonable times, any premises which are the usual place of residence of the applicant or which were his last usual place of residence, and

(b) deal with any personal property of his in any way which is reasonably necessary, in particular by storing it or arranging for its storage.

(2) Where the applicant asks the authority to move his property to a particular location nominated by him, the authority—

(a) may, if it appears to them that his request is reasonable, discharge their responsibilities under section 211 by doing as he asks, and

(b) having done so, have no further duty or power to take action under that section in relation to that property.

If such a request is made, the authority shall before complying with it inform the applicant of the consequence of their doing so.

(3) If no such request is made (or, if made, is not acted upon) the authority cease to have any duty or power to take action under section 211 when, in their opinion, there is no longer any reason to believe that there is a danger of loss of or damage to a person's personal property by reason of his inability to protect it or deal with it.

But property stored by virtue of their having taken such action may be kept in store and any conditions upon which it was taken into store continue to have effect, with any necessary modifications.

(4) Where the authority—

(a) cease to be subject to a duty to take action under section 211 in respect of an applicant's property, or

(b) cease to have power to take such action, having previously taken such action,

they shall notify the applicant of that fact and of the reason for it.

(5) The notification shall be given to the applicant—

(a) by delivering it to him, or

(b) by leaving it, or sending it to him, at his last known address.

(6) References in this section to personal property of the applicant include personal property of any person who might reasonably be expected to reside with him.

213 Co-operation between relevant housing authorities and bodies

(1) Where a local housing authority—

(a) request another relevant housing authority or body, in England, Wales or Scotland, to assist them in the discharge of their functions under this Part, or

(b) request a social services authority, in England, Wales or Scotland, to exercise any of their functions in relation to a case which the local housing authority are dealing with under this Part,

the authority or body to whom the request is made shall co-operate in rendering such assistance in the discharge of the functions to which the request relates as is reasonable in the circumstances.

(2) In subsection (1)(a) 'relevant housing authority or body' means—

(a) in relation to England and Wales, a local housing authority, a new town corporation, a registered social landlord or a housing action trust;

(b) in relation to Scotland, a local authority, a development corporation, a registered housing association or Scottish Homes.

Expressions used in paragraph (a) have the same meaning as in the Housing Act 1985; and expressions used in paragraph (b) have the same meaning as in the Housing (Scotland) Act 1987.

(3) Subsection (1) above applies to a request by a local authority in Scotland under section 38 of the Housing (Scotland) Act 1987 as it applies to a request by a local housing authority in England and Wales (the references to this Part being construed, in relation to such a request, as references to Part II of that Act).

General provisions

214 False statements, withholding information and failure to disclose change of circumstances

(1) It is an offence for a person, with intent to induce a local housing authority to believe in connection with the exercise of their functions under this Part that he or another person is entitled to accommodation or assistance in accordance with the provisions of this Part, or is entitled to accommodation or assistance of a particular description—

(a) knowingly or recklessly to make a statement which is false in a material particular, or

(b) knowingly to withhold information which the authority have reasonably required him to give in connection with the exercise of those functions.

(2) If before an applicant receives notification of the local housing authority's decision on his application there is any change of facts material to his case, he shall notify the authority as soon as possible.

The authority shall explain to every applicant, in ordinary language, the duty imposed on him by this subsection and the effect of subsection (3).

(3) A person who fails to comply with subsection (2) commits an offence unless he shows that he was not given the explanation required by that subsection or that he had some other reasonable excuse for non-compliance.

(4) A person guilty of an offence under this section is liable on summary conviction to a fine not exceeding level 5 on the standard scale.

215 Regulations and orders

(1) In this Part 'prescribed' means prescribed by regulations of the Secretary of State.

(2) Regulations or an order under this Part may make different provision for different purposes, including different provision for different areas.

(3) Regulations or an order under this Part shall be made by statutory instrument.

(4) Unless required to be approved in draft, regulations or an order under this Part shall be subject to annulment in pursuance of a resolution of either House of Parliament.

216 Transitional and consequential matters

(1) The provisions of this Part have effect in place of the provisions of Part III of the Housing Act 1985 (housing the homeless) and shall be construed as one with that Act.

(2) Subject to any transitional provision contained in an order under section 232(4) (power to include transitional provision in commencement order), the provisions of this Part do not apply in relation to an applicant whose application for accommodation or assistance in obtaining accommodation was made before the commencement of this Part.

(3) The enactments mentioned in Schedule 17 have effect with the amendments specified there which are consequential on the provisions of this Part.

217 Minor definitions: Part VII

(1) In this Part, subject to subsection (2)—

'relevant authority' means a local housing authority or a social services authority; and

'social services authority' means a local authority for the purposes of the Local Authority Social Services Act 1970, as defined in section 1 of that Act.

(2) In this Part, in relation to Scotland—

(a) 'local housing authority' means a local authority within the meaning of the Housing (Scotland) Act 1988, and
(b) 'social services authority' means a local authority for the purposes of the Social Work (Scotland) Act 1968.

(3) References in this Part to the district of a local housing authority—

(a) have the same meaning in relation to an authority in England or Wales as in the Housing Act 1985, and
(b) in relation to an authority in Scotland, mean the area of the local authority concerned.

218 Index of defined expressions: Part VII

The following Table shows provisions defining or otherwise explaining expressions used in this Part (other than provisions defining or explaining an expression used in the same section)—

accommodation available for occupation	section 176
applicant	section 183(2)
assistance under this Part	section 183(2)
associated (in relation to a person)	section 178
assured tenancy and assured shorthold tenancy	section 230
district (of local housing authority)	section 217(3)
eligible for assistance	section 183(2)

homeless	section 175(1)
housing functions under this Part (in sections 206 to 209)	section 205(2)
intentionally homeless	section 191
intentionally threatened with homelessness	section 196
local connection	section 199
local housing authority—	
—in England and Wales	section 230
—in Scotland	section 217(2)(a)
minimum period (for purposes of section 193)	section 193(3) and (4)
prescribed	section 215(1)
priority need	section 189
reasonable to continue to occupy accommodation	section 177
registered social landlord	section 230
relevant authority	section 217(1)
social services authority	section 217(1) and (2)(b)
threatened with homelessness	section 175(4)

PART VIII
MISCELLANEOUS AND GENERAL PROVISIONS

Miscellaneous

219 Directions as to certain charges by social landlords

(1) The Secretary of State may give directions to social landlords about the making of service charges in respect of works of repair, maintenance or improvement—

    (a) requiring or permitting the waiver or reduction of charges where relevant assistance is given by the Secretary of State, and

    (b) permitting the waiver or reduction of charges in such other circumstances as may be specified in the directions.

(2) A direction shall not require the waiver or reduction of charges by reference to assistance for which application was made before the date on which the direction was given, but subject to that directions may relate to past charges or works to such extent as appears to the Secretary of State to be appropriate.

(3) Directions which require or permit the waiver or reduction of charges have corresponding effect—

    (a) in relation to charges already demanded so as to require or permit the non-enforcement of the charges, and

    (b) in relation to charges already paid so as to require or permit a refund.

(4) For the purposes of this section 'social landlord' means—

    (a) an authority or body within section 80(1) of the Housing Act 1985 (the landlord condition for secure tenancies), other than a housing co-operative, or

    (b) a registered social landlord.

(5) In this section 'assistance' means grant or other financial assistance of any kind; and directions may specify what assistance is relevant for the purposes of this section, and to what buildings or other land any assistance is to be regarded as relevant.

(6) The provisions of section 220 supplement this section.

220 Directions as to certain charges: supplementary provisions

(1) Directions under section 219 may make different provision for different cases or descriptions of case.

This includes power to make—

  (a) different provision for different social landlords or descriptions of social landlords, and
  (b) different provision for different areas.

(2) Directions under section 219 requiring the reduction of a service charge may specify the amount (or proportion) of the reduction or provide for its determination in such manner as may be specified.

(3) Directions under section 219 permitting the waiver or reduction of a service charge may specify criteria to which the social landlord is to have regard in deciding whether to do so or to what extent.

(4) The Secretary of State shall publish any direction under section 219 relating to all social landlords or any description of social landlords in such manner as he considers appropriate for bringing it to the notice of the landlords concerned.

(5) For the purposes of section 219 'service charge' means an amount payable by a lessee of a dwelling—

  (a) which is payable, directly or indirectly, for repairs, maintenance or improvements, and
  (b) the whole or part of which varies or may vary according to the relevant costs.

(6) The relevant costs are the costs or estimated costs incurred or to be incurred by or on behalf of the social landlord, or a superior landlord, in connection with the matters for which the service charge is payable.

For this purpose costs are relevant costs in relation to a service charge whether they are incurred, or to be incurred, in the period for which the service charge is payable or in an earlier or later period.

(7) In this section—

'costs' includes overheads, and
'dwelling' means a building or part of a building occupied or intended to be occupied as a separate dwelling.

221 Exercise of compulsory purchase powers in relation to Crown land

(1) This section applies to any power to acquire land compulsorily under—

  (a) the Housing Act 1985,
  (b) the Housing Associations Act 1985,

(c) Part III of the Housing Act 1988 (housing action trust areas), or

(d) Part VII of the Local Government and Housing Act 1989 (renewal areas).

(2) Any power to which this section applies may be exercised in relation to an interest in Crown land which is for the time being held otherwise than by or on behalf of the Crown, but only with the consent of the appropriate authority.

(3) In this section 'Crown land' means land in which there is a Crown interest or a Duchy interest.

For this purpose—

'Crown interest' means an interest belonging to Her Majesty in right of the Crown or belonging to a government department or held in trust for Her Majesty for the purposes of a government department; and

'Duchy interest' means an interest belonging to Her Majesty in right of the Duchy of Lancaster or belonging to the Duchy of Cornwall.

(4) For the purposes of this section 'the appropriate authority', in relation to Crown land, is—

(a) in the case of land belonging to Her Majesty in right of the Crown and forming part of the Crown Estate, the Crown Estate Commissioners:

(b) in relation to any other land belonging to Her Majesty in right of the Crown, the government department having the management of that land;

(c) in relation to land belonging to Her Majesty in right of the Duchy of Lancaster, the Chancellor of the Duchy;

(d) in relation to land belonging to the Duchy of Cornwall, such person as the Duke of Cornwall, or the possessor for the time being of the Duchy of Cornwall, appoints;

(e) in the case of land belonging to a government department or held in trust for Her Majesty for the purposes of a government department, that department.

(5) If any question arises as to what authority is the appropriate authority in relation to any land, that question shall be referred to the Treasury, whose decision shall be final.

222 Miscellaneous minor amendments

The enactments mentioned in Schedule 18 have effect with the amendments specified there, which are miscellaneous minor amendments relating to housing.

Part I relates to housing management.

Part II relates to housing finance.

Part III relates to orders in relation to property in family and matrimonial proceedings, etc.

Part IV relates to other housing provisions.

General

223 Offences by body corporate

(1) Where an offence under this Act committed by a body corporate is proved to have been committed with the consent or connivance of a director, manager, secretary or other similar officer of the body corporate, or a person purporting to act in such a capacity, he as well as the body corporate is guilty of an offence and liable to be proceeded against and punished accordingly.

(2) Where the affairs of a body corporate are managed by its members, subsection (1) applies in relation to the acts and defaults of a member in connection with his functions of management as if he were a director of the body corporate.

224 The Common Council of the City of London

(1) The Common Council of the City of London may appoint a committee, consisting of so many persons as they think fit, for any purposes of this Act which in their opinion may be better regulated and managed by means of a committee.

(2) A committee so appointed—

(a) shall consist as to a majority of its members of members of the Common Council, and

(b) shall not be authorised to borrow money or to make a rate,

and shall be subject to any regulations and restrictions which may be imposed by the Common Council.

(3) A person is not, by reason only of the fact that he occupies a house at a rental from the Common Council, disqualified from being elected or being a member of that Council or any committee of that Council; but no person shall vote as a member of that Council, or any such committee, on a resolution or question which is proposed or arises in pursuance of this Act and relates to land in which he is beneficially interested.

(4) A person who votes in contravention of subsection (3) commits a summary offence and is liable on conviction to a fine not exceeding level 4 on the standard scale; but the fact of his giving the vote does not invalidate any resolution or proceeding of the authority.

225 The Isles of Scilly

(1) This Act applies to the Isles of Scilly subject to such exceptions, adaptations and modifications as the Secretary of State may by order direct.

(2) An order shall be made by statutory instrument which shall be subject to annulment in pursuance of a resolution of either House of Parliament.

226 Corresponding provision for Northern Ireland

An Order in Council under paragraph 1(1)(b) of Schedule 1 to the Northern Ireland Act 1974 (legislation for Northern Ireland in the interim period) which states that it is made only for purposes corresponding to those of section 120 (payment of housing benefit to third parties)—

(a) shall not be subject to paragraph 1(4) and (5) of that Schedule (affirmative resolution of both Houses of Parliament), but

(b) shall be subject to annulment in pursuance of a resolution of either House of Parliament.

227 Repeals

The enactments specified in Schedule 19 are repealed to the extent specified.

228 Financial provisions

(1) There shall be paid out of money provided by Parliament—

(a) any expenses of the Secretary of State incurred in consequence of this Act, and

(b) any increase attributable to this Act in the sums payable out of money so provided under any other enactment.

(2) There shall be paid out of the National Loans Fund any increase attributable to this Act in the sums so payable under any other enactment.

(3) Any sums received by the Secretary of State under this Act shall be paid into the Consolidated Fund.

229 Meaning of 'lease' and 'tenancy' and related expressions

(1) In this Act 'lease' and 'tenancy' have the same meaning.

(2) Both expressions include—

(a) a sub-lease or a sub-tenancy, and
(b) an agreement for a lease or tenancy (or sub-lease or sub-tenancy).

(3) The expressions 'lessor' and 'lessee' and 'landlord' and 'tenant', and references to letting, to the grant of a lease or to covenants or terms, shall be construed accordingly.

230 Minor definitions: general

In this Act—

'assured tenancy', 'assured shorthold tenancy' and 'assured agricultural occupancy' have the same meaning as in Part I of the Housing Act 1988;
'enactment' includes an enactment comprised in subordinate legislation (within the meaning of the Interpretation Act 1978);
'housing action trust' has the same meaning as in the Housing Act 1988;
'housing association' has the same meaning as in the Housing Associations Act 1985;
'introductory tenancy' and 'introductory tenant' have the same meaning as in Chapter I of Part V of this Act;
'local housing authority' has the same meaning as in the Housing Act 1985;
'registered social landlord' has the same meaning as in Part I of this Act;
'secure tenancy' and 'secure tenant' have the same meaning as in Part IV of the Housing Act 1985.

Final provisions

231 Extent

(1) The provisions of this Act extend to England and Wales, and only to England and Wales, subject as follows.

(2) The following provisions also extend to Scotland—

Part IV (housing benefit and related matters), and
the provisions of this Part so far as relating to Part IV.

(3) Section 226 (power to make corresponding provision for Northern Ireland) also extends to Northern Ireland.

(4) Any amendment or repeal by this Act of an enactment has the same extent as the enactment amended or repealed, except that—

(a) amendments or repeals of provisions of the Housing Associations Act 1985, other than in consequence of paragraph 1 of Schedule 18 to this Act (repeal of Part IV of the Housing Act 1988), do not extend to Scotland,

(b) amendments or repeals of provisions of the Housing Act 1988 relating to registered housing associations do not extend to Scotland,

(c) amendments or repeals of provisions of the Asylum and Immigration Appeals Act 1993 or the Asylum and Immigration Act 1996 do not extend to Scotland or Northern Ireland, and

(d) repeals of the following provisions do not extend to Scotland—

    (i) section 24(5)(a) and (c) of the Local Government Act 1988,

    (ii) section 182 of the Local Government and Housing Act 1989,

    (iii) paragraph 21(3) of Schedule 6 to the Charities Act 1993, and

    (iv) provisions in Schedule 26 to the Local Government, Planning and Land Act 1980.

(5) Any power conferred by this Act to make consequential amendments or repeals of enactments may be exercised in relation to enactments as they extend to any part of the United Kingdom.

232 Commencement

(1) The following provisions of this Act come into force on Royal Assent—

section 110 (new leases: valuation principles),

section 120 (payment of housing benefit to third parties), and

sections 223 to 226 and 228 to 233 (general provisions).

(2) The following provisions of this Act come into force at the end of the period of two months beginning with the date on which this Act is passed—

sections 81 and 82 (restriction on termination of tenancy for failure to pay service charge),

section 85 (appointment of manager by the court),

section 94 (provision of general legal advice about residential tenancies),

section 95 (jurisdiction of county courts),

section 221 (exercise of compulsory purchase powers in relation to Crown land),

paragraph 24 (powers of local housing authorities to acquire land for housing purposes), paragraph 26 (preserved right to buy) and paragraphs 27 to 29 of Schedule 18 (local authority assistance in connection with mortgages), and

sections 222 and 227, and Schedule 19 (consequential repeals), in so far as they relate to those paragraphs.

(3) The other provisions of this Act come into force on a day appointed by order of the Secretary of State, and different days may be appointed for different areas and different purposes.

(4) An order under subsection (3) shall be made by statutory instrument and may contain such transitional provisions and savings as appear to the Secretary of State to be appropriate.

233 Short title

This Act may be cited as the Housing Act 1996.

SCHEDULES

SCHEDULE 1
REGISTERED SOCIAL LANDLORDS: REGULATION

Section 7

PART I

CONTROL OF PAYMENTS TO MEMBERS, ETC.

Payments by way of gift, dividend or bonus

1 (1) A registered social landlord shall not make a gift or pay a sum by way of dividend or bonus to—

    (a) a person who is or has been a member of the body,

    (b) a person who is a member of the family of a person within paragraph (a), or

    (c) a company of which a person within paragraph (a) or (b) is a director,

except as permitted by this paragraph.

(2) The following are permitted—

    (a) the payment of a sum which, in accordance with the constitution or rules of the body, is paid as interest on capital lent to the body or subscribed by way of shares in the body;

    (b) the payment by a fully mutual housing association to a person who has ceased to be a member of the association of a sum which is due to him either under his tenancy agreement with the association or under the terms of the agreement under which he became a member of the association.

(3) Where an industrial and provident society or a company registered under the Companies Act 1985 pays a sum or makes a gift in contravention of this paragraph, the society or company may recover the sum or the value of the gift, and proceedings for its recovery shall be taken if the Corporation so directs.

Payments and benefits to officers and employees, etc.

2 (1) A registered social landlord which is an industrial and provident society or a company registered under the Companies Act 1985 shall not make a payment or grant a benefit to—

    (a) an officer or employee of the society or company,

    (b) a person who at any time within the preceding twelve months has been a person within paragraph (a),

    (c) a close relative of a person within paragraph (a) or (b), or

    (d) a business trading for profit of which a person falling within paragraph (a), (b) or (c) is a principal proprietor or in the management of which such a person is directly concerned, except as permitted by this paragraph.

(2) The following are permitted—

(a) payments made or benefits granted to an officer or employee of the society or company under his contract of employment with the society or company;

(b) the payment of remuneration or expenses to an officer of the society or company who does not have a contract of employment with the society or company;

(c) any such payment as may be made in accordance with paragraph 1(2) (interest payable in accordance with the rules and certain sums payable by a fully mutual housing association to a person who has ceased to be a member);

(d) the grant or renewal of a tenancy by a co-operative housing association;

(e) where a tenancy of a house has been granted to, or to a close relative of, a person who later became an officer or employee, the grant to that tenant of a new tenancy whether of the same or another house;

(f) payments made or benefits granted in accordance with any determination made by the Corporation.

(3) A determination for the purposes of sub-paragraph (2)(f) may specify the class or classes of case in which a payment may be made or benefit granted and specify the maximum amount.

(4) Where a society or company pays a sum or grants a benefit in contravention of this paragraph, the society or company may recover the sum or value of the benefit; and proceedings for its recovery shall be taken if the Corporation so directs.

Maximum amounts payable by way of fees, expenses, etc.

3 (1) The Corporation may from time to time specify the maximum amounts which may be paid by a registered social landlord which is an industrial and provident society or a company registered under the Companies Act 1985—

(a) by way of fees or other remuneration, or by way of expenses, to a member of the society or company who is not an officer or employee of the society or company, or

(b) by way of remuneration or expenses to an officer of the society or company who does not have a contract of employment with the society or company.

(2) Different amounts may be so specified for different purposes.

(3) Where a society or company makes a payment in excess of the maximum permitted under this paragraph, the society or company may recover the excess, and proceedings for its recovery shall be taken if the Corporation so directs.

PART II

CONSTITUTION, CHANGE OF RULES, AMALGAMATION AND DISSOLUTION

General power to remove director, trustee, etc.

4 (1) The Corporation may, in accordance with the following provisions, by order remove—

(a) a director or trustee of a registered social landlord which is a registered charity,

(b) a committee member of a registered social landlord which is an industrial and provident society, or

(c) a director of a registered social landlord which is a company registered under the Companies Act 1985.

(2) The Corporation may make an order removing any such person if—

(a) he has been adjudged bankrupt or has made an arrangement with his creditors;

(b) he is subject to a disqualification order under the Company Directors Disqualification Act 1986;

(c) he is subject to an order under section 429(2) of the Insolvency Act 1986 (failure to pay under county court administration order);

(d) he is disqualified under section 72 of the Charities Act 1993 from being a charity trustee;

(e) he is incapable of acting by reason of mental disorder;

(f) he has not acted; or

(g) he cannot be found or does not act and his absence or failure to act is impeding the proper management of the registered social landlord's affairs.

(3) Before making an order the Corporation shall give at least 14 days' notice of its intention to do so to the person whom it intends to remove, and to the registered social landlord.

(4) That notice may be given by post, and if so given to the person whom the Corporation intend to remove may be addressed to his last known address in the United Kingdom.

(5) A person who is ordered to be removed under this paragraph may appeal against the order to the High Court.

Restriction on power of removal in case of registered charity

5 (1) The Corporation may make an order under paragraph 4 removing a director or trustee of a registered charity only if the charity has, at any time before the power is exercised—

(a) received financial assistance under section 24 of the Local Government Act 1988 (assistance for privately let housing accommodation),

(b) had property transferred to it on a qualifying disposal under section 135 of the Leasehold Reform, Housing and Urban Development Act 1993, or

(c) received a grant or loan under any of the following provisions.

(2) The provisions are—

section 18 of this Act (social housing grants),

section 22 of this Act or section 58 of the Housing Associations Act 1985 (grants or loans by local authorities),

section 50 of the Housing Act 1988, section 41 of the Housing Associations Act 1985 or any enactment replaced by that section (housing association grant),

section 51 of the Housing Act 1988 or section 54 or 55 of the Housing Associations Act 1985 (revenue deficit grant or hostel deficit grant),

section 79 of the Housing Associations Act 1985 (loans by Housing Corporation),

section 31 of the Housing Act 1974 (management grants), or

any enactment mentioned in paragraph 2 or 3 of Schedule 1 to the Housing Associations Act 1985 (pre-1974 grants and certain loans).

Registered charity: power to appoint new director or trustee

6 (1) The Corporation may by order appoint a person to be a director or trustee of a registered social landlord which is a registered charity—

(a) in place of a person removed by the Corporation,

(b) where there are no directors or no trustees, or

(c) where the Corporation is of the opinion that it is necessary for the proper management of the charity's affairs to have an additional director or trustee.

The power conferred by paragraph (c) may be exercised notwithstanding that it will cause the maximum number of directors or trustees permissible under the charity's constitution to be exceeded.

(2) The Corporation shall only exercise its power under sub-paragraph (1)—

(a) the charity has, at any time before the power is exercised, received financial assistance, had property transferred to it, or received a grant or loan as mentioned in paragraph 5, and

(b) the Corporation has consulted the Charity Commissioners.

(3) A person may be so appointed notwithstanding any restrictions on appointment in the charity's constitution or rules.

(4) A person appointed under this paragraph shall hold office for such period and on such terms as the Corporation may specify; and on the expiry of the appointment the Corporation may renew the appointment for such period as it may specify.

This does not prevent a person appointed under this paragraph from retiring in accordance with the charity's constitution or rules.

(5) A person appointed under this paragraph as director or trustee of a registered charity is entitled—

(a) to attend, speak and vote at any general meeting of the charity and to receive all notices of and other communications relating to any such meeting which a member is entitled to receive,

(b) to move a resolution at any general meeting of the charity, and

(c) to require a general meeting of the charity to be convened within 21 days of a request to that effect made in writing to the directors or trustees.

Company: power to appoint new director

7 (1) The Corporation may by order appoint a person to be a director of a registered social landlord which is a company registered under the Companies Act 1985—

(a) in place of a director removed by the Corporation,

(b) where there are no directors, or

(c) where the Corporation is of the opinion that it is necessary for the proper management of the company's affairs to have an additional director.

(2) A person may be so appointed whether or not he is a member of the company and notwithstanding anything in the company's articles of association.

(3) Where a person is appointed under this paragraph—

(a) he shall hold office for such period and on such terms as the Corporation may specify, and

(b) on the expiry of the appointment the Corporation may renew the appointment for such period as it may specify.

This does not prevent a person from retiring in accordance with the company's articles of association.

(4) A person appointed under this paragraph is entitled—

(a) to attend, speak and vote at any general meeting of the company and to receive all notices of and other communications relating to any general meeting which a member of the company is entitled to receive,

(b) to move a resolution at any general meeting of the company, and

(c) to require an extraordinary general meeting of the company to be convened within 21 days of a request to that effect made in writing to the directors of the company.

Industrial and provident society: power to appoint new committee member

8 (1) The Corporation may by order appoint a person to be a committee member of a registered social landlord which is an industrial and provident society—

(a) in place of a person removed by the Corporation,

(b) where there are no members of the committee, or

(c) where the Corporation is of the opinion that it is necessary for the proper management of the society's affairs to have an additional committee member.

The power conferred by paragraph (c) may be exercised notwithstanding that it will cause the maximum number of committee members permissible under the society's constitution to be exceeded.

(2) A person may be so appointed whether or not he is a member of the society and, if he is not, notwithstanding that the rules of the society restrict appointment to members.

(3) A person appointed under this paragraph shall hold office for such period and on such terms as the Corporation may specify; and on the expiry of the appointment the Corporation may renew the appointment for such period as it may specify.

This does not prevent a person appointed under this paragraph from retiring in accordance with the rules of the society.

(4) A person appointed under this paragraph is entitled—

(a) to attend, speak and vote at any general meeting of the society and to receive all notices of and other communications relating to any general meeting which a member of the society is entitled to receive,

(b) to move a resolution at any general meeting of the society, and

(c) to require a general meeting of the society to be convened within 21 days of a request to that effect made in writing to the committee of the society.

Change of rules, etc. by industrial and provident society

9 (1) This paragraph applies to an industrial and provident society whose registration as a social landlord has been recorded by the appropriate registrar.

(2) Notice shall be sent to the Corporation of any change of the society's name or of the situation of its registered office.

(3) Any other amendment of the society's rules is not valid without the Corporation's consent given by order under the seal of the Corporation.

(4) A copy of that consent shall be sent with the copies of the amendment required by section 10(1) of the Industrial and Provident Societies Act 1965 to be sent to the appropriate registrar.

(5) The Industrial and Provident Societies Act 1965 applies in relation to the provisions of this paragraph as if they were contained in section 10 of that Act (amendment of registered rules).

Change of objects by certain charities

10 (1) This paragraph applies to a registered social landlord—

(a) which is a registered charity and is not a company incorporated under the Companies Act 1985, and
(b) whose registration under this Part of this Act has been recorded by the Charity Commissioners in accordance with section 3(3).

(2) No power contained in the provisions establishing the registered social landlord as a charity, or regulating its purposes or administration, to vary or add to its objects may be exercised without the consent of the Charity Commissioners.

Before giving their consent the Charity Commissioners shall consult the Corporation.

Change of memorandum or articles of association of company

11 (1) This paragraph applies to a company registered under the Companies Act 1985 (including such a company which is also a registered charity) whose registration as a social landlord has been recorded by the registrar of companies.

(2) Notice shall be sent to the Corporation of any change of the company's name or of the address of its registered office.

(3) Any other alteration of the company's memorandum or articles of which notice is required to be given to the registrar of companies is not valid without the Corporation's consent given by order under the seal of the Corporation.

(4) A copy of that consent shall be sent with any copy of the alterations required to be sent to the registrar of companies under the Companies Act 1985.

Amalgamation and dissolution etc. of industrial and provident society

12 (1) This paragraph applies to an industrial and provident society whose registration as a social landlord has been recorded by the appropriate registrar.

(2) The registrar shall not register a special resolution which is passed for the purposes of—

(a) section 50 of the Industrial and Provident Societies Act 1965 (amalgamation of societies),

   (b) section 51 of that Act (transfer of engagements between societies), or

   (c) section 52 of that Act (power of a society to convert itself into, amalgamate with or transfer its engagements to a company registered under the Companies Act 1985),

unless, together with the copy of the resolution, there is sent to him a copy of the Corporation's consent to the amalgamation, transfer or conversion.

(3) Any new body created by the amalgamation or conversion or, in the case of a transfer of engagements, the transferee, shall be deemed to be registered as a social landlord forthwith upon the amalgamation, conversion or transfer taking effect.

(4) If the society resolves by special resolution that it be wound up voluntarily under the Insolvency Act 1986, the resolution has no effect unless—

   (a) before the resolution was passed the Corporation gave its consent to its passing, and

   (b) a copy of the consent is forwarded to the appropriate registrar together with a copy of the resolution required to be so forwarded in accordance with the Companies Act 1985.

(5) If the society is to be dissolved by instrument of dissolution, the appropriate registrar shall not—

   (a) register the instrument in accordance with section 58(5) of the Industrial and Provident Societies Act 1965, or

   (b) cause notice of the dissolution to be advertised in accordance with section 58(6) of that Act,

unless together with the instrument there is sent to him a copy of the Corporation's consent to its making.

(6) The references in this paragraph to the Corporation's consent are to consent given by order under the seal of the Corporation.

Arrangement, reconstruction, etc. of company

13 (1) This paragraph applies to a company registered under the Companies Act 1985 whose registration as a social landlord has been recorded by the registrar of companies.

(2) An order of the court given for the purposes of section 425 of the Companies Act 1985 (compromise or arrangement with creditors or members) is not effective unless the Corporation has given its consent.

A copy of the consent shall be sent to the registrar of companies along with the office copy of the order delivered to him under that section.

(3) An order of the court given for the purposes of section 427 of the Companies Act 1985 (transfer of undertaking or property for purposes of reconstruction or amalgamation) is not effective unless the Corporation has given its consent.

A copy of the consent shall be sent to the registrar of companies along with the office copy of the order delivered to him under that section.

(4) The registrar of companies shall not register any resolution under section 53 of the Industrial and Provident Societies Act 1965 (conversion of company into industrial and

provident society), unless, together with the copy of the resolution, there is sent to him a copy of the Corporation's consent to the conversion.

(5) Where a director, administrator or liquidator of the company proposes to make a voluntary arrangement with the company's creditors under section 1 of the Insolvency Act 1986, the arrangement shall not take effect under section 5 (effect of approval by members and creditors) of that Act unless the Corporation has given its consent to the voluntary arrangement.

(6) If the company resolves by special resolution that it be wound up voluntarily under the Insolvency Act 1986, the resolution has no effect unless—

(a) before the resolution was passed the Corporation gave its consent to its passing, and

(b) a copy of the consent is forwarded to the registrar of companies together with a copy of the resolution required to be so forwarded in accordance with section 380 of the Companies Act 1985.

(7) The references in this paragraph to the Corporation's consent are to consent given by order under the seal of the Corporation.

(8) Where sub-paragraph (3) or (4) applies, the transferee or, as the case may be, any new body created by the conversion shall be deemed to be registered as a social landlord forthwith upon the transfer or conversion taking effect.

Corporation's power to petition for winding up

14 (1) The Corporation may present a petition for the winding up under the Insolvency Act 1986 of a registered social landlord which is—

(a) a company incorporated under the Companies Act 1985 (including such a company which is also a registered charity), or

(b) an industrial and provident society (to which the winding up provisions of the Insolvency Act 1986 apply in accordance with section 55(a) of the Industrial and Provident Societies Act 1965),

on either of the following grounds.

(2) The grounds are—

(a) that the landlord is failing properly to carry out its purposes or objects, or

(b) that the landlord is unable to pay its debts within the meaning of section 123 of the Insolvency Act 1986.

Transfer of net assets on dissolution or winding up

15 (1) This paragraph applies—

(a) where a registered social landlord which is an industrial and provident society is dissolved as mentioned in section 55(a) or (b) of the Industrial and Provident Societies Act 1965 (winding-up under the Insolvency Act 1986 or by instrument of dissolution), and

(b) where a registered social landlord which is a company registered under the Companies Act 1985 is wound up under the Insolvency Act 1986.

(2) On such a dissolution or winding-up, so much of the property of the society or company as remains after meeting the claims of its creditors and any other liabilities arising on or before the dissolution or winding-up shall be transferred to the Corporation or, if the Corporation so directs, to a specified registered social landlord.

The above provision has effect notwithstanding anything in the Industrial and Provident Societies Act 1965, the Companies Act 1985 or the Insolvency Act 1986, or in the rules of the society or, as the case may be, in the memorandum or articles of association of the company.

(3) In order to avoid the necessity for the sale of land belonging to the registered social landlord and thereby secure the transfer of the land under this paragraph, the Corporation may, if it appears to it appropriate to do so, make payments to discharge such claims or liabilities as are referred to in sub-paragraph (2).

(4) Where the registered social landlord which is dissolved or wound up is a charity, the Corporation may dispose of property transferred to it by virtue of this paragraph only to another registered social landlord—

(a) which is also a charity, and
(b) the objects of which appear to the Corporation to be, as nearly as practicable, akin to those of the body which is dissolved or wound up.

(5) In any other case the Corporation may dispose of property transferred to it by virtue of this paragraph to a registered social landlord or to a subsidiary of the Corporation.

(6) Where property transferred to the Corporation by virtue of this paragraph includes land subject to an existing mortgage or charge (whether in favour of the Corporation or not), the Corporation may, in exercise of its powers under Part III of the Housing Associations Act 1985, dispose of the land either—

(a) subject to that mortgage or charge, or
(b) subject to a new mortgage or charge in favour of the Corporation securing such amount as appears to the Corporation to be appropriate in the circumstances.

PART III

ACCOUNTS AND AUDIT

General requirements as to accounts and audit

16 (1) The Corporation may from time to time determine accounting requirements for registered social landlords with a view to ensuring that the accounts of every registered social landlord—

(a) are prepared in a proper form, and
(b) give a true and fair view of—
(i) the state of affairs of the landlord, so far as its housing activities are concerned, and
(ii) the disposition of funds and assets which are, or at any time have been, in its hands in connection with those activities.

(2) The Corporation by a determination under sub-paragraph (1) may lay down a method by which a registered charity is to distinguish in its accounts between its housing activities and other activities.

(3) The accounts of every registered social landlord shall comply with the requirements laid down under this paragraph.

(4) The auditor's report shall state, in addition to any other matters which it is required to state, whether in the auditor's opinion the accounts do so comply.

(5) Every registered social landlord shall furnish to the Corporation a copy of its accounts and auditor's report within six months of the end of the period to which they relate.

Appointment of auditors by industrial and provident societies

17 Section 4 of the Friendly and Industrial and Provident Societies Act 1968 (obligation to appoint qualified auditors to audit accounts and balance sheet for each year of account) applies to every industrial and provident society which is a registered social landlord, without regard to the volume of its receipts and payments, the number of its members or the value of its assets.

Accounting and audit requirements for charities

18 (1) A registered social landlord which is a registered charity shall, in respect of its housing activities (and separately from its other activities, if any), be subject to the following provisions (which impose accounting and audit requirements corresponding to those imposed by the Friendly and Industrial and Provident Societies Act 1968).

This does not affect any obligation of the charity under sections 41 to 45 of the Charities Act 1993 (charity accounts).

(2) The charity shall in respect of its housing activities—

(a) cause to be kept properly books of account showing its transactions and its assets and liabilities, and
(b) establish and maintain a satisfactory system of control of its books of accounts, its cash holdings and all its receipts and remittances.

The books of account must be such as to enable a true and fair view to be given of the state of affairs of the charity in respect of its housing activities, and to explain its transactions in the course of those activities.

(3) The charity shall for each period of account prepare—

(a) a revenue account giving a true and fair view of the charity's income and expenditure in the period, so far as arising in connection with its housing activities, and
(b) a balance sheet giving a true and fair view as at the end of the period of the state of the charity's affairs.

The revenue account and balance sheet must be signed by at least two directors or trustees of the charity.

(4) The charity shall in each period of account appoint a qualified auditor to audit the accounts prepared in accordance with sub-paragraph (3).

A qualified auditor means a person who is eligible for appointment as auditor of the charity under Part II of the Companies Act 1989 or who would be so eligible if the charity were a company registered under the Companies Act 1985.

(5) The auditor shall make a report to the charity on the accounts audited by him, stating whether in his opinion—

 (a) the revenue account gives a true and fair view of the state of income and expenditure of the charity in respect of its housing activities and of any other matters to which it relates, and

 (b) the balance sheet gives a true and fair view of the state of affairs of the charity as at the end of the period of account.

(6) The auditor in preparing his report shall carry out such investigations as will enable him to form an opinion as to the following matters—

 (a) whether the association has kept, in respect of its housing activities, proper books of account in accordance with the requirements of this paragraph,

 (b) whether the charity has maintained a satisfactory system of control over its transactions in accordance with those requirements, and

 (c) whether the accounts are in agreement with the charity's books;

and if he is of opinion that the charity has failed in any respect to comply with this paragraph, or if the accounts are not in agreement with the books, he shall state that fact in his report.

(7) The auditor—

 (a) has a right of access at all times to the books, deeds and accounts of the charity, so far as relating to its housing activities, and to all other documents relating to those activities, and

 (b) is entitled to require from officers of the charity such information and explanations as he thinks necessary for the performance of his duties;

and if he fails to obtain all the information and explanations which, to the best of his knowledge and belief, are necessary for the purposes of his audit, he shall state that fact in his report.

(8) A period of account for the purposes of this paragraph is twelve months or such other period not less than six months or more than 18 months as the charity may, with the consent of the Corporation, determine.

Responsibility for securing compliance with accounting requirements

19 (1) Every responsible person, that is to say, every person who—

 (a) is directly concerned with the conduct and management of the affairs of a registered social landlord, and

 (b) is in that capacity responsible for the preparation and audit of accounts,

shall ensure that paragraph 16 (general requirements as to accounts and audit) and, where applicable, paragraph 18 (accounting and audit requirements for charities) are complied with by the registered social landlord.

(2) If—

 (a) paragraph 16(5) (furnishing of accounts and auditor's report) is not complied with,

 (b) the accounts furnished to the Corporation under that provision do not comply with the accounting requirements laid down under paragraph 16(1),

(c) paragraph 18 (accounting and audit requirements for charities), where applicable, is not complied with,

(d) section 55(9) of the Housing Act 1988 (surplus rental income: power to require information) is not complied with, or

(e) any notice under section 26 (information relating to disposal proceeds fund) is not complied with,

every responsible person, and the registered social landlord itself, commits a summary offence and is liable on conviction to a fine not exceeding level 3 on the standard scale.

(3) In proceedings for an offence under this paragraph it is a defence—

(a) for a responsible person to prove that he did everything that could reasonably have been expected of him by way of discharging the relevant duty;

(b) for a registered social landlord to prove that every responsible person did everything that could reasonably have been expected of him by way of discharging the relevant duty in relation to the registered social landlord.

(4) Proceedings for an offence under this paragraph may be brought only by or with the consent of the Corporation or the Director of Public Prosecutions.

PART IV

INQUIRY INTO AFFAIRS OF REGISTERED SOCIAL LANDLORDS

Inquiry

20 (1) The Corporation may direct an inquiry into the affairs of a registered social landlord if it appears to the Corporation that there may have been misconduct or mismanagement.

For this purpose 'misconduct' includes any failure to comply with the requirements of this Part of this Act.

(2) Any such inquiry shall be conducted by one or more persons appointed by the Corporation.

(3) If one person is appointed he must be a person who is not a member or an employee of the Corporation and has not been such a member or employee within the previous five years; and if more than one person is appointed at least one of them must be such a person.

(4) If the Corporation so directs, or if during the course of the inquiry the person or persons conducting the inquiry consider it necessary, the inquiry shall extend to the affairs of any other body which at any material time is or was a subsidiary or associate of the registered social landlord.

(5) The person or persons conducting the inquiry may, if they think fit during the course of the inquiry, make one or more interim reports on such matters as appear to them to be appropriate.

(6) On completion of the inquiry the person or persons conducting the inquiry shall make a final report on such matters as the Corporation may specify.

(7) An interim or final report shall be in such form as the Corporation may specify.

Power of appointed person to obtain information

21 (1) A person appointed by the Corporation under paragraph 20 to conduct an inquiry (or, if more than one person is so appointed, each of those persons) has, for the purposes of the inquiry, the same powers as are conferred on the Corporation by section 30 (general power to obtain information).

(2) Where by virtue of a notice under that section given by an appointed person any documents are produced to any person, the person to whom they are produced may take copies of or make extracts from them.

(3) Section 31 (enforcement of notice to provide information, etc.) applies in relation to a notice given under this paragraph by an appointed person as it applies in relation to a notice given under section 30 by the Corporation.

Extraordinary audit for purposes of inquiry

22 (1) For the purposes of an inquiry under paragraph 20 the Corporation may require the accounts and balance sheet of the registered social landlord concerned, or such of them as the Corporation may specify, to be audited by a qualified auditor appointed by the Corporation.

(2) A person is a qualified auditor for this purpose if he would be eligible for appointment as auditor of the ordinary accounts of the registered social landlord.

(3) On completion of the audit the appointed auditor shall make a report to the Corporation on such matters and in such form as the Corporation may specify.

(4) The expenses of the audit, including the remuneration of the auditor, shall be paid by the Corporation.

(5) An audit under this paragraph is additional to, and does not affect, any audit made or to be made under any other enactment.

Powers exercisable on interim basis

23 (1) The Corporation may make an order under this paragraph—

  (a) where an inquiry has been directed under paragraph 20 and the Corporation has reasonable grounds to believe—
    (i) that there has been misconduct or mismanagement in the affairs of the registered social landlord, and
    (ii) that immediate action is needed to protect the interests of the tenants of the registered social landlord or to protect the assets of the landlord; or
  (b) where an interim report has been made under paragraph 20(5) as a result of which the Corporation is satisfied that there has been misconduct or mismanagement in the affairs of a registered social landlord.

(2) The orders that may be made under this paragraph are—

  (a) an order suspending any officer, employee or agent of the registered social landlord who appears to the Corporation to have been responsible for or privy to the misconduct or mismanagement or by his conduct to have contributed to or facilitated it;
  (b) an order directing any bank or other person who holds money or securities on behalf of the registered social landlord not to part with the money or securities without the approval of the Corporation;

(c) an order restricting the transactions which may be entered into, or the nature or amount of the payments which may be made, by the registered social landlord without the approval of the Corporation.

(3) An order under this paragraph, if not previously revoked by the Corporation, shall cease to have effect six months after the making of the final report under paragraph 20(6) unless the Corporation renews it, which it may do for a further period of up to six months.

(4) A person suspended by an order under sub-paragraph (2)(a) may appeal against the order to the High Court.

(5) Where a person is suspended by such an order, the Corporation may give directions with respect to the performance of his functions and otherwise as to matters arising from his suspension.

The Corporation may, in particular, appoint a named person to perform his functions.

(6) A person who contravenes an order under sub-paragraph (2)(b) commits an offence and is liable on summary conviction to a fine not exceeding level 5 on the standard scale or imprisonment for a term not exceeding three months, or both.

Proceedings for such an offence may be brought only by or with the consent of the Corporation or the Director of Public Prosecutions.

Powers exercisable as a result of final report or audit

24 (1) Where the Corporation is satisfied, as the result of an inquiry under paragraph 20 or an audit under paragraph 22, that there has been misconduct or mismanagement in the affairs of a registered social landlord, it may make an order under this paragraph.

(2) The orders that may be made under this paragraph are—

(a) an order removing any officer, employee or agent of the registered social landlord who appears to the Corporation to have been responsible for or privy to the misconduct or mismanagement or by his conduct to have contributed to or facilitated it;

(b) an order suspending any such person for up to six months, pending determination whether he should be removed;

(c) an order directing any bank or other person who holds money or securities on behalf of the registered social landlord not to part with the money or securities without the approval of the Corporation;

(d) an order restricting the transactions which may be entered into, or the nature or amount of the payments which may be made, by the registered social landlord without the approval of the Corporation.

(3) Before making an order under sub-paragraph (2)(a) the Corporation shall give at least 14 days' notice of its intention to do so—

(a) to the person it intends to remove, and

(b) to the registered social landlord concerned.

Notice under this sub-paragraph may be given by post, and if so given to the person whom the Corporation intends to remove may be addressed to his last known address in the United Kingdom.

(4) A person who is ordered to be removed under sub-paragraph (2)(a) or suspended under sub-paragraph (2)(b) may appeal against the order to the High Court.

(5) Where a person is suspended under sub-paragraph (2)(b), the Corporation may give directions with respect to the performance of his functions and otherwise as to matters arising from the suspension.

The Corporation may, in particular, appoint a named person to perform his functions.

(6) A person who contravenes an order under sub-paragraph (2)(c) commits an offence and is liable on summary conviction to a fine not exceeding level 5 on the standard scale or imprisonment for a term not exceeding three months, or both.

Proceedings for such an offence may be brought only by or with the consent of the Corporation or the Director of Public Prosecutions.

Disqualification as officer of registered social landlord

25 (1) A person is disqualified from being an officer of a registered social landlord if the Corporation has made an order against him under—

(a) paragraph 24(2)(a) (removal for misconduct or mismanagement), or
(b) section 30(1)(a) of the Housing Associations Act 1985 or section 20(1)(a) of the Housing Act 1974 (corresponding earlier provisions).

(2) The Corporation may, on the application of any such person, waive his disqualification either generally or in relation to a particular registered social landlord or particular class of registered social landlord.

(3) Any waiver shall be notified in writing to the person concerned.

(4) For the purposes of this paragraph the Corporation shall keep, in such manner as it thinks fit, a register of all persons who have been removed from office by the Corporation under the provisions mentioned in sub-paragraph (1).

(5) The register shall be available for public inspection at all reasonable times.

Persons acting as officer while disqualified

26 (1) A person who acts as an officer of a registered social landlord while he is disqualified under paragraph 25(1) commits an offence.

A person guilty of such an offence is liable—

(a) on summary conviction, to imprisonment for a term not exceeding six months or to a fine not exceeding the statutory maximum, or both;
(b) on conviction on indictment, to imprisonment for a term not exceeding two years or to a fine, or both.

(2) Proceedings for an offence under sub-paragraph (1) may be brought only by or with the consent of the Corporation or the Director of Public Prosecutions.

(3) Acts done as an officer of a registered social landlord by a person who is disqualified under paragraph 25(1) are not invalid by reason only of that disqualification.

(4) Where the Corporation is satisfied—

(a) that a person has acted as an officer of a registered social landlord while disqualified under paragraph 25(1), and

(b) that while so acting he has received from the registered social landlord any payments or benefits in connection with his so acting,

it may by order direct him to repay to the registered social landlord the whole or part of any such sums or, as the case may be, to pay to it the whole or part of the monetary value (as determined by it) of any such benefit.

Power to direct transfer of land

27 (1) Where as a result of an inquiry under paragraph 20 or an audit under paragraph 22 the Corporation is satisfied as regards a registered social landlord—

(a) that there has been misconduct or mismanagement in its administration, or
(b) that the management of its land would be improved if its land were transferred in accordance with the provisions of this paragraph,

the Corporation may, with the consent of the Secretary of State, direct the registered social landlord to make such a transfer.

(2) Where the registered social landlord concerned is a charity, the Corporation may only direct a transfer to be made to another registered social landlord—

(a) which is also a charity, and
(b) the objects of which appear to the Corporation to be, as nearly as practicable, akin to those of the registered social landlord concerned.

(3) In any other case the Corporation may direct a transfer to be made to the Corporation or to another registered social landlord.

(4) The transfer shall be on such terms as the Corporation may direct on the basis of principles determined by it.

The consent of the Secretary of State is required both for the terms of the transfer and for the determination of the principles on which it is based.

(5) The price shall not be less than the amount certified by the district valuer to be the amount the property would command if sold by a willing seller to another registered social landlord.

(6) The terms shall include provision as to the payment of debts and liabilities (including debts and liabilities secured on the land).

Availability of powers in relation to registered charities

28 (1) The Corporation may exercise its powers under paragraphs 20 to 26 in relation to a registered charity only if the charity has, at any time before the powers are exercised—

(a) received financial assistance under section 24 of the Local Government Act 1988 (assistance for privately let housing accommodation),
(b) had property transferred to it on a qualifying disposal under section 135 of the Leasehold Reform, Housing and Urban Development Act 1993, or
(c) received a grant or loan under any of the following provisions.

(2) The provisions are—

section 18 of this Act (social housing grant),

section 22 of this Act or section 58 of the Housing Associations Act 1985 (grants or loans by local authorities),

section 50 of the Housing Act 1988, section 41 of the Housing Associations Act 1985 or any enactment replaced by that section (housing association grant),

section 51 of the Housing Act 1988 or section 54 or 55 of the Housing Associations Act 1985 (revenue deficit grant or hostel deficit grant),

section 79 of the Housing Associations Act 1985 (loans by Housing Corporation),

section 31 of the Housing Act 1974 (management grants), or

any enactment mentioned in paragraph 2 or 3 of Schedule 1 to the Housing Associations Act 1985 (pre-1974 grants and certain loans).

(3) In relation to a registered charity paragraphs 20 to 26 have effect with the following adaptations—

(a) references to its affairs are confined to its housing activities and such other activities (if any) as are incidental to or connected with its housing activities;

(b) references to its accounts do not include revenue accounts which do not relate to its housing activities, except so far as such accounts are necessary for the auditing of revenue accounts which do so relate or of the balance sheet;

(c) a person is a qualified auditor for the purpose of paragraph 22 (extraordinary audit) only if he is an auditor qualified for the purposes of paragraph 18 (accounting and audit requirements for charities).

(4) The Corporation shall notify the Charity Commissioners upon the exercise in relation to a registered charity of its powers under—

(a) paragraph 20(1) (inquiry into affairs of registered social landlord),

(b) paragraph 23(2)(a) (interim suspension of person in connection with misconduct or mismanagement), or

(c) paragraph 24(2)(a) or (b) (removal of person in connection with misconduct or mismanagement or suspension with a view to removal).

29 The Corporation may not exercise its powers under paragraph 27 in relation to a registered charity.

SCHEDULE 2
SOCIAL RENTED SECTOR: HOUSING COMPLAINTS
Section 51

Social landlords required to be member of approved scheme

1 (1) A social landlord must be a member of an approved scheme covering, or more than one approved scheme which together cover, all his housing activities.

(2) If a social landlord fails to comply with the duty imposed by this paragraph, the Secretary of State may apply to the High Court for an order directing him to comply within a specified period and the High Court may, if it thinks fit, make such an order.

(3) Nothing in this Schedule shall be construed as restricting membership of an approved scheme to social landlords.

Matters for which scheme must provide

2 (1) A scheme shall not be approved for the purposes of this Schedule unless it makes provision for—

1. The establishment or appointment of an independent person to administer the scheme.

2. The criteria for membership for—

(a) social landlords under a duty to be members of an approved scheme, and

(b) other persons.

3. The manner of becoming or ceasing to be a member.

4. The matters about which complaints may be made under the scheme.

5. The grounds on which a matter may be excluded from investigation, including that the matter is the subject of court proceedings or was the subject of court proceedings where judgment on the merits was given.

6. The descriptions of individual who may make a complaint under the scheme.

7. The appointment of an independent individual to be the housing ombudsman under the scheme.

8. The appointment of staff to administer the scheme and to assist the housing ombudsman and the terms upon which they are appointed.

9. A duty of the housing ombudsman to investigate any complaint duly made and not withdrawn, and a power to investigate any complaint duly made but withdrawn, and where he investigates to make a determination.

10. A power of the housing ombudsman to propose alternative methods of resolving a dispute.

11. The powers of the housing ombudsman for the purposes of his investigations, and the procedure to be followed in the conduct of investigations.

12. The powers of the housing ombudsman on making a determination.

13. The making and publication of annual reports by the housing ombudsman on the discharge of his functions.

14. The manner in which determinations are to be—

(a) communicated to the complainant and the person against whom the complaint was made, and

(b) published.

15. The manner in which the expenses of the scheme are to be defrayed by the members.

16. The keeping and auditing of accounts and the submission of accounts to the Secretary of State.

17. The making of annual reports on the administration of the scheme.

18. The manner of amending the scheme.

(2) The Secretary of State may by order amend sub-paragraph (1) by adding to or deleting from it any item or by varying any item for the time being contained in it.

(3) An order under sub-paragraph (2) shall be made by statutory instrument which shall be subject to annulment in pursuance of a resolution of either House of Parliament.

Approval of scheme, or amendment, and withdrawal of approval

3 (1) An application to the Secretary of State for approval of a scheme shall be made in such manner as the Secretary of State may determine, and shall be accompanied by such information as the Secretary of State may require.

(2) If it appears to the Secretary of State that the scheme—

(a) provides for the matters specified in paragraph 2, and

(b) is a satisfactory scheme for the purposes of this Schedule,

he shall approve the scheme.

(3) An amendment of an approved scheme is not effective unless approved by the Secretary of State.

Sub-paragraph (1) applies in relation to an application for approval of an amendment as it applies to an application for approval of a scheme; and the Secretary of State shall approve the amendment if it appears to him that the scheme as amended meets the conditions in sub-paragraph (2).

(4) The Secretary of State may withdraw his approval of a scheme.

(5) If the Secretary of State proposes to withdraw his approval of a scheme, he shall serve on the person administering the scheme and on the housing ombudsman under the scheme, a notice stating—

(a) that he proposes to withdraw his approval,

(b) the grounds for the proposed withdrawal of his approval, and

(c) that the person receiving the notice may make representations with respect to the proposed withdrawal of approval within such period of not less than 14 days as is specified in the notice;

and he shall, before reaching a decision on whether to withdraw approval, consider any representations duly made to him.

(6) The Secretary of State shall give notice of his decision on a proposal to withdraw approval of a scheme, together with his reasons, to every person on whom he served a notice under sub-paragraph (5).

(7) Withdrawal of approval by the Secretary of State has effect from such date as is specified in the notice of his decision.

(8) Where the person administering a scheme is given notice of a decision to withdraw approval of the scheme, he shall give notice of the decision to every member of the scheme.

Notice to be given of becoming a member of an approved scheme

4 (1) A social landlord who—

(a) becomes a member of an approved scheme, or

(b) is a member of a scheme which becomes an approved scheme,

shall, within the period of 21 days beginning with the date of becoming a member or, as the case may be, of being informed of the Secretary of State's approval of the scheme, give notice of that fact to the Corporation.

(2) The Corporation, on receiving the notice, shall record his membership of an approved scheme.

(3) A person who fails to comply with sub-paragraph (1) commits an offence and is liable on summary conviction to a fine not exceeding level 4 on the standard scale.

Proceedings for such an offence may be brought only by or with the consent of the Corporation or the Director of Public Prosecutions.

Withdrawal from approved scheme

5 (1) A social landlord wishing to withdraw from membership of an approved scheme shall send notice of his proposed withdrawal to the Corporation.

(2) The notice shall specify—

(a) the housing activities in relation to which he is subject to investigation under the scheme,

(b) the approved scheme or schemes of which he is also a member or will, on his withdrawal, become a member, and

(c) under which scheme or schemes the housing activities mentioned in paragraph (a) will be subject to investigation after his withdrawal.

(3) If the Corporation is satisfied that withdrawal by the landlord from the scheme will not result in a failure to comply with his duty under paragraph 1, it shall confirm the landlord's withdrawal from the scheme.

(4) If the Corporation is not so satisfied, it shall withhold confirmation of the landlord's withdrawal from the scheme; and the landlord shall continue to be a member of the scheme and bound and entitled under the scheme accordingly.

Register of approved schemes

6 (1) The Corporation shall maintain a register of schemes approved by the Secretary of State for the purposes of this Schedule and of the social landlords who are members of those schemes.

(2) The Secretary of State shall give notice to the Corporation—

(a) when he grants or withdraws his approval of a scheme, and

(b) when he approves an amendment of a scheme,

and he shall supply the Corporation with copies of any approved scheme or any amendment to a scheme.

(3) A member of the public shall be entitled, upon payment of such fees as the Corporation may determine, to receive a copy of an approved scheme and a list of the social landlords who are members of it.

Determinations by housing ombudsman

7 (1) A housing ombudsman under an approved scheme shall investigate any complaint duly made to him and not withdrawn, and may investigate any complaint duly made but withdrawn, and where he investigates a complaint he shall determine it by reference to what is, in his opinion, fair in all the circumstances of the case.

(2) He may in his determination—

(a) order the member of a scheme against whom the complaint was made to pay compensation to the complainant, and

(b) order that the member or the complainant shall not exercise or require the performance of any of the contractual or other obligations or rights existing between them.

(3) If the member against whom the complaint was made fails to comply with the determination within a reasonable time, the housing ombudsman may order him to publish in such manner as the ombudsman sees fit that he has failed to comply with the determination.

(4) Where the member is not a social landlord, the housing ombudsman may also order that the member—

(a) be expelled from the scheme, and
(b) publish in such manner as the housing ombudsman sees fit that he has been expelled and the reasons for his expulsion.

(5) If a person fails to comply with an order under sub-paragraph (3) or (4)(b), the housing ombudsman may take such steps as he thinks appropriate to publish what the member ought to have published and recover from the member the costs of doing so.

(6) A member who is ordered by the housing ombudsman to pay compensation or take any other steps has power to do so, except that a member which is also a charity shall not do anything contrary to its trusts.

Publication of determinations, etc.

8 (1) A housing ombudsman under an approved scheme may publish—

(a) his determination on any complaint, and
(b) such reports as he thinks fit on the discharge of his functions.

(2) He may include in any such determination or report statements, communications, reports, papers or other documentary evidence obtained in the exercise of his functions.

(3) In publishing any determination or report, a housing ombudsman shall have regard to the need for excluding so far as practicable—

(a) any matter which relates to the private affairs of an individual, where publication would seriously and prejudicially affect the interests of that individual, and
(b) any matter which relates specifically to the affairs of a member of an approved scheme, where publication would seriously and prejudicially affect its interests, unless the inclusion of that matter is necessary for the purposes of the determination or report.

Absolute privilege for communications, etc.

9 For the purposes of the law of defamation absolute privilege attaches to—

(a) any communication between a housing ombudsman under an approved scheme and any person by or against whom a complaint is made to him,
(b) any determination by such an ombudsman, and
(c) the publication of such a determination or any report under paragraph 8.

Appointment and status of housing ombudsman

10 (1) Where an approved scheme provides that it shall be administered by a body corporate, that body shall appoint on such terms as it thinks fit the housing ombudsman for the purposes of the scheme and the appointment and its terms shall be subject to the approval of the Secretary of State.

(2) Where an approved scheme does not so provide—

    (a) the housing ombudsman for the purposes of the scheme shall be appointed by the Secretary of State on such terms as the Secretary of State thinks fit,

    (b) the Secretary of State may by order provide that the housing ombudsman for the purposes of the scheme shall be a corporation sole, and

    (c) the staff to administer the scheme and otherwise assist the ombudsman in the discharge of his functions shall be appointed and employed by him.

(3) The Secretary of State may at any time remove from office a housing ombudsman (whether appointed by him or otherwise).

(4) A housing ombudsman appointed by the Secretary of State or otherwise shall not be regarded as the servant or agent of the Crown or as enjoying any status, privilege or immunity of the Crown or as exempt from any tax, duty, rate, levy or other charge whatsoever, whether general or local, and any property held by him shall not be regarded as property of, or held on behalf of, the Crown.

Subscriptions payable in respect of approved schemes

11 (1) Members of an approved scheme shall pay a subscription, calculated as set out in the scheme, to the person administering the scheme.

(2) If a social landlord fails to comply with his duty under paragraph 1, the Secretary of State may determine—

    (a) which approved scheme or schemes he should have joined, and

    (b) what sums by way of subscription he should have paid,

and may require him to pay those amounts to the person administering the scheme or schemes.

(3) The person administering an approved scheme may recover sums payable under sub-paragraph (1) or (2) as if they were debts due to him.

(4) The Secretary of State or the Corporation may pay grant and provide other financial assistance to—

    (a) a body corporate administering an approved scheme, or

    (b) in a case where paragraph 10(2) applies, to the housing ombudsman under an approved scheme,

for such purposes and upon such terms as the Secretary of State or, as the case may be, the Corporation thinks fit.

SCHEDULE 3
SOCIAL RENTED SECTOR: MINOR AMENDMENTS

Section 55

Finance Act 1981 (c. 35)

1 (1) Section 107 of the Finance Act 1981 (stamp duty payable upon sale of houses at a discount) is amended as follows.

(2) After subsection (3)(e) insert—

'(ea) a registered social landlord within the meaning of Part I of the Housing Act 1996;'.

(3) In subsection (3)(f) for the words from 'registered' to the end substitute

'registered—
(i) in Scotland, under the Housing Associations Act 1985, or
(ii) in Northern Ireland, under Part II of the Housing (Northern Ireland) Order 1992;'.

(4) In subsection (3A) (exclusion of certain sub-sales), for 'subsection (3)(f)' substitute 'subsection (3)(ea) or (f)'.

(5) After subsection (3B) insert—

'(3C) A grant under section 20 or 21 of the Housing Act 1996 (purchase grants in respect of disposals at a discount by registered social landlords) shall not be treated as part of the consideration for a conveyance or transfer to which this section applies made by a body falling within subsection (3)(ea) above.'.

Local Government Finance Act 1982 (c. 32)

2 (1) In Part III of the Local Government Finance Act 1982 (establishment and functions of Audit Commission), after section 28A insert—

'28B General functions of Commission in relation to registered social landlords

(1) The Corporation and the Commission may agree one or more programmes of comparative studies designed to enable the Commission to make recommendations for improving economy, efficiency and effectiveness of registered social landlords.

(2) Where the Corporation and the Commission fail to agree a programme proposed by either of them, either of them may refer the matter to the Secretary of State who may direct that the programme be carried out either without modifications or with modifications specified in the direction.

(3) Where a programme is agreed or is directed to be carried out, the Commission shall ensure that studies giving effect to the programme are carried out by it or on its behalf.

(4) It shall be a term of every such programme that the Corporation make good to the Commission the full costs incurred by the Commission in carrying out the programme.

(5) The Commission shall publish reports on the studies carried out under this section.

(6) Before publishing any such report the Commission shall show a draft of it to the Corporation and shall consider whether to revise the draft in the light of the comments made by the Corporation.

28C Provisions supplementary to s 28B

(1) The Commission may, if authorised to do so by the Corporation—

(a) require a registered social landlord, or any officer or member of a registered social landlord, to supply such information as the Commission may require for the purposes of any study under section 28B above; and

(b) require a registered social landlord included in any such study to make available for inspection such documents as are reasonably required for the purposes of the study.

(2) The Commission may require the information to be supplied, or the documents to be made available, to the Commission or to a person authorised by the Commission for the purposes of this section.

(3) A person who without reasonable excuse fails to comply with a requirement under this section commits an offence and is liable on summary conviction to a fine not exceeding level 3 on the standard scale.

(4) Information obtained by the Commission, or by a person acting on behalf of the Commission, in the course of a study under section 28B above may be disclosed by the Commission to the Corporation notwithstanding anything in section 30 below (general restriction on disclosure of information relating to particular bodies or persons).

28D Functions of Commission in relation to audit of accounts of registered social landlords

(1) The Commission may provide the Corporation with consultancy services relating to the audit of accounts of registered social landlords.

(2) The Commission may recover from the Corporation such costs incurred in providing the services as may be agreed by the Corporation.

28E Meaning of "the Corporation" and "registered social landlord"

In sections 28B to 28D above "the Corporation" and "registered social landlord" have the same meaning as in Part I of the Housing Act 1996.'.

(2) In paragraph 9 of Schedule 3 to the Local Government Finance Act 1982 (the Audit Commission: duty to balance income and expenditure), in sub-paragraph (2) (functions to be managed separately) after sub-paragraph (a) insert—

'(aa) its functions under sections 28B and 28C relating to registered social landlords;
(ab) its functions under section 28D relating to such landlords;'.

Housing Associations Act 1985 (c. 69)

3 Section 33 of the Housing Associations Act 1985 (recognition of central association) shall cease to have effect.

4 In section 69(1) of the Housing Associations Act 1985 (power to vary or terminate certain agreements with housing associations: agreements to which the section applies), omit paragraphs (e) and (g).

5 In section 75(1) of the Housing Associations Act 1985 (general functions of the Corporation) for paragraphs (a) to (c) substitute—

'(a) to facilitate the proper performance of the functions of registered social landlords;
(b) to maintain a register of social landlords and to exercise supervision and control over such persons;
(c) to promote and assist the development of self-build societies (other than registered social landlords) and to facilitate the proper performance of the functions, and to publicise the aims and principles, of such societies;'.

6 In Part III of the Housing Associations Act 1985 (general provisions relating to the Housing Corporation and Housing for Wales), after section 76 (general power of Secretary of State to give directions to Corporation) insert—

'76A Realisation of value of Corporation's loans portfolio

(1) The Corporation may, and if so directed by the Secretary of State (under section 76) shall, enter into arrangements of a description approved by the Secretary of State for the purpose of realising the value of the whole or part of its loans portfolio.

(2) The arrangements may provide for—

  (a) the transfer of any estate or interest of the Corporation, or
  (b) the creation or disposal of economic interests not involving a transfer of an estate or interest,

and may extend to such incidental or ancillary matters as the Corporation or the Secretary of State considers appropriate.

(3) In this section the Corporation's "loans portfolio" means the Corporation's rights and obligations in relation to any loans or related securities.

(4) Nothing in the terms of any loan or related transaction entered into by the Corporation shall be construed as impliedly prohibiting or restricting the Corporation from dealing with its loans portfolio in accordance with arrangements under this section.'.

7 In section 87 of the Housing Associations Act 1985 (financial assistance for formation, management, etc. of housing associations), for subsection (1) substitute—

'(1) The Corporation may give financial assistance to any person to facilitate the proper performance of the functions of registered social landlords or co-operative housing associations.'.

Income and Corporation Taxes Act 1988 (c. 1)

8 (1) The Income and Corporation Taxes Act 1988 is amended as follows.

(2) In section 488 (co-operative housing associations), after subsection (7) insert—

'(7A) The Secretary of State may delegate any of his functions under subsections (6) and (7)—

  (a) to the Housing Corporation, in the case of a body registered as a social landlord in the register maintained by the Housing Corporation under Part I of the Housing Act 1996, and
  (b) to Housing for Wales, in the case of a body registered as a social landlord in the register maintained under that Part by Housing for Wales,

to such extent and subject to such conditions as he may specify.'.

(3) In section 489 (self-build societies), after subsection (5) insert—

'(5A) The Secretary of State may delegate any of his functions under subsections (4) and (5) to—

(a) the Housing Corporation, where the society has its registered office in England for the purposes of the Industrial and Provident Societies Act 1965, and

(b) Housing for Wales, where the society has its registered office in Wales for the purposes of that Act,

to such extent and subject to such conditions as he may specify.'.

Housing (Scotland) Act 1988 (c. 43)

9 After section 2 of the Housing (Scotland) Act 1988 (general functions of Scottish Homes) insert—

'2A Sale of Scottish Homes' loans portfolio

(1) Subject to subsection (2) below, Scottish Homes may enter into arrangements of a description approved by the Secretary of State for the purpose of realising the value of the whole or part of its loans portfolio.

(2) Without prejudice to the power of the Secretary of State to give directions under section 2(10) above, the Secretary of State may direct Scottish Homes to enter into arrangements under this section and it shall be the duty of Scottish Homes to comply with any such direction.

(3) The arrangements may provide for—

(a) the transfer of any estate or interest of Scottish Homes, or

(b) the creation or disposal of economic interests not involving a transfer of an estate or interest,

and may extend to such incidental or ancillary matters as Scottish Homes or the Secretary of State considers appropriate.

(4) In this section, Scottish Homes' "loans portfolio" means Scottish Homes' rights and obligations in relation to any loans or related securities.

(5) Nothing in the terms of any loan or related transaction entered into by Scottish Homes shall be construed as impliedly prohibiting or restricting it from dealing with its loans portfolio in accordance with arrangements under this section.

(6) A direction given under subsection (2) above may be varied or revoked by a subsequent direction given by the Secretary of State.'.

Housing Act 1988 (c. 50)

10 Section 58 of the Housing Act 1988 (application of Housing Acts to certain transactions) shall cease to have effect.

11 In section 79(2) of the Housing Act 1988 (permitted disposals of land by housing action trusts) for paragraph (a) and the word 'or' at the end of the paragraph substitute—

'(a)   to a registered social landlord (within the meaning of Part I of the Housing Act 1996), or'.

SCHEDULE 4
RIGHTS EXERCISABLE BY SURVEYOR APPOINTED BY TENANTS' ASSOCIATION

Section 84

Introductory

1 (1) A surveyor appointed for the purposes of section 84 has the rights conferred by this Schedule.

(2) In this Schedule—

(a)   'the tenants' association' means the association by whom the surveyor was appointed, and

(b)   the surveyor's 'functions' are his functions in connection with the matters in respect of which he was appointed.

Appointment of assistants

2 (1) The surveyor may appoint such persons as he thinks fit to assist him in carrying out his functions.

(2) References in this Schedule to the surveyor in the context of—

(a)   being afforded any such facilities as are mentioned in paragraph 3, or

(b)   carrying out an inspection under paragraph 4,

include a person so appointed.

Right to inspect documents, etc.

3 (1) The surveyor has a right to require the landlord or any other relevant person—

(a)   to afford him reasonable facilities for inspecting any documents sight of which is reasonably required by him for the purposes of his functions, and

(b)   to afford him reasonable facilities for taking copies of or extracts from any such documents.

(2) In sub-paragraph (1) 'other relevant person' means a person other than the landlord who is or, in relation to a future service charge, will be—

(a)   responsible for applying the proceeds of the service charge, or

(b)   under an obligation to a tenant who pays the service charge in respect of any matter to which the charge relates.

(3) The rights conferred on the surveyor by this paragraph are exercisable by him by notice in writing given by him to the landlord or other person concerned.

Where a notice is given to a person other than the landlord, the surveyor shall give a copy of the notice to the landlord.

(4) The landlord or other person to whom notice is given shall, within the period of one week beginning with the date of the giving of the notice or as soon as reasonably practicable thereafter, either—

    (a) afford the surveyor the facilities required by him for inspecting and taking copies or extracts of the documents to which the notice relates, or

    (b) give the surveyor a notice stating that he objects to doing so for reasons specified in the notice.

(5) Facilities for the inspection of any documents required under subparagraph (1)(a) shall be made available free of charge.

This does not mean that the landlord cannot treat as part of his costs of management any costs incurred by him in connection with making the facilities available.

(6) A reasonable charge may be made for facilities for the taking of copies or extracts required under sub-paragraph (1)(b).

(7) A notice is duly given under this paragraph to the landlord of a tenant if it is given to a person who receives on behalf of the landlord the rent payable by that tenant.

A person to whom such a notice is so given shall forward it as soon as may be to the landlord.

Right to inspect premises

4 (1) The surveyor also has the right to inspect any common parts comprised in relevant premises or any appurtenant property.

(2) In sub-paragraph (1)—

'common parts', in relation to a building or part of a building, includes the structure and exterior of the building or part and any common facilities within it;
'relevant premises' means so much of—

    (i) the building or buildings containing the dwellings let to members of the tenants' association, and

    (ii) any other building or buildings,

as constitute premises in relation to which management functions are discharged in respect of the costs of which service charges are payable by members of the association; and
'appurtenant property' means so much of any property not contained in relevant premises as constitutes property in relation to which any such management functions are discharged.

For the purposes of the above definitions 'management functions' includes functions with respect to the provision of services, or the repair, maintenance or insurance of property.

(3) On being requested to do so, the landlord shall afford the surveyor reasonable access for the purposes of carrying out an inspection under this paragraph.

(4) Such reasonable access shall be afforded to the surveyor free of charge.

This does not mean that the landlord cannot treat as part of his costs of management any costs incurred by him in connection with affording reasonable access to the surveyor.

(5) A request is duly made under this paragraph to the landlord of a tenant if it is made to a person appointed by the landlord to deal with such requests or, if no such person has been appointed, to a person who receives on behalf of the landlord the rent payable by that tenant.

A person to whom such a request is made shall notify the landlord of the request as soon as may be.

Enforcement of rights by the court

5 (1) If the landlord or other person to whom notice was given under paragraph 3 has not, by the end of the period of one month beginning with the date on which notice was given, complied with the notice, the court may, on the application of the surveyor, make an order requiring him to do so within such period as is specified in the order.

(2) If the landlord does not, within a reasonable period after the making of a request under paragraph 4, afford the surveyor reasonable access for the purposes of carrying out an inspection under that paragraph, the court may, on the application of the surveyor, make an order requiring the landlord to do so on such date as is specified in the order.

(3) An application for an order under this paragraph must be made before the end of the period of four months beginning with the date on which notice was given under paragraph 3 or the request was made under paragraph 4.

(4) An order under this paragraph may be made in general terms or may require the landlord or other person to do specific things, as the court thinks fit.

Documents held by superior landlord

6 (1) Where a landlord is required by a notice under paragraph 3 to afford the surveyor facilities for inspection or taking copies or extracts in respect of any document which is in the custody or under the control of a superior landlord—

  (a) the landlord shall on receiving the notice inform the surveyor as soon as may be of that fact and of the name and address of the superior landlord, and
  (b) the surveyor may then give the superior landlord notice in writing requiring him to afford the facilities in question in respect of the document.

(2) Paragraphs 3 and 5(1) and (3) have effect, with any necessary modifications, in relation to a notice given to a superior landlord under this paragraph.

Effect of disposal by landlord

7 (1) Where a notice under paragraph 3 has been given or a request under paragraph 4 has been made to a landlord, and at a time when any obligations arising out of the notice or request remain to be discharged by him—

  (a) he disposes of the whole or part of his interest as landlord of any member of the tenants' association, and
  (b) the person acquiring that interest ('the transferee') is in a position to discharge any of those obligations to any extent,

that person shall be responsible for discharging those obligations to that extent, as if he had been given the notice under paragraph 3 or had received the request under paragraph 4.

(2) If the landlord is, despite the disposal, still in a position to discharge those obligations, he remains responsible for doing so.

Otherwise, the transferee is responsible for discharging them to the exclusion of the landlord.

(3) In connection with the discharge of such obligations by the transferee, paragraphs 3 to 6 apply with the substitution for any reference to the date on which notice was given under paragraph 3 or the request was made under paragraph 4 of a reference to the date of the disposal.

(4) In this paragraph 'disposal' means a disposal whether by the creation or transfer of an estate or interest, and includes the surrender of a tenancy; and references to the transferee shall be construed accordingly.

Effect of person ceasing to be a relevant person

8 Where a notice under paragraph 3 has been given to a person other than the landlord and, at a time when any obligations arising out of the notice remain to be discharged by him, he ceases to be such a person as is mentioned in paragraph 3(2), then, if he is still in a position to discharge those obligations to any extent he remains responsible for discharging those obligations, and the provisions of this Schedule continue to apply to him, to that extent.

SCHEDULE 5
TEXT OF PART II OF THE LANDLORD AND TENANT ACT 1987, AS AMENDED

Section 87

'PART II
APPOINTMENT OF MANAGERS BY LEASEHOLD VALUATION TRIBUNAL

21 Tenant's right to apply to tribunal for appointment of manager

(1) The tenant of a flat contained in any premises to which this Part applies may, subject to the following provisions of this Part, apply to a leasehold valuation tribunal for an order under section 24 appointing a manager to act in relation to those premises.

(2) Subject to subsection (3), this Part applies to premises consisting of the whole or part of a building if the building or part contains two or more flats.

(3) This Part does not apply to any such premises at a time when—

(a) the interest of the landlord in the premises is held by an exempt landlord or a resident landlord, or
(b) the premises are included within the functional land of any charity.

(4) An application for an order under section 24 may be made—

(a) jointly by tenants of two or more flats if they are each entitled to make such an application by virtue of this section, and
(b) in respect of two or more premises to which this Part applies;

and, in relation to any such joint application as is mentioned in paragraph (a), references in this Part to a single tenant shall be construed accordingly.

(5) Where the tenancy of a flat contained in any such premises is held by joint tenants, an application for an order under section 24 in respect of those premises may be made by any one or more of those tenants.

(6) An application to the court for it to exercise in relation to any premises any jurisdiction to appoint a receiver or manager shall not be made by a tenant (in his capacity as such) in any circumstances in which an application could be made by him for an order under section 24 appointing a manager to act in relation to those premises.

(7) References in this Part to a tenant do not include references to a tenant under a tenancy to which Part II of the Landlord and Tenant Act 1954 applies.

22 Preliminary notice by tenant

(1) Before an application for an order under section 24 is made in respect of any premises to which this Part applies by a tenant of a flat contained in those premises, a notice under this section must (subject to subsection (3)) be served on the landlord by the tenant.

(2) A notice under this section must—

(a) specify the tenant's name, the address of his flat and an address in England and Wales (which may be the address of his flat) at which the landlord may serve notices, including notices in proceedings, on him in connection with this Part;

(b) state that the tenant intends to make an application for an order under section 24 to be made by a leasehold valuation tribunal in respect of such premises to which this Part applies as are specified in the notice, but (if paragraph (d) is applicable) that he will not do so if the landlord complies with the requirement specified in pursuance of that paragraph;

(c) specify the grounds on which the tribunal would be asked to make such an order and the matters that would be relied on by the tenant for the purpose of establishing those grounds;

(d) where those matters are capable of being remedied by the landlord, require the landlord, within such reasonable period as is specified in the notice, to take such steps for the purpose of remedying them as are so specified; and

(e) contain such information (if any) as the Secretary of State may by regulations prescribe.

(3) A leasehold valuation tribunal may (whether on the hearing of an application for an order under section 24 or not) by order dispense with the requirement to serve a notice under this section in a case where it is satisfied that it would not be reasonably practicable to serve such a notice on the landlord, but the tribunal may, when doing so, direct that such other notices are served, or such other steps are taken, as it thinks fit.

(4) In a case where—

(a) a notice under this section has been served on the landlord, and

(b) his interest in the premises specified in pursuance of subsection (2)(b) is subject to a mortgage,

the landlord shall, as soon as is reasonably practicable after receiving the notice, serve on the mortgagee a copy of the notice.

23 Application to tribunal for appointment of manager

(1) No application for an order under section 24 shall be made to a leasehold valuation tribunal unless—

- (a) in a case where a notice has been served under section 22, either—
  - (i) the period specified in pursuance of paragraph (d) of subsection (2) of that section has expired without the landlord having taken the steps that he was required to take in pursuance of that provision, or
  - (ii) that paragraph was not applicable in the circumstances of the case; or
- (b) in a case where the requirement to serve such a notice has been dispensed with by an order under subsection (3) of that section, either—
  - (i) any notices required to be served, and any other steps required to be taken, by virtue of the order have been served or (as the case may be) taken, or
  - (ii) no direction was given by the tribunal when making the order.

(2) Procedure regulations shall make provision—

- (a) for requiring notice of an application for an order under section 24 in respect of any premises to be served on such descriptions of persons as may be specified in the regulations; and
- (b) for enabling persons served with any such notice to be joined as parties to the proceedings.

24 Appointment of manager by the tribunal

(1) A leasehold valuation tribunal may, on an application for an order under this section, by order (whether interlocutory or final) appoint a manager to carry out in relation to any premises to which this Part applies—

- (a) such functions in connection with the management of the premises, or
- (b) such functions of a receiver,

or both, as the tribunal thinks fit.

(2) A leasehold valuation tribunal may only make an order under this section in the following circumstances, namely—

- (a) where the tribunal is satisfied—
  - (i) that the landlord either is in breach of any obligation owed by him to the tenant under his tenancy and relating to the management of the premises in question or any part of them or (in the case of an obligation dependent on notice) would be in breach of any such obligation but for the fact that it has not been reasonably practicable for the tenant to give him the appropriate notice, and
  - (ii) that it is just and convenient to make the order in all the circumstances of the case;
- (ab) where the tribunal is satisfied—
  - (i) that unreasonable service charges have been made, or are proposed or likely to be made, and
  - (ii) that it is just and convenient to make the order in all the circumstances of the case;

(ac) where the tribunal is satisfied—

  (i) that the landlord has failed to comply with any relevant provision of a code of practice approved by the Secretary of State under section 87 of the Leasehold Reform, Housing and Urban Development Act 1993 (codes of management practice), and

  (ii) that it is just and convenient to make the order in all the circumstances of the case; or

(b) where the tribunal is satisfied that other circumstances exist which make it just and convenient for the order to be made.

(2A) For the purposes of subsection (2)(ab) a service charge shall be taken to be unreasonable—

(a) if the amount is unreasonable having regard to the items for which it is payable,

(b) if the items for which it is payable are of an unnecessarily high standard, or

(c) if the items for which it is payable are of an insufficient standard with the result that additional service charges are or may be incurred.

In that provision and this subsection "service charge" means a service charge within the meaning of section 18(1) of the Landlord and Tenant Act 1985, other than one excluded from that section by section 27 of that Act (rent of dwelling registered and not entered as variable).

(3) The premises in respect of which an order is made under this section may, if the tribunal thinks fit, be either more or less extensive than the premises specified in the application on which the order is made.

(4) An order under this section may make provision with respect to—

(a) such matters relating to the exercise by the manager of his functions under the order, and

(b) such incidental or ancillary matters,

as the tribunal thinks fit; and, on any subsequent application made for the purpose by the manager, the tribunal may give him directions with respect to any such matters.

(5) Without prejudice to the generality of subsection (4), an order under this section may provide—

(a) for rights and liabilities arising under contracts to which the manager is not a party to become rights and liabilities of the manager;

(b) for the manager to be entitled to prosecute claims in respect of causes of action (whether contractual or tortious) accruing before or after the date of his appointment;

(c) for remuneration to be paid to the manager by the landlord, or by the tenants of the premises in respect of which the order is made or by all or any of those persons;

(d) for the manager's functions to be exercisable by him (subject to subsection (9)) either during a specified period or without limit of time.

(6) Any such order may be granted subject to such conditions as the tribunal thinks fit, and in particular its operation may be suspended on terms fixed by the tribunal.

(7) In a case where an application for an order under this section was preceded by the service of a notice under section 22, the tribunal may, if it thinks fit, make such an order notwithstanding—

(a) that any period specified in the notice in pursuance of subsection (2)(d) of that section was not a reasonable period, or

(b) that the notice failed in any other respect to comply with any requirement contained in subsection (2) of that section or in any regulations applying to the notice under section 54(3).

(8) The Land Charges Act 1972 and the Land Registration Act 1925 shall apply in relation to an order made under this section as they apply in relation to an order appointing a receiver or sequestrator of land.

(9) A leasehold valuation tribunal may, on the application of any person interested, vary or discharge (whether conditionally or unconditionally) an order made under this section; and if the order has been protected by an entry registered under the Land Charges Act 1972 or the Land Registration Act 1925, the tribunal may by order direct that the entry shall be cancelled.

(9A) The court shall not vary or discharge an order under subsection (9) on a landlord's application unless it is satisfied—

(a) that the variation or discharge of the order will not result in a recurrence of the circumstances which led to the order being made, and

(b) that it is just and convenient in all the circumstances of the case to vary or discharge the order.

(10) An order made under this section shall not be discharged by a leasehold valuation tribunal by reason only that, by virtue of section 21(3), the premises in respect of which the order was made have ceased to be premises to which this Part applies.

(11) References in this section to the management of any premises include references to the repair, maintenance or insurance of those premises.

24A Jurisdiction of leasehold valuation tribunal

(1) The jurisdiction conferred by this Part on a leasehold valuation tribunal is exercisable by a rent assessment committee constituted in accordance with Schedule 10 to the Rent Act 1977 which when so constituted for the purposes of exercising any such jurisdiction shall be known as a leasehold valuation tribunal.

(2) The power to make regulations under section 74(1)(b) of the Rent Act 1977 (procedure of rent assessment committees) extends to prescribing the procedure to be followed in connection with any proceedings before a leasehold valuation tribunal under this Part.

Such regulations are referred to in this Part as "procedure regulations".

(3) Any order made by a leasehold valuation tribunal under this Part may, with the leave of the court, be enforced in the same way as an order of the county court.

(4) No costs incurred by a party in connection with proceedings under this Part before a leasehold valuation tribunal shall be recoverable by order of any court.

(5) Paragraphs 2, 3 and 7 of Schedule 22 to the Housing Act 1980 (supplementary provisions relating to leasehold valuation tribunals: appeals and provision of information) apply to a leasehold valuation tribunal constituted for the purposes of this section.

(6) No appeal shall lie to the Lands Tribunal from a decision of a leasehold valuation tribunal under this Part without the leave of the leasehold valuation tribunal concerned or the Lands Tribunal.

(7) On an appeal to the Lands Tribunal from a decision of a leasehold valuation tribunal under this Part—

    (a) the Lands Tribunal may exercise any power available to the leasehold valuation tribunal in relation to the original matter, and

    (b) an order of the Lands Tribunal may be enforced in the same way as an order of the leasehold valuation tribunal.

24B Leasehold valuation tribunal: applications and fees

(1) The Secretary of State may make provision by order as to the form of, or the particulars to be contained in, an application made to a leasehold valuation tribunal under this Part.

(2) The Secretary of State may make provision by order—

    (a) requiring the payment of fees in respect of any such application, or in respect of any proceedings before, a leasehold valuation tribunal under this Part; and

    (b) empowering a leasehold valuation tribunal to require a party to proceedings before it to reimburse any other party the amount of any fees paid by him.

(3) The fees payable shall be such as may be specified in or determined in accordance with the order subject to this limit, that the fees payable in respect of any one application or reference by the court together with any proceedings before the tribunal arising out of that application or reference shall not exceed £500 or such other amount as may be specified by order of the Secretary of State.

(4) An order under this section may make different provision for different cases or classes of case or for different areas.

(5) An order may, in particular, provide for the reduction or waiver of fees by reference to the financial resources of the party by whom they are to be paid or met.

Any such order may apply, subject to such modifications as may be specified in the order, any other statutory means-testing regime as it has effect from time to time.

(6) An order under this section shall be made by statutory instrument.

(7) No order altering the limit under subsection (3) shall be made unless a draft of the order has been laid before and approved by a resolution of each House of Parliament.

(8) Any other order under this section, unless it contains only such provision as is mentioned in subsection (1), shall be subject to annulment in pursuance of a resolution of either House of Parliament.'.

SCHEDULE 6

AMENDMENTS OF PART I OF THE LANDLORD AND TENANT ACT 1987

Section 92(1)

PART I

RIGHTS OF FIRST REFUSAL

The following sections are substituted for sections 5 to 10 of the Landlord and Tenant Act 1987—

'Rights of first refusal

Landlord required to serve offer notice on tenants

5 (1) Where the landlord proposes to make a relevant disposal affecting premises to which this Part applies, he shall serve a notice under this section (an "offer notice") on the qualifying tenants of the flats contained in the premises (the "constituent flats").

(2) An offer notice must comply with the requirements of whichever is applicable of the following sections—

section 5A (requirements in case of contract to be completed by conveyance, etc.),
section 5B (requirements in case of sale at auction),
section 5C (requirements in case of grant of option or right of pre-emption),
section 5D (requirements in case of conveyance not preceded by contract, etc.);

and in the case of a disposal to which section 5E applies (disposal for non-monetary consideration) shall also comply with the requirements of that section.

(3) Where a landlord proposes to effect a transaction involving the disposal of an estate or interest in more than one building (whether or not involving the same estate or interest), he shall, for the purpose of complying with this section, sever the transaction so as to deal with each building separately.

(4) If, as a result of the offer notice being served on different tenants on different dates, the period specified in the notice as the period for accepting the offer would end on different dates, the notice shall have effect in relation to all the qualifying tenants on whom it is served as if it provided for that period to end with the latest of those dates.

(5) A landlord who has not served an offer notice on all of the qualifying tenants on whom it was required to be served shall nevertheless be treated as having complied with this section—

(a) if he has served an offer notice on not less than 90% of the qualifying tenants on whom such a notice was required to be served, or
(b) where the qualifying tenants on whom it was required to be served number less than ten, if he has served such a notice on all but one of them.

5A Offer notice: requirements in case of contract to be completed by conveyance, etc.

(1) The following requirements must be met in relation to an offer notice where the disposal consists of entering into a contract to create or transfer an estate or interest in land.

(2) The notice must contain particulars of the principal terms of the disposal proposed by the landlord, including in particular—

(a) the property, and the estate or interest in that property, to which the contract relates,

(b) the principal terms of the contract (including the deposit and consideration required).

(3) The notice must state that the notice constitutes an offer by the landlord to enter into a contract on those terms which may be accepted by the requisite majority of qualifying tenants of the constituent flats.

(4) The notice must specify a period within which that offer may be so accepted, being a period of not less than two months which is to begin with the date of service of the notice.

(5) The notice must specify a further period of not less than two months within which a person or persons may be nominated by the tenants under section 6.

(6) This section does not apply to the grant of an option or right of pre-emption (see section 5C).

5B Offer notice: requirements in case of sale by auction

(1) The following requirements must be met in relation to an offer notice where the landlord proposes to make the disposal by means of a sale at a public auction held in England and Wales.

(2) The notice must contain particulars of the principal terms of the disposal proposed by the landlord, including in particular the property to which it relates and the estate or interest in that property proposed to be disposed of.

(3) The notice must state that the disposal is proposed to be made by means of a sale at a public auction.

(4) The notice must state that the notice constitutes an offer by the landlord, which may be accepted by the requisite majority of qualifying tenants of the constituent flats, for the contract (if any) entered into by the landlord at the auction to have effect as if a person or persons nominated by them, and not the purchaser, had entered into it.

(5) The notice must specify a period within which that offer may be so accepted, being a period of not less than two months beginning with the date of service of the notice.

(6) The notice must specify a further period of not less than 28 days within which a person or persons may be nominated by the tenants under section 6.

(7) The notice must be served not less than four months or more than six months before the date of the auction; and

(a) the period specified in the notice as the period within which the offer may be accepted must end not less than two months before the date of the auction, and

(b) the period specified in the notice as the period within which a person may be nominated under section 6 must end not less than 28 days before the date of the auction.

(8) Unless the time and place of the auction and the name of the auctioneers are stated in the notice, the landlord shall, not less than 28 days before the date of the auction, serve on the requisite majority of qualifying tenants of the constituent flats a further notice stating those particulars.

5C Offer notice: requirements in case of grant or option or right of pre-emption

(1) The following requirements must be met in relation to an offer notice where the disposal consists of the grant of an option or right of pre-emption.

(2) The notice must contain particulars of the principal terms of the disposal proposed by the landlord, including in particular—

(a) the property, and the estate or interest in that property, to which the option or right of pre-emption relates,

(b) the consideration required by the landlord for granting the option or right of pre-emption, and

(c) the principal terms on which the option or right of pre-emption would be exercisable, including the consideration payable on its exercise.

(3) The notice must state that the notice constitutes an offer by the landlord to grant an option or right of pre-emption on those terms which may be accepted by the requisite majority of qualifying tenants of the constituent flats.

(4) The notice must specify a period within which that offer may be so accepted, being a period of not less than two months which is to begin with the date of service of the notice.

(5) The notice must specify a further period of not less than two months within which a person or persons may be nominated by the tenants under section 6.

5D Offer notice: requirements in case of conveyance not preceded by contract, etc.

(1) The following requirements must be met in relation to an offer notice where the disposal is not made in pursuance of a contract, option or right of pre-emption binding on the landlord.

(2) The notice must contain particulars of the principal terms of the disposal proposed by the landlord, including in particular—

(a) the property to which it relates and the estate or interest in that property proposed to be disposed of, and

(b) the consideration required by the landlord for making the disposal.

(3) The notice must state that the notice constitutes an offer by the landlord to dispose of the property on those terms which may be accepted by the requisite majority of qualifying tenants of the constituent flats.

(4) The notice must specify a period within which that offer may be so accepted, being a period of not less than two months which is to begin with the date of service of the notice.

(5) The notice must specify a further period of not less than two months within which a person or persons may be nominated by the tenants under section 6.

5E Offer notice: disposal for non-monetary consideration

(1) This section applies where, in any case to which section 5 applies, the consideration required by the landlord for making the disposal does not consist, or does not wholly consist, of money.

(2) The offer notice, in addition to complying with whichever is applicable of sections 5A to 5D, must state—

  (a) that an election may made under section 8C (explaining its effect), and

  (b) that, accordingly, the notice also constitutes an offer by the landlord, which may be accepted by the requisite majority of qualifying tenants of the constituent flats, for a person or persons nominated by them to acquire the property in pursuance of sections 11 to 17.

(3) The notice must specify a period within which that offer may be so accepted, being a period of not less than two months which is to begin with the date of service of the notice.

6 Acceptance of landlord's offer: general provisions

(1) Where a landlord has served an offer notice, he shall not during—

  (a) the period specified in the notice as the period during which the offer may be accepted, or

  (b) such longer period as may be agreed between him and the requisite majority of the qualifying tenants of the constituent flats,

dispose of the protected interest except to a person or persons nominated by the tenants under this section.

(2) Where an acceptance notice is duly served on him, he shall not during the protected period (see subsection (4) below) dispose of the protected interest except to a person duly nominated for the purposes of this section by the requisite majority of qualifying tenants of the constituent flats (a "nominated person").

(3) An "acceptance notice" means a notice served on the landlord by the requisite majority of qualifying tenants of the constituent flats informing him that the persons by whom it is served accept the offer contained in his notice.

An acceptance notice is "duly served" if it is served within—

  (a) the period specified in the offer notice as the period within which the offer may be accepted, or

  (b) such longer period as may be agreed between the landlord and the requisite majority of qualifying tenants of the constituent flats.

(4) The "protected period" is the period beginning with the date of service of the acceptance notice and ending with—

  (a) the end of the period specified in the offer notice as the period for nominating a person under this section, or

  (b) such later date as may be agreed between the landlord and the requisite majority of qualifying tenants of constituent flats.

(5) A person is "duly nominated" for the purposes of this section if he is nominated at the same time as the acceptance notice is served or at any time after that notice is served and before the end of—

  (a) the period specified in the offer notice as the period for nomination, or

  (b) such longer period as may be agreed between the landlord and the requisite majority of qualifying tenants of the constituent flats.

(6) A person nominated for the purposes of this section by the requisite majority of qualifying tenants of the constituent flats may be replaced by another person so nominated if, and only if, he has (for any reason) ceased to be able to act as a nominated person.

(7) Where two or more persons have been nominated and any of them ceases to act without being replaced, the remaining person or persons so nominated may continue to act.

7 Failure to accept landlord's offer or to make nomination

(1) Where a landlord has served an offer notice on the qualifying tenants of the constituent flats and—

(a) no acceptance notice is duly served on the landlord, or
(b) no person is nominated for the purposes of section 6 during the protected period,

the landlord may, during the period of 12 months beginning with the end of that period, dispose of the protected interest to such person as he thinks fit, but subject to the following restrictions.

(2) Where the offer notice was one to which section 5B applied (sale by auction), the restrictions are—

(a) that the disposal is made by means of a sale at a public auction, and
(b) that the other terms correspond to those specified in the offer notice.

(3) In any other case the restrictions are—

(a) that the deposit and consideration required are not less than those specified in the offer notice, and
(b) that the other terms correspond to those specified in the offer notice.

(4) The entitlement of a landlord, by virtue of this section or any other corresponding provision of this Part, to dispose of the protected interest during a specified period of 12 months extends only to a disposal of that interest, and accordingly the requirements of section 1(1) must be satisfied with respect to any other disposal by him during that period of 12 months (unless the disposal is not a relevant disposal affecting any premises to which at the time of the disposal this Part applies).

8 Landlord's obligations in case of acceptance and nomination

(1) This section applies where a landlord serves an offer notice on the qualifying tenants of the constituent flat and—

(a) an acceptance notice is duly served on him, and
(b) a person is duly nominated for the purposes of section 6,

by the requisite majority of qualifying tenants of the constituent flats.

(2) Subject to the following provisions of this Part, the landlord shall not dispose of the protected interest except to the nominated person.

(3) The landlord shall, within the period of one month beginning with the date of service of notice of nomination, either—

(a) serve notice on the nominated person indicating an intention no longer to proceed with the disposal of the protected interest, or

(b) be obliged to proceed in accordance with the following provisions of this Part.

(4) A notice under subsection (3)(a) is a notice of withdrawal for the purposes of section 9B(2) to (4) (consequences of notice of withdrawal by landlord).

(5) Nothing in this section shall be taken as prejudicing the application of the provisions of this Part to any further offer notice served by the landlord on the qualifying tenants of the constituent flats.

8A Landlord's obligation: general provisions

(1) This section applies where the landlord is obliged to proceed and the offer notice was not one to which section 5B applied (sale by auction).

(2) The landlord shall, within the period of one month beginning with the date of service of the notice of nomination, send to the nominated person a form of contract for the acquisition of the protected interest on the terms specified in the landlord's offer notice.

(3) If he fails to do so, the following provisions of this Part apply as if he had given notice under section 9B (notice of withdrawal by landlord) at the end of that period.

(4) If the landlord complies with subsection (2), the nominated person shall within the period of two months beginning with the date on which it is sent or such longer period beginning with that date as may be agreed between the landlord and that person, either—

(a) serve notice on the landlord indicating an intention no longer to proceed with the acquisition of the protected interest, or

(b) offer an exchange of contracts, that is to say, sign the contract and send it to the landlord, together with the requisite deposit.

In this subsection "the requisite deposit" means a deposit of an amount determined by or under the contract or an amount equal to 10 per cent. of the consideration, whichever is the less.

(5) If the nominated person—

(a) serves notice in pursuance of paragraph (a) of subsection (4), or

(b) fails to offer an exchange of contracts within the period specified in that subsection,

the following provisions of this Part apply as if he had given notice under section 9A (withdrawal by nominated person) at the same time as that notice or, as the case may be, at the end of that period.

(6) If the nominated person offers an exchange of contracts within the period specified in subsection (4), but the landlord fails to complete the exchange within the period of seven days beginning with the day on which he received that person's contract, the following provisions of this Part apply as if the landlord had given notice under section 9B (withdrawal by landlord) at the end of that period.

8B Landlord's obligation: election in case of sale at auction

(1) This section applies where the landlord is obliged to proceed and the offer notice was one to which section 5B applied (sale by auction).

(2) The nominated person may, by notice served on the landlord not less than 28 days before the date of the auction, elect that the provisions of this section shall apply.

(3) If a contract for the disposal is entered into at the auction, the landlord shall, within the period of seven days beginning with the date of the auction, send a copy of the contract to the nominated person.

(4) If, within the period of 28 days beginning with the date on which such a copy is so sent, the nominated person—

(a) serves notice on the landlord accepting the terms of the contract, and
(b) fulfils any conditions falling to be fulfilled by the purchaser on entering into the contract,

the contract shall have effect as if the nominated person, and not the purchaser, had entered into the contract.

(5) Unless otherwise agreed, any time limit in the contract as it has effect by virtue of subsection (4) shall start to run again on the service of notice under that subsection; and nothing in the contract as it has effect by virtue of a notice under this section shall require the nominated person to complete the purchase before the end of the period of 28 days beginning with the day on which he is deemed to have entered into the contract.

(6) If the nominated person—

(a) does not serve notice on the landlord under subsection (2) by the time mentioned in that subsection, or
(b) does not satisfy the requirements of subsection (4) within the period mentioned in that subsection,

the following provisions of this Part apply as if he had given notice under section 9A (withdrawal by nominated person) at the end of that period.

8C Election in case of disposal for non-monetary consideration

(1) This section applies where an acceptance notice is duly served on the landlord indicating an intention to accept the offer referred to in section 5E (offer notice: disposal for non-monetary consideration).

(2) The requisite majority of qualifying tenants of the constituent flats may, by notice served on the landlord within—

(a) the period specified in the offer notice for nominating a person or persons for the purposes of section 6, or
(b) such longer period as may be agreed between the landlord and the requisite majority of qualifying tenants of the constituent flats,

elect that the following provisions shall apply.

(3) Where such an election is made and the landlord disposes of the protected interest on terms corresponding to those specified in his offer notice in accordance with section 5A, 5B, 5C or 5D, sections 11 to 17 shall have effect as if—

(a) no notice under section 5 had been served;

   (b) in section 11A(3) (period for serving notice requiring information, etc.), the reference to four months were a reference to 28 days; and

   (c) in section 12A(2) and 12B(3) (period for exercise of tenants' rights against purchaser) each reference to six months were a reference to two months.

(4) For the purposes of sections 11 to 17 as they have effect by virtue of subsection (3) so much of the consideration for the original disposal as did not consist of money shall be treated as such amount in money as was equivalent to its value in the hands of the landlord.

The landlord or the nominated person may apply to have that amount determined by a leasehold valuation tribunal.

8D Disposal in pursuance of option or right of pre-emption

(1) Where—

   (a) the original disposal was the grant of an option or right of pre-emption, and

   (b) in pursuance of the option or right, the landlord makes another disposal affecting the premises ("the later disposal") before the end of the period specified in subsection (2),

sections 11 to 17 shall have effect as if the later disposal, and not the original disposal, were the relevant disposal.

(2) The period referred to in subsection (1)(b) is the period of four months beginning with the date by which—

   (a) notices under section 3A of the Landlord and Tenant Act 1985 (duty of new landlord to inform tenants of rights) relating to the original disposal, or

   (b) where that section does not apply, documents of any other description—

      (i) indicating that the original disposal has taken place, and

      (ii) alerting the tenants to the existence of their rights under this Part and the time within which any such rights must be exercised,

have been served on the requisite majority of qualifying tenants of the constituent flats.

8E Covenant, etc. affecting landlord's power to dispose

(1) Where the landlord is obliged to proceed but is precluded by a covenant, condition or other obligation from disposing of the protected interest to the nominated person unless the consent of some other person is obtained—

   (a) he shall use his best endeavours to secure that the consent of that person to that disposal is given, and

   (b) if it appears to him that that person is obliged not to withhold his consent unreasonably but has nevertheless so withheld it, he shall institute proceedings for a declaration to that effect.

(2) Subsection (1) ceases to apply if a notice of withdrawal is served under section 9A or 9B (withdrawal of either party from transaction) or if notice is served under section 10 (lapse of landlord's offer: premises ceasing to be premises to which this Part applies).

(3) Where the landlord has discharged any duty imposed on him by subsection (1) but any such consent as is there mentioned has been withheld, and no such declaration as is there mentioned has been made, the landlord may serve a notice on the nominated person stating that to be the case.

When such a notice has been served, the landlord may, during the period of 12 months beginning with the date of service of the notice, dispose of the protected interest to such person as he thinks fit, but subject to the following restrictions.

(4) Where the offer notice was one to which section 5B applied (sale by auction), the restrictions are—

    (a) that the disposal is made by means of a sale at a public auction, and

    (b) that the other terms correspond to those specified in the offer notice.

(5) In any other case the restrictions are—

    (a) that the deposit and consideration required are not less than those specified in the offer notice or, if higher, those agreed between the landlord and the nominated person (subject to contract), and

    (b) that the other terms correspond to those specified in the offer notice.

(6) Where notice is given under subsection (3), the landlord may recover from the nominated party and the qualifying tenants who served the acceptance notice any costs reasonably incurred by him in connection with the disposal between the end of the first four weeks of the nomination period and the time when that notice is served by him.

Any such liability of the nominated person and those tenants is a joint and several liability.

9A Notice of withdrawal by nominated person

(1) Where the landlord is obliged to proceed, the nominated person may serve notice on the landlord (a "notice of withdrawal") indicating his intention no longer to proceed with the acquisition of the protected interest.

(2) If at any time the nominated person becomes aware that the number of the qualifying tenants of the constituent flats desiring to proceed with the acquisition of the protected interest is less than the requisite majority of qualifying tenants of those flats, he shall forthwith serve a notice of withdrawal.

(3) Where notice of withdrawal is given by the nominated person under this section, the landlord may, during the period of 12 months beginning with the date of service of the notice, dispose of the protected interest to such person as he thinks fit, but subject to the following restrictions.

(4) Where the offer notice was one to which section 5B applied (sale by auction), the restrictions are—

    (a) that the disposal is made by means of a sale at a public auction, and

    (b) that the other terms correspond to those specified in the offer notice.

(5) In any other case the restrictions are—

    (a) that the deposit and consideration required are not less than those specified in the offer notice or, if higher, those agreed between the landlord and the nominated person (subject to contract), and

    (b) that the other terms correspond to those specified in the offer notice.

(6) If notice of withdrawal is served under this section before the end of the first four weeks of the nomination period specified in the offer notice, the nominated person and the qualifying tenants who served the acceptance notice are not liable for any costs incurred by the landlord in connection with the disposal.

(7) If notice of withdrawal is served under this section after the end of those four weeks, the landlord may recover from the nominated person and the qualifying tenants who served the acceptance notice any costs reasonably incurred by him in connection with the disposal between the end of those four weeks and the time when the notice of withdrawal was served on him.

Any such liability of the nominated person and those tenants is a joint and several liability.

(8) This section does not apply after a binding contract for the disposal of the protected interest—

(a) has been entered into by the landlord and the nominated person, or

(b) has otherwise come into existence between the landlord and the nominated person by virtue of any provision of this Part.

9B Notice of withdrawal by landlord

(1) Where the landlord is obliged to proceed, he may serve notice on the nominated person (a "notice of withdrawal") indicating his intention no longer to proceed with the disposal of the protected interest.

(2) Where a notice of withdrawal is given by the landlord, he is not entitled to dispose of the protected interest during the period of 12 months beginning with the date of service of the notice.

(3) If a notice of withdrawal is served before the end of the first four weeks of the nomination period specified in the offer notice, the landlord is not liable for any costs incurred in connection with the disposal by the nominated person and the qualifying tenants who served the acceptance notice.

(4) If a notice of withdrawal is served after the end of those four weeks, the nominated person and the qualifying tenants who served the acceptance notice may recover from the landlord any costs reasonably incurred by them in connection with the disposal between the end of those four weeks and the time when the notice of withdrawal was served.

(5) This section does not apply after a binding contract for the disposal of the protected interest—

(a) has been entered into by the landlord and the nominated person, or

(b) has otherwise come into existence between the landlord and the nominated person by virtue of any provision of this Part.

10 Lapse of landlord's offer

(1) If after a landlord has served an offer notice the premises concerned cease to be premises to which this Part applies, the landlord may serve a notice on the qualifying tenants of the constituent flats stating—

(a) that the premises have ceased to be premises to which this Part applies, and

(b) that the offer notice, and anything done in pursuance of it, is to be treated as not having been served or done;

and on the service of such a notice the provisions of this Part cease to have effect in relation to that disposal.

(2) A landlord who has not served such a notice on all of the qualifying tenants of the constituent flats shall nevertheless be treated as having duly served a notice under subsection (1)—

(a) if he has served such a notice on not less than 90% of those tenants, or
(b) where those qualifying tenants number less than ten, if he has served such a notice on all but one of them.

(3) Where the landlord is entitled to serve a notice under subsection (1) but does not do so, this Part shall continue to have effect in relation to the disposal in question as if the premises in question were still premises to which this Part applies.

(4) The above provisions of this section do not apply after a binding contract for the disposal of the protected interest—

(a) has been entered into by the landlord and the nominated person, or
(b) has otherwise come into existence between the landlord and the nominated person by virtue of any provision of this Part.

(5) Where a binding contract for the disposal of the protected interest has been entered into between the landlord and the nominated person but it has been lawfully rescinded by the landlord, the landlord may, during the period of 12 months beginning with the date of the rescission of the contract, dispose of that interest to such person (and on such terms) as he thinks fit.'.

PART II

ENFORCEMENT BY TENANTS OF RIGHTS AGAINST PURCHASER

The following sections are substituted for sections 11 to 15 of the Landlord and Tenant Act 1987—

'Enforcement by tenants of rights against purchaser

11 Circumstances in which tenants' rights enforceable against purchaser

(1) The following provisions of this Part apply where a landlord has made a relevant disposal affecting premises to which at the time of the disposal this Part applied ("the original disposal"), and either—

(a) no notice was served by the landlord under section 5 with respect to that disposal, or
(b) the disposal was made in contravention of any provision of sections 6 to 10,

and the premises are still premises to which this Part applies.

(2) In those circumstances the requisite majority of the qualifying tenants of the flats contained in the premises affected by the relevant disposal (the "constituent flats") have the rights conferred by the following provisions—

section 11A (right to information as to terms of disposal, etc.),
section 12A (right of qualifying tenants to take benefit of contract),
section 12B (right of qualifying tenants to compel sale, etc. by purchaser), and

section 12C (right of qualifying tenants to compel grant of new tenancy by superior landlord).

(3) In those sections the transferee under the original disposal (or, in the case of the surrender of a tenancy, the superior landlord) is referred to as "the purchaser".

This shall not be read as restricting the operation of those provisions to disposals for consideration.

11A Right to information as to terms of disposal, etc.

(1) The requisite majority of qualifying tenants of the constituent flats may serve a notice on the purchaser requiring him—

- (a) to give particulars of the terms on which the original disposal was made (including the deposit and consideration required) and the date on which it was made, and
- (b) where the disposal consisted of entering into a contract, to provide a copy of the contract.

(2) The notice must specify the name and address of the person to whom (on behalf of the tenants) the particulars are to be given, or the copy of the contract provided.

(3) Any notice under this section must be served before the end of the period of four months beginning with the date by which—

- (a) notices under section 3A of the Landlord and Tenant Act 1985 (duty of new landlord to inform tenants of rights) relating to the original disposal, or
- (b) where that section does not apply, documents of any other description—
    - (i) indicating that the original disposal has taken place, and
    - (ii) alerting the tenants to the existence of their rights under this Part and the time within which any such rights must be exercised,

have been served on the requisite majority of qualifying tenants of the constituent flats.

(4) A person served with a notice under this section shall comply with it within the period of one month beginning with the date on which it is served on him.

12A Right of qualifying tenants to take benefit of contract

(1) Where the original disposal consisted of entering into a contract, the requisite majority of qualifying tenants of the constituent flats may by notice to the landlord elect that the contract shall have effect as if entered into not with the purchaser but with a person or persons nominated for the purposes of this section by the requisite majority of qualifying tenants of the constituent flats.

(2) Any such notice must be served before the end of the period of six months beginning—

- (a) if a notice was served on the purchaser under section 11A (right to information as to terms of disposal, etc.), with the date on which the purchaser complied with that notice;
- (b) in any other case, with the date by which documents of any description—
    - (i) indicating that the original disposal has taken place, and
    - (ii) alerting the tenants to the existence of their rights under this Part and the time within which any such rights must be exercised,

    have been served on the requisite majority of qualifying tenants of the constituent flats.

(3) The notice shall not have effect as mentioned in subsection (1) unless the nominated person—

(a) fulfils any requirements as to the deposit required on entering into the contract, and

(b) fulfils any other conditions required to be fulfilled by the purchaser on entering into the contract.

(4) Unless otherwise agreed, any time limit in the contract as it has effect by virtue of a notice under this section shall start to run again on the service of that notice; and nothing in the contract as it has effect by virtue of a notice under this section shall require the nominated person to complete the purchase before the end of the period of 28 days beginning with the day on which he is deemed to have entered into the contract.

(5) Where the original disposal related to other property in addition to premises to which this Part applied at the time of the disposal—

(a) a notice under this section has effect only in relation to the premises to which this Part applied at the time of the original disposal, and

(b) the terms of the contract shall have effect with any necessary modifications.

In such a case the notice under this section may specify the subject-matter of the disposal, and the terms on which the disposal is to be made (whether doing so expressly or by reference to the original disposal), or may provide for that estate or interest, or any such terms, to be determined by a leasehold valuation tribunal.

12B Right of qualifying tenants to compel sale, etc. by purchaser

(1) This section applies where—

(a) the original disposal consisted of entering into a contract and no notice has been served under section 12A (right of qualifying tenants to take benefit of contract), or

(b) the original disposal did not consist of entering into a contract.

(2) The requisite majority of qualifying tenants of the constituent flats may serve a notice (a "purchase notice") on the purchaser requiring him to dispose of the estate or interest that was the subject-matter of the original disposal, on the terms on which it was made (including those relating to the consideration payable), to a person or persons nominated for the purposes of this section by any such majority of qualifying tenants of those flats.

(3) Any such notice must be served before the end of the period of six months beginning—

(a) if a notice was served on the purchaser under section 11A (right to information as to terms of disposal, etc.), with the date on which the purchaser complied with that notice;

(b) in any other case, with the date by which—

(i) notices under section 3A of the Landlord and Tenant Act 1985 (duty of new landlord to inform tenants of rights) relating to the original disposal, or

(ii) where that section does not apply, documents of any other description indicating that the original disposal has taken place, and alerting the tenants to the existence of their rights under this Part and the time within which any such rights must be exercised,

have been served on the requisite majority of qualifying tenants of the constituent flats.

(4) A purchase notice shall where the original disposal related to other property in addition to premises to which this Part applied at the time of the disposal—

(a) require the purchaser only to make a disposal relating to those premises, and

(b) require him to do so on the terms referred to in subsection (2) with any necessary modifications.

In such a case the purchase notice may specify the subject-matter of the disposal, and the terms on which the disposal is to be made (whether doing so expressly or by reference to the original disposal), or may provide for those matters to be determined by a leasehold valuation tribunal.

(5) Where the property which the purchaser is required to dispose of in pursuance of the purchase notice has since the original disposal become subject to any charge or other incumbrance, then, unless the court by order directs otherwise—

(a) in the case of a charge to secure the payment of money or the performance of any other obligation by the purchaser or any other person, the instrument by virtue of which the property is disposed of by the purchaser to the person or persons nominated for the purposes of this section shall (subject to the provisions of Part I of Schedule 1) operate to discharge the property from that charge; and

(b) in the case of any other incumbrance, the property shall be so disposed of subject to the incumbrance but with a reduction in the consideration payable to the purchaser corresponding to the amount by which the existence of the incumbrance reduces the value of the property.

(6) Subsection (5)(a) and Part I of Schedule 1 apply, with any necessary modifications, to mortgages and liens as they apply to charges; but nothing in those provisions applies to a rentcharge.

(7) Where the property which the purchaser is required to dispose of in pursuance of the purchase notice has since the original disposal increased in monetary value owing to any change in circumstances (other than a change in the value of money), the amount of the consideration payable to the purchaser for the disposal by him of the property in pursuance of the purchase notice shall be the amount that might reasonably have been obtained on a corresponding disposal made on the open market at the time of the original disposal if the change in circumstances had already taken place.

12C　Right of qualifying tenants to compel grant of new tenancy by superior landlord

(1) This section applies where the original disposal consisted of the surrender by the landlord of a tenancy held by him ("the relevant tenancy").

(2) The requisite majority of qualifying tenants of the constituent flats may serve a notice on the purchaser requiring him to grant a new tenancy of the premises which were subject to the relevant tenancy, on the same terms as those of the relevant tenancy and so as to expire on the same date as that tenancy would have expired, to a person or persons nominated for the purposes of this section by any such majority of qualifying tenants of those flats.

(3) Any such notice must be served before the end of the period of six months beginning—

(a) if a notice was served on the purchaser under section 11A (right to information as to terms of disposal, etc.), with the date on which the purchaser complied with that notice;

(b) in any other case, with the date by which documents of any description—

(i) indicating that the original disposal has taken place, and

(ii) alerting the tenants to the existence of their rights under this Part and the time within which any such rights must be exercised,

have been served on the requisite majority of qualifying tenants of the constituent flats.

(4) If the purchaser paid any amount to the landlord as consideration for the surrender by him of that tenancy, the nominated person shall pay that amount to the purchaser.

(5) Where the premises subject to the relevant tenancy included premises other than premises to which this Part applied at the time of the disposal, a notice under this section shall—

(a) require the purchaser only to grant a new tenancy relating to the premises to which this Part then applied, and

(b) require him to do so on the terms referred to in subsection (2) subject to any necessary modifications.

(6) The purchase notice may specify the subject-matter of the disposal, and the terms on which the disposal is to be made (whether doing so expressly or by reference to the original disposal), or may provide for those matters to be determined by a leasehold valuation tribunal.

12D Nominated persons: supplementary provisions

(1) The person or persons initially nominated for the purposes of section 12A, 12B or 12C shall be nominated in the notice under that section.

(2) A person nominated for those purposes by the requisite majority of qualifying tenants of the constituent flats may be replaced by another person so nominated if, and only if, he has (for any reason) ceased to be able to act as a nominated person.

(3) Where two or more persons have been nominated and any of them ceases to act without being replaced, the remaining person or persons so nominated may continue to act.

(4) Where, in the exercise of its power to award costs, the court or the Lands Tribunal makes, in connection with any proceedings arising under or by virtue of this Part, an award of costs against the person or persons so nominated, the liability for those costs is a joint and several liability of that person or those persons together with the qualifying tenants by whom the relevant notice was served.

13 Determination of questions by leasehold valuation tribunal

(1) A leasehold valuation tribunal has jurisdiction to hear and determine—

(a) any question arising in relation to any matters specified in a notice under section 12A, 12B or 12C, and

(b) any question arising for determination as mentioned in section 8C(4), 12A(5) or 12B(4) (matters left for determination by tribunal).

(2) On an application under this section the interests of the persons by whom the notice was served under section 12A, 12B or 12C shall be represented by the nominated person; and accordingly the parties to any such application shall not include those persons.

14 Withdrawal of nominated person from transaction under s 12B or 12C

(1) Where notice has been duly served on the landlord under—

section 12B (right of qualifying tenants to compel sale, etc. by purchaser), or

section 12C (right of qualifying tenants to compel grant of new tenancy by superior landlord),

the nominated person may at any time before a binding contract is entered into in pursuance of the notice, serve notice under this section on the purchaser (a "notice of withdrawal") indicating an intention no longer to proceed with the disposal.

(2) If at any such time the nominated person becomes aware that the number of qualifying tenants of the constituent flats desiring to proceed with the disposal is less than the requisite majority of those tenants, he shall forthwith serve a notice of withdrawal.

(3) If a notice of withdrawal is served under this section the purchaser may recover from the nominated person any costs reasonably incurred by him in connection with the disposal down to the time when the notice is served on him.

(4) If a notice of withdrawal is served at a time when proceedings arising under or by virtue of this Part are pending before the court or the Lands Tribunal, the liability of the nominated person for any costs incurred by the purchaser as mentioned in subsection (3) shall be such as may be determined by the court or (as the case may be) by the Tribunal.

(5) The costs that may be recovered by the purchaser under this section do not include any costs incurred by him in connection with an application to a leasehold valuation tribunal.'.

PART III

ENFORCEMENT OF RIGHTS AGAINST SUBSEQUENT PURCHASERS AND TERMINATION OF RIGHTS

The following sections replace sections 16 and 17 of the Landlord and Tenant Act 1987—

'Enforcement by tenants of rights against subsequent purchasers

16 Rights of qualifying tenants against subsequent purchaser

(1) This section applies where, at the time when a notice is served on the purchaser under section 11A, 12A, 12B or 12C, he no longer holds the estate or interest that was the subject-matter of the original disposal.

(2) In the case of a notice under section 11A (right to information as to terms of disposal, etc.) the purchaser shall, within the period for complying with that notice—

(a) serve notice on the person specified in the notice as the person to whom particulars are to be provided of the name and address of the person to whom he has disposed of that estate or interest ("the subsequent purchaser"), and

(b) serve on the subsequent purchaser a copy of the notice under section 11A and of the particulars given by him in response to it.

(3) In the case of a notice under section 12A, 12B or 12C the purchaser shall forthwith—

(a) forward the notice to the subsequent purchaser, and
(b) serve on the nominated person notice of the name and address of the subsequent purchaser.

(4) Once the purchaser serves a notice in accordance with subsection (2)(a) or (3)(b), sections 12A to 14 shall, instead of applying to the purchaser, apply to the subsequent purchaser as if he were the transferee under the original disposal.

(5) Subsections (1) to (4) have effect, with any necessary modifications, in a case where, instead of disposing of the whole of the estate or interest referred to in subsection (1) to another person, the purchaser has disposed of it in part or in parts to one or more other persons.

In such a case, sections 12A to 14—

(a) apply to the purchaser in relation to any part of that estate or interest retained by him, and
(b) in relation to any part of that estate or interest disposed of to any other person, apply to that other person instead as if he were (as respects that part) the transferee under the original disposal.

Termination of rights against purchasers or subsequent purchasers

17 Termination of rights against purchaser or subsequent purchaser

(1) If, at any time after a notice has been served under section 11A, 12A, 12B or 12C, the premises affected by the original disposal cease to be premises to which this Part applies, the purchaser may serve a notice on the qualifying tenants of the constituent flats stating—

(a) that the premises have ceased to be premises to which this Part applies, and
(b) that any such notice served on him, and anything done in pursuance of it, is to be treated as not having been served or done.

(2) A landlord who has not served such a notice on all of the qualifying tenants of the constituent flats shall nevertheless be treated as having duly served a notice under subsection (1)—

(a) if he has served such a notice on not less than 90% of those tenants, or
(b) where those qualifying tenants number less than ten, if he has served such a notice on all but one of them.

(3) Where a period of three months beginning with the date of service of a notice under section 12A, 12B or 12C on the purchaser has expired—

(a) without any binding contract having been entered into between the purchaser and the nominated person, and
(b) without there having been made any application in connection with the notice to the court or to a leasehold valuation tribunal,

the purchaser may serve on the nominated person a notice stating that the notice, and anything done in pursuance of it, is to be treated as not having been served or done.

(4) Where any such application as is mentioned in subsection (3)(b) was made within the period of three months referred to in that subsection, but—

(a) a period of two months beginning with the date of the determination of that application has expired,

(b) no binding contract has been entered into between the purchaser and the nominated person, and

(c) no other such application as is mentioned in subsection (3)(b) is pending,

the purchaser may serve on the nominated person a notice stating that any notice served on him under section 12A, 12B or 12C, and anything done in pursuance of any such notice, is to be treated as not having been served or done.

(5) Where the purchaser serves a notice in accordance with subsection (1), (3) or (4), this Part shall cease to have effect in relation to him in connection with the original disposal.

(6) Where a purchaser is entitled to serve a notice under subsection (1) but does not do so, this Part shall continue to have effect in relation to him in connection with the original disposal as if the premises in question were still premises to which this Part applies.

(7) References in this section to the purchaser include a subsequent purchaser to whom sections 12A to 14 apply by virtue of section 16(4) or (5).'.

PART IV

CONSEQUENTIAL AMENDMENTS

1 In section 4(2) of the Landlord and Tenant Act 1987 (relevant disposals: excluded disposals), in paragraph (aa) (disposals by way of security for a loan) omit the words 'consisting of the creation of an estate or interest'.

2 Before section 19 of the Landlord and Tenant Act 1987, under the heading '*Supplementary provisions*', insert—

'18A The requisite majority of qualifying tenants

(1) In this Part "the requisite majority of qualifying tenants of the constituent flats" means qualifying tenants of constituent flats with more than 50 per cent. of the available votes.

(2) The total number of available votes shall be determined as follows—

(a) where an offer notice has been served under section 5, that number is equal to the total number of constituent flats let to qualifying tenants on the date when the period specified in that notice as the period for accepting the offer expires;

(b) where a notice is served under section 11A without a notice having been previously served under section 5, that number is equal to the total number of constituent flats let to qualifying tenants on the date of service of the notice under section 11A;

(c) where a notice is served under section 12A, 12B or 12C without a notice having been previously served under section 5 or section 11A, that number is equal to the total number of constituent flats let to qualifying tenants on the date of service of the notice under section 12A, 12B or 12C, as the case may be.

(3) There is one available vote in respect of each of the flats so let on the date referred to in the relevant paragraph of subsection (2), which shall be attributed to the qualifying tenant to whom it is let.

(4) The persons constituting the requisite majority of qualifying tenants for one purpose may be different from the persons constituting such a majority for another purpose.'.

3 (1) Section 20(1) of the Landlord and Tenant Act 1987 (interpretation of Part I) is amended as follows.

(2) For the definition of 'acceptance notice' substitute—
' "acceptance notice" has the meaning given by section 6(3);'.

(3) For the definition of 'constituent flat' substitute—
' "constituent flat" shall be construed in accordance with section 5(1) or 11(2), as the case may require;'.

(4) Omit the definition of 'the new landlord'.

(5) After that definition insert—
' "the nominated person" means the person or persons for the time being nominated by the requisite majority of the qualifying tenants of the constituent flats for the purposes of section 6, 12A, 12B or 12C, as the case may require;'.

(6) For the definition of 'the protected interest' substitute—
' "the protected interest" means the estate, interest or other subject-matter of an offer notice;'.

(7) After that definition insert—
' "the protected period" has the meaning given by section 6(4);'.

(8) For the definition of 'purchase notice' substitute—
' "purchase notice" has the meaning given by section 12B(2);'.

(9) After that definition insert—
' "purchaser" has the meaning given by section 11(3);'.

(10) In the definition of 'the requisite majority' for 'section 5(6) and (7)' substitute 'section 18A'.

4 In section 20(2) of the Landlord and Tenant Act 1987, omit the words 'or counter-offer' in each place where they occur.

5 In Part III of the Landlord and Tenant Act 1987 (compulsory acquisition by tenants of their landlord's interest), in section 31 (determination of terms by rent assessment committees)—

    (a) for 'rent assessment committee', wherever occurring, substitute 'leasehold valuation tribunal';
    (b) for 'such a committee' or 'the committee', wherever occurring, substitute 'the tribunal'; and
    (c) omit subsection (5).

6 In section 52(1) of the Landlord and Tenant Act 1987 (jurisdiction of county courts) for 'rent assessment committee' substitute 'leasehold valuation tribunal'.

7 After section 52 of the Landlord and Tenant Act 1987 insert—

'52A Jurisdiction of leasehold valuation tribunal under Part I or III

(1) Any jurisdiction conferred by Part I or III of this Act on a leasehold valuation tribunal is exercisable by a rent assessment committee constituted in accordance with Schedule 10 to the Rent Act 1977 which when so constituted for the purposes of exercising any such jurisdiction shall be known as a leasehold valuation tribunal.

(2) The power to make regulations under section 74(1)(b) of the Rent Act 1977 (procedure of rent assessment committees) extends to prescribing the procedure to be followed in connection with any proceedings before a leasehold valuation tribunal under this Act.

(3) Any application under this Act to a leasehold valuation tribunal must be in such form, and contain such particulars, as the Secretary of State may by regulations prescribe.

(4) Any costs incurred by a party to any such application in connection with the application shall be borne by that party.

(5) Paragraphs 1, 2, 3 and 7 of Schedule 22 to the Housing Act 1980 (supplementary provisions relating to leasehold valuation tribunals: constitution, appeals and provision of information) apply to a leasehold valuation tribunal constituted for the purposes of this section.'.

8 In section 53(2)(b) of the Landlord and Tenant Act 1987 (regulations subject to negative resolution), for the words from 'section 13(2)' to 'section 31)' substitute 'section 52A(3)'.

9 In section 54(4) of the Landlord and Tenant Act 1987 (saving for power under section 20(4)) for 'either of the periods specified in section 5(2)' substitute 'any of the periods specified in section 5A(4) or (5), 5B(5) or (6), 5C(4) or (5), 5D(4) or (5) or 5E(3)'.

10 In section 60(1) of the Landlord and Tenant Act 1987 (general interpretation), omit the definition of 'rent assessment committee'.

11 (1) In Schedule 1 to the Landlord and Tenant Act 1987 (discharge of mortgages, etc.), in paragraph 1 (construction of provisions relating to discharge in pursuance of purchase notice)—

    (a) for the words 'the new landlord' wherever they appear substitute 'the purchaser';
    (b) in the definition of 'consideration payable'—
        (i) for the words 'section 12(4)' substitute 'section 12B(7)', and
        (ii) for the words 'section 16(2) or (3)' substitute 'section 16(4) or (5)';
    (c) in the definition of 'nominated person', for the words 'section 12(1)' substitute 'section 12B(2)'.

(2) In paragraphs 2, 4 and 5 of that Schedule (duty of nominated person to redeem mortgages, payments into court and savings)—

    (a) for the words 'section 12(4)(a)' wherever they appear substitute 'section 12B(5)(a)';
    (b) for the words 'the new landlord' or 'the new landlord's' wherever they appear substitute 'the purchaser' or 'the purchaser's'.

SCHEDULE 7
ASSURED TENANCIES: SCHEDULE INSERTED AFTER SCHEDULE 2 TO
THE HOUSING ACT 1988

'SCHEDULE 2A
ASSURED TENANCIES: NON-SHORTHOLDS

Section 96

Tenancies excluded by notice

1 (1) An assured tenancy in respect of which a notice is served as mentioned in sub-paragraph (2) below.

(2) The notice referred to in sub-paragraph (1) above is one which—

(a) is served before the assured tenancy is entered into,

(b) is served by the person who is to be the landlord under the assured tenancy on the person who is to be the tenant under that tenancy, and

(c) states that the assured tenancy to which it relates is not to be an assured shorthold tenancy.

2 (1) An assured tenancy in respect of which a notice is served as mentioned in sub-paragraph (2) below.

(2) The notice referred to in sub-paragraph (1) above is one which—

(a) is served after the assured tenancy has been entered into,

(b) is served by the landlord under the assured tenancy on the tenant under that tenancy, and

(c) states that the assured tenancy to which it relates is no longer an assured shorthold tenancy.

Tenancies containing exclusionary provision

3 An assured tenancy which contains a provision to the effect that the tenancy is not an assured shorthold tenancy.

Tenancies under section 39

4 An assured tenancy arising by virtue of section 39 above, other than one to which subsection (7) of that section applies.

Former secure tenancies

5 An assured tenancy which became an assured tenancy on ceasing to be a secure tenancy.

Tenancies under Schedule 10 to the Local Government and Housing Act 1989

6 An assured tenancy arising by virtue of Schedule 10 to the Local Government and Housing Act 1989 (security of tenure on ending of long residential tenancies).

Tenancies replacing non-shortholds

7 (1) An assured tenancy which—

 (a) is granted to a person (alone or jointly with others) who, immediately before the tenancy was granted, was the tenant (or, in the case of joint tenants, one of the tenants) under an assured tenancy other than a shorthold tenancy ("the old tenancy"),

 (b) is granted (alone or jointly with others) by a person who was at that time the landlord (or one of the joint landlords) under the old tenancy, and

 (c) is not one in respect of which a notice is served as mentioned in sub-paragraph (2) below.

(2) The notice referred to in sub-paragraph (1)(c) above is one which—

 (a) is in such form as may be prescribed,

 (b) is served before the assured tenancy is entered into,

 (c) is served by the person who is to be the tenant under the assured tenancy on the person who is to be the landlord under that tenancy (or, in the case of joint landlords, on at least one of the persons who are to be joint landlords), and

 (d) states that the assured tenancy to which it relates is to be a shorthold tenancy.

8 An assured tenancy which comes into being by virtue of section 5 above on the coming to an end of an assured tenancy which is not a shorthold tenancy.

Assured agricultural occupancies

9 (1) An assured tenancy—

 (a) in the case of which the agricultural worker condition is, by virtue of any provision of Schedule 3 to this Act, for the time being fulfilled with respect to the dwelling-house subject to the tenancy, and

 (b) which does not fall within sub-paragraph (2) or (4) below.

(2) An assured tenancy falls within this sub-paragraph if—

 (a) before it is entered into, a notice—
   (i)   in such form as may be prescribed, and
   (ii) stating that the tenancy is to be a shorthold tenancy,
  is served by the person who is to be the landlord under the tenancy on the person who is to be the tenant under it, and

 (b) it is not an excepted tenancy.

(3) For the purposes of sub-paragraph (2)(b) above, an assured tenancy is an excepted tenancy if—

 (a) the person to whom it is granted or, as the case may be, at least one of the persons to whom it is granted was, immediately before it is granted, a tenant or licensee under an assured agricultural occupancy, and

 (b) the person by whom it is granted or, as the case may be, at least one of the persons by whom it is granted was, immediately before it is granted, a landlord or licensor under the assured agricultural occupancy referred to in paragraph (a) above.

(4) An assured tenancy falls within this sub-paragraph if it comes into being by virtue of section 5 above on the coming to an end of a tenancy falling within sub-paragraph (2) above.'.

SCHEDULE 8
ASSURED TENANCIES: CONSEQUENTIAL AMENDMENTS

Section 104

Housing Act 1985 (c. 68)

1 In section 553(2) of the Housing Act 1985, for paragraph (c) there shall be substituted—

'(c)   the tenancy is not by virtue of any provision of Part I of the Housing Act 1988 an assured shorthold tenancy;'.

Housing Act 1988 (c. 50)

2 (1) The Housing Act 1988 shall be amended as follows.

(2) In section 14, there shall be inserted at the end—

'(9) This section shall apply in relation to an assured shorthold tenancy as if in subsection (1) the reference to an assured tenancy were a reference to an assured shorthold tenancy.'.

(3) In section 20, for the side-note and subsection (1) there shall be substituted—

'20   Assured shorthold tenancies: pre-Housing Act 1996 tenancies

(1) Subject to subsection (3) below, an assured tenancy which is not one to which section 19A above applies is an assured shorthold tenancy if—

(a)   it is a fixed term tenancy granted for a term certain of not less than six months,
(b)   there is no power for the landlord to determine the tenancy at any time earlier than six months from the beginning of the tenancy, and
(c)   a notice in respect of it is served as mentioned in subsection (2) below.'.

(4) In that section, after subsection (5) there shall be inserted—

'(5A) Subsections (3) and (4) above do not apply where the new tenancy is one to which section 19A above applies.'.

(5) In section 22, in subsection (1), the words from 'in respect of' to 'above' shall be omitted.

(6) In that section, after subsection (5) there shall be inserted—

'(5A) Where—

(a)   an assured tenancy ceases to be an assured shorthold tenancy by virtue of falling within paragraph 2 of Schedule 2A to this Act, and
(b)   at the time when it so ceases to be an assured shorthold tenancy there is pending before a rent assessment committee an application in relation to it under this section,

the fact that it so ceases to be an assured shorthold tenancy shall, in relation to that application, be disregarded for the purposes of this section.'.

(7) In section 34(3), after 'whether or not' there shall be inserted ', in the case of a tenancy to which the provision applies,'.

(8) In section 39(7), after 'whether or not' there shall be inserted ', in the case of a tenancy to which the provision applies,'.

SCHEDULE 9
LOW RENT TEST: EXTENSION OF RIGHTS
Section 106

Right to enfranchisement

1 In the Leasehold Reform Act 1967, after section 1A there shall be inserted—

'1AA Additional right to enfranchisement only in case of houses whose rent exceeds applicable limit under section 4

(1) Where—

    (a) section 1(1) above would apply in the case of the tenant of a house but for the fact that the tenancy is not a tenancy at a low rent, and

    (b) the tenancy falls within subsection (2) below and is not an excluded tenancy,

this Part of this Act shall have effect to confer on the tenant the same right to acquire the freehold of the house and premises as would be conferred by section 1(1) above if it were a tenancy at a low rent.

(2) A tenancy falls within this subsection if—

    (a) it is granted for a term of years certain exceeding thirty-five years, whether or not it is (or may become) terminable before the end of that term by notice given by or to the tenant or by re-entry, forfeiture or otherwise,

    (b) it is for a term fixed by law under a grant with a covenant or obligation for perpetual renewal, unless it is a tenancy by sub-demise from one which is not a tenancy which falls within this subsection,

    (c) it is a tenancy taking effect under section 149(6) of the Law of Property Act 1925 (leases terminable after a death or marriage), or

    (d) it is a tenancy which—

        (i) is or has been granted for a term of years certain not exceeding thirty-five years, but with a covenant or obligation for renewal without payment of a premium (but not for perpetual renewal), and

        (ii) is or has been once or more renewed so as to bring to more than thirty-five years the total of the terms granted (including any interval between the end of a tenancy and the grant of a renewal).

(3) A tenancy is an excluded tenancy for the purposes of subsection (1) above if—

    (a) the house which the tenant occupies under the tenancy is in an area designated for the purposes of this provision as a rural area by order made by the Secretary of State,

(b) the freehold of that house is owned together with adjoining land which is not occupied for residential purposes and has been owned together with such land since the coming into force of section 106 of the Housing Act 1996, and

(c) the tenancy was granted on or before the day on which that section came into force.

(4) Where this Part of this Act applies as if there were a single tenancy of property comprised in two or more separate tenancies, then, if each of the separate tenancies falls within subsection (2) above, this section shall apply as if the single tenancy did so.

(5) The power to make an order under subsection (3) above shall be exercisable by statutory instrument which shall be subject to annulment in pursuance of a resolution of either House of Parliament.'.

2 (1) In consequence of paragraph 1 above, the Leasehold Reform Act 1967 shall be amended as follows.

(2) In section 1(3A)(b) (extension of rights not to apply to existing lettings by charitable housing trusts), after '1A' there shall be inserted ', 1AA'.

(3) In section 3(3) (provision for aggregation of successive tenancies), after 'this Part of this Act' there shall be inserted ', except section 1AA,'.

(4) In section 9(1C) (price payable by tenant on enfranchisement by virtue of section 1A or 1B), after '1A' there shall be inserted ', 1AA'.

(5) In section 9A(1) (compensation payable where right to enfranchisement arises by virtue of section 1A or 1B), after '1A' there shall be inserted ', 1AA'.

(6) In section 32A(1)(b) (extensions to right to enfranchisement not to apply in relation to existing tenancies of property transferred for public benefit), at the end there shall be inserted 'or if section 1AA above were not in force'.

(7) In section 37(4) (treatment for the purposes of Part I of tenancy granted to continue as a periodical tenancy after the expiration of a term of years certain), after 'this Part of this Act' there shall be inserted ', except section 1AA,'.

(8) In Part II of Schedule 3 (procedural provisions), in paragraph 6 (which makes provision about the contents of a tenant's notice under Part I), after sub-paragraph (1) there shall be inserted—

'(1A) Where the tenant gives the notice by virtue of section 1AA of this Act, sub-paragraph (1) above shall have effect with the substitution for paragraph (b) of—
"(b) such particulars of the tenancy as serve to identify the instrument creating the tenancy and show that the tenancy is one in relation to which section 1AA(1) of this Act has effect to confer a right to acquire the freehold of the house and premises;".'.

(9) In that Part of that Schedule, in paragraph 7(4) (admission in landlord's notice of tenant's right to have freehold to be binding on landlord, so far as relating to matters mentioned in section 1(1)(a) and (b)), for 'mentioned in section 1(1)(a) and (b) of this Act' there shall be substituted 'relevant to the existence of that right'.

Right to collective enfranchisement

3 (1) Chapter I of Part I of the Leasehold Reform, Housing and Urban Development Act 1993 (collective enfranchisement in case of tenants of flats) shall be amended as follows.

(2) Section 5 (qualifying tenants) shall be amended as follows—

(a) in subsection (1) (which defines a qualifying tenant as a tenant of a flat under a long lease at a low rent), for 'at a low rent' there shall be substituted 'which is at a low rent or for a particularly long term', and

(b) in subsection (2)(c) (which excludes from the definition a tenant under a lease granted in breach of the terms of a superior lease which is not a long lease at a low rent), after 'rent' there shall be inserted 'or for a particularly long term'.

(3) After section 8 there shall be inserted—

'8A Meaning of "particularly long term"

(1) For the purposes of this Chapter a long lease is for a particularly long term if—

(a) it is granted for a term of years certain exceeding 35 years, whether or not it is (or may become) terminable before the end of that term by notice given by or to the tenant or by re-entry, forfeiture or otherwise,

(b) it is for a term fixed by law under a grant with a covenant or obligation for perpetual renewal (other than a lease by sub-demise from one which is not for a particularly long term),

(c) it takes effect under section 149(6) of the Law of Property Act 1925 (leases terminable after a death or marriage), or

(d) it is a lease which—

(i) is or has been granted for a term of years certain not exceeding 35 years, but with a covenant or obligation for renewal without payment of a premium (but not for perpetual renewal), and

(ii) is or has been renewed on one or more occasions so as to bring to more than 35 years the total of the terms granted (including any interval between the end of a lease and the grant of a renewal).

(2) A long lease which does not fall within subsection (1) above shall nonetheless be treated for the purposes of this Chapter as being for a particularly long term if it is a long lease by virtue of paragraph (c) or (d) of section 7(1).

(3) Where this Chapter applies as if there were a single lease of property comprised in two or more separate leases, then, if each of the separate leases is for a particularly long term, this Chapter shall apply as if the single lease were for such a term.'.

(4) In section 13(3)(e) (particulars to be included in initial notice which relevant to whether person a qualifying tenant), in sub-paragraph (ii), for 'a lease at a low rent' there shall be substituted 'at a low rent or for a particularly long term'.

Right to new lease

4 (1) Chapter II of that Part (individual right of tenant of flat to acquire new lease) shall be amended as follows.

(2) In section 39(3) (provisions of Chapter I which apply for the purposes of Chapter II), at the end of paragraph (c) there shall be inserted ', and

(d) section 8A,'.

(3) In section 42(3) (particulars to be included in notice by qualifying tenant of claim to exercise right), in paragraph (b)(iii), there shall be inserted at the end 'or, in accordance with section 8A (as that section so applies), a lease for a particularly long term'.

5 (1) In Chapter VII of that Part (general), section 94 (Crown land) shall be amended as follows.

(2) In subsection (3) (disapplication of restriction imposed by section 3(2) of the Crown Estate Act 1961 on term for which lease may be granted by Crown Estate Commissioners), in paragraph (a), for 'at a low rent' there shall be substituted 'which is at a low rent or for a particularly long term'.

(3) In subsection (4) (power to shadow statutory rights), for 'at a low rent' there shall be substituted 'which is at a low rent or for a particularly long term'.

(4) For subsection (12) there shall be substituted—

'(12) For the purposes of this section "long lease which is at a low rent or for a particularly long term" shall be construed in accordance with sections 7, 8 and 8A.'.

SCHEDULE 10
SECTION 107: CONSEQUENTIAL AMENDMENTS
Section 107

1 Chapter I of Part I of the Leasehold Reform, Housing and Urban Development Act 1993 shall be amended as follows.

2 In section 1(4) (right to acquire additional property satisfied by grant of rights over that property or other property)—

(a) in paragraph (a), for 'freeholder' there shall be substituted 'person who owns the freehold of that property', and
(b) in paragraph (b), for 'freeholder' there shall be substituted 'person who owns the freehold of that property'.

3 (1) Section 9 (the reversioner and other relevant landlords) shall be amended as follows.

(2) In subsection (1), after 'any premises' there shall be inserted 'the freehold of the whole of which is owned by the same person'.

(3) In subsection (2)—

(a) after 'such claim' there shall be inserted 'as is mentioned in subsection (1)', and
(b) in paragraph (b), after 'premises,' there shall be inserted 'every person who owns any freehold interest which it is proposed to acquire by virtue of section 1(2)(a),'.

(4) After that subsection there shall be inserted—

'(2A) In the case of any claim to exercise the right to collective enfranchisement in relation to any premises the freehold of the whole of which is not owned by the same person—

(a) the reversioner in respect of the premises shall for the purposes of this Chapter be the person identified as such by Part IA of Schedule I to this Act, and
(b) every person who owns a freehold interest in the premises, every person who owns any freehold interest which it is proposed to acquire by virtue of section 1(2)(a), and every person who owns any leasehold interest which it is proposed to acquire under or by virtue of section 2(1)(a) or (b), shall be a relevant landlord for those purposes.'.

(5) In subsection (3), after 'subsection (2)' there shall be inserted 'or (2A)'.

4 (1) Section 10 (premises with a resident landlord) shall be amended as follows.

(2) In subsection (1)(b)—

   (a) for 'the freeholder, or an adult member of the freeholder's' there shall be substituted 'a relevant person, or an adult member of a relevant person's', and

   (b) in sub-paragraph (i), after 'premises' there shall be inserted 'which is a qualifying flat'.

(3) In subsection (2)—

   (a) in paragraph (a)—

      (i) for 'freeholder' there shall be substituted 'relevant person', and

      (ii) after 'Chapter', where it first occurs, there shall be inserted ', or, as the case may be, the amendments of this Chapter made by the Housing Act 1996,', and

   (b) in paragraph (b)—

      (i) for 'freeholder, or an adult member of the freeholder's' there shall be substituted 'relevant person, or an adult member of that person's', and

      (ii) in sub-paragraph (i), after 'premises' there shall be inserted 'which is a qualifying flat'.

(4) In subsection (4)—

   (a) for 'freehold interest' there shall be substituted 'interest of a relevant person', and

   (b) for 'the freeholder' there shall be substituted 'a relevant person'.

(5) After that subsection there shall be inserted—

'(4A) For the purposes of this section a person is a relevant person, in relation to any premises, if he owns the freehold of the whole or any part of the premises.'.

(6) In subsection (6) there shall be inserted at the end—

' "qualifying flat", in relation to a relevant person, or an adult member of a relevant person's family, means a flat the freehold of the whole of which is owned by the relevant person.'.

5 (1) Section 11 (right of qualifying tenant to obtain information about superior interests etc.) shall be amended as follows.

(2) In subsection (1)—

   (a) for 'his immediate landlord', in both places, there shall be substituted 'any immediate landlord of his', and

   (b) for 'the person who owns the freehold of' there shall be substituted 'every person who owns a freehold interest in'.

(3) In subsection (2)(b), for 'the tenant's immediate landlord' there shall be substituted 'any immediate landlord of the tenant'.

(4) In subsection (3), for 'the person who owns the freehold of' there shall be substituted 'any person who owns a freehold interest in'.

(5) In subsection (4), for paragraph (a) there shall be substituted—

'(a) to any person who owns a freehold interest in the relevant premise

(aa) to any person who owns a freehold interest in any such proper
mentioned in subsection (3)(c),'.

(6) In subsection (8)(b)(i), after 'premises' there shall be inserted 'or in any such pro
as is mentioned in subsection (3)(c)'.

(7) In subsection (9), in the definition of 'the relevant premises'—

(a) in paragraph (a), after 'owns', where it second occurs, there shall be inserted ', ،
the persons who own the freehold interests in the flat own,', and

(b) in paragraph (b), after 'owns' there shall be inserted ', or those persons own,'.

6 (1) Section 13 (notice by qualifying tenants of claim to exercise right to collective
enfranchisement) shall be amended as follows.

(2) In subsection (2), in paragraph (a)—

(a) after 'must' there shall be inserted—

'(i) in a case to which section 9(2) applies,',

and

(b) after 'premises;' there shall be inserted 'and
(ii) in a case to which section 9(2A) applies, be given to the person specified in
the notice as the recipient;'.

(3) After that subsection there shall be inserted—

'(2A) In a case to which section 9(2A) applies, the initial notice must specify—

(a) a person who owns a freehold interest in the premises, or

(b) if every person falling within paragraph (a) is a person who cannot be found or
whose identity cannot be ascertained, a relevant landlord,

as the recipient of the notice.'.

(4) In subsection (3)(d)(i), there shall be inserted at the end 'or, if the freehold of the
whole of the specified premises is not owned by the same person, each of the freehold
interests in those premises'.

7 (1) Section 19 (effect of notice under section 13 on subsequent transactions by
freeholder etc) shall be amended as follows.

(2) In subsection (1)(a)—

(a) for 'the person who owns the freehold of the specified premises' there shall be
substituted 'any person who owns the freehold of the whole or any part of the
specified premises or the freehold of any property specified in the notice under
section 13(3)(a)(ii)', and

(b) in sub-paragraph (i), for the words from 'any property' to the end there shall be
substituted 'that property'.

(3) In subsection (2), for paragraph (a) there shall be substituted—

'(a) any person who owns the freehold of the whole or any part of the specified
premises or the freehold of any property specified in the notice under section
13(3)(a)(ii) disposes of his interest in those premises or that property,'.

(4) In subsection (4), for paragraph (a) there shall be substituted—

'(a)   by any person who owns the freehold of the whole or any part of the specified premises or the freehold of any property specified in the notice under section 13(3)(a)(ii),'.

8 (1) Section 21 (reversioner's counter-notice) shall be amended as follows.

(2) In subsection (3)(d), for 'the person who owns the freehold of the specified premises, or any other' there shall be substituted 'any'.

(3) In subsection (4), for 'the person who owns the freehold of the specified premises or of any other' there shall be substituted 'any'.

9 (1) Section 26 (application to court where relevant landlords cannot be found) shall be amended as follows.

(2) In subsection (1)(b), after 'section 9(2)' there shall be inserted 'or (2A)'.

(3) In subsection (3), after 'If' there shall be inserted ', in a case to which section 9(2) applies,'.

(4) After that subsection there shall be inserted—

'(3A) Where in a case to which section 9(2A) applies—

(a)   not less than two-thirds of the qualifying tenants of flats contained in any premises to which this Chapter applies desire to make a claim to exercise the right to collective enfranchisement in relation to those premises, and
(b)   paragraph (b) of subsection (1) does not apply, but
(c)   a copy of a notice of that claim cannot be given in accordance with Part II of Schedule 3 to any person to whom it would otherwise be required to be so given because he cannot be found or his identity cannot be ascertained,

the court may, on the application of the qualifying tenants in question, make an order dispensing with the need to give a copy of such a notice to that person.'.

(5) In subsection (4), for 'or (2)' there shall be substituted ', (2) or (3A)'.

(6) In subsection (7), after '(2)' there shall be inserted 'or (3A)'.

10 In section 30 (effect on acquisition of institution of compulsory acquisition procedures), at the end of subsection (2)(a) there shall be inserted 'or, where the freehold of the whole of the premises is not owned by the same person, any person who owns the freehold of part of them'.

11 (1) Section 34 (conveyance to nominee purchaser) shall be amended as follows.

(2) In subsection (1)—

(a)   after 'specified premises' there shall be inserted ', of a part of those premises', and
(b)   after 'those premises' there shall be inserted ', that part of those premises'.

(3) In subsection (2), after 'premises' there shall be inserted ', the part of the specified premises'.

12 (1) Section 36 (nominee purchaser required to grant leases back to former freeholder) shall be amended as follows.

(2) In subsection (1)—

(a) for 'the freehold of' there shall be substituted 'a freehold interest in', and

(b) for 'freehold', where it second occurs, there shall be substituted 'interest'.

(3) In subsection (2), for 'of the specified premises' there shall be substituted 'interest concerned'.

13 In section 38 (interpretation of Chapter I), in subsection (3), after 'section 9(2)(b)' there shall be inserted 'or (2A)(b)'.

14 In Schedule 1 (conduct of proceedings by reversioner on behalf of other landlords), in Part I (identification of reversioner in case of premises with relevant landlords), in paragraph 1, after '2 to 4,' there shall be inserted 'in a case to which section 9(2) applies,'.

15 In that Schedule, after Part I there shall be inserted—

'PART IA
THE REVERSIONER: PREMISES WITH MULTIPLE FREEHOLDERS

Initial reversioner

5A. Subject to paragraphs 5B to 5D, in a case to which section 9(2A) applies, the reversioner in respect of any premises is the person specified in the initial notice in accordance with section 13(2A) as the recipient.

Change of reversioner

5B. The court may, on the application of all the relevant landlords of any premises, appoint to be the reversioner in respect of those premises (in place of the person designated by paragraph 5A) such person as may have been determined by agreement between them.

5C. If it appears to the court, on the application of a relevant landlord of any premises—

(a) that the respective interests of the relevant landlords of those premises, the absence or incapacity of the person referred to in paragraph 5A or other special circumstances require that some person other than the person there referred to should act as the reversioner in respect of the premises, or

(b) that the person referred to in that paragraph is unwilling to act as the reversioner,

the court may appoint to be the reversioner in respect of those premises (in place of the person designated by paragraph 5A) such person as it thinks fit.

5D. The court may also, on the application of any of the relevant landlords or of the nominee purchaser, remove the reversioner in respect of any premises and appoint another person in his place, if it appears to the court proper to do so by reason of any delay or default, actual or apprehended, on the part of the reversioner.

5E. A person appointed by the court under any of paragraphs 5B to 5D—

(a) must be a relevant landlord; but

(b) may be so appointed on such terms and conditions as the court thinks fit.'.

16 In Schedule 2 (special categories of landlords), in paragraph 1(1), in the definition of 'Chapter I landlord', for 'the reversioner or any other' there shall be substituted 'a'.

17 (1) Part II of Schedule 3 (which makes provision for the giving of copies of the notice under section 13 to relevant landlords) shall be amended as follows.

(2) In paragraph 11, after 'section 9(2)' there shall be inserted 'or (2A)'.

(3) In paragraph 12, in sub-paragraph (1), there shall be inserted at the beginning 'In a case to which section 9(2) applies,'.

(4) After that paragraph there shall be inserted—

'12A (1) In a case to which section 9(2A) applies, the qualifying tenants by whom the initial notice is given shall, in addition to giving the initial notice to the person specified in it as the recipient, give a copy of the notice to every other person known or believed by them to be a relevant landlord of the specified premises.

(2) The initial notice shall state whether copies are being given in accordance with sub-paragraph (1) to anyone other than the person specified in it as the recipient and, if so, to whom.'.

(5) In paragraph 13(3)(a), after '12(2)' there shall be inserted 'or, as the case may be, 12A(2)'.

(6) In paragraph 14(2)(b)—

    (a)   after '12' there shall be inserted ', 12A', and
    (b)   for 'either' there shall be substituted 'any'.

18 (1) Schedule 6 (purchase price payable by nominee purchaser) shall be amended as follows.

(2) In paragraph 1(1) (interpretation)—

    (a)   the definition of 'the freeholder' shall be omitted, and
    (b)   for the definition of 'the valuation date' there shall be substituted—

' "the valuation date" means—

    (a)   the date when it is determined, either by agreement or by a leasehold valuation tribunal under this Chapter, what freehold interest in the specified premises is to be acquired by the nominee purchaser, or
    (b)   if there are different determinations relating to different freehold interests in the specified premises, the date when determinations have been made in relation to all the freehold interests in the premises.'.

(3) In paragraph 2 (price payable for the freehold of the specified premises), in sub-paragraph (1)—

    (a)   after 'this paragraph,' there shall be inserted 'where the freehold of the whole of the specified premises is owned by the same person', and
    (b)   for 'the specified' there shall be substituted 'those'.

(4) In paragraph 3(1A), after paragraph (b) there shall be inserted—

'(ba) an owner of an interest which the nominee purchaser is to acquire in pursuance of section 1(2)(a), or'.

(5) After paragraph 5 there shall be inserted—

'Price payable for freehold of part of specified premises

5A (1) Where different persons own the freehold of different parts of the specified premises—

(a) a separate price shall be payable by the nominee purchaser for the freehold of each of those parts, and
(b) sub-paragraph (2) shall apply to determine the price so payable.

(2) Subject to sub-paragraph (3), the price payable by the nominee purchaser for the freehold of part of the specified premises shall be the aggregate of—

(a) the value of the freeholder's interest in the part as determined in accordance with paragraph 3, modified as mentioned in paragraph 5B, and
(b) the freeholder's share of the marriage value as determined in accordance with paragraph 4, modified as mentioned in paragraph 5C, and
(c) any amount of compensation payable to the freeholder under paragraph 5.

(3) Where the amount arrived at in accordance with sub-paragraph (2) is a negative amount, the price payable by the nominee purchaser for the freehold of the part shall be nil.

5B (1) In its application in accordance with paragraph 5A(2)(a), paragraph 3 shall have effect with the following modifications.

(2) In sub-paragraph (1)(a)(ii), there shall be inserted at the end "so far as relating to the part of the premises in which the freeholder's interest subsists".

(3) In sub-paragraph (1A), after paragraph (a) there shall be inserted—

"(aa) an owner of a freehold interest in the specified premises, or".

(4) In sub-paragraph (4)—

(a) the words "the whole of" shall be omitted, and
(b) for "2(1)(a)" there shall be substituted "5A(2)(a)".

5C (1) In its application in accordance with paragraph 5A(2)(b), paragraph 4 shall have effect with the following modifications.

(2) In sub-paragraph (2)—

(a) after "the specified premises" there shall be inserted "so far as relating to the part of the premises in which the freeholder's interest subsists",
(b) after "participating tenants", where it first occurs, there shall be inserted "in whose flats the freeholder's interest subsists", and
(c) in paragraph (a), for "the", where it second occurs, there shall be substituted "those".

(3) In sub-paragraph (3)—

(a) after "the specified premises" there shall be inserted "so far as relating to the part of the premises in which the freeholder's interest subsists", and

(b) in paragraph (a), for "2(1)(a)" there shall be substituted "5A(2)(a)".

(4) In sub-paragraph (4)(a), after "3(1)", where it first occurs, there shall be inserted "as applied by paragraph 5A(2)(a)".'.

(6) For paragraph 8 there shall be substituted—

'8 (1) Where the owner of the intermediate leasehold interest will suffer any loss or damage to which this paragraph applies, there shall be payable to him such amount as is reasonable to compensate him for that loss or damage.

(2) This paragraph applies to—

(a) any diminution in value of any interest of the owner of the intermediate leasehold interest in other property resulting from the acquisition of his interest in the specified premises; and

(b) any other loss or damage which results therefrom to the extent that it is referable to his ownership of any interest in other property.

(3) Without prejudice to the generality of paragraph (b) of sub-paragraph (2), the kinds of loss falling within that paragraph include loss of development value in relation to the specified premises to the extent that it is referable as mentioned in that paragraph.

(4) In sub-paragraph (3) "development value", in relation to the specified premises, means any increase in the value of the interest in the premises of the owner of the intermediate leasehold interest which is attributable to the possibility of demolishing, reconstructing or carrying out substantial works of construction on, the whole or a substantial part of the premises.'.

(7) In paragraph 9 (owners of intermediate interests entitled to part of marriage value), in sub-paragraph (1), after 'where' there shall be inserted 'paragraph 2 applies and'.

(8) After that paragraph there shall be inserted—

'9A—(1) This paragraph applies where paragraph 5A applies and—

(a) the price payable for the freehold of a part of the specified premises includes an amount in respect of the freeholder's share of the marriage value, and

(b) the nominee purchaser is to acquire any intermediate leasehold interests which subsist in that part.

(2) The amount payable to the freeholder of the part in respect of his share of the marriage value shall be divided between the freeholder and the owners of the intermediate leasehold interests which subsist in that part in proportion to the value of their respective interests in the part (as determined for the purposes of paragraph 5A(2)(a) or paragraph 6(1)(b)(i), as the case may be).

(3) Where an intermediate leasehold interest subsists not only in the part of the specified premises in which the freeholder's interest subsists ("the relevant part") but also in another part of those premises—

(a) the value of the intermediate leasehold interest as determined for the purposes of paragraph 6(1)(b)(i) shall be apportioned between the relevant part and the other part of the specified premises in which it subsists, and

(b) sub-paragraph (2) shall have effect as if the reference to the value of the intermediate leasehold interest in the relevant part as determined for the purposes of paragraph 6(1)(b)(i) were to the value of that interest as determined on an apportionment in accordance with paragraph (a).

(4) Where the owner of an intermediate leasehold interest is entitled in accordance with sub-paragraph (2) to any part of the amount payable to the freeholder in respect of the freeholder's share of the marriage value, the amount to which he is so entitled shall be payable to him by the freeholder.'.

(9) For paragraph 13 there shall be substituted—

'13—(1) Where the owner of any such freehold or leasehold interest as is mentioned in paragraph 10(1) or (2) ('relevant interest') will suffer any loss or damage to which this paragraph applies, there shall be payable to him such amount as is reasonable to compensate him for that loss or damage.

(2) This paragraph applies to—

(a) any diminution in value of any interest in other property belonging to the owner of a relevant interest, being diminution resulting from the acquisition of the property in which the relevant interest subsists; and

(b) any other loss or damage which results therefrom to the extent that it is referable to his ownership of any interest in other property.

(3) Without prejudice to the generality of paragraph (b) of sub-paragraph (2), the kinds of loss falling within that paragraph include loss of development value in relation to the property in which the relevant interest subsists to the extent that it is referable to his ownership of any interest in other property.

(4) In sub-paragraph (3) 'development value', in relation to the property in which the relevant interest subsists, means any increase in the value of the relevant interest which is attributable to the possibility of demolishing, reconstructing or carrying out substantial works of construction on, the whole or a substantial part of the property.'.

(10) In paragraph 14 (valuation of freehold and intermediate leasehold interests), in sub-paragraph (1)—

(a) in paragraph (a), for 'the', where it second occurs, there shall be substituted 'a' and for 'in accordance with paragraph 3' there shall be substituted 'for the relevant purposes',

(b) in paragraph (b), for 'in accordance with paragraph 7' there shall be substituted 'for the relevant purposes', and

(c) for 'the relevant' there shall be substituted 'those'.

(11) In that paragraph, after sub-paragraph (3) there shall be inserted—

'(3A) Where sub-paragraph (2) applies—

(a) for the purposes of paragraph 5A(2)(a), and

(b) in relation to an intermediate leasehold interest in relation to which there is more than one immediately superior interest,

any reduction in value made under that sub-paragraph shall be apportioned between the immediately superior interests.'.

(12) In that paragraph, in sub-paragraph (5)(a)—

  (a) for 'the', where it first occurs, there shall be substituted 'a', and

  (b) after '2(1)(a)' there shall be inserted 'or, as the case may be, 5A(2)(a)'.

(13) In paragraph 15 (calculation of marriage value), there shall be inserted at the end—

'(4) References in this paragraph to paragraph 4(2), (3) or (4) extend to that provision as it applies in accordance with paragraph 5A(2)(b).'.

(14) In paragraph 16 (apportionment of marriage value), in sub-paragraph (2), for 'the', where it first occurs, there shall be substituted 'a'.

(15) In paragraph 17 (adjustment of compensation), in sub-paragraph (4)(a), after '2(1)(c)' there shall be inserted ', 5A(2)(c)'.

(16) In that paragraph, there shall be inserted at the end—

'(6) Where any reduction in value under sub-paragraph (2) of paragraph 14 is apportioned in accordance with sub-paragraph (3A) of that paragraph, any amount of compensation payable by virtue of this paragraph shall be similarly apportioned.'.

19 In Schedule 7 (conveyance to nominee purchaser on enfranchisement), in paragraph 1—

  (a) for sub-paragraphs (a) and (b) there shall be substituted—

   '(a) "the relevant premises" means, in relation to the conveyance of any interest, the premises in which the interest subsists;

   (b) "the freeholder" means, in relation to the conveyance of a freehold interest, the person whose interest is to be conveyed;',

    and

  (b) for sub-paragraph (d) there shall be substituted—

   '(d) "the appropriate time" means, in relation to the conveyance of a freehold interest, the time when the interest is to be conveyed to the nominee purchaser.'.

20 (1) Schedule 9 (grant of leases back to former freeholder) shall be amended as follows.

(2) In paragraph 1—

  (a) for the definition of 'the appropriate time' there shall be substituted—

   ' "the appropriate time", in relation to a flat or other unit contained in the specified premises, means the time when the freehold of the flat or other unit is acquired by the nominee purchaser;', and

  (b) for the definition of 'the freeholder' there shall be substituted—

   ' "the freeholder", in relation to a flat or other unit contained in the specified premises, means the person who owns the freehold of the flat or other unit immediately before the appropriate time;'.

(3) In paragraph 2, in sub-paragraph (1), for 'contained in the specified premises' there shall be substituted 'falling within sub-paragraph (1A)', and after that sub-paragraph there shall be inserted—

'(1A) A flat falls within this sub-paragraph if—

(a) the freehold of the whole of it is owned by the same person, and

(b) it is contained in the specified premises.'.

(4) In paragraph 3, in sub-paragraph (1), for 'contained in the specified premises' there shall be substituted 'falling within sub-paragraph (1A)', and after that sub-paragraph there shall be inserted—

'(1A) A flat falls within this sub-paragraph if—

(a) the freehold of the whole of it is owned by the same person, and

(b) it is contained in the specified premises.'.

(5) In paragraph 5, in sub-paragraph (1), for 'contained in the specified premises' there shall be substituted 'falling within sub-paragraph (1A)', and after that sub-paragraph there shall be inserted—

'(1A) A unit falls within this sub-paragraph if—

(a) the freehold of the whole of it is owned by the same person, and

(b) it is contained in the specified premises.'.

(6) In paragraph 6, for sub-paragraphs (1) and (2) there shall be substituted—

'(1) Sub-paragraph (2) applies where, immediately before the freehold of a flat or other unit contained in the specified premises is acquired by the nominee purchaser—

(a) those premises are premises with a resident landlord by virtue of the occupation of the flat or other unit by the freeholder of it, and

(b) the freeholder of the flat or other unit is a qualifying tenant of it.

(2) If the freeholder of the flat or other unit ("the relevant unit") by notice requires the nominee purchaser to do so, the nominee purchaser shall grant to the freeholder a lease of the relevant unit in accordance with section 36 and paragraph 7 below; and, on the grant of such a lease to the freeholder, he shall be deemed to have surrendered any lease of the relevant unit held by him immediately before the appropriate time.'.

(7) In that paragraph, in sub-paragraph (3), for '(1)(c)' there shall be substituted '(1)(b)'.

SCHEDULE 11
COMPENSATION FOR POSTPONEMENT OF TERMINATION IN CONNECTION WITH INEFFECTIVE CLAIMS

Section 116

Claims under Part I of the Leasehold Reform Act 1967

1 (1) After section 27 of the Leasehold Reform Act 1967 there shall be inserted—

'27A Compensation for postponement of termination in connection with ineffective claims

(1) This section applies where, on or after 15th January 1999—

(a) a tenant of any property makes a claim to acquire the freehold or an extended lease of it, and

(b) the claim is not made at least two years before the term date of the tenancy in respect of which the claim is made ("the existing tenancy").

(2) The tenant shall be liable to pay compensation if the claim is not effective and—

    (a) the making of the claim caused a notice served under paragraph 4(1) of Schedule 10 to the Local Government and Housing Act 1989 to cease to have effect and the date on which the claim ceases to have effect is later than four months before the termination date specified in the notice,

    (b) the making of the claim prevented the service of an effective notice under paragraph 4(1) of Schedule 10 to the Local Government and Housing Act 1989 (but did not cause a notice served under that provision to cease to have effect) and the date on which the claim ceases to have effect is a date later than six months before the term date of the tenancy, or

    (c) the existing tenancy is continued under paragraph 3(1) of Schedule 3 to this Act by virtue of the claim.

(3) Compensation under subsection (2) above shall become payable at the end of the appropriate period and be the right of the person who is the tenant's immediate landlord at that time.

(4) The amount which the tenant is liable to pay under subsection (2) above shall be equal to the difference between—

    (a) the rent for the appropriate period under the existing tenancy, and

    (b) the rent which might reasonably be expected to be payable for that period were the property to which the existing tenancy relates let for a term equivalent to that period on the open market by a willing landlord on the following assumptions—

        (i) that no premium is payable in connection with the letting,

        (ii) that the letting confers no security of tenure, and

        (iii) that, except as otherwise provided by this paragraph, the letting is on the same terms as the existing tenancy.

(5) For the purposes of subsection (2) above, a claim to acquire the freehold or an extended lease is not effective if it ceases to have effect for any reason other than—

    (a) the acquisition in pursuance of the claim of the interest to which it relates, or

    (b) the lapsing of the claim under any provision of this Act excluding the tenant's liability for costs.

(6) For the purposes of subsections (3) and (4) above, the appropriate period is—

    (a) in a case falling within paragraph (a) of subsection (2) above, the period—

        (i) beginning with the termination date specified in the notice mentioned in that paragraph, and

        (ii) ending with the earliest date of termination which could have been specified in a notice under paragraph 4(1) of Schedule 10 to the Local Government and Housing Act 1989 served immediately after the date on which the claim ceases to have effect, or, if the existing tenancy is terminated before then, with the date of its termination;

    (b) in a case falling within paragraph (b) of subsection (2) above, the period—

        (i) beginning with the later of six months from the date on which the claim is made and the term date of the existing tenancy, and

        (ii) ending six months after the date on which the claim ceases to have effect, or, if the existing tenancy is terminated before then, with the date of its termination; and

(c) in a case falling within paragraph (c) of subsection (2) above, the period for which the existing tenancy is continued under paragraph 3(1) of Schedule 3 to this Act.

(7) For the purposes of this section—

(a) references to a claim to acquire the freehold or an extended lease shall be taken as references to a notice of a person's desire to acquire it under Part I of this Act and as including a claim made by a tenant not entitled to acquire it, and

(b) references to the date on which a claim ceases to have effect shall, in relation to a notice which is not a valid notice, be taken as references to the date on which the notice is set aside by the court or withdrawn or would, if valid, cease to have effect, that date being taken, where the notice is set aside, or would (if valid) cease to have effect, in consequence of a court order, to be the date when the order becomes final.

27B Modification of section 27A where change in immediate reversion

(1) Where a tenant's liability to pay compensation under section 27A above relates to a period during which there has been a change in the interest immediately expectant on the determination of his tenancy, that section shall have effect with the following modifications.

(2) For subsections (3) and (4) there shall be substituted—

"(3) Compensation under subsection (2) above shall become payable at the end of the appropriate period and there shall be a separate right to compensation in respect of each of the interests which, during that period, have been immediately expectant on the determination of the existing tenancy.

(4) Compensation under subsection (2) above shall—

(a) in the case of the interest which is immediately expectant on the determination of the existing tenancy at the end of the appropriate period, be the right of the person in whom that interest is vested at that time, and

(b) in the case of an interest which ceases during the appropriate period to be immediately expectant on the determination of the existing tenancy, be the right of the person in whom the interest was vested immediately before it ceased to be so expectant.

(4A) The amount which the tenant is liable to pay under subsection (2) above in respect of any interest shall be equal to the difference between—

(a) the rent under the existing tenancy for the part of the appropriate period during which the interest was immediately expectant on the determination of that tenancy, and

(b) the rent which might reasonably be expected to be payable for that part of that period were the property to which the existing tenancy relates let for a term equivalent to that part of that period on the open market by a willing landlord on the following assumptions—

(i) that no premium is payable in connection with the letting,

(ii) that the letting confers no security of tenure, and

(iii) that, except as otherwise provided by this paragraph, the letting is on the same terms as the existing tenancy."

(3) In subsection (6), for "(3) and (4)" there shall be substituted "(3) to (4A)".'

(2) In section 21(1) of that Act (matters to be determined by leasehold valuation tribunal), after paragraph (c) there shall be inserted—

'(ca) the amount of any compensation payable under section 27A;'.

*Claims under Chapter I of Part I of the Leasehold Reform, Housing and Urban
Development Act 1993*

2 (1) After section 37 of the Leasehold Reform, Housing and Urban Development Act 1993 there shall be inserted—

'*Landlord's right to compensation in relation to ineffective claims*

37A Compensation for postponement of termination in connection with ineffective claims

(1) This section applies where a claim to exercise the right to collective enfranchisement in respect of any premises is made on or after 15th January 1999 by tenants of flats contained in the premises and the claim is not effective.

(2) A person who is a participating tenant immediately before the claim ceases to have effect shall be liable to pay compensation if—

(a) the claim was not made at least two years before the term date of the lease by virtue of which he is a qualifying tenant ("the existing lease"), and

(b) any of the conditions mentioned in subsection (3) is met.

(3) The conditions referred to above are—

(a) that the making of the claim caused a notice served under paragraph 4(1) of Schedule 10 to the Local Government and Housing Act 1989 in respect of the existing lease to cease to have effect and the date on which the claim ceases to have effect is later than four months before the termination date specified in the notice,

(b) that the making of the claim prevented the service of an effective notice under paragraph 4(1) of Schedule 10 to the Local Government and Housing Act 1989 in respect of the existing lease (but did not cause a notice served under that provision in respect of that lease to cease to have effect) and the date on which the claim ceases to have effect is a date later than six months before the term date of the existing lease, and

(c) that the existing lease has been continued under paragraph 6(1) of Schedule 3 by virtue of the claim.

(4) Compensation under subsection (2) shall become payable at the end of the appropriate period and be the right of the person who is the tenant's immediate landlord at that time.

(5) The amount which a tenant is liable to pay under subsection (2) shall be equal to the difference between—

(a) the rent for the appropriate period under the existing lease, and

(b) the rent which might reasonably be expected to be payable for that period were the property to which the existing lease relates let for a term equivalent to that period on the open market by a willing landlord on the following assumptions—

    (i) that no premium is payable in connection with the letting,

    (ii) that the letting confers no security of tenure, and

    (iii) that, except as otherwise provided by this paragraph, the letting is on the same terms as the existing lease.

(6) For the purposes of subsections (4) and (5), the appropriate period is—

(a) in a case falling within paragraph (a) of subsection (3), the period—

    (i) beginning with the termination date specified in the notice mentioned in that paragraph, and

    (ii) ending with the earliest date of termination which could have been specified in a notice under paragraph 4(1) of Schedule 10 to the Local Government and Housing Act 1989 in respect of the existing lease served immediately after the date on which the claim ceases to have effect, or, if the existing lease is terminated before then, with the date of its termination;

(b) in a case falling within paragraph (b) of subsection (3), the period—

    (i) beginning with the later of six months from the date on which the claim is made and the term date of the existing lease, and

    (ii) ending six months after the date on which the claim ceases to have effect, or, if the existing lease is terminated before then, with the date of its termination; and

(c) in a case falling within paragraph (c) of subsection (3), the period for which the existing lease is continued under paragraph 6(1) of Schedule 3.

(7) In the case of a person who becomes a participating tenant by virtue of an election under section 14(3), the references in subsections (3)(a) and (b) and (6)(b)(i) to the making of the claim shall be construed as references to the making of the election.

(8) For the purposes of this section—

(a) references to a claim to exercise the right to collective enfranchisement shall be taken as references to a notice given, or purporting to be given (whether by persons who are qualifying tenants or not), under section 13,

(b) references to the date on which a claim ceases to have effect shall, in the case of a claim made by a notice which is not a valid notice under section 13, be taken as references to the date on which the notice is set aside by the court or is withdrawn or would, if valid, cease to have effect or be deemed to have been withdrawn, that date being taken, where the notice is set aside, or would, if valid, cease to have effect, in consequence of a court order, to be the date when the order becomes final, and

(c) a claim to exercise the right to collective enfranchisement is not effective if it ceases to have effect for any reason other than—

    (i) the application of section 23(4), 30(4) or 31(4),

    (ii) the entry into a binding contract for the acquisition of the freehold and other interests falling to be acquired in pursuance of the claim, or

    (iii) the making of an order under section 24(4)(a) or (b) or 25(6)(a) or (b) which provides for the vesting of those interests.

37B Modification of section 37A where change in immediate reversion

(1) Where a tenant's liability to pay compensation under section 37A relates to a period during which there has been a change in the interest immediately expectant on the determination of his lease, that section shall have effect with the following modifications.

(2) For subsections (4) and (5) there shall be substituted—

"(4) Compensation under subsection (2) shall become payable at the end of the appropriate period and there shall be a separate right to compensation in respect of each of the interests which, during that period, have been immediately expectant on the determination of the existing lease.

(5) Compensation under subsection (2) above shall—

(a)   in the case of the interest which is immediately expectant on the determination of the existing lease at the end of the appropriate period, be the right of the person in whom that interest is vested at that time, and

(b)   in the case of an interest which ceases during the appropriate period to be immediately expectant on the determination of the existing lease, be the right of the person in whom the interest was vested immediately before it ceased to be so expectant.

(5A) The amount which the tenant is liable to pay under subsection (2) above in respect of any interest shall be equal to the difference between—

(a)   the rent under the existing lease for the part of the appropriate period during which the interest was immediately expectant on the determination of that lease, and

(b)   the rent which might reasonably be expected to be payable for that part of that period were the property to which the existing lease relates let for a term equivalent to that part of that period on the open market by a willing landlord on the following assumptions—

(i) that no premium is payable in connection with the letting,

(ii) that the letting confers no security of tenure, and

(iii) that, except as otherwise provided by this paragraph, the letting is on the same terms as the existing lease."

(3) In subsection (6), for "(4) and (5)" there shall be substituted "(4) to (5A)".'

(2) In section 91(2) of that Act (matters to be determined by leasehold valuation tribunal), after paragraph (c) there shall be inserted—

'(ca) the amount of any compensation payable under section 37A;'.

Claims under Chapter II of Part I of the Leasehold Reform, Housing and Urban Development Act 1993

3 (1) After section 61 of the Leasehold Reform, Housing and Urban Development Act 1993 there shall be inserted—

'Landlord's right to compensation in relation to ineffective claims

61A Compensation for postponement of termination in connection with ineffective claims

(1) This section applies where, on or after 15th January 1999—

(a) a tenant of a flat makes a claim to acquire a new lease of the flat, and

(b) the claim is not made at least two years before the term date of the lease in respect of which the claim is made ("the existing lease").

(2) The tenant shall be liable to pay compensation if the claim is not effective and—

(a) the making of the claim caused a notice served under paragraph 4(1) of Schedule 10 to the Local Government and Housing Act 1989 to cease to have effect and the date on which the claim ceases to have effect is later than four months before the termination date specified in the notice,

(b) the making of the claim prevented the service of an effective notice under paragraph 4(1) of Schedule 10 to the Local Government and Housing Act 1989 (but did not cause a notice served under that provision to cease to have effect) and the date on which the claim ceases to have effect is a date later than six months before the term date of the existing lease, or

(c) the existing lease is continued under paragraph 5(1) of Schedule 12 by virtue of the claim.

(3) Compensation under subsection (2) shall become payable at the end of the appropriate period and be the right of the person who is the tenant's immediate landlord at that time.

(4) The amount which the tenant is liable to pay under subsection (2) shall be equal to the difference between—

(a) the rent for the appropriate period under the existing lease, and

(b) the rent which might reasonably be expected to be payable for that period were the property to which the existing lease relates let for a term equivalent to that period on the open market by a willing landlord on the following assumptions—

(i) that no premium is payable in connection with the letting,

(ii) that the letting confers no security of tenure, and

(iii) that, except as otherwise provided by this paragraph, the letting is on the same terms as the existing lease.

(5) For the purposes of subsections (3) and (4), the appropriate period is—

(a) in a case falling within paragraph (a) of subsection (2), the period—

(i) beginning with the termination date specified in the notice mentioned in that paragraph, and

(ii) ending with the earliest date of termination which could have been specified in a notice under paragraph 4(1) of Schedule 10 to the Local Government and Housing Act 1989 served immediately after the date on which the claim ceases to have effect, or, if the existing lease is terminated before then, with the date on which it is terminated;

(b) in a case falling within paragraph (b) of subsection (2), the period—

(i) beginning with the later of six months from the date on which the claim is made and the term date of the existing lease, and

(ii) ending six months after the date on which the claim ceases to have effect, or, if the existing lease is terminated before then, with the date of its termination; and

(c) in a case falling within paragraph (c) of subsection (2), the period for which the existing lease is continued under paragraph 5(1) of Schedule 12.

(6) For the purposes of subsection (2), a claim to a new lease is not effective if it ceases to have effect for any reason other than—

(a) the application of section 47(1) or 55(2), or

(b) the acquisition of the new lease in pursuance of the claim.

(7) For the purposes of this section—

(a) references to a claim to acquire a new lease shall be taken as references to a notice given, or purporting to be given (whether by a qualifying tenant or not), under section 42, and

(b) references to the date on which a claim ceases to have effect shall, in the case of a claim made by a notice which is not a valid notice under section 42, be taken as references to the date on which the notice is set aside by the court or is withdrawn or would, if valid, cease to have effect or be deemed to have been withdrawn, that date being taken, where the notice is set aside, or would, if valid, cease to have effect, in consequence of a court order, to be the date when the order becomes final.

61B Modification of section 61A where change in immediate reversion

(1) Where a tenant's liability to pay compensation under section 61A relates to a period during which there has been a change in the interest immediately expectant on the determination of his lease, that section shall have effect with the following modifications.

(2) For subsections (3) and (4) there shall be substituted—

"(3) Compensation under subsection (2) shall become payable at the end of the appropriate period and there shall be a separate right to compensation in respect of each of the interests which, during that period, have been immediately expectant on the determination of the existing lease.

(4) Compensation under subsection (2) above shall—

(a) in the case of the interest which is immediately expectant on the determination of the existing lease at the end of the appropriate period, be the right of the person in whom that interest is vested at that time, and

(b) in the case of an interest which ceases during the appropriate period to be immediately expectant on the determination of the existing lease, be the right of the person in whom the interest was vested immediately before it ceased to be so expectant.

(4A) The amount which the tenant is liable to pay under subsection (2) above in respect of any interest shall be equal to the difference between—

(a) the rent under the existing lease for the part of the appropriate period during which the interest was immediately expectant on the determination of that lease, and

(b) the rent which might reasonably be expected to be payable for that part of that period were the property to which the existing lease relates let for a term equivalent to that part of that period on the open market by a willing landlord on the following assumptions—

(i) that no premium is payable in connection with the letting,

(ii) that the letting confers no security of tenure, and

(iii) that, except as otherwise provided by this paragraph, the letting is on the same terms as the existing lease."

(3) In subsection (5), for "(3) and (4)" there shall be substituted "(3) to (4A)".'

(2) In section 91(2) of that Act (matters to be determined by leasehold valuation tribunal), after paragraph (c) there shall be inserted—

'(cb) the amount of any compensation payable under section 61A;'.

SCHEDULE 12
ADMINISTRATION OF HOUSING BENEFIT, ETC.
Section 121

Administration of housing benefit

1 (1) Section 134 of the Social Security Administration Act 1992 (arrangements for housing benefit) is amended as follows.

(2) For subsection (1) (administering authority and form of benefit) substitute—

'(1) Housing benefit provided by virtue of a scheme under section 123 of the Social Security Contributions and Benefits Act 1992 (in this Part referred to as "the housing benefit scheme") shall be funded and administered by the appropriate housing authority or local authority.

(1A) Housing benefit in respect of payments which the occupier of a dwelling is liable to make to a housing authority shall take the form of a rent rebate or, in prescribed cases, a rent allowance funded and administered by that authority.

The cases that may be so prescribed do not include any where the payment is in respect of property within the authority's Housing Revenue Account.

(1B) In any other case housing benefit shall take the form of a rent allowance funded and administered by the local authority for the area in which the dwelling is situated or by such other local authority as is specified by an order made by the Secretary of State.'.

(3) In subsection (2)(b) omit the words 'or rates'.

(4) Omit subsections (3), (4), (6) and (7).

(5) For subsection (5) (agreements with other authorities for carrying out of functions) substitute—

'(5) Authorities may—

(a) agree that one shall discharge functions relating to housing benefit on another's behalf; or

(b) discharge any such functions jointly or arrange for their discharge by a joint committee.

(5A) Nothing in this section shall be read as excluding the general provisions of the Local Government Act 1972 or the Local Government (Scotland) Act 1973 from applying in relation to the housing benefit functions of a local authority.'.

(6) In subsection (9) for the words from 'the rebates or allowances' to the end substitute 'the housing benefit which will be paid by the authority in any year will not exceed the permitted total or any subsidiary limit specified by order of the Secretary of State.'.

(7) In subsection (11) for the words from 'the rebates or allowances' to the end substitute 'the housing benefit paid by them during the year exceeds the permitted total or any subsidiary limit specified by order of the Secretary of State.'.

(8) For subsection (12) substitute—

'(12) The Secretary of State—

    (a)   shall by order specify the permitted total of housing benefit payable by any authority in any year; and

    (b)   may by order specify one or more subsidiary limits on the amount of housing benefit payable by any authority in any year in respect of any matter or matters specified in the order.

The power to specify the permitted total or a subsidiary limit may be exercised by fixing an amount or by providing rules for its calculation.'.

Administration of council tax benefit

2 In section 138 of the Social Security Administration Act 1992 (council tax benefit: nature of benefit), at the end of subsection (1) insert—

'References in any enactment or instrument (whenever passed or made) to payment, in relation to council tax benefit, include any of those ways of giving the benefit.'.

3 (1) Section 139 of the Social Security Administration Act 1992 (arrangements for council tax benefit) is amended as follows.

(2) For subsections (4) and (5) (agreements with other authorities for carrying out of functions) substitute—

'(4) Nothing in this section shall be read as excluding the general provisions of the Local Government Act 1972 or the Local Government (Scotland) Act 1973 from applying in relation to the council tax benefit functions of a local authority.'.

(3) In subsection (7) for the words from 'the benefits which will be allowed' to the end substitute 'the amount of benefit which will be paid by them in any year will not exceed the permitted total or any subsidiary limit specified by order of the Secretary of State.'.

(4) In subsection (9) for the words from 'the benefits allowed by it' to the end substitute 'the amount of benefit paid by them in any year exceeds the permitted total or any subsidiary limit specified by order of the Secretary of State.'.

(5) For subsection (10) substitute—

'(10) The Secretary of State—

    (a)   shall by order specify the permitted total of council tax benefit payable by any authority in any year; and

    (b)   may by order specify one or more subsidiary limits on the amount of council tax benefit payable by any authority in any year in respect of any matter or matters specified in the order.

The power to specify the permitted total or a subsidiary limit may be exercised by fixing an amount or by providing rules for its calculation.'.

Subsidy

4 After section 140 of the Social Security Administration Act 1992 insert—

'*Subsidy*

140A Subsidy

(1) For each year the Secretary of State shall pay a subsidy to each authority administering housing benefit or council tax benefit.

(2) He shall pay—

- (a) rent rebate subsidy to each housing authority;
- (b) rent allowance subsidy to each local authority; and
- (c) council tax benefit subsidy to each billing authority or levying authority.

(3) In the following provisions of this Part "subsidy", without more, refers to subsidy of any of those descriptions.

140B Calculation of amount of subsidy

(1) The amount of subsidy to be paid to an authority shall be calculated in the manner specified by order made by the Secretary of State.

(2) Subject as follows, the amount of subsidy shall be calculated by reference to the amount of relevant benefit paid by the authority during the year, with any additions specified in the order but subject to any deductions so specified.

In the case of a housing authority in England and Wales, any Housing Revenue Account rebates paid by them shall be excluded from the total.

(3) The order may provide that the amount of subsidy in respect of any matter shall be a fixed sum or shall be nil.

(4) The Secretary of State may deduct from the amount which would otherwise be payable by way of subsidy such amount as be considers it unreasonable to pay by way of subsidy.

(5) The Secretary of State may pay to an authority as part of the subsidy an additional amount in respect of the costs of administering the relevant benefit.

Any such additional amount shall be a fixed sum specified by, or shall be calculated in the manner specified by, an order made by the Secretary of State.

(6) In this section "relevant benefit" means housing benefit or council tax benefit, as the case may be.

(7) Nothing in this section shall be taken to imply that any such addition or deduction as is mentioned in subsection (2) or (4) above may not be determined by reference to—

- (a) the amount of relevant benefit paid by the authority during a previous year; or

(b) the amount of subsidy paid to the authority in respect of a previous year, under this section.

(8) The amount of subsidy payable to an authority shall be calculated to the nearest pound, disregarding an odd amount of 50 pence or less and treating an odd amount exceeding 50 pence as a whole pound.

140C Payment of subsidy

(1) Subsidy shall be paid by the Secretary of State in such instalments, at such times, in such manner and subject to such conditions as to claims, records, certificates, audit or otherwise as may be provided by order of the Secretary of State.

(2) The order may provide that if an authority has not, within such period as may be specified in the order, complied with the conditions so specified as to claims, records, certificate, audit or otherwise, the Secretary of State may estimate the amount of subsidy payable to the authority and employ for that purpose such criteria as he considers relevant.

(3) Where subsidy has been paid to an authority and it appears to the Secretary of State—

(a) that subsidy has been overpaid; or
(b) that there has been a breach of any condition specified in an order under this section,

he may recover from the authority the whole or such part of the payment as he may determine.

Without prejudice to other methods of recovery, a sum recoverable under this subsection may be recovered by withholding or reducing subsidy.

(4) An order made by the Secretary of State under this section may be made before, during or after the end of the year or years to which it relates.

140D Rent rebate subsidy: accounting provisions

(1) Rent rebate subsidy is payable—

(a) in the case of a local authority in England and Wales, for the credit of a revenue account of theirs other than their Housing Revenue Account or Housing Repairs Account;
(b) in the case of a local authority in Scotland, for the credit of their rent rebate account;
(c) in the case of a development corporation in England and Wales or the Development Board for Rural Wales, for the credit of their housing account; and
(d) in the case of a new town corporation in Scotland or Scottish Homes, for the credit of the account to which rent rebates granted by them, or it, are debited.

(2) Every local housing authority in England and Wales shall for each year carry to the credit of their Housing Revenue Account from some other revenue account of theirs which is not a Housing Repairs Account an amount equal to the aggregate of—

(a) so much of each Housing Revenue Account rebate paid by them during the year as was paid—

      (i) in the exercise of a discretion conferred by the housing benefit scheme; or

     (ii) in pursuance of any modification of that scheme under section 134(8)(b) above; and

  (b) unless the authority otherwise determine, so much of each such rebate as was paid in pursuance of such modifications of that scheme as are mentioned in section 134(8)(a) above.

Supplementary provisions

140E Financing of joint arrangements

(1) Where two or more authorities make arrangements for the discharge of any of their functions relating to housing benefit or council tax benefit—

  (a) by one authority on behalf of itself and one or more other authorities; or

  (b) by a joint committee,

the Secretary of State may make such payments as he thinks fit to the authority or committee in respect of their expenses in carrying out those functions.

(2) The provisions of sections 140B and 140C (subsidy: calculation and supplementary provisions) apply in relation to a payment under this section as in relation to a payment of subsidy.

(3) The Secretary of State may (without prejudice to the generality of his powers in relation to the amount of subsidy) take into account the fact that an amount has been paid under this section in respect of expenses which would otherwise have been met in whole or in part by the participating authorities.

140F No requirement for annual orders

(1) Any power under this Part to make provision by order for or in relation to a year does not require the making of a new order each year.

(2) Any order made under the power may be revoked or varied at any time, whether before, during or after the year to which it relates.

140G Interpretation: Part VIII

In this Part, unless the context otherwise requires—

    "Housing Repairs Account" means an account kept under section 77 of the Local Government and Housing Act 1989;

    "Housing Revenue Account" means the account kept under section 74 of the Local Government and Housing Act 1989, and—

      (a) references to property within that account have the same meaning as in Part VI of that Act, and

      (b) "Housing Revenue Account rebate" means a rebate debited to that account in accordance with that Part;

    "rent rebate subsidy" and "rent allowance subsidy" shall be construed in accordance with section 134 above;

    "year" means a financial year within the meaning of the Local Government Finance Act 1992.'.

Transitional provision

5 (1) The Secretary of State may by order make such transitional provision, and such consequential provision and savings, as appear to him appropriate in connection with the coming into force of the provisions of this Schedule.

(2) Without prejudice to the generality of that power, the order may provide for the recovery by the withholding or reduction of subsidy payable under the provisions inserted by paragraph 4 above of any amount which would have been recoverable under the provisions of Part VIII of the Social Security Administration Act 1992 repealed by this Act.

(3) Section 189(3) to (7) of the Social Security Administration Act 1992 (general provisions as to regulations and orders) apply in relation to the power conferred by sub-paragraph (1) as they apply in relation to a power conferred by that Act to make an order.

(4) A statutory instrument containing an order under this paragraph shall be subject to annulment in pursuance of a resolution of either House of Parliament.

SCHEDULE 13
HOUSING BENEFIT AND RELATED MATTERS: CONSEQUENTIAL AMENDMENTS

Section 123

Rent Act 1977 (c.42)

1 In section 63(7) of the Rent Act 1977 (expenditure on rent officers to be met by Secretary of State), in paragraph (a), for 'or an order under section 121 of the Housing Act 1988' substitute 'or an order under section 122 of the Housing Act 1996'.

Housing Act 1985 (c.68)

2 In section 425(2)(b) of the Housing Act 1985 (housing subsidy: local contribution differential), for 'section 135' substitute 'section 140A'.

Social Security Administration Act 1992 (c.5)

3 (1) The Social Security Administration Act 1992 is amended as follows.

(2) In section 5(3) (regulations about benefit: information required by a rent officer), for 'section 121 of the Housing Act 1988' substitute 'section 122 of the Housing Act 1996'.

(3) In section 116(4) (legal proceedings for offences: definition of 'appropriate authority')—

   (a) omit paragraph (a);
   (b) in paragraph (b), for 'that subsection' substitute 'section 134 below'; and
   (c) in paragraph (c), for 'that subsection' substitute 'that section'.

(4) In section 176 (consultation with representative organisations), in subsection (1)(b) for 'section 134(12), 135, 139 or 140 above' substitute 'any provision of Part VIII above'.

(5) In section 189(8) (requirement for consent of the Treasury), for '135, 140' substitute '140B, 140C'.

(6) In section 191 (interpretation: general)—

(a) at the appropriate place insert—

' "council tax benefit scheme" shall be construed in accordance with section 139(1) above;';

(b) in the definition of 'rate rebate', 'rent rebate' and 'rent allowance', omit the reference to rate rebate;

(c) omit the definitions of 'rates' and 'rating authority'.

Leasehold Reform, Housing and Urban Development Act 1993 (c.28)

4 In section 135(8) of the Leasehold Reform, Housing and Urban Development Act 1993 (programmes for disposals of dwelling-houses by local authorities), for 'section 135(1) of the Social Security Administration Act 1992 (housing benefit finance)' substitute 'section 140A of the Social Security Administration Act 1992 (subsidy)'.

SCHEDULE 14
INTRODUCTORY TENANCIES: CONSEQUENTIAL AMENDMENTS
Section 141(1)

Housing Act 1985 (c.68)

1 In section 88(1) of the Housing Act 1985 (cases where the secure tenant is a successor) after paragraph (e) insert 'or

(f) the tenancy was previously an introductory tenancy and he was a successor to the introductory tenancy.'.

2 In section 104(2) of the Housing Act 1985 (provision of information about secure tenancies) for the words 'on the grant of the tenancy' substitute 'when the secure tenancy arises'.

3 After section 115 of the Housing Act 1985 insert—

'115A Meaning of "introductory tenancy"

In this Part "introductory tenancy" has the same meaning as in Chapter I of Part V of the Housing Act 1996.'.

4 In section 117 of the Housing Act 1985 (index of defined expressions: Part IV) insert at the appropriate place—

'introductory tenancy   section 115A'.

5 In Schedule 1 to the Housing Act 1985 (tenancies which are not secure tenancies) after paragraph 1 insert—

'Introductory tenancies

1A. A tenancy is not a secure tenancy if it is an introductory tenancy or a tenancy which has ceased to be an introductory tenancy—

(a) by virtue of section 133(3) of the Housing Act 1996 (disposal on death to non-qualifying person), or

(b) by virtue of the tenant, or in the case of a joint tenancy every tenant, ceasing to occupy the dwelling-house as his only or principal home.'.

SCHEDULE 15
ARREST FOR ANTI-SOCIAL BEHAVIOUR: POWERS OF HIGH COURT AND COUNTY COURT TO REMAND

Section 155(6)

Introductory

1 (1) The provisions of this Schedule apply where the court has power to remand a person under section 155(2) or (5) (arrest for breach of injunction, etc.).

(2) In this Schedule 'the court' means the High Court or a county court and includes—

(a) in relation to the High Court, a judge of that court, and
(b) in relation to a county court, a judge or district judge of that court.

Remand in custody or on bail

2 (1) The court may—

(a) remand him in custody, that is, commit him to custody to be brought before the court at the end of the period of remand or at such earlier time as the court may require, or
(b) remand him on bail, in accordance with the following provisions.

(2) The court may remand him on bail—

(a) by taking from him a recognizance, with or without sureties, conditioned as provided in paragraph 3, or
(b) by fixing the amount of the recognizances with a view to their being taken subsequently, and in the meantime committing him to custody as mentioned in sub-paragraph (1)(a).

(3) Where a person is brought before the court after remand, the court may further remand him.

3 (1) Where a person is remanded on bail, the court may direct that his recognizance be conditioned for his appearance—

(a) before that court at the end of the period of remand, or
(b) at every time and place to which during the course of the proceedings the hearing may from time to time be adjourned.

(2) Where a recognizance is conditioned for a person's appearance as mentioned in sub-paragraph (1)(b), the fixing of any time for him next to appear shall be deemed to be a remand.

(3) Nothing in this paragraph affects the power of the court at any subsequent hearing to remand him afresh.

4 (1) The court shall not remand a person for a period exceeding 8 clear days, except that—

- (a) if the court remands him on bail, it may remand him for a longer period if he and the other party consent, and
- (b) if the court adjourns a case under section 156(1) (remand for medical examination and report), the court may remand him for the period of the adjournment.

(2) Where the court has power to remand a person in custody it may, if the remand is for a period not exceeding 3 clear days, commit him to the custody of a constable.

Further remand

5 (1) If the court is satisfied that a person who has been remanded is unable by reason of illness or accident to appear or be brought before the court at the expiration of the period for which he was remanded, the court may, in his absence, remand him for a further time.

This power may, in the case of a person who was remanded on bail, be exercised by enlarging his recognizance and those of any sureties for him to a later time.

(2) Where a person remanded on bail is bound to appear before the court at any time and the court has no power to remand him under sub-paragraph (1) the court may in his absence enlarge his recognizance and those of any sureties for him to a later time.

The enlargement of his recognizance shall be deemed to be a further remand.

(3) Paragraph 4(1) (limit of period of remand) does not apply to the exercise of the powers conferred by this paragraph.

Postponement of taking of recognizance

6 Where under paragraph 2(2)(b) the court fixes the amount in which the principal and his sureties, if any, are to be bound, the recognizance may afterwards be taken by such person as may be prescribed by rules of court, with the same consequences as if it had been entered into before the court.

SCHEDULE 16
ALLOCATION OF HOUSING ACCOMMODATION: CONSEQUENTIAL AMENDMENTS

Section 173

Housing Act 1985 (c.68)

1 In section 106 of the Housing Act 1985 (information about allocation of secure tenancies) at the end insert—

'(6) The provisions of this section do not apply to a landlord authority which is a local housing authority so far as they impose requirements corresponding to those to which such an authority is subject under sections 166 and 168 of the Housing Act 1996 (provision of information about housing registers and allocation schemes).'.

2 (1) Schedule 1 to the Housing Act 1985 (tenancies which are not secure tenancies) is amended as follows.

(2) In paragraph 2 (premises occupied in connection with employment) at the beginning of sub-paragraph (1), (2) and (3) insert in each case 'Subject to subparagraph (4B)'.

(3) In sub–paragraph (4) of that paragraph—

(a) at the beginning insert 'Subject to sub-paragraph (4A) and (4B)', and
(b) omit the words from 'until' to the end.

(4) After sub-paragraph (4) of that paragraph insert—

'(4A) Except where the landlord is a local housing authority, a tenancy under sub-paragraph (4) shall become a secure tenancy when the periods during which the conditions mentioned in sub-paragraph (1), (2) or (3) are not satisfied with respect to the tenancy amount in aggregate to more than three years.

(4B) Where the landlord is a local housing authority, a tenancy under sub-paragraph (1), (2), (3) or (4) shall become a secure tenancy if the authority notify the tenant that the tenancy is to be regarded as a secure tenancy.'.

(5) In paragraph 5 (temporary accommodation for persons taking up employment) in sub-paragraph (1)—

(a) for the words from the beginning to first 'grant' substitute 'Subject to sub-paragraphs (1A) and (1B), a tenancy is not a secure tenancy', and
(b) omit from 'unless' to the end.

(6) After sub-paragraph (1) of that paragraph insert—

'(1A) Except where the landlord is a local housing authority, a tenancy under sub-paragraph (1) shall become a secure tenancy on the expiry of one year from the grant or on earlier notification by the landlord to the tenant that the tenancy is to be regarded as a secure tenancy.

(1B) Where the landlord is a local housing authority, a tenancy under sub-paragraph (1) shall become a secure tenancy if at any time the authority notify the tenant that the tenancy is to be regarded as a secure tenancy.'.

(7) In paragraph 10 (student lettings) in sub-paragraph (1)—

(a) for the words from the beginning to 'sub-paragraph (3)' substitute 'Subject to sub-paragraphs (2A) and (2B), a tenancy of a dwelling-house is not a secure tenancy', and
(b) omit from 'unless' to the end.

(8) After sub-paragraph (2) of that paragraph insert—

'(2A) Except where the landlord is a local housing authority, a tenancy under sub-paragraph (1) shall become a secure tenancy on the expiry of the period specified in sub-paragraph (3) or on earlier notification by the landlord to the tenant that the tenancy is to be regarded as a secure tenancy.

(2B) Where the landlord is a local housing authority, a tenancy under sub-paragraph (1) shall become a secure tenancy if at any time the authority notify the tenant that the tenancy is to be regarded as a secure tenancy.'.

(9) In sub-paragraph (3) of that paragraph for the words 'sub-paragraph (1)' substitute 'sub-paragraph (2A)'.

3 (1) Section 9 of the Asylum and Immigration Act 1996 (entitlement to housing accommodation and assistance) is amended as follows.

(2) In subsection (1) (entitlement to housing accommodation)—

   (a) for 'housing authority' substitute 'local housing authority within the meaning of the Housing Act 1985', and

   (b) for 'the accommodation Part' substitute 'Part II of that Act'.

(3) After subsection (4) insert—

'(5) This section does not apply in relation to any allocation of housing accommodation to which Part VI of the Housing Act 1996 (allocation of housing accommodation) applies.'

SCHEDULE 17
HOMELESSNESS: CONSEQUENTIAL AMENDMENTS

Section 216(3)

Local Authority Social Services Act 1970 (c.42)

1 In Schedule 1 to the Local Authority Social Services Act 1970 (enactments conferring functions assigned to Social Services Committee) for the entry relating to the Housing Act 1985 substitute—

'Housing Act 1996	Co-operation in relation to
Section 213(1)(b)	homeless persons and persons
	threatened with homelessness.'.

Greater London Council (General Powers) Act 1984 (c.xxvii)

2 In section 39 of the Greater London Council (General Powers) Act 1984 (occupants removed from buildings to have priority housing need) for 'Part III of the Housing Act 1985 (housing the homeless)' substitute 'Part VII of the Housing Act 1996 (homelessness)'.

Housing Act 1985 (c.68)

3 In Schedule 1 to the Housing Act 1985 (tenancies which are not secure tenancies), for paragraph 4 (accommodation for homeless persons) substitute—

'Accommodation for homeless persons

4. A tenancy granted in pursuance of any function under Part VII of the Housing Act 1996 (homelessness) is not a secure tenancy unless the local housing authority concerned have notified the tenant that the tenancy is to be regarded as a secure tenancy.'.

Housing (Scotland) Act 1987 (c.26)

4 In section 42 of the Housing (Scotland) Act 1987 (application of Part II to cases arising in England and Wales: request for co-operation)—

(a) in subsection (1) for 'section 67(1) of the Housing Act 1985' substitute 'section 198(1) of the Housing Act 1996'; and

(b) in subsections (2) and (3) for 'section 72 of the Housing Act 1985' substitute 'section 213 of the Housing Act 1996'.

SCHEDULE 18
MISCELLANEOUS PROVISIONS

Section 222

PART I

HOUSING MANAGEMENT

Repeal of Part IV of the Housing Act 1988

1 Part IV of the Housing Act 1988 (change of landlord: secure tenants) is hereby repealed.

Payments to encourage local housing authority tenants to move to other accommodation

2 (1) A local housing authority may make payments to or for the benefit of a tenant or licensee of a dwelling-house within its Housing Revenue Account with a view to assisting or encouraging that person to move to qualifying accommodation.

(2) In sub-paragraph (1) 'qualifying accommodation' means a dwelling-house made available to the person concerned as tenant or licensee by any of the following—

(a) the local housing authority making the grant or any other local housing authority; or

(b) a registered social landlord.

(3) The reference in sub-paragraph (1) to a dwelling-house being within the Housing Revenue Account of a local housing authority is to a dwelling-house to which section 74(1) of the Local Government and Housing Act 1989 for the time being applies.

(4) In this paragraph—

'dwelling-house' has the meaning given by section 112 of the Housing Act 1985; and 'tenant' does not include a tenant under a long tenancy as defined in section 115 of that Act.

Consultation with respect to housing management

3 (1) Part II of the Housing Act 1985 (provision of housing accommodation) is amended as follows.

(2) After section 27B insert—

'*Consultation with respect to housing management*

27BA Consultation with respect to management

(1) The Secretary of State may make regulations for imposing requirements on a local

housing authority to consult tenants, or to consider representations made to them by tenants, with respect to the exercise of their management functions (including proposals as to the exercise of those functions), in relation to any of the authority's houses or other land held for a related purpose.

(2) The regulations may include provision requiring a local housing authority to consult tenants, or consider representations made by tenants, with respect to—

(a) the terms of a written specification to be prepared by the authority of functions proposed to be exercised by the authority or another person;

(b) a proposal of the authority to exercise management functions themselves;

(c) any person whom the authority propose to invite to submit a bid to exercise any of their management functions;

(d) the standards of service for the time being achieved by the authority or (as the case may be) the person with whom they have entered into a management agreement;

(e) a proposal to enforce the standards of service required by a management agreement.

(3) The requirements imposed on a local housing authority by the regulations may include provision with respect to—

(a) the tenants to be consulted or whose representations are to be considered;

(b) the means by which consultation is to be effected (including the arrangements to be made for tenants to consider the matters on which they have been consulted);

(c) the arrangements to be made for tenants to make representations to the authority;

(d) the action to be taken by the authority where representations are made.

(4) The regulations may include provision requiring a local housing authority to consult representatives of tenants, or to consider representations made to them by such representatives, as well as (or instead of) the tenants themselves; and accordingly, references in subsections (1) to (3) above to tenants include references to such representatives.

(5) The regulations may include provision for particular questions arising under them to be determined by a local housing authority on whom they impose requirements.

(6) Nothing in subsections (2) to (5) above shall be taken as prejudicing the generality of subsection (1).

(7) Regulations under this section—

(a) may make different provision with respect to different cases or descriptions of case, including different provision for different areas,

(b) may contain such incidental, supplementary or transitional provisions as appear to the Secretary of State to be necessary or expedient, and

(c) shall be made by statutory instrument which shall be subject to annulment in pursuance of a resolution of either House of Parliament.

(8) Except as otherwise provided by the regulations, in the case of secure tenants, the provisions of the regulations shall apply in place of the provisions of section 105 (consultation on matters of housing management).

(9) Except as otherwise provided by the regulations, in the case of introductory tenants, the provisions of the regulations shall apply in place of the provisions of section 137 of the Housing Act 1996 (consultation on matters of housing management).

(10) References in this section to the management functions of a local housing authority in relation to houses or land shall be construed in the same way as references to any such functions in section 27.'.

(3) In section 20(1) (application of housing management provisions) for 'section 27B' substitute 'section 27BA'.

(4) In section 27 (management agreements), after subsection (5) insert—

'(5A) Nothing in section 6 of the Local Government Act 1988 (restrictions on authority carrying out functional work) shall apply in relation to any management functions which, in pursuance of a management agreement, are carried out by the manager as agent of the local housing authority.'.

(5) In section 27AB (management agreements with tenant management organisations), in subsection (7)(b)(i), for the words from 'section 27A' to the end substitute 'regulations under section 27BA (consultation with respect to management)'.

PART II

HOUSING FINANCE

Housing Revenue Account: directions as to certain matters

4 (1) In Part VI of the Local Government and Housing Act 1989 (housing finance), after section 78 (directions as to proper accounting practices) insert—

'78A Directions as to treatment of service charges etc.

(1) The Secretary of State may give directions as to what items or amounts are to be regarded as referable to property within a local housing authority's Housing Revenue Account where one or more parts of a building have been disposed of but the common parts remain property within that account.

(2) Any such direction also has effect for the purposes of any Housing Repairs Account kept by the authority.

(3) Directions under this section may give the authority a discretion as to whether items or amounts are accounted for in the Housing Revenue Account or any Housing Repairs Account or in another revenue account.

(4) In this section 'common parts' includes the structure and exterior of the building and common facilities provided, whether in the building or elsewhere, for persons who include the occupiers of one or more parts of the building.

78B Directions as to accounting for work subject to competitive tendering

(1) This section applies where work is carried out by a local housing authority which has successfully bid for the work on a competitive basis.

(2) The Secretary of State may give directions—

(a) to secure that the amount debited to the Housing Revenue Account or any Housing Repairs Account of the authority in respect of the work reflects the amount of the authority's successful bid for the work rather than expenditure actually incurred;

(b) allowing an authority to credit to its Housing Revenue Account any surpluses reasonably attributable to work undertaken on or in connection with property within that account.

(3) Directions under subsection (2)(a) may make provision for determining the amount to be treated as the amount of the authority's successful bid.

References in this Part to expenditure shall be construed as references to the amount falling to be debited in accordance with the directions.

(4) Directions under subsection (2)(b) may make provision as to the ascertainment of the surpluses referred to and the circumstances in which a surplus is or is not to be taken to be attributable to property within an authority's Housing Revenue Account.'.

(2) The above amendment has effect for the financial year beginning on 1st April 1997 and subsequent financial years.

Housing Revenue Account subsidy: final decision on amount

5 (1) In Part VI of the Local Government and Housing Act 1989 (housing finance), after section 80 (calculation of Housing Revenue Account subsidy) insert—

'80A Final decision on amount of Housing Revenue Account subsidy

(1) The Secretary of State shall, as soon as he thinks fit after the end of the year, make a final decision as to the amount (if any) of Housing Revenue Account subsidy payable to a local housing authority for that year and notify the authority in writing of his decision.

(2) Once notified to the authority the decision is conclusive as to the amount (if any) payable by way of subsidy and shall not be questioned in any legal proceedings.

(3) Where the amount of Housing Revenue Account subsidy paid to an authority is less than the amount finally decided, the authority is entitled to be paid the balance.

(4) Where Housing Revenue Account subsidy has been paid to an authority in excess of the amount finally decided, the Secretary of State may recover the excess, with interest from such time and at such rates as he thinks fit.

Without prejudice to other methods of recovery, a sum recoverable under this subsection may be recovered by withholding or reducing subsidy.

(5) Nothing in this section affects any power of the Secretary of State to vary a determination as to the amount of subsidy before the final decision is made.'.

(2) The above amendment applies in relation to the amount of subsidy payable—

(a) to authorities in England for the financial year beginning on 1st April 1996 and subsequent years; and

(b) to authorities in Wales for such financial years as the Secretary of State may specify by order made by statutory instrument.

Abolition of exchequer contributions for agricultural housing

6 (1) No contribution shall be made by the Secretary of State by virtue of Part II of Schedule 15 to the Housing Act 1985 (exchequer contributions for agricultural housing) in respect of any year after the year ending on 31st March 1996.

(2) Part II of Schedule 15 to that Act is amended as follows.

(3) For the heading substitute—

'ANNUAL GRANTS FOR AGRICULTURAL HOUSING'

(4) For paragraph 1 substitute—

'Annual grants by local housing authorities

1.—(1) Annual grants shall, notwithstanding the abolition of exchequer contributions by paragraph 6(1) of Schedule 18 to the Housing Act 1996, continue to be payable by local housing authorities in respect of agricultural housing provided in pursuance of arrangements made under section 46 of the Housing (Financial Provisions) Act 1958.

(2) Subject to the provisions of this Part of this Schedule, such annual grants are payable, in respect of any house as to which the Secretary of State originally undertook to make annual contributions under section 46 of the Housing (Financial Provisions) Act 1958, for the remainder of the 40 year period for which that undertaking was given.

(3) The amount paid by way of annual grant to the owner of a house shall not be less than the amount of the last annual contribution paid by the Secretary of State in respect of the house.'.

(5) For paragraph 2(1) substitute—

'Conditions of payment of annual grant

2.—(1) It is a condition of the payment of a grant in respect of a house in any year that throughout the year the house—

(a) is reserved for members of the agricultural population, and

(b) if let, is let at a rent not exceeding the limit applicable in accordance with the following provisions of this paragraph,

and that in the opinion of the local housing authority all reasonable steps have been taken to secure the maintenance of the house in a proper state of repair during the year.'.

(6) In paragraph 3(1), for 'contribution' substitute 'grant'.

(7) For paragraph 4 substitute—

'4. A grant shall not be made or shall be reduced, as the local housing authority think fit, if (before the grant is paid) the local housing authority are of the opinion that during the whole or the greater part of the period to which the payment of the grant is referable the house has not been available as a dwelling fit for habitation, unless the authority is satisfied that that could not with reasonable diligence have been achieved.'.

(8) In paragraph 5 omit the words 'the Secretary of State or'.

(9) After paragraph 5 insert—

'Commutation of future annual grant

6.—(1) A local authority may make an offer in writing to the person who is for the time being the owner of a house as respects which annual grant is payable under this Part of this Schedule to pay a lump sum in lieu of—

(a) the annual grant payable for the year in which the offer is accepted; and
(b) any further payments of annual grant that would (apart from this paragraph) be payable for the remainder of the period for which the original arrangements under section 46 of the Housing (Financial Provisions) Act 1958 were made.

(2) An owner may accept an offer made under this paragraph by notice in writing to the local housing authority.

(3) Subject to sub-paragraph (4) below, where such an offer is accepted the local housing authority shall pay to the owner a lump sum calculated in such manner as the authority may determine.

(4) A lump sum shall not be paid as respects a house unless the local housing authority are satisfied that the conditions in this Part of this Schedule have been observed throughout the year preceding the date on which the lump sum would otherwise be paid.

(5) On payment of a lump sum under this paragraph to the owner of a house—

(a) no further annual grants under this Part of this Schedule shall be payable in respect of the house; and
(b) the conditions described in this Part of this Schedule shall cease to apply to the house.'.

(10) Nothing in this paragraph affects the operation of Part II of Schedule 15 to the Housing Act 1985 in respect of any year ending before 1st April 1996.

PART III

ORDERS IN RELATION TO PROPERTY IN FAMILY AND MATRIMONIAL PROCEEDINGS ETC.

Housing Act 1980 (c.51)

7 In section 54(2) of the Housing Act 1980 (prohibition on assignment of protected shorthold tenancy or protected tenancy of dwelling-house), for 'except in pursuance of an order under section 24 of the Matrimonial Causes Act 1973' substitute—

'except in pursuance of an order under—

    (a) section 24 of the Matrimonial Causes Act 1973 (property adjustment orders in connection with matrimonial proceedings),

    (b) section 17(1) of the Matrimonial and Family Proceedings Act 1984 (property adjustment orders after overseas divorce, etc.), or

    (c) paragraph 1 of Schedule 1 to the Children Act 1989 (orders for financial relief against parents).'.

Housing Act 1985 (c.68)

8 (1) Section 39 of the Housing Act 1985 (exempted disposals) is amended as follows.

(2) In subsection (1), for paragraph (c) substitute—

'(c) it is a disposal of the whole of the house in pursuance of any such order as is mentioned in subsection (3);'.

(3) After subsection (2) add—

'(3) The orders referred to in subsection (1)(c) are orders under—

    (a) section 24 or 24A of the Matrimonial Causes Act 1973 (property adjustment orders or orders for the sale of property in connection with matrimonial proceedings),

    (b) section 2 of the Inheritance (Provision for Family and Dependants) Act 1975 (orders as to financial provision to be made from estate),

    (c) section 17 of the Matrimonial and Family Proceedings Act 1984 (property adjustment orders or orders for the sale of property after overseas divorce, etc.), or

    (d) paragraph 1 of Schedule 1 to the Children Act 1989 (orders for financial relief against parents).'.

9 In section 88(2) of the Housing Act 1985 (cases where secure tenant is a successor) after 'proceedings)' insert 'or section 17(1) of the Matrimonial and Family Proceedings Act 1984 (property adjustment orders after overseas divorce, etc.)'.

10 In section 89 of the Housing Act 1985 (succession to periodic tenancy), for subsection (3) substitute—

'(3) Where there is no person qualified to succeed the tenant, the tenancy ceases to be a secure tenancy—

    (a) when it is vested or otherwise disposed of in the course of the administration of the tenant's estate, unless the vesting or other disposal is in pursuance of an order made under—

        (i) section 24 of the Matrimonial Causes Act 1973 (property adjustment orders made in connection with matrimonial proceedings),

        (ii) section 17(1) of the Matrimonial and Family Proceedings Act 1984 (property adjustment orders after overseas divorce, etc.), or

        (iii) paragraph 1 of Schedule 1 to the Children Act 1989 (orders for financial relief against parents); or

    (b) when it is known that when the tenancy is so vested or disposed of it will not be in pursuance of such an order.'.

11 In section 90(3) of the Housing Act 1985 (devolution of secure tenancy), for paragraph (a) and the word 'or' at the end of the paragraph substitute—

'(a) the vesting or other disposal is in pursuance of an order made under—
  (i) section 24 of the Matrimonial Causes Act 1973 (property adjustment orders in connection with matrimonial proceedings),
  (ii) section 17(1) of the Matrimonial and Family Proceedings Act 1984 (property adjustment orders after overseas divorce, etc.), or
  (iii) paragraph 1 of Schedule 1 to the Children Act 1989 (orders for financial relief against parents), or'.

12 In section 91(3) of the Housing Act 1985 (cases where assignment of secure tenancy permitted), for paragraph (b) substitute—

'(b) an assignment in pursuance of an order made under—
  (i) section 24 of the Matrimonial Causes Act 1973 (property adjustment orders in connection with matrimonial proceedings),
  (ii) section 17(1) of the Matrimonial and Family Proceedings Act 1984 (property adjustment orders after overseas divorce, etc.), or
  (iii) paragraph 1 of Schedule 1 to the Children Act 1989 (orders for financial relief against parents);'.

13 In section 99B(2) of the Housing Act 1985 (persons qualifying for compensation for improvements) for paragraph (e) substitute—

'(e) a person to whom the tenancy was assigned by the improving tenant in pursuance of an order made under—
  (i) section 24 of the Matrimonial Causes Act 1973 (property adjustment orders in connection with matrimonial proceedings),
  (ii) section 17(1) of the Matrimonial and Family Proceedings Act 1984 (property adjustment orders after overseas divorce, etc.), or
  (iii) paragraph 1 of Schedule 1 to the Children Act 1989 (orders for financial relief against parents);'.

14 In section 101(3) of the Housing Act 1985 (rent not increased on account of tenant's improvements: qualifying persons) for paragraph (c) substitute—

'(c) a person to whom the tenancy was assigned by the tenant in pursuance of an order made under—
  (i) section 24 of the Matrimonial Causes Act 1973 (property adjustment orders in connection with matrimonial proceedings),
  (ii) section 17(1) of the Matrimonial and Family Proceedings Act 1984 (property adjustment orders after overseas divorce, etc.), or
  (iii) paragraph 1 of Schedule 1 to the Children Act 1989 (orders for financial relief against parents);'.

15 (1) Section 160 of the Housing Act 1985 (exempted disposals in relation to right to buy) is amended as follows.

(2) In subsection (1), for paragraph (c) substitute—

'(c) it is a disposal of the whole of the dwelling–house in pursuance of any such order as is mentioned in subsection (3);'.

(3) After subsection (2) add—

'(3) The orders referred to in subsection (1)(c) are orders under—

    (a) section 24 or 24A of the Matrimonial Causes Act 1973 (property adjustment orders or orders for the sale of property in connection with matrimonial proceedings),

    (b) section 2 of the Inheritance (Provision for Family and Dependants) Act 1975 (orders as to financial provision to be made from estate),

    (c) section 17 of the Matrimonial and Family Proceedings Act 1984 (property adjustment orders or orders for the sale of property after overseas divorce, etc.), or

    (d) paragraph 1 of Schedule 1 to the Children Act 1989 (orders for financial relief against parents).'.

16 In section 171B(4)(b) of the Housing Act 1985 (extent of preserved right to buy: qualifying successors of tenant), after sub-paragraph (ii) insert—

'or

    (iii) a property adjustment order under section 17(1) of the Matrimonial and Family Proceedings Act 1984 (property adjustment orders after overseas divorce, etc.), or

    (iv) an order under paragraph 1 of Schedule 1 to the Children Act 1989 (orders for financial relief against parents),'.

17 In paragraph 1(2) of Schedule 6A to the Housing Act 1985 (obligation to redeem landlord's share: excluded disposals), for paragraph (c) substitute—

'(c) it is a disposal in pursuance of an order under—

    (i) section 24 or 24A of the Matrimonial Causes Act 1973 (property adjustment orders or orders for the sale of property in connection with matrimonial proceedings),

    (ii) section 2 of the Inheritance (Provision for Family and Dependants) Act 1975 (orders as to financial provision to be made from estate),

    (iii) section 17 of the Matrimonial and Family Proceedings Act 1984 (property adjustment orders or orders for the sale of property after overseas divorce, etc.), or

    (iv) paragraph 1 of Schedule 1 to the Children Act 1989 (orders for financial relief against parents),'.

Landlord and Tenant Act 1987 (c.31)

18 In section 4(2) of the Landlord and Tenant Act 1987 (right of first refusal: excluded disposals), for paragraph (c) substitute—

'(c) a disposal in pursuance of an order made under—

    (i) section 24 of the Matrimonial Causes Act 1973 (property adjustment orders in connection with matrimonial proceedings),

    (ii) section 24A of the Matrimonial Causes Act 1973 (orders for the sale of property in connection with matrimonial proceedings) where the order includes provision requiring the property concerned to be offered for sale to a person or class of persons specified in the order,

    (iii) section 2 of the Inheritance (Provision for Family and Dependants) Act 1975 (orders as to financial provision to be made from estate),

   (iv) section 17(1) of the Matrimonial and Family Proceedings Act 1984 (property adjustment orders after overseas divorce, etc.),

   (v) section 17(2) of the Matrimonial and Family Proceedings Act 1984 (orders for the sale of property after overseas divorce, etc.) where the order includes provision requiring the property concerned to be offered for sale to a person or class of persons specified in the order, or

   (vi) paragraph 1 of Schedule 1 to the Children Act 1989 (orders for financial relief against parents);'.

Housing Act 1988 (c.50)

19 (1) Paragraph 4 of Schedule 11 to the Housing Act 1988 (repayment of discount on disposal: exempted disposals) is amended as follows.

(2) In sub-paragraph (1), for paragraph (c) substitute—

   '(c) it is a disposal of the whole of the house in pursuance of any such order as is mentioned in sub-paragraph (4) below;'.

(3) After sub-paragraph (3) add—

   '(4) The orders referred to in sub-paragraph (1)(c) above are orders under—

   (a) section 24 or 24A of the Matrimonial Causes Act 1973 (property adjustment orders or orders for the sale of property in connection with matrimonial proceedings),

   (b) section 2 of the Inheritance (Provision for Family and Dependants) Act 1975 (orders as to financial provision to be made from estate),

   (c) section 17 of the Matrimonial and Family Proceedings Act 1984 (property adjustment orders or orders for the sale of property after overseas divorce, etc.), or

   (d) paragraph 1 of Schedule 1 to the Children Act 1989 (orders for financial relief against parents).'.

PART IV

OTHER HOUSING PROVISIONS

Abolition of consent requirements for exercise of certain housing powers

20 Section 16 of the Housing Act 1985 (consent requirements for exercise of certain housing powers) shall cease to have effect.

Amendments of section 133 of the Housing Act 1988

21 (1) Section 133 of the Housing Act 1988 (consent required for certain subsequent disposals) is amended as follows.

(2) After subsection (1) insert—

   '(1A) This section does not apply if the original disposal was made before the date on which this section comes into force.'.

The amendment made by this sub-paragraph shall be deemed always to have had effect.

(3) After subsection (2) insert—

'(2A) Consent required for the purposes of this section may be given either generally to all persons who may require such consent or to any particular person or description of person who may require such consent.'.

(4) After subsection (5) insert—

'(5A) A person seeking any consent required by virtue of this section is not required to consult a tenant of the land or house proposed to be disposed of if—

    (a)   consent is sought for the disposal of the land or house to that tenant or to persons including that tenant; or

    (b)   consent is sought subject to the condition that the land or house is vacant at the time of the disposal;

and, accordingly, subsection (5) does not apply in either case.'.

Abolition of requirements for Treasury consent

22 (1) Any requirement in the following enactments for the consent or approval of the Treasury shall cease to have effect—

    (a)   in the Rent Act 1977—

        section 63(2) (schemes for appointment of rent officers), and
        Schedule 10 (rent assessment committees);

    (b)   Schedule 26 to the Local Government, Planning and Land Act 1980 (urban development corporations);

    (c)   in the Housing Act 1985—

        section 156(4) (liability to repay discount: approved lending institutions), and
        section 429A (financial assistance for persons concerned with housing management);

    (d)   in the Housing Associations Act 1985—

        section 85(2) (meaning of 'recognised body'), and
        paragraphs 5 and 6 of Schedule 6 (remuneration, allowances and pensions);

    (e)   Schedule 7 to the Housing Act 1988 (constitution of housing action trusts);

    (f)   Schedule 17 to the Leasehold Reform, Housing and Urban Development Act 1993 (constitution of the Urban Regeneration Agency).

(2) In Schedule 10 to the Rent Act 1977 (rent assessment committees), in paragraph 9(c), for 'the Minister for the Civil Service' substitute 'the Secretary of State'.

(3) The amendments in this paragraph do not extend to Scotland.

Disposal of dwelling-houses subject to secure tenancies: consultation requirements

23 In section 106A of the Housing Act 1985 (consultation before disposal to private sector landlord) at the end insert—

'(3) That Schedule, and this section, do not apply in relation to any disposal of an interest in land by a local authority if—

(a) the interest has been acquired by the authority (whether compulsorily or otherwise) following the making of an order for compulsory purchase under any enactment, other than section 290 (acquisition of land for clearance),

(b) the order provides that the interest is being acquired for the purpose of disposal to a registered social landlord, and

(c) such a disposal is made within one year of the acquisition.

(4) In this section "registered social landlord" has the same meaning as in Part I of the Housing Act 1996.'.

Powers of local housing authorities to acquire land for housing purposes

24 (1) In section 17(2) of the Housing Act 1985 (acquisition of land for housing purposes) at end insert 'or facilities which serve a beneficial purpose in connection with the requirements of persons for whom housing accommodation is provided'.

(2) In section 74(3)(b) of the Local Government and Housing Act 1989 (land excluded from Housing Revenue Account) at end insert 'or facilities which serve a beneficial purpose in connection with the requirements of persons for whom housing accommodation is provided'.

Housing action trusts

25 (1) In section 63 of the Housing Act 1988 (objects etc of housing action trusts)—

(a) in subsection (1)(d) after 'conditions' insert 'of those living'; and

(b) after subsection (2) insert—

'(2A) For the avoidance of doubt it is hereby declared that it is immaterial for the purposes of this section whether action taken by a housing action trust for achieving its objects or exercising the powers conferred on it by subsection (2) above also—

(a) benefits persons who do not live in the designated area; or

(b) improves the social conditions or general environment of an area outside the designated area.'.

(2) In section 64 of that Act (proposals for area of housing action trust) in subsections (1) and (5) after 'in' insert 'relation to'.

Preserved right to buy

26 (1) In section 171B of the Housing Act 1985 (qualifying persons in relation to preserved right to buy)—

(a) in subsection (4)(a), at the end insert 'or in whom that assured tenancy vested under section 17 of the Housing Act 1988 (statutory succession to assured tenancy)'; and

(b) in subsection (5)(b), for 'subsection (4)(a) or (b)' substitute 'subsection (4)'.

(2) The amendment made by sub-paragraph (1)(a) does not apply in relation to qualifying disposals (within the meaning of Part V of the Housing Act 1985) made before,

or made under a contract entered into before, the day on which this paragraph comes into force.

Local authority assistance in connection with mortgages

27 (1) Section 442 of the Housing Act 1985 (agreements by local authority to indemnify mortgagees) is amended as follows.

(2) In subsection (1)—

(a) for the words from the beginning to 'house' (in the second place it appears) substitute 'A local authority may enter into an agreement with a person or body making an advance on the security of a house (or a building to be converted into a house)';

(b) for 'society or body' (in both places) substitute 'mortgagee'.

(3) After subsection (1) insert—

'(1A) The local authority may only enter into the agreement if the advance is for one or more of the purposes specified in subsection (1) of section 435; and subsections (2) to (4) of that section apply in relation to power to enter into such an agreement as they apply to the power to make an advance under that section.'.

(4) In subsection (2) for 'building society or recognised body' substitute 'mortgagee';

(5) Subsections (4) and (5) shall cease to have effect.

28 In section 443 of the Housing Act 1985 (local authority contributions to mortgage costs)—

(a) in subsection (1), for 'a building society or recognised body' substitute 'any person or body'; and

(b) subsections (2) and (3) shall cease to have effect.

29 (1) For section 444 of the Housing Act 1985 (meaning of 'recognised body' and 'relevant advance') substitute—

'444 Relevant advances for the purposes of section 443

The expression 'relevant advance' in section 443 (contributions to mortgage costs) means an advance made to a person whose interest in the house (or building to be converted into a house) on the security of which the advance is made is, or was, acquired by virtue of a conveyance of the freehold, or a grant or assignment of a long lease, by a housing authority.'.

(2) Any reference in an agreement made under section 442 of the Housing Act 1985 before the date on which this paragraph comes into force which defines the expression 'recognised body' by reference to section 444 of that Act shall (notwithstanding the amendment made by sub-paragraph (1) of this paragraph) continue to have the same meaning as it had immediately before that date.

30 In paragraph 21(d) of Schedule 13 to the Local Government (Wales) Act 1994 (Residuary Body a local authority for purposes of section 442 of Housing Act 1985—

(a) omit the words from '(so' to 'subsection (1)(b))', and

(b) after 'local authority' insert 'agreement to indemnify mortgagee and'.

SCHEDULE 19
REPEALS

Section 227

PART I
SOCIAL RENTED SECTOR

Chapter	*Short title*	*Extent of repeal*
1985 c. 69.	Housing Associations Act 1985.	Sections 3 to 8. Section 9(1) and (4). Section 11. Sections 13 to 33. Section 36A. Section 67. Section 69(1)(e) and (g). Schedules 2 and 3.
1988 c. 9.	Local Government Act 1988.	Section 24(5)(a) and (c).
1988 c. 50.	Housing Act 1988.	Sections 48 and 49. Section 55(1)(a). Section 58. Section 79(6) to (10). In section 92(2), the words from 'but' to the end. In Schedule 6, paragraphs 3 to 6 and 9 to 23.
1989 c. 42.	Local Government and Housing Act 1989.	Section 182.
1993 c. 10.	Charities Act 1993.	In Schedule 6, paragraph 21(3).
1993 c. 28.	Leasehold Reform, Housing and Urban Development Act 1993.	Section 134.

PART II
HOUSES IN MULTIPLE OCCUPATION

Chapter	Short title	Extent of repeal
1985 c. 68.	Housing Act 1985.	In section 365(5), the words 'and (e)'. In section 368(3), the words from 'and if' to the end. Part XII. Section 619(1).
1989 c. 42.	Local Government and Housing Act 1989.	In Schedule 9— (a) paragraphs 45 to 47 and 53(2), (b) in paragraph 53(3) the words from 'after' to '(2A)' and' and the words 'of that subsection', (c) paragraphs 55(2), 63, 66 and 68(2). In Schedule 11, paragraphs 75 and 76.

PART III
TENANTS' RIGHTS

Chapter	Short title	Extent of repeal
1985 c. 70.	Landlord and Tenant Act 1985.	In section 19(3), the words 'within the meaning of Part I of the Arbitration Act 1996'. Section 19(4).
1987 c. 31.	Landlord and Tenant Act 1987.	In section 4(2)(aa), the words 'consisting of the creation of an estate or interest'. In section 20(1), the definition of 'the new landlord'. In section 20(2), the words 'or counter-offer' in each place where they occur. Section 24(2)(a)(ii). Section 31(5). In section 60(1), the definition of 'rent assessment committee'.
1996 c. 23.	Arbitration Act 1996.	In Schedule 3, paragraph 43.

PART IV
ASSURED TENANCIES

Chapter	Short title	Extent of repeal
1985 c. 68.	Housing Act 1985.	In section 553(2)(b), the words 'or under section 20(1)(c) of that Act (notice served in respect of assured shorthold tenancies)'.
1988 c. 50.	Housing Act 1988.	Section 20(7).
		In section 22, in subsection (1), the words from 'in respect of' to 'above' and, in subsection (2), the word 'or' after paragraph (a).
		In Schedule 17, paragraph 60(c).

PART V
LEASEHOLD REFORM

Chapter	Short title	Extent of repeal
1993 c. 28.	Leasehold Reform, Housing and Urban Development Act 1993.	In section 1, in subsection (3), the words 'the freehold of it is owned by the person who owns the freehold of the relevant premises and' and, in subsection (7), the definition of 'the freeholder'.
		In section 3(1)(a), the words 'and the freehold of the whole of the building or of that part of the building is owned by the same person'.
		In section 10(6), the definition of 'the freeholder'.
		In section 11(4)(i), the words 'as is mentioned in subsection (3)(c)'.
		In section 13, in subsection (3)(a)(iii), the words 'of the person who owns the freehold of the specified premises' and 'by him' and subsections (4), (6) and (7).
		In section 39, in subsection (3), the word 'and' at the end of paragraph (b), and subsection (6).
		In Schedule 6, in paragraph 1(1), the definition of 'the freeholder'.

PART VI
HOUSING BENEFIT AND RELATED MATTERS

Chapter	Short title	Extent of repeal
1988 c. 50.	Housing Act 1988.	Section 121.
1988 c. 43.	Housing (Scotland) Act 1988.	Section 70.
1992 c. 4.	Social Security Contributions and Benefits Act 1992.	Section 130(5).
1992 c. 5.	Social Security Administration Act 1992.	Section 116(4)(a). In section 134— (a) in subsection (2)(b), the words 'or rates'; (b) subsections (3), (4), (6) and (7). Sections 135 to 137. Section 140. In section 191— (a) in the definition of 'rate rebate', 'rent rebate' and 'rent allowance', the reference to rate rebate; (b) the definitions of 'rates' and 'rating authority'.
1992 c. 6.	Social Security (Consequential Provisions) Act 1992.	In Schedule 2, paragraph 104.
1992 c. 14.	Local Government Finance Act 1992.	In Schedule 9, paragraph 21.
1994 c. 39.	Local Government etc. (Scotland) Act 1994.	In Schedule 13, in paragraph 175, in sub-paragraph (3) the words '138(1), 139(2), (5) and (6) and 140(1), (2), (4) and (7)' and sub-paragraph (4).

PART VII
ALLOCATION OF HOUSING ACCOMMODATION

Chapter	Short title	Extent of repeal
1985 c. 68.	Housing Act 1985.	Section 22. In Schedule 1, in paragraph 2(4) the words from 'until' to the end and in paragraphs 5(1) and 10(1) the words from 'unless' to the end.
1996 c. 49.	Asylum and Immigration Act 1996.	In section 9(4), the definitions of 'the accommodation Part', 'housing authority' and 'licence to occupy' and, in the definition of 'tenancy' the words ', in relation to England and Wales,'.

PART VIII
HOMELESSNESS

Chapter	Short title	Extent of repeal
1985 c. 68.	Housing Act 1985.	Part III.
1985 c. 71.	Housing (Consequential Provisions) Act 1985.	In Schedule 2, paragraphs 19 and 60(3).
1986 c. 63.	Housing and Planning Act 1986.	Section 14.
1987 c. 26.	Housing (Scotland) Act 1987.	In Schedule 23, paragraph 30(1).
1988 c. 50.	Housing Act 1988.	Section 1(6) and (7). Section 70.
1993 c. 23.	Asylum and Immigration Appeals Act 1993.	Sections 4 and 5. Schedule 1.
1994 c. 39.	Local Government etc. (Scotland) Act 1994.	In Schedule 13, paragraph 142(2).
1996 c. 49.	Asylum and Immigration Act 1996.	In section 9, subsection (2), in subsection (3)(a) the words 'or assistance' and in subsection (4) the definition of 'the homelessness Part'.

PART IX
CHANGE OF LANDLORD: SECURE TENANTS

Chapter	Short title	Extent of repeal
1985 c. 68.	Housing Act 1985.	In section 32(1) and 43(1), the words from 'and Part IV' to 'tenants)'.
1985 c. 69.	Housing Associations Act 1985.	In section 9(1), the word ', 105(6)'.
1988 c. 50.	Housing Act 1988.	In section 79(2)(a), the words 'either' and 'or under section 94 below'. Sections 93 to 114. In Schedule 2, in Ground 6, the paragraph beginning 'For the purposes of this ground, every acquisition under Part IV'. Schedule 12. In Schedule 17, paragraphs 38 and 39.
1989 c. 42.	Local Government and Housing Act 1989.	Section 174. In Schedule 11, paragraphs 107 and 109.
S.I. 1990/ 778.	Local Authorities (Capital Finance) (Consequential Amendments) Order 1990.	In the Schedule, paragraph 2.
1993 c. 28.	Leasehold Reform, Housing and Urban Development Act 1993.	Section 124(4) to (6). In Schedule 10, paragraph 1(2)(d).
1995 c. 8.	Agricultural Tenancies Act 1995.	In the Schedule, paragraph 33.
1995 c. 38.	Civil Evidence Act 1995.	In Schedule 1, paragraph 14.

PART X
CONSULTATION WITH RESPECT TO HOUSING MANAGEMENT

Chapter	Short title	Extent of repeal
1985 c. 68.	Housing Act 1985.	Sections 27A and 27AA.
1993 c. 28.	Leasehold Reform, Housing and Urban Development Act 1993.	Sections 130 and 131.

PART XI
ABOLITION OF EXCHEQUER CONTRIBUTIONS FOR AGRICULTURAL HOUSING

Chapter	Short title	Extent of repeal
1985 c. 68.	Housing Act 1985.	In section 432, the entry for Part II of Schedule 15. In Schedule 15, Part II.

PART XII
ABOLITION OF CERTAIN CONSENT REQUIREMENTS

Chapter	Short title	Extent of repeal
1985 c. 68.	Housing Act 1985.	Section 16.

PART XIII
REMOVAL OF TREASURY CONSENT REQUIREMENTS

Chapter	Short title	Extent of repeal
1977 c. 42.	Rent Act 1977.	In section 63(2)(a), the words 'with the consent of the Treasury'. In Schedule 10, in paragraphs 7, 7A and 8, the words 'with the consent of the Minister for the Civil Service'.
1980 c. 65.	Local Government Planning and Land Act 1980.	In Schedule 26, in paragraphs 8, 9 and 10, the words 'with the consent of the Minister for the Civil Service' and, in paragraph 12(5), the words 'given with the consent of the Minister for the Civil Service'.
1985 c. 68.	Housing Act 1985.	In section 156(4), the words 'with the consent of the Treasury'. In section 429A, in subsections (1) and (3), the words 'with the consent of the Treasury' and 'with the like consent' and, in subsection (5), the words 'with the consent of the Treasury'.
1985 c. 69.	Housing Associations Act 1985.	In section 85(2), the words 'with the consent of the Treasury'. In Schedule 6, in paragraphs 5(1) and 6(1), the words 'with the consent of the Treasury'.
1988 c. 50.	Housing Act 1988.	In Schedule 7, in paragraph 8, the words 'with the approval of the Treasury', in paragraph 9, the words 'with the approval of the Treasury' and 'with that approval', in paragraphs 10 and 12(2), the words 'with the approval of the Treasury' and, in paragraph 12(5), the words 'given with the consent of the Treasury'.
1993 c. 28.	Leasehold Reform, Housing and Urban Development Act 1993.	In Schedule 17, paragraphs 2(4) and 3(8) and, in paragraph 5(5), the words 'with the approval of the Treasury'.

PART XIV
LOCAL AUTHORITY ASSISTANCE IN CONNECTION WITH MORTGAGES

Chapter	Short title	Extent of repeal
1974 c. 39.	Consumer Credit Act 1974.	In section 16(1)(ff), '444(1)'.
1985 c. 68.	Housing Act 1985.	Section 442(4) and (5). Section 443(2) and (3). In section 459, the entry for 'recognised body'.
1986 c. 53.	Building Societies Act 1986.	In Schedule 18, paragraph 18(2).
1994 c. 19.	Local Government (Wales) Act 1994.	In Schedule 13, in paragraph 21(d) the words from '(so' to 'subsection (1) (b))'.

INDEX